Combined Arms Warfare in Ancient Greece

Combined Arms Warfare in Ancient Greece examines the timelines of military developments that led from the hoplite-based armies of the ancient Greeks to the hugely successful and multi-faceted armies of Philip II, Alexander the Great, and his Successors. It concentrates on the introduction and development of individual units and their tactical coordination and use in battle in what is termed "combined arms": the effective integration of different unit types into one cohesive battle plan and army allowing each unit to focus on its strengths without having to worry about its weaknesses.

This volume traces the development, and argues for the vital importance, of the use of combined arms in Greek warfare from the Archaic period onwards, especially concerning the Macedonian hegemony, through to its developmental completion in the form of fully "integrated warfare" at the battle of Ipsus in 301 BCE. It argues crucially that warfare should never be viewed in isolation in individual states, regions, conflicts, or periods but taken as a collective whole, tracing the mutual influence of other cultures and the successful innovations that always result.

Wrightson analyses Greek and Macedonian warfare through the lens of modern military theoretical terminology, making this study accessible to those with a general interest in military history as well as those studying this specific period.

Graham Wrightson is Assistant Professor of History at South Dakota State University, USA. His research focuses primarily on Macedonian military history with a special focus on military manuals and the sarissa phalanx. He also examines comparative warfare between cultures and eras and their influence on each other. He has published multiple articles and papers on Macedonian warfare, has jointly edited three books, and has produced a textbook for the standard US university first-year survey course Western Civilization 1.

Routledge Monographs in Classical Studies

Titles include:

Juvenal's Global Awareness
Circulation, Connectivity, and Empire
Osman Umurhan

The Greek and Roman Trophy
From Battlefield Marker to Icon of Power
Lauren Kinnee

Rethinking 'Authority' in Late Antiquity
Authorship, Law, and Transmission in Jewish and Christian Tradition
Edited by A. J. Berkovitz and Mark Letteney

Thinking the Greeks
A Volume in Honour of James M. Redfield
Edited by Bruce M. King and Lillian Doherty

Pushing the Boundaries of Historia
Edited by Mary C. English and Lee M. Fratantuono

Greek Myth and the Bible
Bruce Louden

Combined Arms Warfare in Ancient Greece
From Homer to Alexander the Great and his Successors
Graham Wrightson

Power Couples in Antiquity
Transversal Perspectives
Edited by Anne Bielman Sánchez

For more information on this series, visit: www.routledge.com/classicalstudies/series/RMCS

Combined Arms Warfare in Ancient Greece

From Homer to Alexander the Great and his Successors

Graham Wrightson

Routledge
Taylor & Francis Group

LONDON AND NEW YORK

First published 2019
by Routledge
2 Park Square, Milton Park, Abingdon, Oxon OX14 4RN

and by Routledge
605 Third Avenue, New York, NY 10017

First issued in paperback 2021

Routledge is an imprint of the Taylor & Francis Group, an informa business

© 2019 Graham Wrightson

The right of Graham Wrightson to be identified as author of this work has been asserted by him in accordance with sections 77 and 78 of the Copyright, Designs and Patents Act 1988.

All rights reserved. No part of this book may be reprinted or reproduced or utilised in any form or by any electronic, mechanical, or other means, now known or hereafter invented, including photocopying and recording, or in any information storage or retrieval system, without permission in writing from the publishers.

Trademark notice: Product or corporate names may be trademarks or registered trademarks, and are used only for identification and explanation without intent to infringe.

Publisher's Note
The publisher has gone to great lengths to ensure the quality of this reprint but points out that some imperfections in the original copies may be apparent.

British Library Cataloguing-in-Publication Data
A catalogue record for this book is available from the British Library

Library of Congress Cataloging-in-Publication Data
A catalog record for this book has been requested

ISBN 13: 978-1-03-209358-1 (pbk)
ISBN 13: 978-1-138-57459-5 (hbk)

Typeset in Times New Roman
by Apex CoVantage, LLC

Printed in the United Kingdom
by Henry Ling Limited

For Dorie and my parents

Contents

List of figures xii
Acknowledgements xiii

Introduction part 1: the purpose and methodology of the study 1
   Putting Greek warfare in context 2
   The theory of combined arms 4
     Methodology and terminology – a conceptual methodological framework 4
   Combined arms in the ancient world: a developmental continuum 7
   "Integrated warfare" 8
   The process of moving from a basic use of combined arms to integrated warfare 8
   A methodology for examining this process 9
   The focus of this study 9

Introduction part 2: the theory of combined arms 13
   Combined arms vs. integrated warfare 13
   The effect of terrain on warfare and units 14
     Unit categorisation and subdivisions 14
   Infantry – the hands, arms, and chest of the army 15
   Regular heavy infantry – the chest and breastplate of the army 15
   Elite heavy infantry – the hands of the army 17
   Light infantry – the arms of the army 17
   Missile troops 18
     Archers 18
     Javelin men 19
     Slingers 19

Peltasts 19
Elite light infantry – the elbows of the army 20
Cavalry – the feet of the army according to Iphicrates 20
Heavy cavalry – the feet of the army 21
Chariots – earlier feet of the army 22
Elephants – the joints of the army 23
Light cavalry – the legs of the army 24
Non-missile light cavalry 25
Horse archers 25
Field artillery 26
Conclusions: the benefit of combined arms
  and integrated warfare 26

SECTION 1
The hoplite revolution in Greece 31

1 Homeric warfare and the introduction of the hoplite 33
Primary sources for Greek warfare 33
Homeric warfare 34
Sources 34
Heavy infantry 35
Missile infantry 37
Infantry combined arms 38
Chariots 39
Cavalry 39
Combined arms conclusions 40

2 Archaic Greece – the dominance of the heavy infantry phalanx 45
Sources 45
Infantry 46
Hoplites and the phalanx 46
Hoplites as individual soldiers 47
The crucial importance of maintaining balance
  in hoplite combat 50
Early hoplites 53
Tactical separation of light and heavy infantry 59
Chariots 62
Cavalry 62
Combined arms 63

3   Persia vs. Greece – the advantages of the heavy infantryman   69
  The Persian Empire and its (mis)use of a
    combined arms army   69
    Sources   69
    Infantry   70
    Cavalry   73
    Combined arms   74
  The Persian Wars: the mirage of the hoplite's
    superiority   76
    Sources   76
  Persian armies exposed without using combined
    arms properly – Marathon   76
    Combined arms conclusions   83
  The beginnings of successful combined arms in
    Greek armies – Plataea   83
    Xerxes' army   84
    The Greek army   86
    Infantry   86
    Cavalry   88
    The battle   89
    Combined arms   91
  Combined arms conclusions   92

SECTION 2
The implementation of combined arms in Greek warfare   101

4   The Peloponnesian War – combined arms innovation on the battlefield   103
  Sources   103
  Infantry   104
  Cavalry   104
  Combined arms   107
  Sicily and the Athenian siege of Syracuse – large-scale
    combined arms in practice   114
    Sources   114
    Early warfare in Sicily   114
    The Athenian campaign   116
    Combined arms   121
  Combined arms conclusions   124

Contents

5 **The Corinthian War and Iphicrates: light infantry integration** 132
   Sources 132
   Infantry 133
   Cavalry 142
   Combined arms 143
   Combined arms conclusions 146

6 **The Theban hegemony – the inclusion of heavy cavalry** 150
   Sources 150
   Infantry 150
   Cavalry 152
   Combined arms 154
   Combined arms conclusions 156

SECTION 3
Macedon and integrated warfare 159

7 **Philip II – the sarissa phalanx and heavy cavalry** 161
   Sources 161
   Infantry 161
   Cavalry 167
   Field artillery 168
   Combined arms 169
   Chaeronea – Macedonian combined arms
      vs. Greek diverse units 171
      Sources 172
      The battle 172
      Combined arms 173
      Combined arms conclusions 174

8 **Alexander the Great – linking the heavy cavalry and the phalanx** 178
   Sources 178
   Infantry 178
   Cavalry 184
   Artillery 185
   Combined arms 186
   Combined arms conclusions 190
   Issus and Gaugamela: integrated warfare in action 191
      Sources 191
      Issus 191
      Combined arms 193
      Gaugamela 193
      Combined arms 195
   Combined arms conclusions 196

9 The Successors – war elephants and integrated warfare 202
Sources 202
Combined arms 203
Paraetacene 205
Combined arms 206
Gabiene 207
Combined arms 208
Ipsus 210
Combined arms 211
Combined arms conclusions 212

**Conclusion – Greece, Persia, and Macedon:
the success of combined arms and integrated warfare** 216

Bibliography 222
Index 240
Index of battles 247

Figures

2.1	Sack of Troy. Red-figure Kylix by the Brygos painter. Louvre Paris (G 152).	50
2.2	The Amathus bowl, silverwork; possibly Assyrian or Phoenician (c. 710–675).	54
2.3	The Chigi vase. Middle Protocorinthian olpe by the Macmillan painter (c. 650).	57
2.4	Sherd of black-figure middle Corinthian column Krater, attributed to the Cavalcade painter (c. 600–575).	60
2.5	Black figure aryballos by the Macmillan painter (the "Macmillan aryballos"), Middle Protocorinthian (c. 650).	61
4.1	Battle map of Delium showing the crucial movement of Pagondas' cavalry around the hill to win the battle.	106
6.1	Map of Leuctra showing the crucial innovation of the oblique formation and the deep phalanx led by the Sacred Band under Pelopidas.	151
7.1	The battle of Chaeronea showing the Macedonian oblique formation and the withdrawal up the hill of Philip's phalanx followed by Alexander's charge into the resultant gap.	173

Acknowledgements

I especially would like to thank my PhD supervisor, friend, and mentor Waldemar Heckel for giving me so much support and good advice throughout the years and for his invaluable insight concerning the many early drafts of this book as my PhD dissertation. Many thanks in particular to Eric Howell for his last-minute drawings of some of the figures in this book. Thanks also to Freddy Moran Jr. for his tireless work on the battle of Delium map in the book and on others that did not make the cut, and for listening to my complaints. Thanks to Dan Powers for numerous discussions on many of these themes over the years and for his invaluable military insights. I would like to thank my parents for supporting me to go down the long road of endless studying that eventually led to this. Finally, I especially want to thank my amazing wife Dorie for putting up with all the long days with the kids while I was working and for encouraging me to discuss matters with her over the years.

Introduction part 1

The purpose and methodology of the study

Greek warfare after the introduction of the hoplite remained tactically static for centuries. A number of factors created this circumstance: the geography of Greece, the political climate, the lack of external spheres of conflict or military influence, and the lack of any necessity to develop other styles of warfare, to name a few. During the Peloponnesian War, Greek poleis began to make use of other units in battle and develop innovative tactics not wholly reliant on a hoplite phalanx as the new demands, resources, and operational theatres of war required. This process eventually led to the multi-faceted armies employed by Alexander the Great and his Successors.

The main focus of this book is an examination of Greek warfare from the archaic period through to the wars of Alexander's Successors, tracing the development and importance of "combined arms" in land warfare.[1] In order to examine combined arms and the process of the implementation of "integrated warfare" in Greece, this study will concentrate on the introduction and development of individual units and their coordination and use in battle. This will start with the beginnings of hoplite warfare in the seventh century and end at the battle of Ipsus in 301[2].

The battle of Ipsus is a good terminal point for a number of reasons: By 301 most units found in ancient armies had come into being and been used effectively; few new tactics involving combined arms occur afterwards; and after Ipsus primary source material becomes fragmentary and less reliable, especially concerning tactical details.

This study will provide a detailed analysis of all the trends and developments in Greek land warfare from Homeric warfare through to 301. It will demonstrate the importance of combined arms to warfare in general as well as examining specific examples of its influence on Greek warfare in particular. The overall result will be a comprehensive timeline of Greek warfare showing how each innovation in tactics and armament and different battles led to the eventual adoption of combined arms in every state in Greece. My aim is to demonstrate that different styles and periods of Greek warfare should be taken as a whole and not dealt with individually, and that the whole picture represents the widespread understanding of the need for the implementation of combined arms.

2   *The purpose and methodology of the study*

Examining Greek warfare through the lens of combined arms tactics will also shed more light on the independent culture of the Classical Greeks and how that culture shaped, or was shaped by, warfare reliant on the hoplite to the detriment of the implementation of combined arms tactics. It is this analytical tool that I hope will create the foundation for future examinations of Greek culture and serve as one means of assessment for its rather slow adoption of aspects of other cultures, both military and other.

Putting Greek warfare in context

Much has been written on Greek warfare in general and on specific armies, battles, and units. But when scholars discuss battle tactics or unit types, there is no concept of a tactical continuum or concern for unit evolution over the whole period. Even works intended as overviews of all Greek or ancient warfare often view each conflict independently with only a few threads of development followed throughout.

Very rarely in any society does warfare ever exist in a vacuum, isolated from outside influences on tactics or technology. Once an innovation occurs that significantly alters the outcomes of battles other states must adopt, or adapt to, this new practice or weapon in order to survive. Moreover, one innovation usually leads to many more in the future. There is always the drive to create better ways of waging war or to perfect what already exists. Carl von Clausewitz stated as much in *On War* in 1832: "War is more than a true chameleon that slightly adapts its characteristics to the given case". Mansoor rightly summarises:

> as Clausewitz stated nearly two centuries ago, although war changes its characteristics in various circumstances, in whatever way it manifests itself, war is still war. War in the twenty-first century has been and will remain a complex phenomenon, but its essence has not and will not change.[3]

The classical Greeks did not develop their style of war isolated from all other cultures and eras, and so before examining hoplite warfare it is necessary also to be familiar with earlier Greek practices as well as contemporary warfare elsewhere. It is especially important to understand the methods of war in influential societies that had direct or indirect contact with early Greece, in particular the Persian Empire. The beginnings of combined arms can be seen in Homeric Greece, and therefore the subsequent shift of focus in Classical Greece to an army reliant on heavy infantry alone becomes that much more significant.

At the collapse of the Bronze Age, the Greeks regressed in military style to a simpler army structure reliant on hoplites loosely supported by light infantry and light cavalry, which, though simple, was better at effective conflict resolution. This change can be explained by a number of factors, such as the nature of the polis and consequent parochialism, Greece's mountainous terrain and isolated position, and the fact that war was primarily used for defence and resolving local disputes but not conquest. As Greek poleis expanded their influence outside their immediate area, rival states or different terrain prompted changes in military style. This necessitated a return to combined arms and led to the integrated warfare of the Macedonian-style armies of the fourth century.

The concept of combined arms in Greek warfare is touched on occasionally by scholars, in particular with regards to the armies of Philip and Alexander, but it is rarely dealt with in detail and in the context of a continuum of developments in Greek warfare.[4] The most focused study on combined arms in a specific period of Greek warfare is Robert B. Pederson's *A Study of Combined Arms Warfare by Alexander the Great* (US Army Command and General Staff College and Penny Hill Press: December 6, 2015). But it is not a scholarly work, ignoring many of the aspects of ancient military history still debated by scholars and taking the sources at face value. However, no one previously has discussed in detail the importance of combined arms in Greek warfare as a whole[5] or made clear the importance of recognising a continuum concerning the level of combined arms utilised at any time.

The best summary of combined arms in the context of a continuum of historical development is Archer Jones' *The Art of War in the Western World* (Chicago, 1987). However, he does not provide any background to earlier developments in combined arms warfare. Nevertheless, his account is valuable in relating ancient warfare to modern military theory, in particular the importance of combined arms in overcoming the strength of the enemy. Perhaps the best work that does trace the development of combined arms throughout the ancient world is Arther Ferrill's *The Origins of War: From the Stone Age to Alexander the Great* (New York, 1986).

Ferrill begins with early man and briefly outlines Mesopotamian warfare before detailing Greek warfare up to and including Alexander. However, he does not mention combined arms specifically despite the use of modern military theoretical terms, such as firepower or fighting in column versus line. Ferrill praises the armies of Persia and Alexander because of their level of integration and criticises the hoplite phalanxes of Classical Greece because of their tactical simplicity. He is advocating the use of combined arms in warfare and to some degree tracing its development in the ancient world, but he never spells out if this is his aim. Nor does he provide any reasons for his preference for integrated armies or discuss what these actually entailed in each case. Moreover, in ending with Alexander, Ferrill fails to recognise the crucial developments in army integration that occurred under Alexander's Successors. In trying to write a general history Ferrill does not engage in detailed tactical analysis of the intricacies of army integration, and his arguments suffer as a result.

This book details the timeline in Greek warfare of innovative developments in armaments or tactics and how everything combined to lead to the integrated armies of Macedon in the late fourth century. Combined arms theory is the methodological lens through which we will examine in detail the various advances in Greek warfare leading up to the intricate and complicated armies of Alexander the Great and his Successors.

4   *The purpose and methodology of the study*

The theory of combined arms

Combined arms has a relatively modern application in military theory, but although the specific term is new, its application is not.[6]

> The concept of combined arms in ground combat has existed for centuries, but the nature of that combination and the organizational level at which it occurred have varied greatly. . . . Since then twentieth-century warfare . . . developed to the point where some form of combined arms is essential for survival, let alone victory.[7]

Similarly, post-traumatic stress disorder is a modern name for an illness, the symptoms of which are visible throughout history.[8] "Total war" is another modern term that is often used to describe the all-encompassing warfare of the nineteenth and twentieth centuries. More recently it has been ascribed to the Napoleonic period and even the US Civil War.[9] However, many, if not all, of the aspects of war that are collated in this succinct name can be seen in the ancient world, but that is for another discussion.[10]

The model of combined arms warfare as outlined next serves as a way of analysing battles from a tactical perspective. It is very useful in detailing the intricacies of a battle where such information is not necessarily provided in the sources. This is particularly relevant in ancient warfare, where the number, focus, and reliability of sources is problematic for any tactical reconstruction and analysis. Using the complete implementing of combined arms as the end point for the most advanced and successful tactical realisation in battle, here referred to as integrated warfare, it is possible to review all battles through a comparative lens. Combined arms allows historians the means of comparing the tactical efficiencies of armies and commanders throughout the history of warfare. Here the focus is on Greece and the Near East, but this model of analysis is just as relevant for discussions of Roman or mediaeval warfare.

In this study there is no space for any detailed analysis of generalship in the ancient world and the ancient knowledge of the theory of combined arms. Nor is this study focused on strategy in ancient warfare. Here my focus is limited to the application of tactics in battle as the simplest way of assessing the level and importance of combined arms in ancient warfare.

Methodology and terminology – a conceptual methodological framework

Combined arms warfare

> The very term "combined arms" means different things to different people, or it is left undefined and vague . . . the combined arms concept is the basic idea that different combat arms and weapons systems must be used in concert to maximize the survival and combat effectiveness of the others. The strengths of one system must be used to compensate for the weaknesses of others. The specific

arms and weapons included in this concept have varied greatly among national armies and over time.[11]

For the purposes of this study the term "combined arms" refers to the process of moving from an army centred on a simple unit to a diverse and multi-faceted army, as well as to the tactical uses and deployment of two or more units in combination in battle.[12] This includes integrating all the diverse units into a successful tactical plan on the battlefield.[13] The goal of combined arms is to enable a coordination of action in a battle that brings each unit into offensive or defensive action to mutually support the rest of the army "working in concert towards a common objective to destroy or disrupt the enemy forces".[14] It is intended "to achieve an effect on the enemy that is greater than if each arm was used against the enemy independently".[15]

The US Army *Field Manual 100–5* specifies the nine principles of war that govern the US Army.[16] The sixth principle regarding unity of command stresses that "[u]nity of command obtains unity of effort by the coordinated action of all forces towards a common goal. While coordination may be attained by cooperation, it is best achieved by vesting a single commander with the requisite authority".[17] This statement aptly summarises the purpose of combined arms, to achieve success "by the coordinated action of all forces towards a common goal".

Most armies today are organised around combined arms. "Imagine a modern army on today's battlefield not utilising combined arms, an idea that simply doesn't seem plausible to even the most inexperienced warrior".[18] Yet according to Herbert, the idea of combined arms was not a formal part of US Army training until the 1976 edition of the field manual, *FM 100–5*.[19] Even though the US Army did not officially recognise combined arms until 40 years ago, it has been used variously throughout the history of war with varying degrees of success and expertise; it just did not have a specific term.[20]

The *US Army Field Manual* outlining strategic and tactical operations says the following concerning the modern application of combined arms warfare:

> Combined arms warfare is the simultaneous application of combat, CS [combat support], and CSS [combat service support] toward a common goal. These arms and services are integrated horizontally at each command echelon, normally battalion through corps, and vertically between these command echelons. Combined arms warfare produces effects that are greater than the sum of the individual parts. The combined arms team strives to conduct fully integrated operations in the dimensions of time, space, purpose, and resources. . . . The goal is to confuse, demoralize, and destroy the enemy with the coordinated impact of combat power.[21]

This *Field Manual* also outlines that the qualities of any successful military force involve an understanding of combined arms warfare.

> Once the force is engaged, superior combat power derives from the courage and competence of soldiers, the excellence of their training, the capability of

their equipment, the soundness of their combined arms doctrine, and, above all, the quality of their leadership.[22]

In addition to this the manual argues that "commanders fight combined arms battles and engagements employing every tactical means available". This shows that today the application of combined arms is a complicated process that requires significant levels of training for soldiers and commanders alike but is fundamental to the actions and successes of the army as a whole.[23] The same is true also for the application of combined arms in the ancient world. Perhaps more so, since much of the specific tactics and the level of training required to implement the system did not exist originally.

There is a crucial difference between a combined arms army making full, and the best, use of every unit in the battle plan, and an army made up of diverse units. Diversity in an army does not equal combined arms. Diversity is a starting point for an army to develop combined arms, but if there is no tactical integration of units then there is no use of combined arms. This is an important factor in tracing the development of combined arms in the ancient world. As discussed next, the Persian army is the best example of a diverse army that was not integrated tactically and therefore lacked the benefits of combined arms in battle. Tactical integration is the most important aspect of combined arms in an army in battle.

Combined arms should also be distinguished from support arms.

> Combined arms hits the enemy with two or more arms simultaneously in such a manner that the actions he must take to defend himself from one make him more vulnerable to another. In contrast supporting arms, is hitting the enemy with two or more arms in sequence, or if simultaneously, then in such a combination that the actions the enemy must take to defend himself from one also defends him from the other(s). Combined arms . . . seeks to strike at the enemy psychologically as well as physically. . . . The distinction between combined arms and supporting arms is important because combined arms take no more firepower, but will usually be much more effective.[24]

A commander utilising supporting arms makes use of different units in battle but does not achieve the best tactical coordination of them in order to disadvantage the enemy in battle. It is the level of tactical coordination that is important in employing combined arms on the battlefield.[25]

Modern military theory makes a clear distinction between combined arms (two or more combat arms acting jointly), combined operations (two or more countries fighting as allies), and joint operations (two or more services, such as the navy and army, acting together).[26] Here, when dealing with the ancient world, only the first is of prime concern. In modern armies, combat arms are air defence artillery, armour, aircraft, cavalry, field artillery, infantry, and special-forces regiments.[27] Of these, only infantry, cavalry, and to some extent field artillery, are present on the ancient battlefield.

In the study of the ancient world it is necessary to divide the list of combat arms even further. The list includes infantry, both light and heavy; cavalry, both light and heavy, including chariots and elephants; missile troops; and to a lesser degree field artillery. Within each category there are many other types of unit available depending on their armament, armour, or training. All of these units have different strengths and weaknesses and different effectiveness in battle. In effect ancient military practices can be divided into their use of these four weapon systems: heavy infantry, heavy cavalry, light infantry, and light cavalry.[28] Not every type of unit was readily available to every state in the ancient world, or in Greece in particular, but they were all used somewhere at some time.

It is also necessary in the ancient world to distinguish between the tactical application of combined arms on the battlefield and the strategic use of combined arms in a campaign setting. This study is concerned with the tactics of combined arms only. The strategical use of combined arms, for example in waging a war using the navy and army together, is another aspect of this topic, but one that should be reserved for a fuller discussion elsewhere. Battles are the basic foundation for any military activity on which all other aspects of war depend. Especially in the ancient world, campaigns or wars could rarely be concluded without a battle. As a result, any detailed analysis of ancient warfare should focus on battles first, and then address strategy and the larger implications of war. In my view it is crucial to distinguish between the tactics and strategy of combined arms in order to be fully able to analyse its development throughout the ancient world. Combined arms theory forms the basis for a comparative discussion of all aspects of warfare, but the starting point should be tactics in battle.

Combined arms in the ancient world: a developmental continuum

The modern term of combined arms refers to military action in a tactical setting. In today's world, where almost every army has the same units and weapons technology, there need be no differentiation between stages of combined arms. However, in the ancient world this is far from true. The simplest form of combined arms is the use of two arms together. This can be infantry and cavalry, infantry and missile troops, cavalry and artillery, or any other combination. Even the earliest armies for which we have records apparently used a basic form of combined arms. The Sumerians used chariots alongside infantry. However, there is a clear difference between the armies of the Sumerians and those of Alexander and his Successors. Both use combined arms but at very different levels of sophistication.

In the ancient world it is absolutely necessary to differentiate between armies employing combined arms at different levels of sophistication. The simplest way to do this is to view combined arms as a continuum ranging from the most basic use of combined arms—two units acting in concert—to an army that fully integrates a large number of different units in battle. Different levels on the sliding scale represent varied amounts of unit expertise and successful coordinated action

8 *The purpose and methodology of the study*

in battle. The final point on this continuum is the successful integration of all the diverse troop types available into one army in order to get the best use out of each unit. Such an army is one that fulfils a number of criteria:

1   It is as diverse as possible in terms of the different units incorporated in it and includes every individual type of unit that is available.
2   Each unit demonstrates the perfection of warfare within its own style, such as Agrianian javelin men or Cretan archers.
3   The general is able to make the best use of each and every unit in a coordinated battle plan, calling on his own knowledge of the latest tactical and strategic knowledge.

The term "integrated warfare" is used here to describe the style of battle employed by an army that has reached the end of the continuum of combined arms.

Just as with modern armies using combined arms in battle, in the ancient world employing integrated warfare in battle was a difficult thing to achieve. "The application of combined arms in this manner is complex and demanding. It requires detailed planning and violent execution by highly trained soldiers and units who have been thoroughly rehearsed".[29] Combined arms in this study refers both to the integration of two or more units in battle and the process of developing a multi-faceted and fully integrated army.

"Integrated warfare"

In modern military terminology, integrated warfare is "The conduct of military operations in any combat environment wherein opposing forces employ non-conventional weapons in combination with conventional weapons".[30] The term is most commonly used in relation to Integrated Warfare Systems, the electronic programmes or devices that allow modern armed forces to use different weapons systems.[31]

Since this modern term is largely irrelevant for ancient warfare where electronic systems did not exist, I use it to refer to an army that has made full use of combined arms in battle. Integrated warfare is how an army has perfected the coordinated use of the maximum available variety of different units in battle according to the basic principles of combined arms.

The process of moving from a basic use of combined arms to integrated warfare

As mentioned earlier, military innovations occur at different times throughout history and usually lead to further advancements in technology or tactics. An army at any time can only utilise units or tactics that are available until an innovation occurs. As states or commanders become acquainted with new tactics, technologies, or units, they see the benefits of incorporating them into their own army. This is the process that is interesting to historians.

Once the specific military innovations are identified and their development traced, it is possible to suggest answers to a number of important questions. To what extent do military advances shift the balance of power in war? How quickly do different types of innovation spread? Why do some states or armies not embrace the changes? To what extent can an understanding of the science and history of ancient warfare influence war today?

A methodology for examining this process

Combined arms cannot occur when there is only one type of soldier available in war. As different units are invented or encountered, they should be integrated into the battle plan in order to keep pace with military science. To examine the development of combined arms in Greek warfare as a whole, it is necessary to look at two different things. First, the study must detail specific innovations in tactics or technology and analyse their significance in advancing combined arms warfare. Second, it is crucial to discuss when, how, where, and why individual units first appear in order to see the combined arms of different units in action on the battlefield within an army.

A simple examination of the development of combined arms will detail the specific innovations and units as they occur historically and link them on a continuous timeline of military science. A more detailed examination will propose reasons for any new advances in warfare and assess their significance. Where there is a break in the timeline – for example in Greece, where military science favoured warfare focused on heavy infantry – it is necessary to determine the factors that influenced this anomaly.[32] Overall, in tracing the development of combined arms it is possible to create a thorough account of the tactical and technological advancements in military science throughout history.

The focus of this study

This book will examine the following: the development of combined arms; why it developed; when it was used and what impact it had; when, where and why new units were introduced; and what influence they had on warfare. This will involve problems such as regional terrain variance, cultural variance, social variance, and outside contact with other military systems. The discussion of particular battles will show exactly how combined arms impacts warfare.

This study will use modern terminology to analyse Greek history in order to examine the overall development of warfare in the Greek world and demonstrate that individual poleis, regions, conflicts, or periods should not be viewed in isolation but taken as a collective whole. The main focus is on an army on the battlefield and not elsewhere. As a result, campaign logistics, training practices, siege warfare, naval warfare, biological warfare, and terror tactics are not of concern here.

The analysis will be anchored by an examination of tactics and deployment on the battlefield and will use certain battles as case studies. Battles for study are selected either because significant changes occur or because the sources are particularly good in documenting aspects of warfare. All types of source available pose difficulties in interpretation. Neither inscriptions nor historical works are usually specifically concerned with military matters, and archaeology can rarely show how something was used in battle. Excavations at a site can to some degree illustrate the events of a battle, but there is always the possibility that the finds moved over time, either on purpose or accidentally.

Through the lens of combined arms theory, I will examine the development of combined arms in Greek warfare and create a detailed tactical analysis of Greek armies from Homer to Alexander's Successors.[33]

Notes

1 What is meant by the terms "combined arms" and "integrated warfare" will be discussed below, alongside an outline of the specific terminology to be used. The principal focus of this study is land warfare, in particular the specific tactics employed in battle. As a result, naval and siege warfare, as well as other aspects of war and the modern application of combined arms, do not feature in this discussion. See below for a detailed discussion of what is meant by combined arms.
2 All dates below are BCE unless otherwise stated.
3 Murray and Mansoor (2012: 1).
4 Most works on Greek warfare deal with specific time periods in isolation rather than focusing on how one era influences the next. For example, Hans van Wees' magisterial work deals only with early hoplites, *Greek Warfare: Myths and Realities*, Duckworth 2005. The most recent book of Christopher Matthew (*An Invincible Beast: Understanding the Hellenistic Pike Phalanx in Action*, Barnsley: Pen and Sword, 2015) deals with Macedonian warfare in detail. Likewise, Stephen English's two works on Alexander's army, *The Army of Alexander the Great* (Pen and Sword 2009) and *The Field Campaigns of Alexander the Great* (Pen and Sword 2011), do not comment on how Alexander arrived at utilising combined arms. Lonsdale mentions briefly the use of combined arms in the armies of Philip and Alexander but goes no further than that: *Alexander Killer of Men: Alexander and the Macedonian Way of War* (New York: Constable, 2004) and *Alexander the Great: Lessons in Strategy* (London: Routledge, 2007). Likewise, Karunanithy mentions it only in passing without sufficiently explaining the theory and why it is relevant to understand the successes of the Macedonian military machine: *The Macedonian War Machine 359–281 BC* (Barnsley: Pen and Sword 2013).
5 Oorthuys (2007) discusses Agricola's use of combined arms in his campaigns in Britain, but he is concerned more with combined operations involving the army and navy than combined arms on the battlefield.
6 See House (1984); Spiller (1992) and in particular House (2001).
7 House (2001: 3).
8 See for example Shay (1994); Shay et al. (2003); Tritle (2000).
9 Bell (2007); Förster and Nagler (1997). For a general history of total war see Power and Tremain (1988).
10 There is a firm belief that in the ancient world sieges or conflicts involving the whole population were very rare. Technology was limited and biological or chemical warfare alongside the use of terror was rarely practiced. Religion and propaganda, as well as deceit and politics, are integral to total war and are often noticeably lacking in early warfare. However, the Neo-Assyrian Empire repeatedly captured cities through sieges, often using terror tactics such as diverting or polluting the water supply or

fostering disease among the beleaguered population. Throughout history mass executions, enslavements, or deportations were often used as a way of subduing a captured region or population.
11 House (2001: 4).
12 Very little has been written about combined arms warfare in the ancient world, but much has been written about twentieth-century warfare.
13 As House (2001: 5) aptly summarises, the exact application of combined arms tactics in battle "is the area that is of most concern to professional soldiers, yet it is precisely this area where historical records and tactical manuals often neglect important details".
14 Pederson (1998: xii).
15 Pederson (1998: xii).
16 US Army (1993).
17 As quoted in Matloff (1969: 7).
18 Pederson (1998: vii). See for example US Army (1992a).
19 Herbert (1988: 7). Matloff's great work tracing the US Army's development from its instigation to 1969 never refers to combined arms. His reference to the then current *FM 100-5* (1969: 6–7) demonstrates the novelty of the 1976 edition in using combined arms theory as a basis for army doctrine, as discussed by Herbert in 1988.
20 Arguably the first full use of combined arms in modern warfare (i.e. using mobile field artillery alongside infantry, cavalry (tanks), and static artillery) was the German First World War offensive at Amiens in March 1918 (Matloff 1969: 385). It was the success of this German offensive that prompted the Allied forces to create a unified command system. In the end it was the British refusal to give ground easily that slowed the advance of the Germans enough to call off the various assaults on the Allied lines. Amiens certainly marks a significant shift in the practice of battle in modern warfare to becoming reliant on combined arms combat teams utilising infantry, cavalry, and artillery together and finally ended trench warfare. For more information on the German uses of combined arms in the First World War and afterwards, see in particular Citino (1999).
21 US Army (1993: 2.3).
22 US Army (1993: 2.12).
23 The German use of combined arms at Amiens in 1918 was so extraordinary because these "new tactics put a premium on courage, stamina, initiative, and co-ordination, qualities which, for lack of time, the Germans could instil in only about two dozen specially selected divisions. These were pulled from the line, filled out with men from other divisions, and put through an intensive training program." Matloff (1969: 385).
24 Lind (1985: 20–1).
25 The term "coordinated arms" is not in use in military theory as "combined arms" is preferred.
26 For a clear distinction see Pederson (1998: xii). The operational field manual clarifies the terms in the glossary, defining combined arms as the "application of several arms, such as infantry, armor, artillery, and aviation" and combined operation as "an operation conducted by forces of two or more allied nations acting together for the accomplishment of a single mission" (US Army 1993: glossary 2). For joint operations see US Department of Defense (2001). Any work on modern warfare utilises this terminology. See for example House (1984); Herbert (1988); Spiller (1992) and recently Kretchik (2011).
27 See US Army (1990).
28 For a clear description in modern military theory terms of combat arms in the ancient world through the four weapon systems see Jones (1987: 39–45). See also below for a detailed analysis of the units discussed here.
29 US Army (1993: 2.3).
30 US Department of Defense (2005).

31 Ranstorp and Normark (2009). The navy is the only US military force that has a specific office dealing with Integrated Warfare and appoints a program executive officer to oversee its application: Arnold (2012).
32 In the Near East there is never a break from continual advancement of military science. From Sumer's infantry-based armies through to the large Persian armies containing many different units, warfare constantly advanced and embraced any innovations, admittedly with varying degrees of success.
33 Bar Kochva (1976) provides a similar review for the Hellenistic Seleucid armies in particular.

Introduction part 2
The theory of combined arms

Combined arms vs. integrated warfare

As mentioned earlier, combined arms is the effective integration of different unit types into one cohesive battle plan and army. It allows each unit to focus on its strengths without having to worry about its weaknesses. "Combined arms" does not mean that each unit fights independently supported by the other units; rather it is the focused communal action towards the same goal that gives the army its strength.

Although the basic form of combined arms only requires the effective use of two of the three main types of unit – cavalry/chariots, infantry, and missile troops – the full implementation of combined arms makes the best use of all the sub-categories of unit type in an army. That is to say that if an army has many types of cavalry, infantry, and missile troops, a general will make use of each individual unit in the best way possible to achieve the overall aim of victory. I have termed this integrated warfare, the most advanced coordinated action of an army, in order to differentiate it from the most basic uses of combined arms, and everything in between. Combined arms here is used to describe the basic theory of mutual action of different units, as well as the process of developing an army that makes use of fully integrated warfare, the end point of the process.

The obvious benefit to a general in using combined arms in any form is that he has his bases covered. He can attack or defend against the enemy in a variety of ways as the situation demands. This adaptability is a priceless asset for any general in enabling him to cope better with the tactics and strategy of the enemy. Perhaps most importantly, the adaptability does not come at a cost in offensive power or effectiveness. Each unit has different strengths and weaknesses depending on its armament, training, and all the other factors that influence military ability. All of these things should be incorporated into the battle plan. Despite (or perhaps as a result of) the many styles of unit in the army, integrated warfare allows for harmonious action, and in doing so actually increases effectiveness.

The main drawback of using any level of combined arms is the large amount of coordination, training, and trust required for an army to use the system successfully. Each unit has not only to be very good at what it does, but also must be able to understand how its role fits into the grand scheme of battle. It also has to believe wholeheartedly that the other units will cover up its own flaws while they do the same for them, all working towards the common goal.

Integrated warfare is a complicated system, and only an army with sufficient training is able to implement it successfully, hence its relatively late appearance in western warfare. Furthermore, if any one of the parts of the system breaks down or is overcome, then the whole military machine collapses along with it. Because each unit's strengths protect the weaknesses of others, once one fails the other is exposed to the danger.

So we can see that combined arms is a difficult system to implement fully and successfully. But when employed as integrated warfare it is a highly effective way of neutralising any weaknesses and enhancing the overall ability of the army, whether in attack or defence.

The effect of terrain on warfare and units

Terrain strongly influences warfare and battles in particular. Good generals adapt their battle plans to the terrain on which they are to fight. But topography also influenced the style of unit developed. "Geography had much to do with the development of regional or national models of warfare, as seen with the Greeks, the Persians, and the Parthians".[1] As discussed next, the flat terrain of Thessaly, Boeotia, and Macedon allowed those Greek states to develop a reliable cavalry force alongside infantry. The mountainous terrain of Aetolia led to a dependence on light infantry.[2] Despite terrain restrictions armies had to adopt other styles of warfare in order to make use of combined arms. In this study terrain will be discussed in detail wherever it is important for a particular battle or for the development of specific units.

Unit categorisation and subdivisions

Each of the basic types of unit used in combined arms can be subdivided into heavy and light (that is heavily armed and lightly armed) and even further into various armaments or fighting styles. In order to fully appreciate the varying abilities of each unit, we have to describe their normal equipment and primary function.[3] Before beginning the historical analysis of the development of combined arms, it is necessary to briefly outline the many unit types present in ancient warfare with a particular focus on Greece.

Plutarch (*Pelopidas* 2.1) provides a metaphor of the army as a body: "as Iphicrates analyzed the matter, the light-armed troops are like the hands, the cavalry like the feet, the phalanx itself like the chest and breastplate, and the general like the head".[4] Plutarch's purpose in quoting Iphicrates is to show that generals were foolish who did not realise their own survival was of paramount importance for the success of their army. However, it also shows us how Plutarch, Iphicrates, and their audiences viewed each part of an army in terms of its purpose in battle. Iphicrates' metaphor adequately explains the system of combined arms in one of its most basic forms, using light and heavy infantry and light cavalry. It does not, however, go far enough in providing a function for all the different units employed in an advanced system of combined arms. Let us take each of the military arms in turn – infantry and missile troops, and cavalry – and expand on Iphicrates' body metaphor to cover the whole range of units in an army.

Infantry – the hands, arms, and chest of the army

Infantry are the glue that all armies require. They are usually the base foundation on which all the other units are added. The heavy infantry, in Greece in particular, are often the main force of an army, hence Plutarch's association with the chest. Light infantry and missile infantry, although usually more numerous, typically had little to do with the outcome of a battle, yet were very useful in war, hence their association with the arms in my description. Elite heavy infantry, something akin to modern special-forces units, usually delivered the heavy infantry's offensive force, the punch from the hands. This section will deal with all the types of infantry that appear in the ancient world in turn. Specific, and more detailed, analysis will be reserved for the appearance of each unit in the historical development chapters that follow.

Regular heavy infantry – the chest and breastplate of the army

As Iphicrates stated, it is the heavy infantry that fill the role of the chest, or body, of the army. They are often its principal defence, since they are called "the breastplate" (Plutarch, *Pelopidas* 2.1). Whether that heavy infantry is a sarissa phalanx, such as the Macedonians used, a hoplite phalanx in the Greek style, or the Roman legionary, does not change its main role. Some armies relied on the heavy infantry more than others.[5] Few armies can be repeatedly successful in all aspects of warfare without including some form of heavy infantry as a foundation.[6]

What makes a heavy infantryman? Is the definition one of weight of armour or weight of attack? To many admirers of the Greek hoplite it is certainly the former. Herodotus (9.62.3) states that the Persians at Plataea were weakened by their lack of armour and could not hope to win a battle as *anhoploi* against *hoplitai*. He goes on (9.63.2) to describe the Persians as lightly armed (*gymnetes*). He also describes the armament of the Persians as having an iron scale corselet but no metal helmet or greaves and only a wicker shield (7.61.1). Herodotus is ignoring the fact that the Persians used scale armour, especially in their elite units, and believes that the bronze panoply of the hoplite was greatly superior. To Herodotus, then, it was the armour of the Greeks that made them so successful as a heavy infantry unit. However, the Persians, Egyptians, Assyrians, and other eastern civilisations did field infantry armed with spear, shield, helmet, and some form of effective body armour, just like hoplites. Why are these not classed as heavy infantry by Herodotus?

Perhaps the difference is the weight of attack. Some of the reasons that the Persians were defeated by the Greek hoplites are the relative shortness of Persian spears and the size and construction of their wicker shields. The fact that they did not fight in a dense formation such as the phalanx also made their attack much less penetrative and their defence much less effective. The early Egyptians apparently lacked any form of good defensive armour. Contrary to Herodotus' belief, the Persian spearmen were heavy infantry; they were simply not as heavy as Greek hoplites.[7]

Snodgrass, when discussing the Macedonian sarissa phalanx, states that the infantry did not wear bronze corselets and "they were thus in no real sense heavy infantry".[8] But they did have helmets and bronze-faced shields, and perhaps greaves. By the mid-sixth century the Greek hoplite was usually armed with a linen corselet rather than a bronze breastplate. Since the Macedonian phalangite was also equipped with a linen corselet, in this respect the Greek hoplite is certainly not much more protected than his northern counterpart. The main difference between the two is the use of a sarissa and smaller shield instead of the hoplite spear (*dory*) and shield (*hoplon*). Both should be classed as heavy infantry because of their roles and abilities in battle regardless of their armour.

The sarissa phalanx was preeminent in warfare throughout the Hellenistic Age, suggesting a Macedonian superiority over the Greek hoplite in both attack and defence in many situations. The battles of Chaeronea in 338 and Megalopolis in 331 are perhaps the best examples of the relative abilities of the sarissa and hoplite phalanx.[9] Despite the perceived relative lack of armour, the soldiers of the sarissa phalanx achieved the prime function of a heavy infantry unit to excel in hand-to-hand combat, albeit at a greater distance because of the length of the sarissa.

In my view a heavy infantryman is determined by the use and effectiveness of defensive armour *as well as* his abilities in close-quarter combat. Perhaps a better definition is any foot soldier whose defensive and offensive abilities in a battle are very high and whose main function in battle is to engage in close combat or hand-to-hand warfare. He may have metal armour and large shield or simply a large weapon.[10] There were many varieties of heavy infantry in the ancient and mediaeval worlds, but each is usually intended to be successful in battle at close quarters. The main armaments of a heavy infantryman are usually some form of body armour, a shield, and an assault weapon of some form.

Whatever armament a heavy infantry unit employs, its strengths and weaknesses remain almost the same. In most cases a unit will function more effectively when fighting in a formation with its flank and rear protected, especially Greek heavy infantry armed with spear and shield.[11] Even when not deployed in formation, the heavy infantry was often the most important part of the army in the majority of battles in the ancient world. It was the heavy infantry of Rome that created and maintained its empire.

The main weaknesses of most heavy infantry units are their slow movement and lack of flexibility. Phalanxes especially were vulnerable when attacked on their exposed flank and rear.[12] The more professional armies instituted a number of drills to allow them to change face in an instant to counter that threat.[13] A unit relying on heavy armour or a large weapon loses mobility in a trade-off for a greater frontal offensive force. In the same way, a unit armed with lighter armour and a sword or other smaller assault weapon is more flexible in its formation and mobility on the battlefield, but often has less of an impact in a frontal attack. Once at close quarters, with the enemy unable or unwilling to get away, the heavy infantryman is in his element. He can hack or stab at will behind the relative safety of his armour and is very effective with his expertise in hand-to-hand warfare. Getting to that point, if the enemy does not want to do so, is the difficult part.

Since this study centres on Greek warfare, most of the focus is on Greek heavy infantry units. These are mainly the hoplites and the sarissa phalangites. But the various units used by the Persians also appear. A closer examination of the specific armaments and tactics of the various units in this study will be given as they appear in the historical record.

Elite heavy infantry – the hands of the army

Most societies throughout history maintained a force of elite infantry that was tasked with the most arduous aspects of battle and campaigning and which usually delivered the offensive thrust of the infantry. In Greece these were the Spartan *Homoioi* (Similars) or the Theban Sacred Band, and in Macedon the hypaspists and argyraspids. In Persia they were the Immortals. They are the hands of our body metaphor, as they could carry out all the necessary tasks for an army on campaign while also delivering the knockout punch when required.

Usually taken out of the ranks of the regular infantry, these were the most professional and experienced units in the army. They usually fought in the front ranks in battle, just as the Sacred Band at Leuctra, and were usually the first over the walls in sieges, just as the hypaspists under Alexander the Great. Due to their greater skill, training, discipline, and experience these troops generally were more mobile than regular heavy infantry, as they were fitter and more used to the difficulties of warfare. The hypaspists under Alexander even ran alongside cavalry into battle while still fighting on foot as heavy infantry. The units specific to each society will be discussed in more detail as they appear in the following chapters.

Light infantry – the arms of the army

Iphicrates equates the light infantry with the hands of the body. This fits with their role as the general dogsbodies of an army, doing all the necessary but unglamorous work behind the scenes. However, this ignores the action of the hands in punching the enemy. Light infantry on their own were rarely capable of delivering a knockout blow to an enemy force. I have, therefore, adjusted their metaphorical place to the arms and making the elite infantry the hands.

Light infantry are a much more diverse collection of troops than heavy infantry. They range from the peasant armed only with what he could find to a professional, well-armed, and experienced mercenary peltast. Missile troops are an integral part of light infantry and often are the only such troops in an army. The principal role of the light infantryman was to support the heavy infantry and protect them in their vulnerable areas, usually on the flanks. Light infantry are also very effective

18 *The theory of combined arms*

against cavalry, and particularly chariots, as they have the agility and flexibility to crowd or avoid the mounted soldier and to drag, or shoot, him off his horse or chariot.

The great disadvantage of light infantry is their vulnerability in close-quarter situations. Although some armies, such as the Assyrians, used heavily armed archers in order to increase their effectiveness at close quarters, most archers wore no armour or protective gear at all. Consequently, they were very exposed if the enemy were able to close them down, and in such cases a great number of casualties ensued. This is why a force of non-missile light infantry unable to attack and maintain their distance, unless they have an overwhelming superiority in numbers, cannot function as the main thrust of an army opposed by heavy infantry.[14] In using light infantry, the trade-off is for a highly mobile force excelling at skirmishing and rapid attacks but that is also ineffective in close combat.

Missile troops

The primary focus of missile troops is to engage the enemy at a distance before the two opposing forces close hand to hand. There are many specific tactical uses for missile troops ranging from pre-battle skirmishing and harassing an enemy's march to covering the movements of other units. Their main use in a battle is to protect the flanks of heavy infantry and cavalry, as well as forming a screen in front of the whole line. They are most successful at breaking up enemy attacks, especially cavalry or chariot charges, using the sheer numbers of their missiles to expose both horse and rider.[15] With time to concentrate their missiles on densely packed formations of infantry they can also cause significant damage. Just like other forms of light infantry, missile troops are often ineffective in hand-to-hand conflict. It is for this reason that eastern armies began to protect archers with metal armour and equip them also with assault weapons, such as swords, axes, or spears. Such soldiers could act as heavy infantry fighting successfully at close quarters while also being just as able to engage at a distance.[16]

The problem with most ancient missile weapons is that their penetrative effectiveness was rather limited.[17] So the offensive ability of missile troops was not necessarily to kill or disable a significant number of the enemy, but rather to break up attacks and give cover to allow the decisive units to enter the fray. Archers, slingers, and javelin men were the principal types of missile troops used in ancient warfare. Individual units will be discussed in more detail as they appear. Here it is enough to provide a brief discussion of each type of unit.

Archers

Archery required large amounts of practice to master, and as a result skilled archers were in demand in the ancient world. East of the Aegean archery was popular and often decided battles especially after the invention of the composite bow. The professional troops of most eastern empires, such as the Assyrians and Persians, were archers and archery was favoured as an aristocratic pursuit.

The Persians relied more on archers in their army than any other form of infantry.[18] However, in Greece archery was ignored for the most part in favour of the hoplite. In the more isolated parts of Greece this was not the case. Crete, in particular, promoted archery and its archers were often hired as mercenaries throughout the Mediterranean.[19]

Javelin men

Before the advent and widespread adoption of the effective composite bow, javelins were the principal missile weapon in an army. The Sumerians armed their chariot warriors with javelins, and even after the adoption of the highly effective composite bow chariots maintained a quiver of javelins. Drews (1993) argues that it was the arrival of northern armies armed with the javelin that prompted the downfall of Mycenaean Greece and other states reliant on the chariot in battle. This is unlikely, but in the east the javelin was for the most part abandoned in favour of the more expensive, and difficult to master, composite bow. The use of a javelin required comparatively little training and was therefore the principal weapon given to missile troops.

Slingers

Slingers rarely appear in Greek warfare.[20] They are often classed alongside other missile troops as the light infantry in an army. Elsewhere a number of ancient armies made use of slingers, particularly in the east and western Europe.[21] According to Pritchett's summary, ancient sources state "that the range of the slinger was longer than that of the bow and javelin".[22] Lead bullets, usually between 30 and 40 grams, could penetrate the body and were hard to extract.[23] Plato (*Laws* 794c, 834a) even lists the use of a sling as one of the main arts a child should learn in his ideal state, suggesting slingers had their uses in war, probably to defend cities or on ships.

The biblical tale of David and Goliath is a perfect example of a slinger in battle and reveals both the low status of slingers as well as their existence in many armies of the ancient world. Rhodes became synonymous with slingers in the ancient world.[24] Xenophon (*Anabasis* 3.3.16) states that "their missile carries no less than twice as far as those from the Persian slings". The city of Aspendus was so proud of its greatest export, the mercenary slinger, that it put his image on its coins.[25] The art of the slinger is difficult to master, needs space to be used in battle and, until the manufacture of lead bullets, caused limited damage to an armoured opponent.[26] These factors reduced the need for slingers in battle in Greece in particular, where the hoplite's armour would protect him from all but the most precise volley from a slinger.

Peltasts

Peltasts are a hybrid light infantry unit that functions somewhere between missile and non-missile infantry.[27] Armed with a small shield, or *pelte*, javelins, and a helmet, they repeatedly proved their effectiveness in battle using hit-and-run tactics.[28] They could also be called on to engage in hand-to-hand combat and were usually armed with a small sword or dagger for this purpose, and perhaps under Iphicrates a long thrusting spear.[29] The peltast was the main type of soldier in Thrace, along with light cavalry.[30]

The terrain of Thrace and the north of Greece was ill-suited to hoplite warfare.[31] The successes of Thracian peltasts against Greek hoplite armies that were unsupported by light infantry or missile troops caused the widespread adoption of peltasts into all Greek warfare by the end of the Peloponnesian War.[32] Other types of light infantry never reached the same level of importance as peltasts and gradually were superseded by them.

Elite light infantry – the elbows of the army

Some armies extensively used special forces of light infantry alongside elite units of heavy infantry. In our metaphor they are the elbows of the army as they link the regular infantry with the elite infantry, especially in the army of Alexander, and also maintain a significant offensive prowess in combat when supported by heavy infantry: using the elbows to strike at an opponent.

The most famous example is Alexander the Great's use of his Agrianes javelin men. This unit of allied Thracian light infantry accompanied Alexander's elite heavy infantry regiment, the hypaspists, on all the difficult or fast parts of his campaign as well as having a heightened role in battle over other light infantry. It was their expertise and discipline that made them so reliable for Alexander, and he used them to link the fast attacks of cavalry with the slower heavy infantry and to deliver offensive attacks especially on fortified positions or vulnerable enemy units in a battle.

There are few other examples of elite light infantry in Greek warfare except for Iphicrates' and Chabrias' mercenary peltasts in the Corinthian War and later. As shown best by the battle of Lechaeum and Chabrias' action outside Thebes, these peltasts were so well trained, experienced, and disciplined they could defeat a whole regiment of Spartan hoplites, or kneel to await the attack of heavy infantry. Later societies maintained elite regiments of light infantry, especially in terrain more suited to light infantry actions. It was not a great concern in Greek warfare and so is discussed sparingly here.

Cavalry – the feet of the army according to Iphicrates

The cavalry are the feet of the army if we follow Iphicrates. Iphicrates equating light infantry and cavalry to the same level of body parts (hands and feet) shows that in his time cavalry were not used as an offensive force. They were used in the same way as light infantry. Usually this was to harass the enemy or as a screen, while for the most part the winning of the battle was done by the heavy infantry. The problem here comes that, unlike with the infantry, Iphicrates does not differentiate between light and heavy or missile cavalry. In this case, unlike with the infantry, missile cavalry and light cavalry do have different functions on a battlefield, and do exist in armies together, and so should be accounted for separately. If we continue with Iphicrates' body metaphor, we must propose independent roles for the heavy, light, and missile cavalry. Again, let us deal with heavy cavalry first since here, just as with the infantry, the separation between light and heavy is significant. The chariot and the elephant are generally used in the same way as heavy cavalry and will receive a separate discussion next.

Heavy cavalry – the feet of the army

Iphicrates did not provide a role for heavy cavalry in his body metaphor, since for him cavalry in Greek armies all had the same role and armament as light cavalry. If the cavalry as a whole are the legs of the army body, the heavy cavalry are the feet used to kick the opponent. Their purpose is to attack the enemy at speed and cause as much damage as possible in a short space of time. Heavy cavalry are usually larger men riding bigger horses, wearing more armour, and fighting with stronger weapons.[33] Just as with the heavy infantry, the definition rests with the excellence of heavy cavalry at close quarters rather than necessarily more armour or armament. Armoured horse archers are still classed as missile cavalry if they are not expected to fight in hand-to-hand combat.

The main strength of a heavy cavalry force is the charge. A close formation of heavy cavalry charging at full gallop is an awe-inspiring sight, even for a well-drilled professional in the phalanx. Most cavalry charges succeed because the frightened infantryman does not stand to receive the huge force he can see coming but turns and runs before, or just as, contact is made.[34] The heavy cavalry is best used in repeated charges over short distances and falling back to charge again once the impetus has gone. The clear advantage of the fully armoured horse and rider is in the added impact of the charge. However, the extra weight of the armour of both rider and horse usually meant that they could only charge once or twice in a battle, and this rather reduced their repeated effectiveness.[35]

Another important strength of the heavy cavalry is its rapid movement and ability to change the focus of attack. Although slower than light cavalry, their flexibility in attack is a key benefit for an army in a battle.[36] Heavy cavalry can also use its strength and power in defence to withstand the cavalry or infantry of the enemy or to counterattack quickly. It is normally a very resilient unit because of the strength of both men and horses, and as a result has great stamina in close combat.

The disadvantages of heavy cavalry are few, but significant. Horses will not charge headlong into a dense mass of people especially if that mass is bristling with weapons. If the defenders can manage to stop a heavy cavalry charge in its tracks, then the stationary cavalryman becomes vulnerable to the mass of infantry.[37] Obviously the horseman has a height advantage over a man on foot, but once he is immobile he is far less effective. Heavy cavalry rely on the force of a sudden impact, and once this is removed they become much more vulnerable.

Another very important problem is the vulnerability of the horse itself. This is why many later armies began to protect their horses with armour. A heavy cavalry unit is also ineffective against missile cavalry as long as the latter can stay just out of reach and make use of its greater speed of movement. The trade-off for heavy cavalry to have an impact at close quarters is the lack of prolonged speed of movement. The weight of the rider and his armour, plus any armour placed on the horse, significantly reduces the stamina of the animal and limits the timescale of its effectiveness in battle. Light cavalry can fight for much longer periods of time without causing their mounts to go lame from exhaustion.

Chariots – earlier feet of the army

Before the advent of cavalry, the chariot was the cutting edge of the battle line. Then it functioned as the feet of the army, the role taken on by heavy cavalry. Chariots were still used in some areas even after cavalry replaced chariots as the striking force of an army on the battlefield.

There are a number of different types of chariot, especially in warfare before cavalry.[38] Chariots could have four wheels or two and range from very small mobile chariots pulled by one or two horses to large cart-like vehicles drawn by four or more. Early chariots were pulled by onagers before the harnessing of the horse and as a result were rather cumbersome and slow. Slower or larger chariots were often used as firing platforms for archers or javelin men and this was almost certainly their first use in battle.[39] They also functioned as mobile platforms to transport elite infantrymen to different parts of the battle, whether these men were aristocratic heroes, such as in Homer, or professional elite troops, just as in Assyria and the Hittite Empire.[40]

Some chariots could hold only the driver and one other warrior; others could hold four men in total. As chariots became faster and more reliable, they became more useful as a rapid attack force. Archers and other missile troops could ride in the chariot and quickly bring massive firepower to any point in the battle line, in order to assault the enemy or prevent defeat. This, it seems, was the use favoured by the Egyptian pharaohs on the open plains of North Africa and the Levant.[41] Armies in very early Greece used the chariot in a number of these different styles.[42] However, it seems from a lack of archaeological evidence that chariots were rarely used in Greek warfare after the Mycenaean period.[43] In eastern armies chariots retained their prevalence throughout.

Chariots also have limited use in rough terrain or bad weather. Darius, after preparing the ground at Gaugamela, was forced to attack prematurely when Alexander marched his army away from the levelled area and the chariots of the Indian king Porus became stuck in mud.[44] The greater mobility given to the archers in a chariot without problems with terrain could be achieved by horse archers at a much reduced expense. Once blades were added to the wheels of a chariot it was given a whole new offensive capability.[45] Scythed chariots could cause incredible carnage when charging into infantry in disorder or not in a strong formation.[46] Celtic tribal societies, particularly in Britain, continued using chariots as aristocratic status symbols and elite fighting platforms.[47]

Later Seleucid armies had scythed chariots in their armies that were increased in size to be drawn by as many as six horses. The drivers and horses were all heavily armoured in order to protect against missiles. The greater size allowed more archers to be included as well as increasing the power of its charge.[48] Despite these alterations the chariot had limited success. Antiochus III never used them in battle against Greek opponents, and when he tried to use them against the Romans at Magnesia, Eumenes the king of Pergamum told his enemy how to deal with them successfully; it was the last use of them in battle.[49] In fact, as Bar Kochva summarises, it was "the disaster inflicted on the whole force at Magnesia by the retreat of the chariots [that] persuaded the Seleucids to withdraw them for good".[50]

Scythed chariots in particular were successful in a battle when directed against a disordered mass of infantry who could not disperse. However, against a compact formation of heavy infantry their effectiveness was significantly reduced.[51] They were unable to penetrate and use their scythed wheels if the phalanx's flanks were protected. The chariot also can be easily overcome by light troops and missiles. The most problematic use of scythed chariots is the devastation they could cause on their own army in a panicked retreat, as happened to Antiochus III at Magnesia. Overall, the inclusion of scythed chariots in an army caused more harm than good. The usefulness of chariots in warfare in the Mediterranean virtually ended with the conquest of the Persian Empire by Alexander.[52]

Elephants – the joints of the army

The elephant is a form of heavy cavalry. If we were to expand on Iphicrates' metaphor once more, we may propose that elephants are the knees of the cavalry leg. They are a solid force that provides a base for the flexible movement of the cavalry and light infantry. They are usually a more defensive option, often being employed as movable mini-castles within a battle line from which to fire missiles or hold the line. The strength of the elephants provides a solid foundation for offensive or defensive action against the enemy but does not provide the flexibility of rapid action afforded by other heavy cavalry units. But they can attack if necessary, and with a greater penetrative power than heavy cavalry, in our body metaphor using a knee as an offensive move in a fight. However, the charge of the elephants often led to disaster if the lead animal was downed or they were stopped and goaded into turning on their own side.

Elephants came into western warfare through the Persian Empire after their conquest of India in particular. The Egyptian pharaohs do not seem to have made much use of elephants in battle despite their prevalence in Africa. The main uses of elephants were as shock troops and as missile-firing platforms.[53] The former use was very effective against disorganised infantry, and to some extent against cavalry where the horses were unused to the animals. The shock value was often maximised by purple cloths, or elephant armour consisting of head pieces and leg guards.[54] In certain cases the elephant's tusks were reinforced with iron.[55]

Against heavy infantry in a compact formation, the elephants' first charge had only limited success and the animals were vulnerable once they had lost their impetus.[56] If the lead elephant was killed, then the other animals would lose heart. Once an elephant was wounded or enraged, it was just as likely to attack its own side as the enemy. Elephants could also be utilised in a siege. They were able to use their trunks to pull apart wooden palisades or to force a city gate.[57] However, they were ineffective against stone foundations and were vulnerable to spiked planks, or caltrops, placed in their path, as Polyperchon found out at Megalopolis.[58] This defensive tactic could also be used on the battlefield, as most effectively seen in Ptolemy I's defeat of Demetrius at Gaza.[59]

As a firing platform, elephants were similar to chariots although the elephants themselves were more defensively sound to protect the missile troops. These missile troops sat on the elephants and later in the early third century wooden towers were built on their backs to better protect the soldiers.[60] Up to four soldiers could be placed in the tower on an Indian elephant but probably only two on the smaller north African elephants.[61] The Seleucids may have armed some men with sarissas in the elephant platform alongside the missile troops.[62]

Usually elephants were drawn up in battles intermingled with light infantry and missile troops. They acted as protection for the flanks or as a frontal screen. In a battle the defensive qualities of the elephants proved to be much more useful than their offensive thrust.[63] The effectiveness of elephants against troops who were used to them was very little and gradually they went out of use. The Parthians did not use elephants and after the 140s the Seleucid and Ptolemaic Empires abandoned them also.[64]

Light cavalry – the legs of the army

Light cavalry are the units that link the heavy infantry to the heavy cavalry and support the light infantry, or if we expand on Iphicrates' body part metaphor, they are the main limbs of the cavalry legs. Primarily used for screening the army in the vanguard or the rear or acting as flank guards, the main strength of light cavalry is their flexibility in speed of movement.[65] The other forces in the army are given the time and space to advance to the attack because of the actions and movability of light cavalry.

In Greece in particular, cavalry was not available in large numbers and there was rarely an occasion where the enemy's position or numbers were not known beforehand, reducing the opportunities for light cavalry as scouts.[66] Eumenes and Antigonus both made use of light cavalry as scouting screens when engaged in their strategic marches around Paraetacene and Gabiene, and Eumenes used his light cavalry in a flanking attack to defeat Antigonus' superior cavalry on the left wing at Paraetacene.[67]

Light cavalry as an offensive force are best unleashed on a retreating enemy to chase down the tired soldiers, where they can utilise their speed without worrying about engaging anyone in close combat.[68] Just as light infantry, light cavalry are ineffective at close quarters. In a battle they are useful to break up an attack by chariots or to harass elephants and often are used as flank guards or to screen movements.[69]

The main difference in most cases between light and heavy cavalry is primarily their tactics in battle, as well as the amount of armour worn by the rider and the horse. Some heavy cavalry used javelins or bows despite their advantage in battle relying on the impact of the charge. Light cavalry usually required less armour because of their peripheral roles in battle of scouting or screening deployments, and the choice of arms and armour often rested with the individual soldier. Light cavalry were principally reserved for scouting, in pursuit, or on the march, but nevertheless they are an indispensable force in an army. Again, there are many types of light cavalry both missile and not.

Non-missile light cavalry

Xenophon *On The Cavalry Commander* recommends that cavalry should use the javelin and not the spear. It is difficult to find many examples of non-javelin light cavalry, particularly after the widespread adoption of effective body armour by infantry and cavalry alike. Light cavalry were lightly armoured. Not expected to engage often in hand-to-hand combat light cavalry would not have needed much defensive armour in order to maintain their speed of movement. This is the trade-off: rapid movement for minimal defensive armament.

The effectiveness of such lightly armoured non-missile cavalry in battle was limited and their tactical battlefield roles could easily be provided by missile cavalry. Scouting, shielding the army's movements, pre-battle skirmishing and chasing a defeated enemy can all be achieved by missile cavalry. Because of this, light cavalry often took the form of missile cavalry of various sorts. Here light cavalry using the javelin as a throwing weapon would be classed as missile cavalry alongside horse archers.

Horse archers

Horse archers rarely appeared in Greece except in the Persian armies of Mardonius, and in Alexander's army at the end of his conquest of Persia. Although such cavalry did not play a very important role in warfare in Greece until the fourth century, it was very common in the east. Athens used some of these horsemen as mercenaries in the latter stages of the Peloponnesian War.[70] The ability of some missile cavalry units to wheel in a circle while shooting obviously has great benefits, as Crassus' death at Carrhae shows,[71] and led to the widespread use of horse archers in the east and eventually in the Roman Empire.

The most notable of these eastern horse archers were the Scythians.[72] Horse archers were often not expected to engage at close quarters and so wore little armour. Some horse archers, particularly in Assyria and Persia, were more heavily armoured since they were the main battle force and were usually expected to engage in hand-to-hand combat before or after using their bows. These are classed as heavy cavalry because their principal role in battle was to excel in close-quarter combat and use the bow as a secondary weapon before the charge. Usually horse archers were held out of the battle to engage from afar and so did not require much armour.

Field artillery

In the ancient world artillery was primarily reserved for sieges because of the relative paucity of reliable and easily manoeuvrable field artillery pieces.[73] There are very few instances of machines being used on the battlefield at all until the fourth century and even then it was a rare event.[74] The static nature of artillery did not fit with the flexible battle plans of the Hellenistic Era. Even in situations where artillery could have been used to disrupt the phalanx, the adoption of elephants fulfilled this goal.

Artillery pieces were static and so could easily be attacked and outflanked.[75] They were also very expensive, and few generals could afford to lose them by risking them in battle. Philip and Alexander certainly had artillery in their armies, and its use is recorded on occasion but not regularly enough to prompt a detailed analysis.[76] Nevertheless, a true system of combined arms should make use of artillery if it is available and easily deployable without negative effects on the battle plan, just as the Romans did.

Conclusions: the benefit of combined arms and integrated warfare

The system of combined arms is the modern term used to describe the coordinated use of different units in battle. It allows each unit to focus on its strengths without having to worry about its weaknesses since it is supported by others. In ancient warfare different units appear, or are developed, at different times. As a result, combined arms also refers to the process of developing a completely integrated army focusing on the appearance and incorporation of new, or foreign, units into the army. Why, when, and how each unit is introduced into Greek warfare, in particular, is at the centre of the discussion of combined arms here, as well as how each innovation leads to the implementation of integrated warfare.

There were many different units in use in the ancient world. Each type of unit has both strengths and weaknesses. Each "has its own special capability and relative dominance".[77] It is clear how each unit can complement and improve the other. Heavy infantry are much more secure and forceful when fighting with flanks protected by light infantry, cavalry, or missile troops, and so are able to concentrate on their offensive central thrust. Heavy cavalry are more effective when they can attack an enemy already weakened by missile troops, or one held in place by the advance of the heavy infantry. If their charge is stopped, they can rely on the heavy infantry to come to their rescue in a static close combat situation. Missile troops, both cavalry and infantry, and other light infantry are better when able to concentrate on their background roles and let the melee work be done by the more heavily armed troops. Finally, light cavalry are much more effective when retained to be unleashed fresh onto a retreating enemy or to scout the enemy's position.

Every unit has its uses but there is an exchange of abilities in each case. Those soldiers who fight well in a rigid formation at close quarters, such as the phalanx, are vulnerable on the flanks and in the rear. Those who do not need a formation are more vulnerable to concerted direct assaults and often lack organisation. Those who excel at distance fighting are limited when it comes to hand-to-hand conflict. Those who rely on speed of movement in attack or defence become less effective when their mobility is reduced. All of these trade-offs can be made redundant by the other units in an army if the commander knows how to do so — the basic principle of combined arms.

So, we can see that integrated warfare, the full realisation of combined arms, is a difficult system to implement successfully. However, when employed correctly it is a highly effective way of neutralising any weaknesses and enhancing the overall ability of the army, whether in attack or defence. It also makes it very hard for an enemy army to find any weak spots, as the different unit types mutually protect one another and eliminate all the vulnerable areas. Its implementation creates a complete package and is the forerunner of the modern professional armed forces.

Notes

1 Jones (1987): 41.
2 See Best (1969). For the style of warfare practiced in Aetolia as viewed by Messenians at Naupactus see Thucydides 3.94.3–5. Also see the battle of Spartolus below.
3 Part of this latter process involves looking at the ideology of war in societies and poleis. For example, in most Greek states the hoplite was the primary unit in an army regardless of the strategic or tactical situation. In Macedonia, by contrast, the aristocratic heavy cavalry unit was the most important. The ideology of the state regarding the qualities and uses of various units affects the employment of those troops in a battle. These problems will be dealt with in the historical chapters below.
4 See also Polyaenus 3.9.22.
5 The Greek poleis in the Classical period often fielded armies of hoplites exclusively. Whereas the armies of the late Achaemenid Persian Empire, as discussed below, tended to put their hope of victory in the heavy cavalry and archers, and relegated their spearmen to purely defensive functions.
6 Iphicrates and his victories over hoplites with only peltasts, such as at Lechaeum in 390 (Xenophon, *Hellenika* 4.5.11–17; Diodorus 14.91.2; Plutarch, *Agesilaus* 22.2), is the exception that proves the rule. Since, if the Spartans had also had light troops or cavalry used properly, they would not have suffered so badly and if Iphicrates had used his heavy infantry to follow up the decimation caused by his peltasts, then even more of the Spartans would have died. It was a chance occasion where each side only fought with one style of unit and because of the locale, the peltasts emerged victorious. The victories of eastern armies using missile cavalry and heavy cavalry demonstrate the possibility of winning battles without much heavy infantry. However, close-quarter infantry such as axemen or spearmen were used by the eastern empires, as discussed below. But these infantry were not armoured enough to be truly considered heavy infantry as the Persian defeats at the hand of hoplites demonstrated. In general, to be successful in sieges or to occupy territory requires infantry. Infantry are usually better able to excel in hand-to-hand combat the more heavily armed and armoured they are.
7 A distinction can be made between heavy infantry and medium infantry. The latter would be the Persian and Near Eastern infantry and the former the hoplite. However, in Greek warfare medium infantry rarely appear or have an important role, and so the distinction is not a focus of this study.

28 The theory of combined arms

8. Snodgrass (1999): 117
9. Chaeronea: Diodorus 16.85–6; Polyaenus 4.2.2; Demosthenes 20.2. Megalopolis: Diodorus 17.62–3; Curtius 6.1.1–16.
10. Saxon Husscaarls, who used only a double-handed axe for attack and defence, are just one example of a heavy infantry unit that did not need defensive armour or shield to be effective: Bennett et al. (2005); Poss (2011).
11. The successes of the Saxon shield wall show this in the early mediaeval period. One soldier held a shield defensively overlapping with his neighbour while from behind archers, spearmen and men armed with two-handed axes attacked the enemy. Despite relatively little body armour the shield wall was able to stand firm against repeated attacks from various types of troops. See Bennett et al. (2005); Poss (2011).
12. The defeat of Eumenes' victorious phalanx at Paraetacene (Diodorus 19.30.7–10) when attacked in the flank and rear by Antigonus' cavalry shows this well, and there are many other examples, such as Delium (Thucydides 4.90–6) and Ipsus (Plutarch *Demetrius* 29.3–5; Appian *Syrian Wars* 55).
13. The best example would be Alexander's manoeuvres of the phalanx when faced with superior numbers of Illyrians (Arrian 1.6.1–5). Xenophon (*CL* 11.8) discusses the training of the Spartan phalanx to be able to change face in an instant so that the best hoplites are always facing the enemy line. Asclepiodotus (10.1–22) and the later tactical writers describe in detail the variety of manoeuvres that could be employed by a phalanx.
14. In many instances non-missile light infantrymen are an unnecessary inclusion in an army. Their roles can easily be taken on by armoured missile troops, who provide the added bonus of being able to cause damage to the enemy at a distance using hit-and-run tactics. Nevertheless, it is necessary to mention them as many ancient armies did use them in great number because of their ready availability and cheapness.
15. This is how Alexander used them at Gaugamela, as well as to protect his vulnerable flanks (Arrian, *Anabasis* 3.8–15; Curtius 4.9.9–16; Diodorus 17.56–61; Plutarch, *Alexander* 32–3). For a full discussion of Alexander's tactical uses of light infantry, see below.
16. The best example of these dual purpose soldiers is the Persian Immortals, as discussed in detail below.
17. See Wheeler (2001). The thousands of Athenian peltasts on Sphacteria took a whole day to kill just half of 400 Spartan hoplites, if we believe our source (Thucydides 4.26–39), and Iphicrates' peltasts at Lechaeum in 390 only killed half of the Spartans there, albeit in a shorter space of time (Xenophon, *Hellenika* 4.5.11–17; Diodorus 14.91.2; Plutarch, *Agesilaus* 22.2). For references and a discussion of each battle, see below.
18. For example, the Persian elite force of 10,000 so-called Immortals was armed with spear and bow. The common organisation of the base Persian infantry unit of ten was one spearman with large shield protecting nine archers behind him. See Sekunda (1992: 16–7).
19. Cf. Thucydides 6.25.2.
20. Pritchett (1971–91: vol. V.1–67) lists all the references to slingers in the Greek and Roman worlds.
21. Echols (1949–50): 227–230.
22. Pritchett (1971–91: V.56).
23. Pritchett (1971–91: V.43).
24. Xenophon *Anabasis* 3.3.16–20; cf. Diodorus 15.85.4–5 on the training of slingers.
25. Pritchett (1971–91: V.37, 46–7).
26. Vigors (1888).
27. Griffith (1981) argues that peltasts, particularly from Thrace, influenced the Macedonian phalanx of Philip II. However, the phalanx was still a unit of heavy infantry and the evidence for Macedonian peltasts is scarce.
28. I will deal with many aspects of their uses in the historical examples below. The specific history of their development in Greek warfare has been dealt with well by Best (1969).

29 See Best (1969: 3–7) for a discussion of the early Thracian peltast's armament. See below for a discussion of Iphicrates' so-called peltast reforms.
30 Hoddinott (1981); Webber (2011).
31 Hoplites were vulnerable in wide plains and mountainous regions; the former because the phalanx could easily be outflanked and the latter because the phalanx could not maintain its rigid formation or move quickly.
32 Thucydides (6.22) has Nicias say in his speech before the campaign is launched argues that the Athenians should take "great numbers also of archers and slingers, to make head against the Sicilian horse". See Chapter 4 below for a full discussion of the Athenian campaign against Syracuse.
33 In the British army of the nineteenth century, the Heavy Brigade consisted entirely of men over six feet tall riding larger horses and wearing a large breastplate, even though rifles effectively made them defensively useless. Of course, it did not take long for the Heavy Brigade to fall out of use as the lancer and mounted rifleman became a much more efficient cavalry force in the changing style of nineteenth-century warfare. The Heavy Brigade remained for so long merely to maintain the awe of a heavy cavalry charge. Such a charge on an infantryman, even in formation, more often than not resulted in the defeat of the infantry. See Muir (2000).
34 Darius' two flights from Alexander's charge at Issus (Diodorus, 17.34.6–8; Plutarch, *Alexander* 20) and Gaugamela (Arrian, *Anabasis* 3.8–15; Curtius 4.9.9–16; Diodorus 17. 61; Plutarch, *Alexander* 33.4–5) are good examples of the effectiveness of the Macedonian heavy cavalry. For a full discussion of each battle, see the case studies in Chapter 4.
35 At Magnesia, Antiochus' cavalry and cataphracts on the right wing easily routed the opposing Roman infantry and chased them to their camp but could not be turned for another charge in time to save his defeated phalanx (Livy 37.37–44; Appian, *Syrian Wars* 30–6).
36 At Paraetacene, Antigonus' rapid attack with his heavy cavalry on Eumenes won him the battle and his kingdom (Diodorus 19. 30.7–10).
37 The defeat of the French knights at Crecy, Poitiers, and Agincourt show this, as does that of the English at Bannockburn. See Bennett et al. (2005).
38 For a detailed discussion of the various types of chariot used in ancient warfare see Cotterell (2005).
39 Moorey (1986); Anthony (1995).
40 Anderson (1975); Noble (1990); Nardo (2008).
41 Littauer and Crouwel (1985); Spalinger (2003).
42 See in particular Anderson (1965, 1975); Littauer (1972); Greenhalgh (1973); Crouwel (1981); Nefedkin (2001).
43 Also see in particular Greenhalgh (1973); Littauer (1972).
44 Chariots at Gaugamela: Arrian, *Anabasis* 3.13.2. Heckel et al. (2010). Porus: Arrian, *Anabasis* 5.14.3–15.2.
45 Nefedkin (2004).
46 For Darius III's use of scythed chariots in the battle of Gaugamela see Heckel et al. (2010).
47 Boudicca famously used chariots in her conflicts with the Romans in Britain as late as 61 CE. Anderson (1965).
48 At the parade at Daphne 100 six-horse chariots, but only 40 four-horse chariots were arrayed. Polybius (30.25.11) even records one drawn by elephants. These chariots may all have been retained for purely ceremonial reasons Bar Kochva (1976: 84).
49 Livy 37.41.6–42. The chariots were stationed on the left wing and their defeat and subsequent retreat threw the whole wing into chaos causing the rout of the whole army.
50 Bar Kochva (1976: 83).
51 Antiochus III had chariots in his Seleucid army and used them against the Romans at the battle of Magnesia as a surprise. It did not work (Livy 37.37–44; Appian, *Syrian*

Wars 30–6). He never used chariots against Macedonian style armies because of their ineffectiveness against a phalanx.
52 Cotterell (2005).
53 See Scullard (1974); Kistler (2007); Nossov and Dennis (2008).
54 Kistler (2007).
55 Appian, *Punica* 9.581–3.
56 See Charles (2008).
57 Scullard (1974); Kistler (2007).
58 Diodorus 18.71.2–3.
59 Diodorus 19.80–4; Plutarch, *Demetrius* 5. See Devine (1989b).
60 Scullard (1974); Kistler (2007)
61 Kistler (2007).
62 See Scullard (1974); Kistler (2007).
63 Glover (1948). As discussed below, the effective use of elephants in a battle was not perfected until Ipsus in 301 BCE, where Seleucus used them as a screen to hold back Demetrius' cavalry (Plutarch *Demetrius* 29.3–5; Appian *Syrian Wars* 55). Other defensive alignments did not work, such as Porus' defensive wall at the Hydaspes (Arrian 5.8–19; Curtius 8.13–14; Diodorus 17.87–9; Plutarch, *Alexander* 60–2) or the static screens adopted by Eumenes and Antigonus at Paraetacene (Diodorus 19.26–31) and Gabene (Diodorus 19.39–43; Plutarch, *Eumenes* 16).
64 Glover (1944).
65 There are many examples of this practice. See for example Alexander's uses of light cavalry at Gaugamela (Arrian, *Anabasis* 3.8–15; Curtius 4.9.9–16; Diodorus 17. 61; Plutarch, *Alexander* 33.4–5).
66 Spence (1993); Gaebel (2002).
67 Paraetacene: Diodorus 19.26–31. Gabiene: Diodorus 19.39–43; Plutarch, *Eumenes* 16.
68 There are of course many examples of cavalry turning defeat into a rout. The first in the Greek world was the battle of Inessa in 426–425 BCE during the Peloponnesian War (Thucydides 3.103). Perhaps the most significant in the Greek world was the defeat of Lysander at Haliartus. There the Theban cavalry turned his defeat into a complete rout (Xenophon, *Hellenika* 3.5.17–20; Diodorus 14.81.1–3; Plutarch, *Lysander* 28).
69 Alexander made great use of light cavalry as flank guards in battles, especially at Gaugamela where he used them to extend his line beyond the Persian wing (Arrian, *Anabasis* 3.8–15; Curtius 4.9.9–16; Diodorus 17. 61; Plutarch, *Alexander* 33.4–5). In this situation their lack of ability at close quarters did not matter since they were only required to fight other light cavalry.
70 Sulimirski (1952).
71 Sampson (2008).
72 Gardiner-Garden (1987); Karasulas (2004).
73 Small and reliable machines did not really come into play in Greek warfare until the fourth century. By then the Macedonians relied on the flexibility of their battle lines for victory. The benefits of static artillery were outweighed by the manoeuvrability of missile infantry and cavalry. See Marsden (1969).
74 See Marsden (1969).
75 Machanidas' defeat by the Achaeans at Mantinea in 207 (Polybius 16.36–7; Pausanias 3.10) and the success of the Romans at Thermopylae (Livy 36.15–19; Appian, *Syrian Wars* 17–20; Plutarch, *Cato the Elder* 13–14) and Aous Gorge (Livy 32.5–6, 10–12; Plutarch, *Flamininus* 3–5) show the vulnerability of static artillery.
76 See Keyser (1994) and below.
77 Jones (1987: 39–45) provides a detailed discussion of the relative merits of each of the four basic types of unit in battle against the others.

Section 1
The hoplite revolution in Greece

1 Homeric warfare and the introduction of the hoplite

Primary sources for Greek warfare

Before we can begin any discussion on the history of Greece, we must first discuss the quality of the sources from which we draw our information. Whether the source is a historical account, such as Thucydides' *Peloponnesian War*, or a biography, such as one of Plutarch's various *Lives*, we have to assess the reliability of the account. The nature and purpose of the source, the bias of the author, the origin of the source, the purpose of the information – all these have to be assessed to determine the value of the piece of history.

In view of the large time period this study covers, it is necessary to use many types of sources. But very few of these accounts are concerned specifically with military information. Even a history of Alexander that describes his battles in detail and which was written by an experienced military leader, such as Arrian's *Anabasis*, spends more time glorifying the man and his achievements rather than examining thoroughly the mechanics of his army or campaign. The biographies of Plutarch provide a significant amount of character detail but were never written for the purpose of pure history. As a result, we have to use every type of available source whatever its form and function. Our ability to reliably reconstruct the tactics and events of a particular battle is significantly reduced as a result of all these factors.[1] As Hans van Wees succinctly summarises:

> the problem with the study of Greek warfare of any period is that so many ancient authors tell us about military ideals, of which they often needed to remind themselves and their audiences, whereas so few of them tell us about the humdrum military realities with which they were only too familiar. If there is one common failing in modern work on the subject, it is that it underestimates how wide the gap between ideal and reality could be.[2]

Despite the many problems of historiography associated with our sources, the accuracy of most ancient historical accounts, in Greece in particular, was considerable in terms of many of the specific details of a battle. It is likely that locals went to observe battles nearby as a function of human curiosity, just as schoolchildren flock to observe the fight in the playground, or villagers follow the fire engine or police car to the scene of an accident.³ Much of the information in our primary sources is reliable, especially if it is corroborated elsewhere by archaeology or contemporary inscriptions. In my view we must be careful not to hinder the effectiveness of modern historical interpretations on account of too many limits placed on the reliability of our sources through an obsession with historiography.⁴

In this book, I will engage in a detailed discussion of sources only where the purpose, nature, or any other aspect of the historiography impacts considerably the analysis of combined arms or a particular battle. Each section will begin with a discussion of the merits of all the primary sources relevant to that particular period.

Homeric warfare

There is still a debate today whether the warfare depicted in Homer represents Mycenaean practice or that of the poet's own time (c. 750–700 BCE), or perhaps somewhere in between.⁵ It is very difficult to determine the style of warfare used without any definitive statement to that effect by the poet himself, which has led Pritchett to conclude: "Doubtless many periods of warfare are represented in the *Iliad*".⁶ We see the events of a war fought in the Mycenaean period narrated by a much later poet, but since the style of warfare described could have occurred at either time period we cannot draw any firm conclusions.⁷ This longstanding debate is not crucial here since the primary concern is an analysis of combined arms warfare, and a surface analysis of warfare in Homer's poems serves well.⁸

Since it is clear that Homeric battles were infantry based, it is not necessary to wade deeply into the debate of the precise era of warfare and culture represented in Homer. Suffice it to say that whatever period or amalgamation of battle styles, Homer is not describing a combined arms army integrating close-combat infantry and missile troops with chariots or cavalry. However, the close combat infantry do fight alongside and intermingled with missile troops, and this will be the focus of the following discussion.

It is difficult to garner any comprehensive picture of the overall style of battle in Homer since his focus, and that of his audience, is on the individual heroes. Nevertheless, it is necessary to examine briefly the style of infantry warfare shown in Homer in order to demonstrate the lack of combined arms integrating cavalry or chariots in Greece between the Mycenaean period and the Peloponnesian War.

Sources

The main written sources for any discussion of Homeric warfare are obviously the two epic poems, the *Iliad* and the *Odyssey*. There are also many images on pottery from later periods. Epic poets may have described the past in detail but they also had to take into account the familiarities of their audience: "the society depicted by Homer, for all its apparent remoteness in time, had to make sense to a contemporary audience".[9] Homer's narration of battle scenes and the descriptions of armour and armaments reveal as much about the information expected to be understood by his audience as the poet himself. He spends little time detailing large-scale battle tactics and the actions of the mass of troops because his audience would be expected to know that already. Such scenes are also not required for his focus on the heroic deeds of his individual characters.

His principal concern, and the main interest of his audience, was the deeds of the heroes. Homer does not want to describe the specific tactics of battle in the *Iliad* because it would take away from his narrative, and he does not need to do so since his audience would understand how battle worked.[10]

Heavy infantry

Homer's concern was for the heroes, the aristocratic generals in the Greek and Trojan armies. Once battle was joined, the fighting became a melee and the level of organisation within each army was very low, as shown by Van Wees.[11] Thus battle in Homer's accounts was very much an initial order of marshalled infantry and then disorganised chaos. The main question regarding infantry in the Homeric epics is whether hoplites are described.

A Greek hoplite was a heavy infantryman, usually wearing a bronze helmet and breastplate. Primarily made of bronze to begin with, the breastplate was eventually replaced with the lighter, but just as durable, leather or linen cuirass. Arm guards and greaves to cover the shins were optional extras for the wealthier soldiers. The main armaments were a nine-foot spear, or *dory*, and a wooden shield faced with bronze called a *hoplon*. This shield was three feet in diameter, and convex so that it could rest on the fighting man's left shoulder. These armaments together are referred to as the hoplite panoply.[12]

The hoplite panoply is alluded to occasionally in the *Iliad*. Hector wears the hoplite bronze corselet he took from Patroclus when he is killed by Achilles' spear thrust into his throat, the only part of him exposed (*Iliad* 22.320–9). The bronze also gleamed on the breast of Achilles as he ran (*Iliad* 22.32). Paris puts on greaves and corselet as well as a horse-plumed, well-wrought helmet and carries a heavy and sturdy shield to face Menelaus, who also arms himself in the same manner (*Iliad* 3.330–340). The fullest description is the arming of Agamemnon in Book 11 of the *Iliad* where he clearly uses a hoplite panoply (*Iliad* 11.15–45). This includes a bronze embossed shield that covers two men on each side, perhaps a reference to the width of the *hoplon* or at the very least to a large, heroically sized, hand-grip shield.

Hoplite warfare tactics of the dense phalanx also may appear. The Greeks, ready for inspection, bristle with shields and spears in blue-black phalanxes (*Iliad* 4.274), and the Greeks with shining armour clash with the Trojans, a fight of bronze-corseleted men (*Iliad* 8.60–65). But, as discussed extensively by Van Wees, none of Homer's descriptions necessarily implies the hoplite phalanx familiar from the Classical period.[13]

There are certainly aspects of the warfare described in Homer that remind us of hoplite battle, but these allusions are interspersed with numerous references to Mycenaean and pre-hoplite era weapons and armour. Priam in his appeal to Hector bemoans the time "when some man by thrust or cast of the sharp bronze hath reft my limbs of life" (*Iliad* 22.67–8) and that a young man "slain in battle, that he lie mangled by the sharp bronze" is prey to dogs (*Iliad* 22.72–3). These are just two instances of the many that show Homer referring to bronze-tipped weapons rather than iron ones, perhaps artistically but certainly anachronistically. Homer's military descriptions are confusing at best since they amalgamate hoplite arms and armour and aspects of pre-hoplite warfare. Some problems also come when trying to determine whether the pre-hoplite warfare he describes details Mycenaean battle or fighting styles in Archaic Greece.[14]

An example of the junction of various historical fighting styles is the argument for Hector using a body-shield (*Iliad* 6.117–8) when he withdraws from the fighting.[15] Homer states that his neck and ankles were tired from the black hide beating on them. This must refer to the body-shield, even though Homer (*Iliad* 6.118) states his pain was from the hard leather rim that ran around the bossed shield, a type of hand-grip shield addition. Another example (*Iliad* 7.238–240) is Hector stating that he knows "well how to wield to right, and well how to wield to left my shield of seasoned hide, which I deem a sturdy thing to wield in a fight", showing that Homer is describing the use of the tactics of a hand-grip shield rather than the less manoeuvrable *hoplon*, even though elsewhere (*Iliad* 13.803–4) Hector's shield is described as round and bronze faced.

It is also at the end of the Geometric period that the hand-grip round shield is replaced by the large, circular, and convex shield associated with Classical hoplites. Hoplite tactics are implied in Homer but there are no clear references to the *hoplon* as separate from the more general bronze-faced, round hand-grip shield. Hoplite shields are represented on Attic vases from the 730s,[16] and we should conclude that the implementation of hoplite warfare was a gradual process throughout the last few decades of the eighth century. That no reference is made to the *hoplon* explicitly in Homer shows that its use was not favoured above the hand-grip shield at the time of the composition of the poems, and the concept of a hoplite using a *hoplon* in a phalanx did not exist as such even if the armaments did.

Differences also occur in attacking weapons. Heroes in Homer's works use swords, single thrusting spears, and throwing spears. This is different from the hoplite reliance on the thrusting spear, with a sword as a last resort. However, the *Iliad* always depicts heroes fighting with swords only after they have used spears or other weapons first. For example, Hector, having thrown his spear at Achilles, draws his sword, "a great sword and a mighty" (*Iliad* 22.307), only after his appeal to the imaginary Deiphobus to give him another spear is unsuccessful (*Iliad* 22.294–5). Menelaus breaks his sword on Paris' shield after the exchange of throwing spears (*Iliad* 3.360–4). The sword was the weapon of last resort to a Homeric hero, just as it was to hoplites. This is despite many of the heroes in the Homeric epics having elaborate swords.

Homeric warfare and the hoplite 37

The throwing spear became common in the early Geometric period (c. 750), and scenes in art often show spears flying through the air.[17] Agamemnon arms himself with two spears (*Iliad* 11.44) but fights with a thrusting spear (*Iliad* 11.95–99) first before throwing his spear and using a sword (*Iliad* 11.107–9). Paris has two spears at the start of Book 3 (*Iliad* 3.19), but he and Menelaus throw only one spear each in their duel before Menelaus charged at Paris with a sword (*Iliad* 3.345–365). Achilles, when he defeats Hector, throws his spear, but in order to kill his opponent later with a spear thrust, is made to have Athena return his thrown spear to him (*Iliad* 22.273–7). Telemachos fetches two spears each in preparation for the attack on the suitors only for them to be shown using a single thrusting spear later (*Odyssey* 22.110; 144; 292). Van Wees argues that the use of weapons in Homer mirrors their use in Archaic Greek warfare, and I agree.[18]

Images of infantry in Greek art in the ninth and eighth centuries show the prominent use of swords rather than spears.[19] Large numbers of swords have been found in graves from this period.[20] Infantry are also shown using throwing spears and bows, sometimes while also wearing a helmet and using a shield.[21] After 700 the spear was used in favour of the sword eventually becoming the main weapon of the hoplite.[22]

Another problem is the number of references to iron. Homer only mentions an iron sword five times in his works, clearly showing he is describing the Bronze Age when iron was still a precious metal. However, iron can be seen in each poem, for example the description of a smith working iron (*Iliad* 18.475) and iron drawing a man to battle (*Odyssey* 16.294). By the eighth century iron was the main metal for weapons, although bronze was retained for facing shields and constructing armour.[23] Homer knew that his characters lived in an age before iron and so usually described them in terms of bronze.[24]

Missile infantry

The bow is not as common a weapon in Homer as a melee armament, and yet on occasion it is afforded greater importance in war than hand-to-hand weapons. Philoctetes had to be brought to Troy in order for his expertise with the bow to bring the Greeks victory (*Iliad* 2.720; cf. Sophocles, *Philoctetes*). Paris rejoices in shooting Diomedes in the foot during his *aristeia* and is the only one who forces him to leave the battlefield (*Iliad* 6.375–9). Even the greatest hero, Achilles, is killed by an arrow in his foot, although this is never mentioned by Homer (Ovid, *Metamorphoses* 12.580–619). Odysseus fights the suitors armed with a single spear and hand-grip shield (*Odyssey* 16.295; 22.292–3) but is more renowned for his prowess as an archer who can string a huge bow (*Odyssey* Book 21; cf. 8.215–25), a distinctly Mycenaean theme. These few examples show that the bow still held significant importance in the warfare described in the Homeric epics.[25]

It is, however, difficult to determine whether archery features in Homer because it still played a part in battles of the poet's own time or because Homer wanted his audience to appreciate its role in earlier Mycenaean warfare.[26] The bow certainly remained a useful weapon in Greek warfare, but the tendency of Greeks to alienate or belittle archers has led to the belief that they were not used in warfare. Snodgrass has argued that archery disappeared in Greece in the Dark Ages on account of the relatively few arrows that have been excavated.[27] But Van Wees shows that a third of weapons pictured in Greek art between 850 and 700 are drawn bows, suggesting a continued reliance on archery in battle.[28]

Archers are occasionally portrayed by Homer as cowardly soldiers who fight unheroically from a safe distance. Homer has Diomedes berate Paris with a number of abuses, the first of which is "you archer!" (*Iliad* 11.385). This deprecating view of archery is prevalent in Classical Greek histories, as Hornblower summarises succinctly.[29] Despite this tendency to denigrate the role of the archer in battle in Greece, archery must have been used, especially to protect the city, even if sieges were rare until the fourth century. Archers were also very successful on board ships, where they could pick off the unarmoured sailors at will or force immobilised crews to surrender.[30] Athens records the deaths of barbarian archers alongside citizen dead with no apparent distinction in status or importance in war.[31] Certainly archery was not as important in hoplite warfare but in Homer's time, and certainly in the historical setting of the Trojan War, archers must have been part of battle. As Van Wees states, "Homer, in other words, is aware of the older, more prominent, role of archers, but is also familiar with the archaic practice".[32]

Infantry combined arms

The armaments of the infantry in Homer represent a mixture of different fighting styles. As a result, soldiers are described using a variety of different weapons from bows and throwing spears to spears and swords. There is no detail given on specific formations of troops or uses of missile and heavy and light infantry separately as tactical units. Rather, all the infantry fight together on the battlefield using whatever weapon they have at hand in whatever way that weapon was most useful. Heroes fought hand to hand but could use the bow, and archers hid behind individual spearmen on the battlefield.

It is impossible to draw conclusions about any standard armament or organised and separated tactical infantry practice of Homer's time.[33] Instead we must conclude that infantrymen were the principal forces in the warfare described by Homer, armed in a variety of ways, and that specialised archers and other missile troops, if there were any, fought dispersed among the ranks of other infantry in a haphazard fashion. This is definitively not a utilisation of combined arms, where the different types of troops (here heavy infantry and missile infantry) are integrated separately into a combined battle plan to maximise the strengths and weaknesses of each unit.

Chariots

Homer principally describes chariots being used to convey heroes to the front lines to collect their trophies, but he also records reminiscences of chariot battles.[34] Nestor tells his chariots to keep in line as they advance (*Iliad* 4.300) and Hector repeatedly orders the chariots to charge at the Greeks (e.g. *Iliad* 15.346; 16.833). It is possible that until one side broke ranks chariots did indeed convey men to the front as well as, or instead of, functioning as manoeuvrable firing platforms.[35] Once one side retreated, chariots were used to save the fleeing heroes or to enable a faster and more destructive pursuit of the defeated.[36]

Here it is likely that we have references in Homer to two styles of warfare that used chariots differently. Chariots perhaps were still used for transport to the battlefield in Homer's time and after, as the mid-seventh-century Chigi vase suggests as discussed next, but they may also be an anachronistic addition by the poet in order to take the audience back to an age of chariot supremacy. Suffice it to say that there is no firm evidence that chariots in Homer fight alongside the infantry, and therefore they are never used in a system of combined arms.

The well-armed elite fought on foot, and as a result the chariot was not a significant feature of Greek warfare.[37] It certainly was never integrated into the battle tactics of Greek warfare after the Mycenaean period and was quickly abandoned even by the elite in favour of riding the cheaper and more practical horse. As discussed next, the Archaic Greek use of horses was as heavy infantry transports in the same way as Homer describes the use of the chariot.

Cavalry

In Homer there are no references to cavalry. There are images of armoured men riding horses in Dark Age Greece, however, the probable time of the composition of the poems. Greenhalgh has shown that it is very likely that the images of such heavily armed cavalrymen depicted soldiers who would ride to battle attended by a squire and dismount to fight.[38] This is proven by the fact that most of the weapons excavated from the Proto-Geometric and Geometric periods involve hand-to-hand combat, something that did not become common cavalry practice until the eighth or seventh centuries even in the Near East where cavalry was first developed and deployed extensively.

Worley argues that cavalry did fight in battle on horseback in Dark Age Greece, as they did in contemporary Assyria, and that their importance in warfare in Greece is overlooked, but his argument is based on comparative evidence rather than any Greek evidence.[39] It is possible that once the hoplite phalanx was created existing cavalry forces were hastily abandoned everywhere and as a result have left us little evidence of their use. Perhaps the Spartan unit called the *hippeis*, described by Lazenby as an elite unit of hoplites in the classical period,[40] is a remnant of this earlier system of an aristocratic cavalry. Aristotle (*Politics* 1297b) stated that early Greek fighting between poleis involved the cavalry, *hippeis*, of each side because the infantry were not yet ordered into a phalanx and without this formation hoplites are useless. This supports this conclusion, however, cavalry as used in the east, as scouts or as mounted archers, are never shown in images of early Greek warfare. It is enough to conclude that cavalry played a very limited role, if at all, in the warfare in Greece from the fall of the Mycenaeans through to the late eighth century and perhaps even later.[41]

Combined arms conclusions

Whether Homer describes hoplite warfare or Mycenaean warfare, or something in between, it is clear, as Van Wees states, that his

> battle narrative cuts back and forth between close-ups of the deeds of a few men somewhere along the front and panoramic images of the entire mass of men in action, exchanging missiles and trading blows. . . . In the fluid, open-order action of the epic, mass fighting takes place at close range and long range at the same time.[42]

Van Wees has shown that Homeric warfare involved missiles and hand-to-hand combat at different times.[43] The heroes in Homer almost always fight as heavy infantry in hand-to-hand combat while also throwing their spears, and the rest of the army probably did the same. Fighting style varied during the ebb and flow of the battle, sometimes involving missile duels and sometimes close-quarter melees in separate parts of the field.[44] The soldiers wandered in and out of the battle, and even heroes are shown in the rear ranks resting or encouraging others to fight.

> To the modern reader, unfamiliar with the kind of fighting described by the poet, the panoramic scene of "shields clashing" at the beginning of the first battle (4.446–56) may suggest a collision of two close-order phalanxes, while the missiles which fly all morning at the beginning of the third battle (11.90–1) may sound like long range skirmishing. But to audiences who understood how the heroes fought it would have been obvious that such images simply represented two sides of the same coin.[45]

It is likely that this style of battle was usual in Homer's time before the advent of a hoplite phalanx, which saw a more regimented fighting style. Nevertheless, Homeric warfare does not involve any use of combined arms tactics of infantry and chariots in coordination. The missile infantry fight alongside the close combat troops without any apparent regimentation or even differentiation between the two.

The army familiar to Homer's audience had little in the way of hierarchical organisation and is thought to have been united under the command of the local leader.[46] Battles at this time involved armies commanded by the king, or general, fighting en masse in a disorganised melee of infantry. Van Wees conjectures that

Homeric warfare and the hoplite 41

any concept of military hierarchy came into place with the implementation of military alliances between *poleis* in the sixth century.[47] The well-armed, perhaps chariot-driven aristocrats fought independently throughout the battle separated from the rest of the infantry.[48] Crucially for the purpose of this study all soldiers fought alternately as missile or close combat infantry. This makes it very difficult to propose any tactical use of combined arms.

There was no idea of units fighting collectively or independently, and certainly no integration of cavalry or chariots into the army. All types of non-aristocratic soldiers fought side by side, and it was every man for himself. Once the close order of the phalanx was implemented a hierarchical command structure became necessary in order to maintain strict discipline within the formation. Before this, any use of combined arms in warfare was accidental as the infantry fought using missiles and melee weapons at their discretion. That Odysseus is famed for use of the bow but fights the suitors as a spearman (*Odyssey* Books 21 and 22) demonstrates that there was no differential in Homeric warfare between missile troops and close-quarter combat infantry. Therefore, battle in Homer cannot be said to demonstrate the use of combined arms.

Notes

1 The more military-focused accounts of the tactical manuals provide few particulars of tactics on the battlefield. Our examination of the development of combined arms does not allow for a detailed focus on logistics, training, and internal army hierarchical organisation. As a result, very little evidence from the tactical manuals is required, and so I will not focus on the historiography of this type of source.
2 Van Wees (2005: 2).
3 Homer's descriptions of Helen identifying to Priam the Greek leaders as they both watched the battle from the city walls is perhaps the earliest example (*Iliad* 3.145–245). Women often accompanied the Persian army on campaign (Xenophon *Cyropaedia* 3.3.67; 4.1.17, 2.2), and Justin (1.6.13–14) records an instance of the women condemning their men as cowards for turning to flee while the battle was still raging. In the more modern era there are numerous examples of an audience for battles, such as the yachts of British tourists watching a naval battle in the Balkans during the Crimean War (Ponting 2004: 45), Russian families eating their picnics during the Crimean War (Royle 2000: 219), or prominent Americans travelling in coaches from Washington to watch the First Battle of Manassas (or Bull Run) in the US Civil War (Commager 1995: 106–9).
4 For a good discussion of all the controversies surrounding the use of ancient sources to reconstruct the events of battles see Sabin (2009: 3–15).
5 One of the earliest discussions is Lorimer (1947). See in particular Snodgrass (1965); Pritchett (1985: 7–33); Singor (1991).
6 Pritchett (1985: 30).
7 See in particular Van Wees (1992) for a detailed discussion of the influence on warfare in the Homeric epics of Homer, his audience and epic style. Latacz (1977) is still a good discussion of hoplites in the *Iliad*.
8 Kirk (1968); Van Wees (2005) argues that warfare in Homer is that of the poet's time with a few archaising elements of armour. I agree that archaic and dark age Greek warfare involved open battles where missiles and close-quarter combat occurred at

42 The hoplite revolution in Greece

the same time. It is perhaps going too far to conclude that Mycenaean war was even more open since there is so little evidence at all for Mycenaean battle tactics. Rather we should conclude that armour was inferior in Mycenaean times but the style of battle may have changed very little by Homer's time despite the beginning of the introduction of the so-called hoplite panoply. As discussed below, hoplite tactics were not introduced in Greece until after the composition of the Homeric epics.

9 Hall (2007: 26).
10 "The nature of Homeric warfare cannot be categorized as either mere myth or history, but becomes comprehensible only through knowledge about the conditions of oral poetry and epic delivery, in which in an era of nascent literacy oral bards sang to mostly aristocratic and reactionary audiences folk tales that evolved over centuries". Hanson (2007: 19). See also Latacz (1977); Van Wees (1992).
11 Van Wees (1986). In describing why Homer's descriptions do not focus on the actions of the immediate retinues of individual heroes, Van Wees (1986: 300) states that "[w]e must conclude that contingents and their leaders disappear in battle because they are alien to the poet's conception of army organisation".
12 Any work on Classical Greek warfare describes a hoplite. See Snodgrass (1964, 1999) for an examination of the archaeological history of the different armaments. For a good summary of the use of these weapons in battle see Anderson (1991). See recently Kagan and Viggiano (2013a).
13 Van Wees (2005). See also Van Wees (1986, 1988, 1992, 1994, 1997).
14 I agree with Van Wees (2005) that Homer did not know the hoplite phalanx since this was not implemented until 650. However, the hoplite panoply was prevalent in his day and it is this that prompted allusions to hoplites in the Homeric epics. The problem for historians and commentators comes amid <u>confusion as to whether equipment or tactics define a hoplite</u>. I believe the hoplite existed as a type of heavy infantry before the implementation of phalanx tactics into Greek warfare and the <u>tactics did not cause the invention of the hoplite panoply</u>. This view will be discussed in more detail below.
15 Van Wees (2005) argues that Homer views tower shields as impenetrable and not to describe earlier armaments. This is possible but not certain and so I include the different terms for shields as evidence of ambiguity in Homer. Lorimer (1950) distances these shields from the *hoplon* as does Hanson (1991a) who argues that hoplites, and the phalanx, are described by Homer. As will be seen below, this is the only part of Van Wees' interpretation of Homeric warfare with which I do not fully agree.
16 Snodgrass (1999).
17 The evidence and importance of two throwing spears will be discussed in detail in the next chapter.
18 Van Wees (2005: 251–2). Contra Hanson (1991a), who argues for the hoplite phalanx existing in the *Iliad* alongside Mycenaean elements.
19 Van Wees (1994: 144 table 1).
20 Snodgrass (1964: 180).
21 Ahlberg (1971).
22 Van Wees (2005: 251). "The spear clearly developed from being primarily a missile in the eighth century, via becoming as much a thrusting weapon as a missile in the early seventh, to taking on its classical role as exclusively a hand-weapon by the end of the seventh century – and what we find in Homer corresponds to the middle phase of the evolution, to be dated *c.* 700–640 BC".
23 Snodgrass (1999).
24 This evidence is often used to prove Homer described different periods (e.g. Lorimer 1950). Van Wees (2005) does not address this problem.
25 See Hijmans (1976); Sutherland (2001).
26 Ahlberg (1971: 107) states: "Archers are more distinctly connected with sea fights than with fighting on land and then mostly as defenders of a ship". Contra Hijmans (1976),

who believes that archery is more important to the action in the *Iliad* than is generally accepted.
27 Snodgrass (1964: 141–56; 1999: 80–4).
28 Van Wees (1994: 144).
29 "Later writers voice much the same attitude. Thucydides describes the mocking by Athenian allies of some Spartan prisoners taken to Athens: 'Did all the brave gentlemen among you die, then?', implying that the survivors were cowards. One Spartan replies 'the spindle, meaning the arrow, would be a fine weapon if it could tell brave men from cowards' (4.40.2). Part of the point of this good retort consists in the feminine associations of 'spindle' (atrakton). Manly hoplites, unlike marginal archers, stand their ground and fight at close quarters on behalf of their polis". Hornblower (2007: 40–1).
30 Jordan (1975: 208–9). Cf. Thucydides 1.50.1.
31 Bradeen (1974 nos. 14.35, 17.27, and 22.252).
32 Van Wees (2005: 252).
33 We may be able to state that the absence of the *hoplon* from Homer's poems does demonstrate that they were composed before the addition of this type of shield to the panoply of a hoplite.
34 On chariots in Homer see in particular Anderson (1975); Greenhalgh (1973: 7–17); Kirk (1985: 360–3).
35 See Anderson (1965).
36 See Littauer (1972); Hooker (1976: 90); Greenhalgh (1982: 89).
37 Later, as argued by Hanson (1983), the heavy infantryman was common because of the growth in urbanisation centred on sedentary agriculture in Greece. However, in Mesopotamia, where agriculture was first employed on a large scale, archers still remained more important than heavy armed infantry.
38 Greenhalgh (1973: 40–61).
39 Worley (1994: 21–3).
40 Lazenby (1985: 10–12).
41 The nature of cavalry in Greece will be discussed in more detail in the next chapter. Spence (1993) argues that cavalry in Athens were limited by social and ideological factors, although Worley (1994) believes cavalry were more important in Greek warfare than is often accepted. Gaebel (2002) argues for an increase in the use of cavalry through the classical period but agrees that their use was limited in the Dark Ages.
42 Van Wees (2005: 157). See also Van Wees (1994).
43 Van Wees (2005: 153–65).
44 This is similar to some battles in the English Wars of the Roses in the fifteenth century. The battle of Tewkesbury lasted over a day and the battle of Towton lasted for over 12 hours, Bennett et al. (2005). Clearly in battles of this length soldiers, especially heavily armoured knights, had to fight in relays to preserve their effectiveness, just as the Roman legions did. Van Wees (2005) uses the warfare practiced in Papua New Guinea as evidence for this style of battle. There are no clear examples of this in the ancient world since information is scarce concerning Greek battle tactics before the classical period and after the implementation of the hoplite phalanx Greek warfare was distinctly different. Since most of the fullest sources for battles in the ancient world are Greek and Roman our understanding of ancient warfare is focused on the decisive hand-to-hand engagements they describe. As Drews (1993: 97) summarises: "Warfare in the preclassical world is a subject on which we evidently will never know very much . . . we can imagine at least the outlines of battles fought by Archaic Greeks and Romans. But beyond ca. 700 questions begin to multiply, and about the second millennium we are grossly ignorant".
45 Van Wees (2005: 157).

46 Van Wees (1986: 301): "The epic army, then, is an organizational compromise. If the poet had wanted to retain the real-life unity of the army under one man's authority, he would have had to forget about regional leaders and the notion of regions as political entities. This would have meant, first, a serious loss of status for all the great heroes.... Second, it would have meant imposing political unity both on heroic Greece and on Asia Minor – a rather bold move. If, on the other hand, he had wanted to retain the legendary regions and regional leadership, he would have had to forsake the unified command and divide the army – or rather, construct a divided army by putting several ordinary armies side by side, and adding an imaginary level of command for the most powerful of the commanders".
47 Van Wees (1986: 302): "Homeric warfare should also pre-date the development of symmachies. In times when battles were regularly fought by alliances of states, each contributing its own contingent and its own commander, no poet would have had any conceptual difficulties with the organisation of the Greek army before Troy".
48 This style of battle is similar to mediaeval Europe where nobles bring their personal retinues to battle but do not necessarily fight alongside their retainers. Instead the nobles may fight alongside each other as a concentrated cavalry force, just as in the French armies at Agincourt, Crecy, and Poitiers. See Bennett et al. (2005).

2 Archaic Greece – the dominance of the heavy infantry phalanx

Archaic warfare in Greece saw the development of the hoplite that is familiar from the Classical period. The focus of this section, just as that dealing with Homeric warfare, is on the nature of the tactics employed by hoplites, the existence of the phalanx formation, and the level of integration in battle of light infantry and cavalry with the hoplite.

Sources

There are few contemporary written sources for this period of Greek history, and those that exist are poetical. Classical writers who cover the period, such as Herodotus, summarise the history without providing their sources.[1] Fortunately the archaic poems that survive, such as those by Archilochus and Tyrtaeus, are military in theme and at least provide solid evidence for the mindset and culture of battle in Greece if not specific tactical details.[2] The historiographic difficulties of these sources, such as their poetic nature and the problems of determining exact dates of origins, in this instance do not prevent using them to examine Archaic Greek warfare.

Images on pots provide a great deal of information about armaments and troop types in Archaic Greece. Hoplites, archers, light infantry, and chariots all appear in various guises in these images. As with most artistic representations it is difficult to determine the intended image of the artist or to disentangle mythological, or non-contemporary, scenes from the current reality of the painter. For military tactics this is problematic. As discussed previously, the Homeric epics confuse our understanding of both Dark Age and Mycenaean warfare because the intention of the author is not explicitly clear. Images have no other context to aid analysis and thus blur the timelines of the adoption of certain weapons or tactics, most crucially the hoplite phalanx.

Nevertheless, the images and written sources can provide important information regarding warfare in the Archaic period. That hoplites are shown wearing the familiar classical Greek panoply allows us to see the growth in the importance of heavy infantry in Greece. The repeated representations of archers and other missile troops, often alongside hoplites, show that the hoplite phalanx had not fully developed, as discussed in more detail in the following.

Infantry

The principal question concerning early Greek hoplites is when the phalanx formation was adopted – the so-called hoplite revolution. This problem has concerned scholars for decades. Although this debate is not crucial for an analysis of the use of combined arms, it does have some impact on the roles of missile troops and tactics in battle. If all types of soldiers fought together in a melee without regimentation of unit types, as is the case before the hoplite phalanx, then combined arms cannot occur. So if there was no phalanx in the Archaic period, there was also no use of combined arms.

Hoplites and the phalanx

Generally, opinion on the first implementation of a phalanx is divided into two schools of thought.[3] The first hypothesis argues that phalanx tactics were adopted suddenly around 700 with the invention of the double grip for the concave shield, the *hoplon*.[4] The second and more generally accepted theory emphasises that the individual armaments of the hoplite panoply were adopted gradually over a number of decades, as suggested by the distribution of archaeological finds, and this eventually led to the phalanx.[5]

Victor Davis Hanson presents an alternate view that the adoption of phalanx tactics in the eighth century or earlier caused the invention of the new shield grip and its concave nature as well as the use of a butt spike. He argues that the double grip and concave shield were unnecessary in non-formation battle and must have been invented to aid in the success of the phalanx.[6] He begins his argument stating that tactics prompt new inventions in armament and thus the new shield and butt spike "were representative of the response of technology to a pre-existing practice throughout Greece to fight in massed array".[7] His interpretation of the evidence is based solely on the assumption that tactics usually prompt new weapons technology and not the other way around. He concludes that

> Military technology in the Greek world – despite what most scholars think – usually *reacted* [his italics] to the demands of the changing battlefield in the form of new or improved weapons.[8]

Hanson admits:

> True, on occasion, an innovative breakthrough (e.g. gunpowder, rifling) can sometimes suggest new tactical implications, but this is rarer, and is usually a matter of modifying, rather than creating, tactics.[9]

Yet there are many examples where this is not true. In my opinion, history is full of examples of new weapons prompting the adoption of new tactics, and that

> a fundamental change in weaponry, equipment, or technology, be it the adoption of gunpowder, the rifle musket, the airplane, the tank, or the atomic

bomb, will affect the traditional modes of fighting and reverberate throughout the institutional framework.¹⁰

To give just a few examples in ancient warfare, the chariot must have been invented before the tactics of its use in battle; the latter cannot occur until the former exists. The same can be said for massed archery occurring only after the invention of the bow. Perhaps a more relevant example is that the tactics of a shock cavalry charge in a wedge formation could not be used until horsemen were armed and sufficiently proficient at riding to be able to directly assault the enemy line. Similarly, in mediaeval warfare the longbow was deployed on a battlefield before the English chanced upon the best defensive formation to make the most out of the devastating archery barrage, a formation that became standard English deployment for over 100 years. Admittedly, subsequently the perfection of tactics on the battlefield often led to modifications of weapons, but revolutionary inventions have to come before the tactics to use them.¹¹

Hanson's misunderstanding of other comparative examples continues to his dismissal of aristocrats wearing the hoplite panoply and riding horses to battle only to fight on foot. Hanson asks:

> Are we to believe a knight would "suit up" in the panoply, dismount (so unlike his medieval cousin), and then stab away or cast with his spear in single combat on the ground against non-hoplites, with such liabilities as reduced vision, comfort, and mobility?¹²

Not only does this practice appear in Homer, but Hanson's reference to mediaeval knights is wrong. In fourteenth- and fifteenth-century England it was indeed standard practice for the knights, including royalty, to dismount and fight on foot with reduced vision, comfort, and mobility often against unarmoured opponents and peasants.¹³ To give just one example, the Earl of Warwick, nicknamed the Kingmaker, was killed at the battle of Barnet in 1471 because he was fighting on foot in the front lines and did not have a chance to reach his horse at the rear of the battlefield once the battle was lost.¹⁴ In fact the latter half of the Hundred Years' War saw the French alter their entire style of warfare from heavily armoured knights on horseback to knights on foot, lest the longbowmen's arrows have the same devastating effect on horses as they did at the battles of Crecy and Poitiers.

Hoplites as individual soldiers

Hanson recently has added to this fallacy by stating that "it is still not altogether clear how an ancient hoplite of 120–150 pounds, with even nearly 50 pounds of offensive and defensive gear, could have fought deftly out of formation".¹⁵ Yet, there are numerous examples in history of heavily armoured individuals wearing very heavy armour fighting on foot as individuals, not just mediaeval men-at-arms as discussed previously. A greater size of armour was beneficial for an infantryman in a melee and for those able to practice daily, such as wealthy aristocrats in Greece or feudal Europe they became used to fighting and even running in such armour.

Hanson also dismisses the likelihood that soldiers heavily armed in a hoplite panoply would fight as individuals in a general infantry melee as the hoplite shield requires a phalanx to function best. Though the phalanx is the best tactic to get the most out of the *hoplon*, hence the Greek obsession with that formation from the sixth century onwards, the shield can be used without it. This is a common source of disagreement among scholars of hoplite warfare. Hanson, and others of the orthodox view, described most succinctly by Schwartz,[16] argue that the heavy and large hoplite shield with a double grip (an arm strap at the elbow and hand grip at the rim), as well as the shield needing to lean on the shoulder, meant that it was incapable of being used in individual combat. Yet Krentz has shown conclusively that the total weight of the panoply is at most 22 kilograms or 48.5 pounds.[17] For an experienced and well-trained soldier this is a small weight of equipment to carry into battle.

Modern soldiers in the US infantry regularly go into combat carrying anywhere between 65 pounds and 170 pounds of equipment depending on their role. The body armour alone weighs 25–30 pounds; added to that are the weapon and magazines plus extra ammunition, water, food rations, and other items. A machine gun team leader carries ammunition for the weapon plus the heavy and cumbersome gun, tripod, and lube. Now these soldiers are not advancing to fight in hand-to-hand combat, but they are trained to do so when necessary. They may ditch their weapons to fight in close combat but would still be wearing all the heavy equipment while trying to use their physical attributes and practiced skills to overcome their opponent. Additionally, no mitigation in weight of equipment is made for smaller soldiers in modern armies. Many are the same size or less than Classical Greeks would have been and still, with the requisite training of carrying the equipment, are perfectly capable of keeping up with larger colleagues. Schwartz is too disparaging of shorter people when he assumes that the smaller stature of hoplites meant that the weight of their equipment was too great to allow manoeuvrability or individual combat.[18] This modern evidence shows that hoplites were comparatively lightly equipped compared with today's infantry soldiers. The veterans I interviewed expressed a firm belief that hoplites carrying 50 pounds of equipment who drilled or were experienced enough could easily run 50 to 100 yards into battle and still fight or could march long distances if needed with the requisite endurance training.[19]

It is important to note the crucial problem with the two published academic experiments in having students or athletes fight mock hoplite battles to see for how long they could fight in heavy equipment under the hot sun.[20] Hand-to-hand combat while carrying a significant amount of equipment is something that requires extensive and specific training. Athletes or young students who go to the gym would not have anywhere near the same level of capabilities as someone trained specifically for the combat role. That is why even today boot camp and basic training for infantry soldiers, especially in elite infantry regiments, has a high drop-out rate.[21] It is incredibly physically demanding. As a veteran of an elite regiment in the US Army stated in my interview with him concerning the hoplites running 1,500 metres into battle at Marathon: "you need soldiers not football players – it could totally be done, even for a mile".[22] Well-trained and experienced soldiers would be able to fight and move relatively easily in the hoplite panoply; they would be accustomed to the weight and would get used quickly to the size of the shield and how best to use it in combat.

Despite Schwartz commenting that he corresponded repeatedly with a group of hoplite reenactors, no one from the orthodox camp has given evidence of trying to use a hoplite shield in combat to see what can be achieved.[23] I built hoplite shields for a class constructed out of much heavier plywood than the poplar or willow used in antiquity, and yet with practice anyone, especially someone with martial arts experience as some of my students had, is able to move around agilely to counter attacks with a sword and a spear. Krentz draws attention to the YouTube videos of a martial arts expert wielding the hoplite shield to all sides and all angles after training for a year in its use.[24] Moreover, the reenactor is using a shield that is heavier than Classical Greek ones were (9 kg instead of 5 kg), indicating that all the techniques he uses would have been easier for Classical Greeks to accomplish.

In my experience with my shield, after a time, if it is tightly attached to the arm in the arm grip, the porpax, it becomes almost an extension of the arm, and though it is more comfortable to rest it on the shoulder for brief periods it is possible to thrust it out at arm's length to counter opponent's thrusts. In fact, when I carry it back from class it is often more comfortable to fully extend the elbow and carry the shield hanging at my side rather than resting on my shoulder with a bent arm.[25] I have yet to see any convincing argument to disprove the practical evidence of reenactors that the size and weight of the hoplite shield meant that it could not be used in single combat by an experienced practitioner.

Indeed, some images on pots show hoplites holding double-grip shields with the arm fully extended. The best example is on a red-figure Kylix by the Brygos painter showing the sack of Troy (Figure 2.1).[26] There in the centre, a hoplite shown in full garb, rather than heroically nude, has swung out his shield at arm's length just before he stabs his opponent with his sword. It seems from the stance of the hoplite leaning over a prone adversary whose head is knocked back as far as it can go that the hoplite has used his shield to knock the head of his opponent to create the opening for the sword thrust that is coming. The shield is pictured behind the head and shoulder of the enemy but slightly overlapping his shoulder and chin. I can think of no other martial action that would lead to his shield being held thus and the opponent's head thrown back other than swinging it into the head of the enemy. So, any arguments made that the shield was too bowl shaped and heavy to be used as smaller shields in combat and that it had to always remain rested on the shoulder ignores the evidence.

Figure 2.1 Sack of Troy. Red-figure Kylix by the Brygos painter. Louvre Paris (G 152). Drawing by Eric Howell. The hoplite has used his shield to knock back the head of his opponent to create an opening for his sword thrust.

The crucial importance of maintaining balance in hoplite combat

The group of scholars who argue for the use of a hoplite shield in individual combat, headed by Van Wees, use as evidence for a hoplite's individual manoeuvrability the importance in Greek culture of Pyrrhic dancing and the *hoplitodromos* (the competitive running race in full hoplite armour). Schwartz argued against this extensively, concluding that

> ultimately the question of the value of dancing for hoplite combat cannot be assessed with any certainty; but so far as can be judged from the textual sources, it contributed only indirectly and insignificantly to the hoplite's weapon skills, but probably to a great degree to overall suppleness, agility and bodily strength.[27]

While I agree there is no way to prove with certainty the association of dancing with hoplite combat, that is true of most things concerning hoplite warfare. That is why books continue to be written on the subject. The evidence in no way can conclusively show anything. However, despite his long discussion and correct analogy to martial arts practices Schwartz never mentions the all-important issue of balance.[28]

Balance in hand-to-hand combat, whether in a formation or as an individual, was arguably the most important skill. If you fell down in the battle line in full armour, it was difficult to get up again and you were at the mercy of your opponent.[29] Fallen heroes feature on many occasions in Homer's poems and in Classical texts or in iconography. Moreover, balance is crucial also throughout mediaeval warfare and into modern warfare. The US Army handbook for hand-to-hand combat techniques lists the very first item under basic principles as physical balance.[30]

> a *Physical Balance.* Balance refers to the ability to maintain equilibrium and to remain in a stable, upright position. A hand-to-hand fighter must maintain his balance both to defend himself and to launch an effective attack. Without balance, the fighter has no stability with which to defend himself, nor does he have a base of power for an attack. The fighter must understand two aspects of balance in a struggle:
>
> (1) *How to move his body to keep or regain his own balance.* A fighter develops balance through experience, but usually he keeps his feet about shoulder-width apart and his knees flexed. He lowers his centre of gravity to increase stability.
> (2) *How to exploit weaknesses in his opponent's balance.* Experience also gives the hand-to-hand fighter a sense of how to move his body in a fight to maintain his balance while exposing the enemy's weak points.

Modern scholars often forget that the hoplite was a soldier equipped for close combat. The nature of the phalanx formation does not diminish that fact. Thus hoplites, just as all soldiers before the era of gunpowder, had to become well-versed and experts in the techniques of hand-to-hand combat in order to survive. And the most important skill of all was being able to keep your balance under any circumstances, weather, or terrain and simultaneously try to throw your enemy off his. The phalanx, with the pressure of those behind and the pressure exerted on the large hoplite shield, made maintaining balance even more important, and the best way to practice was dancing.

Balance is also one of the key features of martial arts training and combat. Whether combative types such as jiujitsu or judo, or more passive styles like tai chi and yoga, balance is crucial and perhaps the one common element in all of them. The Greek enthusiasm for wrestling and the no-holds-barred version pankration was likely for the same reason: to teach the importance and techniques of maintaining balance and getting the opponent to the ground. Since these events started well before hoplite warfare in Greece and continued long afterwards into the modern sports of wrestling, it is clear that balance was crucial to all hand-to-hand combat throughout history.

Schwartz's discussion of the "Thessalian feint", where a hoplite moves a shield back quickly to throw off an opponent and expose his vulnerable side to a death blow, is crucial because the opponent is thrown off balance.[31] Everything else that happens is a result of the loss of balance. Likewise, Schwartz's detailed discussion of the problem of a hoplite being hit on the head emphasises loss of consciousness but ignores the crucial aspect of momentarily being knocked off-balance.[32] One moment is likely all it would take in combat for a defender to succumb to his opponent, whether in a phalanx formation, a general melee, or in a duel of individuals.

To my mind the crucial importance of the Pyrrhic dancing in Greek warfare was maintaining balance in all situations. Mediaeval knights and men-at-arms were expected to be good at music and dancing, not just because it was part of the courtly chivalrous routine but because being a good dancer made you light on your feet and so better balanced in hand-to-hand combat.[33] Almost every ancient and mediaeval culture around the world features some form of military themed often ritual dance.[34] Some of the most successful boxers and mixed martial arts (MMA) fighters in history have a background in dancing, from ballet to capoeira.[35]

The importance of military dancing was not necessarily being able at all times to employ every movement of the dance in battle, but to be able and comfortable to use whatever movement was necessary at any moment in order to maintain balance and perhaps in turn to take advantage of an opponent being off-balance or cause them to be so. This is how martial arts work in combat. It is both offensive and defensive in using techniques and routines learned to counter an opponent's movements and gain the advantage. This is very similar to Xenophon's advice for a cavalryman to practice what is now termed dressage in order perfect the riding technique and responsiveness of the horse, crucial factors in battle on horseback.[36] Now dressage is seen as dancing on a horse, but in the ancient and mediaeval eras it was intended purely as military training.

As Schwartz states, "Plato informs us that there were two basic types of dance: one which imitated defensive fighting (evasive manoeuvres such as dodging, jumping, ducking, retreating, parrying), and one which emulated attacking (blows, feints, counterthrusts etc.)".[37] Xenophon records a dance he witnessed in Thrace where the audience actually thought one of the participants was dead, such was the realism of the dance.[38] This must prove that this particular dance was intended to mimic actual combat techniques. Yet Schwartz, conveniently for his argument, confines this episode to a footnote and does not discuss it.[39] However, Schwartz concludes from evidence that women and children also were taught the dance steps, that the dance "was used not so much as a direct exercise for fighting in the phalanx: rather, it was thought of as a fitness exercise or a beautiful dance, including (although not exclusively) moves vaguely mimicking fighting of a rather generic kind".[40] Contrary to proving that the steps taught by Pyrrhic dancing would not be used in combat, Schwartz has in fact emphasised the crucial importance of movement and balance in all combat and the importance of dance to teaching this especially to children who were unlikely to train in combat specific techniques until later but could learn the movements as soon as they could walk, as in modern martial arts.

Archaic Greece – the heavy infantry phalanx 53

Though this does not prove the hoplite shield could be used in individual combat, it also does not disprove it. These steps and movements learned in the Pyrrhic dance allowed the hoplite to get used to moving his feet, body position, and shield in all directions and thus was able to counter attacks from all around. Schwartz misunderstands the importance of the feet in moving the shield to counter opponent's attacks. Yes, the single hand-grip shield could be thrust out further and more easily to counter enemy thrusts, but the hoplite could adjust to any attack just as easily by moving his feet and whole body. In fact, the greater size of the shield, which allows the hoplite to hide his whole head and torso behind the shield, actually gives significant defensive advantages in single combat over smaller shields. It makes it first and foremost a lot harder for an opponent to find an opening to deliver a blow to the hoplite hiding behind the shield, and a hoplite who has the balance and agility to prevent his rear from exposure can counter the enemy's moves easily.

Early hoplites

Infantry in early Greece fought in hand-to-hand warfare using armour, helmets, and large shields but not in a phalanx formation. The spearmen of Egypt had large body-shields and the spearmen on the Warrior vase in Mycenae use similar shields. The concave nature of the *hoplon* does not automatically require soldiers engaged in hand-to-hand combat to fight in a phalanx formation. In fact, the extra weight that requires the new grip and shape probably aided an offensive use of the shield individually as well as deflecting missiles.[41]

The large hoplite double-grip shield, the *hoplon*, was adopted probably sometime between 750 and 700, but its use did not alone force the implementation of hoplite phalanx tactics.[42] A large shield can be used offensively by an individual warrior, just as the Romans used their large, concave *scutum*.[43] The *secutor* fighting as a Roman gladiator was trained to fight as an individual relying on his large shield for victory.[44] Reliance on formation developed in order to get the best results out of the new shield but the one does not necessarily presuppose the other. Bardunias and Ray have described well the process of individual heavy infantry hoplites gradually collecting on a battlefield as their numbers increased in order to seek protection of others as well as improving the melee fighting ability of the whole force.[45] As aristocratic well-armed hoplites led their retainers to battle, the poorer armed individuals sought protection behind the hoplites' shields, and the hoplites gathered together to protect their flanks with their neighbours' shields. To keep the different troop types separated required significant central organisation, training, and discipline that were all likely lacking from early Greek armies.

> The rules for hoplites thus need not be more complex than: men with shields tend to stand beside men with shields to protect their flanks and archers tend to stand behind men with shields. . . . This type of formation puts more heavily armored men, who may throw missiles themselves, in front of unarmored missile troops to act as a wall or screen. Segregation like this is natural to

54 *The hoplite revolution in Greece*

tribal war bands in which richer, better equipped men lead a troupe of progressively poorer and lighter equipped warriors into battle. It would actually take more discipline to keep troop types evenly mixed than to clump in this manner.[46]

Luraghi has shown that Greek soldiers wearing the hoplite panoply were employed as mercenaries in Asia by the end of the eighth century.[47] Assyrian documents, the first dating to c. 738, show Ionian military involvement within the Assyrian Empire that had to be countered. This culminated in Sennacherib's invasion of Cilicia in 696 when he incorporated Ionian Greeks into the royal Assyrian army.[48] Clearly hoplites were common throughout the Greek world by the early seventh century. Hoplites and the many advantages of heavy armed infantrymen were appreciated by the Assyrians and other states lacking their own close-quarter heavy infantry units.[49]

Luraghi discusses a Phoenician bowl, of a type usually dated to between 710 and 675, which shows hoplites fighting alongside Assyrian archers in a siege in Asia (Figure 2.2).[50] This bowl was found in a chamber tomb on Cyprus near Amathus.[51] The four hoplites pictured attacking the city seem to be marching in step

Figure 2.2 The Amathus bowl, silverwork; possibly Assyrian or Phoenician (c. 710–675). British Museum, London (ANE 123053). Drawing after Myres *JHS* 53 (1933). The four hoplites pictured attacking the city seem to be marching in step in a phalanx formation. Other hoplites defend the city.

in a phalanx formation. Other hoplites defend the city. Luraghi concludes that "this is the earliest depiction of a hoplite phalanx".[52] I do not agree that we see a phalanx, since such a formation would be useless in a siege even on approach to the walls.[53] Rather, the image depicts hoplites simply advancing in formation to the ladder that is awaiting their ascent of the walls where they are opposed by an enemy hoplite. Marching close together would reduce the impact of missiles on the hoplites on their approach, just as a Roman testudo, and was a sensible move but does not prove they fought a pitched battle in a phalanx formation. Fighting in a phalanx formation is different from simply marching in close formation. Schwartz and Ober have argued that hoplite equipment prevents hoplites from climbing siege ladders,[54] but the hypaspists in Alexander the Great's army ascended ladders armed in the hoplite panoply and others did so in Carthaginian and Sicilian Greek sieges. Hale argues that hoplites were incorporated into the Assyrian army because they were useful as heavy infantry fighting in siege warfare.[55] Again, there is likely a misunderstanding of modern scholars as to how far training and experience could go to make a hoplite very capable of wielding his large shield in different terrain and situations.

Hale, following on from Luraghi, has provided more evidence from the eastern Mediterranean that hoplites in the eighth century were fighting as mercenaries in the armies of the great empires of Assyria and later Babylonia, and Egypt.[56] He argues that these were Ionian Greeks who began as hoplite pirates ravaging the shores and who were then incorporated into the armies of the kingdoms they raided, most notably the Assyrians.[57] He rightly draws the comparison with the Vikings, who raided European coasts and rivers before being employed as mercenaries throughout, most notably as the famous Varangian Guard in the Byzantine Empire.[58]

Just as the Vikings, these Ionian Greeks probably sailed in groups of ships owned by a wealthy aristocrat who led on his force of retainers to seek wealth and fame.[59] These aristocrats, just as the Homeric heroes, wore expensive hoplite armour and would have ridden horses but fought on foot alongside their less well-armed followers. This fits well with the evidence of Van Wees for the eighth-century "phalanx" seeing lighter armed troops dispersed among the hoplites. These aristocrats would have competed among themselves with their bands of soldiers to gain the most wealth and fame for their military exploits and thus increase the number of their retainers. This is similar to the Homeric heroes,[60] as well as the Vikings and the Turkish Ghazis of the fourteenth century.

As mercenaries these men were professional hoplites serving abroad. The archaic warrior poet Archilochus provides us with the best examples of the ethos of these soldiers who win sustenance from their weapons but ditch them, even the shield, if necessary for survival.[61] The stigma of throwing away the shield, or *rhipsaspia*, developed in the Classical period. There are numerous sources that detail the shame attached to a hoplite in the phalanx leaving his shield behind. Schwartz discusses the evidence, including the Archaic poetry of Archilochus, Alcaeus, and Anakreon, that proudly boasts of discarding the shield to stay alive. He concludes that the tone of the poetry is intended to show it is bucking the trend rather than describing normal behaviour, which was to keep hold of the shield at all costs. Schwartz is right that in the Classical period the Greeks did attach stigma including actual legal punishments for rhipsaspia,[62] but that does not mean it did not happen. Clearly intended to stop citizen soldiers in the phalanx throwing their shield and fleeing in the middle of combat, it is not at all relevant when the whole phalanx flees en masse. There are countless examples of phalanxes fleeing, presumably with a number of soldiers throwing away their shield in their flight, but I know of no occasion where a city punished their whole phalanx for this behaviour.

These laws concerning rhipsaspia were intended to discourage individual cowardice in the phalanx which would threaten the integrity of the whole formation. Archilochus ditching his shield to escape a defeat, as a professional mercenary hoplite, was perhaps normal considering the well-known phrase "a dead mercenary costs nothing". When it was citizens fighting for their own state, loyalty to the battle line and city came before personal safety. For the Archaic poets as mercenary hoplites that was not the case. Nor is this a case of individual cowardice among professional hoplites not in a phalanx. These poets were fleeing a defeat and trying to escape the presumed pursuit in order to live to fight another day, important since that was their means of making a living. It does not refer to soldiers ditching their shield when the battle was still raging, the true act of cowardice despised by Greeks. In fact, Schwartz[63] comments offhand later in his book that hoplites fleeing after a defeat "probably had discarded their shields and whatever else they could and were running for their lives" and this must surely have been the norm in Greek, and indeed all ancient and mediaeval, warfare.

As a corps of soldiers fighting amidst the many other types of unit in the armies of the eastern Mediterranean armies these hoplites need not have fought in a phalanx formation in order to prove themselves valuable, especially in siege warfare where the heavier armament was an advantage. Nor did the whole army have to fight in a combined arms style in order to benefit from the great abilities of hoplites in hand-to-hand combat. Again, unfortunately, we have no evidence of the tactics of Near Eastern battles in this period, but the poet Alcaeus praises his brother for defeating a Goliath-esque enemy champion as a hoplite.[64] This was undoubtedly in single combat showing that the hoplite panoply could function expertly in single combat, as discussed previously.

Snodgrass has argued that archaeological evidence of finds and images proves that the hoplite phalanx did not occur before 650, and Van Wees has more recently argued that hoplites fighting in a close-order phalanx did not occur until just before the Persian Wars at the end of the sixth century.[65] Certainly a number of images in Greek art show hoplites armed with two spears, which may be fitted with a throwing-loop.[66] Archilochus and Callinus refer to battle as combat using javelins.[67] If soldiers equipped with the hoplite panoply used throwing spears they cannot have fought in a tight formation and so the hoplite must have existed before the tactics of the phalanx, as is the commonly held view.

Archers are also shown to fight side by side with hoplites but are shown as unarmoured light infantry.[68] This is a clear difference from the archers in Homer and Dark Age images, who are just as armoured as those fighting with swords and thrusting spears. The number of archers seen in Greek art of the seventh and sixth centuries is low, but this is symptomatic of their reduced status in society and war.[69] Arrowheads appear in enough quantity from this period to prove the use of archery never disappeared entirely in Greek warfare, contrary to Snodgrass' assertion.[70]

The fact that archers and light infantry are shown fighting alongside the heavy armed hoplites suggests that battle was fought in an open formation. Perhaps the best example of this is the well-known Chigi vase, a Corinthian jug from around 640 (Figure 2.3).[71] This vase has numerous scenes depicted, one of which is a battle scene showing a line of spearmen armed as hoplites going into battle.

Figure 2.3 The Chigi vase. Middle Protocorinthian olpe by the Macmillan painter (c. 650). Villa Giulia, Rome (22679). Drawing by Eric Howell. Hoplites holding two spears marching to battle accompanied by chariots and flute player.

58 The hoplite revolution in Greece

However, these hoplites carry two spears rather than one, and are accompanied by a chariot behind. If this is not a mythological scene and does depict contemporary warfare, then we must conclude that chariots and two spears were the complement of hoplites still in the mid-seventh century.

The image could be dismissed as referring to the *Iliad*, hence the chariot and two spears, but it is more likely, as Van Wees has suggested,[72] that it depicts contemporary warfare. It certainly does not represent a hoplite phalanx in close-quarter combat.[73] The phalanx warfare of the fifth century had not yet been implemented and heavy armed hoplites fought alongside light infantry in a more open order of battle. The wealthy elite may still have been conveyed to battle on horses or in chariots, as they were in Homeric warfare.[74]

Tyrtaeus' poetry reveals that towards the end of the seventh century hoplites abandoned the use of throwing spears and preferred fighting hand to hand with a single spear and sword. The best example is the often quoted passage (8.29–34):

> Go near, strike with a long spear or a sword at close range, and kill a man. Set foot against foot, press shield against shield, fling crest against crest, helmet against helmet, and chest against chest, and fight a man, gripping the hilt of a sword or a long spear.

Missile infantry still fight alongside the hoplites but are clearly now visibly distinguished from hoplites in battle, though not tactically, noticeably lacking in any defensive armour: "You, light-armed, squatting under a shield here and there, must throw great rocks and hurl smooth javelins while you stand close by the heavy-armed" (Tyrtaeus 8.35–8).

Schwartz, and others, have argued that Tyrtaeus' poetry does not show a mixed phalanx but the traditional hoplite-only phalanx.[75] While he is right that fragment eight does not necessarily state that the light armed fought intermingled with the hoplites, it also does not definitively state they were separated. But I take issue when Schwartz states that

> the terrifying crash of many shields being smashed together on impact, is likely to have occurred when two determined phalanxes met in a head-on collision, whereas a meeting between two open formations is unlikely to have entailed anything like a collision.[76]

I do not know if he has ever seen movies depicting mediaeval combat or read the accounts of mediaeval battles, but on each occasion massed armies of heavily armed infantry run at each other at full speed and literally smash into each other.[77] The sound created by the massed impacts was indeed a terrifying crash. Both sides would try to knock their individual opponent backwards in order to gain the advantage, and to knock them off-balance and then go to hand-to-hand combat with the various weapons at their disposal. This is surely to what Tyrtaeus refers when he exhorts the Spartans to plant their feet and not give ground, not to weaken the phalanx formation but not to create a bridgehead for the enemy infantry. Massed hoplites out of a phalanx formation running at each other would have been no different.

Tactical separation of light and heavy infantry

The lack of tactical separation between light and heavy infantry in Greek armies is proven by Herodotus' assertion (1.103.1) that the Median king Cyaxares was the first to tactically separate spearmen, archers, and cavalry. To Herodotus' readers this would be understandable if their own knowledge of earlier Greek warfare revealed no such division. This continues the practice evident in Homeric battle descriptions, as discussed previously, and definitively proves that combined arms could not be used. What we know of the Messenian Wars between Sparta and Messenia shows this style of warfare remained. The Battle of the Trench, where the Spartans forced their men to stand and fight lest they fall into a trench behind their lines, would have been named differently had a phalanx operated without need for ditch in the rear.[78]

Sixth-century evidence is scarce, but images on pots show hoplites fighting in small groups sometimes joined by archers or horses.[79] Nothing suggests the existence of a regular formation and the separation of light infantry from the phalanx. These images are often dismissed as heroic or mythological anachronisms without citing any convincing evidence for this view.[80] Significant numbers of Athenian pots in the sixth century show archers in combination with hoplites. Van Wees estimates that archers "featured on some 750 surviving vases, . . . and on about a hundred vases they take an active part in battle or ambush amongst the heavy infantry".[81] Most of these Athenian images show "barbarian" archers distinguished by their foreign dress. These Scythian archers were probably employed as mercenaries in the Athenian army but they were not necessarily separated tactically in battle.[82] Clearly light infantry retained some importance in Greek warfare throughout the archaic period and representations of them fighting among hoplites suggest the phalanx was not yet established.

Schwartz has argued that there are so few images even in Classical Greece that depict a phalanx that it is incorrect to discount earlier images as phalanxes.[83] He discusses in particular a Middle Corinthian krater attributed to the Cavalcade painter (Figure 2.4), the Chigi vase (Figure 2.3), and two works by the Macmillan painter (Figure 2.5) as well as the Amathus bowl (Figure 2.2) to argue phalanxes are shown. To me the krater shows the second line running into battle to support the already engaged front line. This is incompatible with a phalanx in practice since the whole phalanx is intended to engage the enemy at the same time. The Chigi vase shows hoplites marching and fighting in separate lines and not necessarily fighting in a dense phalanx, which are different things. The two images from the Macmillan painter (one not pictured here) show hoplites engaged in combat in different phases. Again, they are in only a single line but there is no way of knowing if this is intended to be a full phalanx. Schwartz is perhaps right that "analyses founded chiefly in iconography should be set forth with extreme caution".[84]

Figure 2.4 Sherd of black-figure middle Corinthian column Krater, attributed to the Cavalcade painter (c. 600–575). Metropolitan Museum of Art, New York (12.229.9; gift of John Marshall, 1912). The second line of hoplites running into battle to support the already engaged front line.

Unfortunately, there is no information for any eighth-century battles abroad, and no tactical specific details for those in Greece, and so it is possible the phalanx did exist. However, I generally follow Van Wees that the Greek evidence for the same timeframe never shows a full phalanx of hoplites in operation. Nevertheless, hoplites were employed in Near Eastern armies from the middle of the eighth century onwards, demonstrating their abilities as effective heavy infantry but not necessarily the existence of the phalanx until perhaps 650 or later. Hoplites fought in battles and sieges throughout the Mediterranean from the eighth century onwards but not always relying on the tactics of the phalanx. For combined arms this is the important point. Hoplites and other types of soldiers have to be employed on the battlefield in separate roles and positions in order for true combined arms to occur.

Once the Greeks adopted the hoplite panoply as the main equipment for a heavy infantryman, the tactics specific to heavy infantry began to develop naturally. It is usual for a soldier on the battlefield to seek the protection afforded to him by his neighbour's shield. Homer often describes groups of men fighting together and emphasises the benefit of fighting side by side. "We may do some good even if there are only two of us, for even the poorest fighters can display

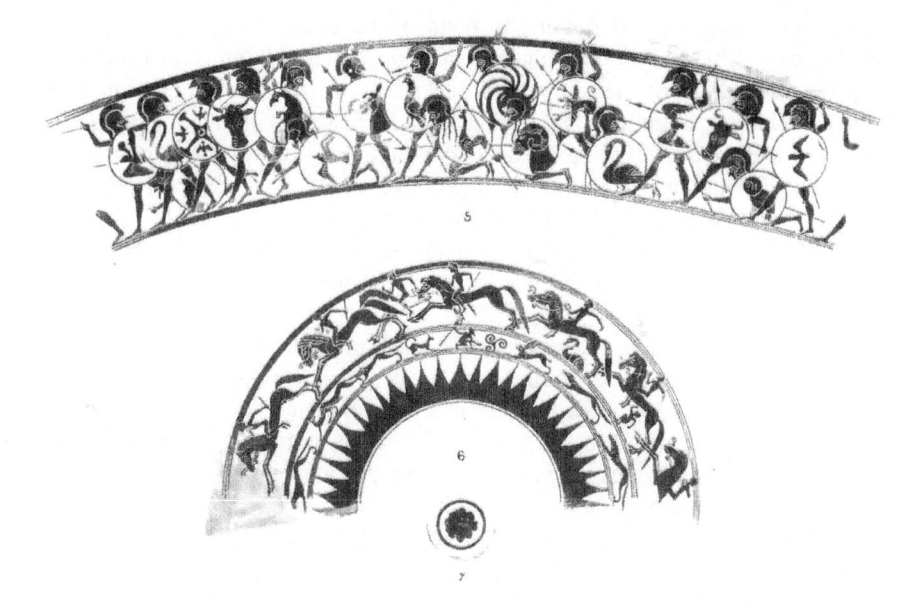

Figure 2.5 Black figure aryballos by the Macmillan painter (the "Macmillan aryballos"), Middle Protocorinthian (c. 650). British Museum, London (1889.4–18.1). Drawing from F. Anderson. 1889. "A Small Archaic Lekythos, (plate V)" *JHS* X: 253 Pl. V. Groups of hoplites fighting but no way to know if they are in a phalanx or more simple lines.

combined prowess" (*Iliad* 13.236–7). The group of hoplites on the Amathus bowl (Figure 2.2) shows the same seeking of protection, against missiles especially.

As Greek warfare moved to favour close hand-to-hand combat and as more people could afford the hoplite panoply, heavy infantry began to cooperate in battle, and this in turn led to the development of the phalanx formation. Van Wees has shown that the rise in numbers of hoplites in Greek poleis did not occur until around the start of the fifth century.[85] Until then states could field only small numbers of hoplites and so dispersed the thousands of light infantry among them in the battle line.

Van Wees argues that it was not until the Persian Wars that the Greeks became reliant on the close formation of the phalanx.[86] Even then Herodotus (9.28–9) describes the helots fighting as light infantry alongside their Spartan masters in great numbers at Plataea, showing that rarely were light infantry completely absent in Greek battles. Rather, hoplites became the most important type of soldier and the roles in battle of the other types of units were subordinated to a great degree.

When infantry combat took the form of a general melee with light and heavy infantry mixed together and not in independent formations, it was impossible for a flanking manoeuvre to occur. To flank the enemy is to attack the sides of the battle line. If there is no obvious line but rather a mass of soldiers fighting everywhere, then there is nothing to flank. Flank attacks developed as a possibility only when the hoplite phalanx developed. Then infantry or cavalry of any type could attack the vulnerable flanks and rear of an enemy formation. When attacking a melee light infantry and cavalry would be exposed to one-on-one combat with a hoplite and that would almost always turn out well for the hoplite.[87] Hoplites were rarely used to deliver flanking attacks. As Kagan and Viggiano summarise well, "Greek generals of the fifth century avoided using the flank attack as an offensive strategy of his own. Should a general detach a body of hoplites from the rest of the line to attack the flank of the enemy, he might expose the flanks of his own army".[88]

Until types of soldiers are separated on the battlefield in position as well as roles, combined arms by definition cannot occur. So in Archaic Greece, when light infantry fought alongside hoplites in a general melee, just as in most mediaeval battles, combined arms was not used. The separation of unit types is the decisive factor in allowing combined arms to happen on the battlefield. Until then, the heavy infantryman was always preeminent in the close-quarter combat of the infantry melee whether fighting in a phalanx or not.

Chariots

Many late sixth-century pots show the chariot being used to transport a hoplite to or from battle.[89] Among these "one remarkable painting shows three lines of seven running hoplites, each group about to be joined by an eighth running hoplite whose horses are galloping beside him. The horses are envisaged as mingling with the infantry in the epic manner".[90] These images have been suggested as representing myths anachronistically.[91] Van Wees argues that these pots depict contemporary practice and that the chariot was used to transport hoplites to and from battle as late as the early fifth century.[92] If these images do depict contemporary practice then the compact hoplite phalanx as seen in the Peloponnesian War did not become common until well into the fifth century. Nevertheless, chariots were never used in a combined arms tactic in battle in conjunction with infantry.

Cavalry

A number of images show hoplites riding horses in Archaic Greece. Greenhalgh provides the fullest discussion of these images. He concludes that horses were used as transports to and from the battle for the wealthier individuals in the same way as chariots were earlier.[93] A number of the hoplites riding horses carry two spears rather than the hoplite's customary one.[94] This is further evidence of open order battle in Archaic Greek warfare where the elites rely on throwing spears. The use of cavalry in Archaic Greece was never combined with the infantry and so is not important for the discussion of combined arms.

Combined arms

As Van Wees states, "Archaic infantry combat was in many ways closer to Homer's heroic clashes than to the battles of the classical period".[95] Greek warfare in this period made no use of cavalry or chariots and it is probable that missile troops were distributed among the heavy close combat infantry, just as they were in Homeric or Dark Age warfare. The principal difference is that light infantry in Archaic Greece were unarmoured in contrast to the heavily armoured hoplite, likely because of cost. Hoplites still made use of throwing spears but rarely used bows, as the heavily armoured heroes did in Homer. Archers and slingers, and later javelin men, gradually became a visibly distinct group of infantry although they were not tactically separated.

This lack of tactical separation of units in Archaic Greece precludes the existence of combined arms warfare. Distinct units can only be combined in battle if they are regarded as separate entities to begin with. "The strict separation of hoplites, light-armed, and horsemen characteristic of the classical phalanx, therefore, may not have emerged until the very end of the archaic period".[96] Although missile and heavy infantry fought together in battle there certainly was no idea of united action or a coordinated and combined tactical military action. Just as with Homeric warfare, any use of combined arms was purely accidental arising from the existence of both missile and heavy infantry in the army.

Regardless of the lack of tactical separation between hoplites and light infantry, the hoplite, as the embodiment of heavy infantry, was quickly appreciated as a vital component in battle. It is the creation of a heavy infantryman able to excel in close-quarter combat that prompted other states to utilise Greek mercenaries, not the phalanx tactics and organisation that appeared later. Even a few hoplites fighting among the usual forces of the Assyrian Empire would have significantly improved the offensive capabilities of Assyrian infantry in battles and sieges because of their superior arms. This likely explains the large number of hoplites depicted on the Amathus bowl when compared with the other troops present.

The hoplite was the first heavy infantryman fielded in large numbers in the west and Near East despite the lack of combined arms in Greece. It was not the tactics of the phalanx that allowed hoplites to excel on the battlefield but their superior armament and abilities in hand-to-hand combat. The success of the hoplites led the Eastern states to incorporate them into the army and make up for their own lack of heavy infantry, a crucial stage in the development of combined arms. The hoplite revolution, whenever it occurred precisely, revealed the benefit of having a superior heavy infantry force in an army. It does not matter the exact nature of the armaments or the tactics employed; the heavy infantryman tactically became the most important unit in all subsequent Greek and Mediterranean warfare for the next thousand years until the third century CE saw the decline of the Roman legionary in favour of cavalry.

Notes

1. Perhaps the best example is Aristotle's assertion that early Greek warfare revolved around the use of cavalry but the archaeological evidence for this suggests otherwise. See Greenhalgh (1973).
2. Van Wees (2005: 166–77).
3. The recent work *Men of Bronze* (Kagan and Viggiano 2013a) brings together scholars from both sides in the most recent attempt to address this divide and settle its impact on other topics of hoplite warfare. It is by far the best description of the differences and impact of the two hypotheses. See especially the two chapters by Kagan and Viggiano, and Hanson; those by Viggiano and Van Wees, Snodgrass, and Viggiano are also informative.
4. Lorimer (1950) first argued this theory. Cartledge (1977) and Greenhalgh (1973) expand on the arguments. Hanson's two famous works (1991b and 1999) also detail this theory.
5. This view is well argued by Snodgrass (1965). See also Donlan (1970); Garlan (1976); Salmon (1977). On the archaeological finds see Snodgrass (1964: 59–60).
6. Hanson (1991a).
7. Hanson (1991a: 64).
8. Hanson (1991a: 74).
9. Hanson (1991a: 79 n. 5). Hanson continues to say that musketry may have come from a desire for greater missile velocity and First World War fighter planes developed from a need for new aerial combat methods. The latter is probably true, but gunpowder had to have been invented for musketry to be used at all, and the aeroplane had to have been designed for aerial combat to exist in the first place. He is right that weapons do not arrive "without some consideration for the battlefield", but to argue that almost all new weapons come in response to already existing tactics is taking things too far.
10. Matloff (1969: 3).
11. To expand on Hanson's own example about air combat (1991a: 64), the aeroplane had to come first to enable dogfights in the air, as did the machine gun before it could be fixed to a plane, just as he says. But it is also impossible for tactics of air combat to occur before air combat was possible. He seems to be confused at the difference between tactics and technology. Tactics involving tanks in battle could not occur until tanks existed, just as aircraft. So tactics reliant on a large hoplite shield could not be finalised before a hoplite shield existed. If – as Hanson here and Schwartz elsewhere (Schwartz 2009: 104–5) believe – the phalanx formation and hoplite shield are indispensable to each other, then either they both arrived in Greek warfare simultaneously or one came first. Which it was is impossible to know, but most interpretations of the existing evidence prove the existence of the shield well before any single piece of evidence can prove the existence of the tactic. I find it inconceivable for anyone to believe that tactics explicitly connected solely to a revolutionary new weapon or technology can possibly come before the invention of that weapon. Microwave dinners cannot come before the microwave, and missile silos cannot come before missiles!
12. Hanson 1991a: 84 n. 28.
13. Bennett et al. 2005.
14. Hicks 1998.
15. Hanson 2013: 266.
16. Schwartz 2013. See also Schwartz 2009: 32–54.
17. Krentz 2013: 135–6.
18. Schwartz 2013.
19. Freddy Moran Sr. and Freddy Moran Jr., in person interview by author, June 27, 2018. Dan Powers, email conversation with author, June 27, 2018.
20. Donlan and Thompson 1976, 1979; Hanson 2000.

21 Government statistics in the United States put the rate at 11%–14% of recruits who fail to make it through basic training, though not always because of the physical and mental demands. An article published in the *Daily Telegraph* by Sean Rayment (24 February 2008: www.telegraph.co.uk/news/uknews/1579703/Record-numbers-of-Army-recruits-drop-out.html) states that the drop-out rate of recruits into the British army was over 34% in 2007, though the comparison to the US Army is less relevant since the rate of pay is much less in the UK and there is no GI Bill providing such a good pension for life after demobilisation. As a result, many UK recruits leave for monetary rather than fitness issues. In the United States a new test in 2017 to streamline recruits to the jobs for which they are best suited has raised the on-time graduation rate to 93% and has seen injuries drop by 17%, but still 25%–29% of male recruits are injured physically in basic training (www.armytimes.com/news/your-army/2017/10/18/early-numbers-show-the-armys-new-fitness-test-is-reducing-injuries-in-basic-training-3/). But crucially the US Army has completely revamped its basic training in infantry school in order to produce better disciplined and fitter soldiers (www.armytimes.com/news/your-army/2018/04/09/fitter-deadlier-soldiers-this-is-how-the-army-plans-to-prepare-you-for-tomorrows-wars/). This extra emphasis on fitness raises the passing bar from 50% on each test to 60%, and includes a 33% increase in hand-to-hand combat training (www.armytimes.com/news/your-army/2018/02/09/land-nav-iron-sights-and-more-discipline-big-changes-are-coming-to-army-basic-training/). Combat fitness is very different from general fitness. The US Army Ranger School uses statistics in its training manual that show that between 2000 and 2012 almost 29% of all cadets failed in the first RAP (Ranger Assessment Phase) week of physical testing (www.benning.army.mil/infantry/rtb/content/PDF/Ranger%20School%20web11.pdf). That is 57% of all cadets who failed. Fifty-one percent of all cadets failed Ranger School, and these were on average already serving soldiers with 2.3 years of experience and 23 years of age. Passing basic training is hard; passing extra leadership training to enter elite regiments (which is what Ranger School is) is extremely hard, and it was likely just as hard for Spartan hoplites. All in all, combat fitness is very different from normal fitness, and Greeks through practice became very fit for the harsh conditions of hoplite combat. Like the veterans I interviewed, I have no doubt that hoplites, especially professional or experienced soldiers, could fight or march for an extended period and run with their equipment if necessary or in a charge. They were certainly fit enough to be able to wield their shield easily and use it in hand-to-hand combat out of a phalanx and in a siege.
22 From the 82nd Airborne, and 19th Special Forces Group.
23 Schwartz 2009: 35 n. 103.
24 Krentz 2013: 139 and 151 n. 30.
25 Admittedly I have a very bad shoulder and constantly bending the arm to rest the shield in that position makes it worse, but it is not so heavy that carrying it with an extended arm is impossible as many scholars argue. In fact, it is also easier to walk with the shield held like that since the rim does not constantly bump into the thigh when walking.
26 Schwartz 2009: 87 fig. 12. Louvre, Paris (G 152).
27 Schwartz 2009: 53. 46–53 for his full discussion of the hoplite armour race and Pyrrhic dancing.
28 Schwartz 2009: 50–1.
29 Xenophon (*Hellenika* 5.4.33) states that the Spartan king Cleonymos fell down and got up three times in the phalanx before he was killed. Clearly depending on circumstances, it was not always instantly fatal to lose your footing. But this story is told precisely because it was unusual. Schwartz (2009: 184) rightly comments that "once a man had fallen to the ground inside the phalanx, it was exceedingly difficult to get up again", and Hanson (1991a: 67–74) discusses how hoplites further back in the

66 *The hoplite revolution in Greece*

phalanx could use their butt spikes to dispatch fallen opponents beneath them. Yet neither scholar focuses on the importance of balance to prevent this. Schwartz (2009: 191) does mention "the risk of throwing the attacker off balance" (and again briefly at 192) but goes no further even though doing so would help his arguments concerning the phalanx's shoving, the *othismos*.

30 US Army 1992b: 1. The whole section is of interest in addition to what is quoted previously, especially: "g. *Leverage*. A fighter uses leverage in hand-to-hand combat by using the natural movement of his body to place his opponent in a position of unnatural movement. The fighter uses his body or parts of his body to create a natural mechanical advantage over parts of the enemy's body. He should never oppose the enemy in a direct test of strength; however, by using leverage, he can defeat a larger or stronger opponent".

31 Schwartz 2009: 41–5.

32 Schwartz 2009: 34–5.

33 Forrest (1999: 90) in his book about the history of Morris dancing states that it developed from combat forms. Though not dance to benefit combat, the combat practices informed the dance steps similarly to Pyrrhic dancing. "This metamorphosis has several important aspects from the point of view of the developmental history of the dance. What is happening here is that the basic forms of mediaeval combat have gradually become surrounded by dramatic trappings until the aesthetic forms have completely usurped the martial".

34 There are too many examples from cultures all over the world to list further reading here, but some of the most famous are the war dances of the Plains Indians in North America, the Scottish Highland sword dance, and Kabuki dance in Japan.

35 To my knowledge there are no detailed books (though many internet articles) focused solely on the benefit of dancing to boxing and MMA, but biographies of famous fighters like Sugar Ray Leonard and Muhammad Ali emphasise their reliance on dancing before boxing. See for example https://evolve-vacation.com/blog/why-dancing-may-be-the-missing-ingredient-of-your-fight-game/

36 Xenophon *On Horsemanship*.

37 Schwartz 2009: 51. The Plato reference is to *Leg.* 815a.

38 Xenophon *Anabasis* 6.1.12.

39 Schwartz 2009: 51 n. 163.

40 Schwartz 2009: 51.

41 Van Wees (2005); Krentz (2013). See also Anderson (1991: 15); Lazenby and Whitehead (1996).

42 Snodgrass (1964); Snodgrass (1999); Everson (2004).

43 Anglim et al. (2002).

44 Wisdom (2001).

45 Bardunias and Ray (2016: 109–12). They use crowd dynamics to discuss early warfare structures and battlefield formations.

46 Bardunias and Ray (2016: 111).

47 Luraghi (2006). Mercenaries existed in Minoan Knossos also. See Driessen and Macdonald (1984).

48 Berossus *FgrHist* 680 F 7, 31 and Abydenus *FgrHist* 685 F 5, 6.

49 The use of hoplites as mercenaries in the Near East very soon after the adoption of the hoplite panoply demonstrates that the hoplite was the most effective heavy infantry soldier available anywhere at the time. This supports the argument that eastern armies were deficient in heavy infantry despite using combined arms, something I intend to discuss in detail elsewhere.

50 Luraghi (2006: 36–7).

51 Myres (1933).

52 Luraghi (2006: 37). Schwartz (2009: 130–3) echoes Luraghi in believing this is a phalanx formation even arguing that the scenes show sequential actions of an invasion with hoplites fighting a pitched battle not hoplites advancing to assault the walls. To me this is untenable.
53 The hoplites depicted are clearly shown to be attacking the city walls. Hale (2013: 182–4) follows Luraghi in adding another detailed analysis of the bowl but does not state openly whether he agrees with the interpretation of the men being in a phalanx.
54 Schwartz (2009: 133); Ober (1991: 180–3).
55 Hale (2013: 182).
56 The Egyptian evidence provided by Herodotus (2.152, 2.163, 2.30, etc.) and discussed by Hale (2013: 184–5) is for the last half of the seventh century. The Babylonians and Egyptians in 605 both field hoplites in a campaign against each other.
57 Hale (2013: 180–1).
58 Hale (2013: 181, 186–7). Hale rightly points out in the latter section the similarity between the ritualised agreed conflicts of Vikings within Scandinavia and hoplite battles in Greece. But the raiding is what made Vikings famous and had the most influence, just as the Greeks. "As it was in Scandinavia from AD 800 to 1000, so it had been, I would suggest, in Archaic Greece". Hale (2013: 187).
59 Hale (2013: 187–91).
60 See Homer's *Odyssey* 14.210–51 for an account of a Cretan aristocrat leading a band of retainers in nine ships to raid eastern shores and gain martial fame.
61 See for example Archilochus fr. 1, 2 and 5, Gerber as quoted in Hale (2013: 179). The losing of a shield was something that famously riled Classical hoplites, with Spartan mothers famously imploring their sons to come back "with their shield or on it". Alcaeus also was happy to admit to losing his shield in combat: Herodotus 5.95. To early mercenaries, as Hale emphasises, there appears no stigma attached to survival without a shield.
62 Schwartz (2009: 147–55). Schwartz is trying to use rhipsaspia to prove his argument that the hoplite shield could only be used in a phalanx formation. So, the stigma was attached in the Archaic period also because they also fought in a phalanx. However, I believe the shield did not necessitate a phalanx formation and so the stigma for rhipsaspia may not have always been present in Greek warfare, as Van Wees and others have argued elsewhere. Nonetheless, rhipsaspia was not relevant when whole armies turned and fled and so is irrelevant as a criticism of the passages of Archaic poetry.
63 Schwartz (2009: 214).
64 Alcaeus fr. 19, Edmonds as quoted in Hale (2013: 185).
65 Snodgrass (1965: 110), "the adoption of the 'hoplite panoply' was a long drawn out, piecemeal process, which did not at first entail any radical change in tactics". See also Van Wees (2005: 166–84). In particular, 177, "the Greek style of fighting throughout the sixth century remained much the same as in the time of Tyrtaeus. The first hints of change come only at the end of the century: mounted hoplites begin to fade from the vase-painters' repertoire, soon followed by hoplites with throwing spears and Boeotian shields, and from about 500 BC Spartan archer figurines no longer kneel in combat pose, but instead stand up straight, with their bows unstrung. . . . The strict separation of hoplites, light-armed, and horsemen characteristic of the classical phalanx, therefore, may not have emerged until the very end of the archaic period".
66 Van Wees (2000a: 147–9).
67 Archilochus F 139.6, West; and Callinus F 1.14, West.
68 Snodgrass (1964: fig. 15); Van Wees (2000a: 152–4).
69 This aspect of archers in Greek warfare is discussed previously.
70 Snodgrass (1964: 250, 1999: 81).
71 See in particular Hurwit (2002: 14–16).
72 Van Wees (2000a: 134–9).

68 *The hoplite revolution in Greece*

73 Lorimer (1947); Snodgrass (1964: 138); Cartledge (1977); Salmon (1977); Krentz (1985a).
74 Greenhalgh (1973).
75 Schwartz (2009: 121).
76 Schwartz (2009: 121).
77 In Hollywood such scenes always show the first ranks jumping up into the air or over the enemy's shields and doing somersaults in full armour. Clearly unlikely in actual combat, but the initial contact was still huge.
78 See the scholiast to Aristotle, *Nichomachean Ethics* 1116a36-b1; Tyrtaeus F 9.23.5, 23a.19 West; Pausanias 4.6.2, 17.2–7.
79 Van Wees (2005: 174–7) provides a good discussion of the specific images.
80 See for example Cartledge (1977).
81 Van Wees (2005: 175).
82 Van Wees (2005: 175–6).
83 Schwartz (2009: 123–35).
84 Schwartz (2009: 130).
85 Van Wees (2013: 240–5). Foxhall (2013) supports this view by showing that in archaeology of Archaic Greece there is little sign of a rise in numbers of those able to afford hoplite arms, the so-called yeoman farmers of Hanson. Contra see recently Viggiano (2013); Hanson (2013).
86 Van Wees (2005: 177–83). His argument is convincing that Herodotus emphasised the role of helots at Plataea because it was unusual to his readers. This will be discussed in more detail in the following chapter. Contra Schwartz (2009: 135–46).
87 Archaic cavalry was not heavy cavalry and so the advantage remained with the heavy unit over the light. Hale suggests an individual hoplite. "Should a horse come too close, even a lone hoplite stood a chance of fending the animal off with his heavy convex shield, or even inflicting a wound with a slash of the shield's blade-like rim". Hale (2013: 190). Herodotus 5.111–2 records the anecdote that the Persian general Artybius had trained his horse to rear up and use his feet and teeth to attack an infantryman. Surely, he was not alone in this practice so cavalry could face down individual hoplites. However, the fate of Artybius, his horse's legs cut off when resting on the hoplite's shield, suggests even then the large shield gave hoplites a decisive advantage as Hale argues.
88 Kagan and Viggiano (2013c: 9).
89 See Webster (1972: 190–5) for a list of pots displaying chariots and hoplites together.
90 Van Wees (2005:177).
91 Lissarrague (1990).
92 Van Wees 2005: (176–7).
93 Greenhalgh (1973).
94 Greenhalgh (1973: figs. 47, 53, 60, 66, 71, 73, 74).
95 Van Wees (2005: 166).
96 Van Wees (2005: 177).

3 Persia vs. Greece – the advantages of the heavy infantryman

The Persian Empire and its (mis)use of a combined arms army

The Persian Empire, despite its size and the lessons of the Assyrian Empire, failed to adopt a complete system of combined arms. Since the Persian king controlled so many different territories, which had to supply troops to the royal army, the Persian military consisted of every type of unit that existed at the time. However, the one thing that prevented their military system from being truly one of combined arms is that never were all the types of unit integrated successfully to mutually support each other. Instead, each unit fought semi-independently and the Persian commanders almost always relied on the elite Persian aristocratic cavalry to give them victory, and to a lesser extent the professional royal infantry bodyguard of 10,000 Immortals.

Sources

Unfortunately, most of the sources that detail the army of the Persian Empire are written from a western perspective. For the most part these focus on the Persian invasion of Greece and later the Macedonian conquest of Persia. It is very difficult to paint a true picture of the Persian military system without encountering western bias towards warfare focused on heavy infantry. Images that adorn Persian temples and buildings can provide significant detail of the armaments and dress of individuals and units but rarely show their use in battle.[1] Persian written sources take the form of royal inscriptions and commands along similar lines to those of earlier Mesopotamian civilisations, such as the Hittites and Assyria. Because of this it is necessary to engage with the western sources and attempt to piece information together despite their biased representations.

Xenophon's account of the Persian army of Cyrus the Great in the *Cyropaedaia* is written from a philosophical perspective, drawing more on the author's own knowledge and idealisation of the Spartan army than on any historical reality. Herodotus' account of the Persians before and during the Persian invasion of Greece is clearly slanted towards explaining Greek superiority over barbarians.

70 *The hoplite revolution in Greece*

The surviving histories of Alexander's campaign in Persia were written so long after the event that any specific details they present are shrouded in uncertainty. Nevertheless, it is possible to create a picture of the make-up of the Persian army and the tactics employed on the battlefield. This is especially true on occasions where the western bias of the author does not affect the details. In Herodotus, for example, descriptions of battles fought between two barbarian armies are not treated with the disdain shown for those involving Greek hoplites and are perhaps more reliable as a result.

Infantry

The Persian army was so large that most of the units that the king summoned did not even join the fight. Either the battle was won before reinforcements were needed or the whole force began to flee and every unit joined the rout.[2] Herodotus (9.68) states that after the battle of Plataea most of the contingents in the Persian army

> made their escape without striking a blow or doing any service whatever. It is perfectly obvious that everything depended on the Persians: the rest of Mardonius' army took to their heels simply because they saw the Persians in retreat, and before they had even come to grips with the enemy.

Infantry were the largest force in the Persian army. Herodotus (3.25) states that Cambyses took a force of 50,000 infantry, excluding his Greek mercenaries, against Ethiopia. In Darius' invasion of Scythia, the Scythian cavalry repeatedly overcame their Persian counterparts with their arrows but were forced to retreat once the Persian cavalry were supported at close quarters by the infantry.[3] In the Persian retreat, the Scythian horsemen overtook them because "the greater part of the Persian army was travelling on foot".[4]

Persian archers were the most important "national" infantry unit.[5] The three divisions of fief holdings in the Persian administration system were chariots, cavalry, and archers.[6] Just as in Assyria, the bow was the principal weapon of Persian royalty since Darius I boasted of his abilities with the bow on foot and on horseback, just as Assyrian kings did.[7] Darius I also minted coins for his kingdom featuring a kneeling archer, crowned and robed.[8]

This obsession with archery meant that any national Persian troops were armed with the bow as their principal weapon. Against unarmoured or poorly armoured opponents, massed archery was very successful when combined with assaults by heavy cavalry. This was the style of warfare practised by the Assyrians, and neighbouring states such as Media and Scythia used the same system.

The emphasis on archery in eastern armies can be seen in Herodotus' description of the battle between the Neo-Assyrian army of Sennacherib and the Egyptians (2.141). There field mice swarmed over Sennacherib's camp and ate all the quivers, bow strings, and shield handles, leaving them with no arms to fight the battle. Even if this account is fictitious, it demonstrates Herodotus' belief that archery was the main method of warfare for non-Greeks.[9] His belief is emphasised in the Persian attack on the Scythian Massagetae. This invasion culminated in a battle described by Herodotus as beginning with "the two armies coming to a halt within range of each other and exchanging shots with bows and arrows until their arrows were used up; after which there was a long period of close fighting with spears and daggers, neither side being willing to retreat".[10] Both sides relied first and foremost on archery, and when that failed they resorted to seemingly disorganised close-quarter combat until one side turned and fled.

Herodotus (1.103) states that it was not until the reign of the Median King Cyaxares that the army was divided into separate units of archers, spearmen, and cavalry: a prerequisite for combined arms in battle. Previously all the soldiers in the army were mixed together en masse. Fighting in this way allowed for a reliance on archery. Arrows would take their toll on a large mass of soldiers in an unregimented army and there was no need to develop or use different tactics. After the regimentation of the army Persian tactics still relied on massed archery from both infantry and cavalry. Only after the enemy had been sufficiently weakened by the missile barrage did the Persians engage in hand-to-hand combat. Cook concludes that "usually the Persian infantry seems to have expected to make short work of an enemy who had already been harassed and softened up by cavalry and missiles".[11]

As a consequence of the emphasis on archers as well as their many successes, the Persians never really used heavy infantry. Most of the levies in the Persian army were light infantry.[12] The majority of these used bows or javelins but were armed also with small shields and swords or daggers for close-quarter combat. The only Persian unit of heavy infantry was the Royal Bodyguard of 10,000. This unit was nicknamed the Immortals by the Greek historians because their total number was never lower than 10,000 (Herodotus, 7.83). These men were armed with bows first and foremost but were accustomed to use shields and spears if necessary. They were heavily armoured with a long coat of mail and helmet.

The deployment of the Persian infantry usually consisted of a line of spearmen holding large shields at the front protecting a number of archers and missile troops behind.[13] That is not to say that the Persian spearmen were not well-armoured soldiers who were highly skilled in individual combat. Persian spearmen, just as their Assyrian counterparts, were very able close-quarter warriors. However, very rarely were they required to fight in a close formation. Each soldier fought independently in the melee protecting his section of the shield wall, supported by the archers and light infantry behind him. At the battle of Mycale Herodotus states (9.102):

> The Persians, as long as their line of shields remained intact, successfully repelled all attacks and had by no means the worst of things; . . . They [the Athenians] burst through the line of shields and fell upon the enemy in a mass assault. For a time, indeed, the assault was held, but in the end the Persians were forced to retreat within the protection of the barricade.

The Persians were very able individual warriors at close quarters, especially protected behind their shield wall, but against an organised and disciplined mass of well-armoured heavy infantry their shortcomings could be exposed.

The concept of individual heroism permeated the Persian military society. Nobles strived to excel at fighting as individuals with the bow, javelin, and spear.[14] The Immortals were well-armed individuals who could fight effectively as archers or spearmen in close quarters. But they did not fight in any tactical formation.[15] At Thermopylae the Greek hoplites held off repeated Persian assaults for two days and successfully repulsed the Immortals without suffering too many casualties. Even this elite unit of well-armed infantry was not a match for true heavy infantry fighting in a compact formation due to the narrowness of the terrain.[16] As a result the Immortals were almost always employed as missile troops alongside the rest of the Persian infantry and joined the melee as spearmen only when archery became less effective.

At the battle of Marathon, Herodotus states that the Persians and Sacae put up the most resistance to the Athenian hoplites. This was perhaps because these were the main infantry units, along with the Assyrians, that were well armed and so could, and did, fight ably in hand-to-hand combat if required. Likely they were also the men whom the veterans would remember most clearly.[17] Herodotus (7.61–4) outlines the armaments of these units when describing the forces arrayed by Xerxes in 480, and shows they were well equipped for melee fighting.[18] They were also used as marines in Xerxes' navy alongside hoplites from Ionia, suggesting they could act as true heavy infantry (i.e. not archers) when required.

Herodotus (7.61) states that the Persians (and the Medians) were armed with "large wicker shields, quivers slung below them, short spears, powerful bows with cane arrows, and daggers swinging from belts beside the right thigh". According to Herodotus, there is no differentiation between units and all Persians, that is all ethnically Persian soldiers, were armed in the same way.[19]

As for defensive armour, the Persian style of scaled bronze or iron sewn onto a leather or linen jerkin ("a coat of mail looking like the scales of a fish" as Herodotus [7.61] describes it) was effective enough against arrows and light infantry. Until Darius' attack on Greece, the Persian military had not encountered well-armed, organised infantry en masse.[20] Against the concerted thrust of a hoplite's spear a Persian soldier's wicker shield and body armour offered significantly less protection than a bronze breastplate and *hoplon*.

Other than mercenary hoplites, there were a number of Greek subject states that supplied heavy infantry to the Persian army, but these were from maritime powers for the most part, and therefore these hoplites would probably have been used mainly as marines. The Egyptians (when they were used on land rather than as marines), the Assyrians, and the Sacae were the only units of non-hoplite heavy infantry in the regular army according to Herodotus' description (7.61–81). Even the Assyrians and Sacae used the bow first before fighting in the melee with axes or spears.

The majority of Persian armies consisted of infantry raised from a number of different states under Achaemenid control. All of these different national units were arrayed in the battle line and fought in the same manner, using a barrage of arrows to weaken the enemy before closing for hand-to-hand warfare. The Persian style of infantry combat did allow for the regimentation of archers and spearmen, after Cyaxares if we believe Herodotus 1.103, but still relied on massed archery first and foremost, rather than using tactics involving spearmen and archers in combination.

Cavalry

The most important unit in the Persian army was the elite cavalry. According to Herodotus, Croesus, the king of Lydia, intended to defeat the Persian army because his cavalry was superior.[21] This suggests that the battle was intended to be decided by a clash of cavalry, only for Croesus to be undone by Cyrus' use of camels.

The importance of the Persian heavy cavalry is clear. The royal bodyguard unit under Xerxes was listed by Herodotus (7.40–42) as comprising

> a thousand horsemen, picked out from all Persia, followed by a thousand similarly picked spearmen with spears reversed. . . . Then came the king himself. . . . Behind him marched a thousand spearmen, their weapons pointing upwards in the usual way – all men of the best and noblest Persian blood; then a thousand picked Persian cavalry, then – again chosen for quality out of all that remained – a body of Persian infantry ten thousand strong. . . . The ten thousand infantry were followed by a squadron of ten thousand Persian horse.

The cavalry were principally armed with the bow but could also use clubs and their javelins as spears in close-quarter combat.[22] A list of the required equipment for a cavalry fief holder at Uruk under Darius II in 422 includes "horse and harness, saddle-cloth, iron cuirass, helmet with felt neck guard, shield, 130 arrows, an iron shield attachment, and an iron club and two javelins".[23] The heavy cavalry were well armoured, wearing mail coat and helmet and using a shield. The bow is obviously understood to have been used and there is a noticeable omission of a sword.

The main tactic of the Persian cavalry, as the battle of Plataea demonstrates (Herodotus 9.49), was to wheel in front of the enemy lines discharging their missiles. Persian armies contained levies from throughout the empire and so included many different units of cavalry. However, most units were either light cavalry accustomed to using missiles, such as Scythian horse archers, or heavy cavalry that relied on firing arrows before closing in to fight with the spear or axe. As a result, all of the cavalry in the Persian army was utilised tactically in the same way as archers.

The heavy cavalry were so well armed that they could also function as close combat troops, either acting as shock troops in a charge or fighting hand to hand in a static engagement. At the battle of Plataea (Herodotus 9.49) the cavalry engaged in a bitter hand-to-hand struggle over the body of their fallen commander, charging repeatedly at the Greek line, but the Greek hoplites eventually forced them to retreat. At the battle of Malene, the Greek rebels under Histiaeus were defeated only when the Persian cavalry attacked them in the rear after arriving late at the battlefield (Herodotus 6.29). It is possible, as Hammond states, that the cavalry engaged the Greeks at close quarters. However, Herodotus does not state that the cavalry charged into the Greek lines but suggests more simply that their arrival is what sparked the Greek flight. The simple presence of cavalry at the exposed rear of a phalanx would be enough to cause panic in the ranks of Greek hoplites, and any missiles fired from that position would cause significant casualties.

Nefedkin convincingly argues that after the wars with Greece the Persian cavalry changed to adopt shock assault tactics and were regularly armed with a thrusting spear, or *pelte*, for this purpose.[24] These shock tactics were certainly favoured by the Persian cavalry in the armies of Darius III in the fourth century, as discussed next, and proved a match for the Macedonian and Thessalian cavalry of Alexander.[25] Exactly when these tactics were adopted is difficult to determine, but likely the ineffectiveness of arrows against Greek hoplites prompted a tactical shift in the military mindset of the Persians.

Although they had the ability to engage the enemy at close quarters the Persian cavalry usually relied on firing missiles from a distance, just as did the infantry until the fourth century when they began to use the tactics of the charge into close-quarter combat. The Persian cavalry was always the most important unit in the Persian army before and after the adoption of assault tactics.

Combined arms

Even though a Persian army contained many types of soldiers, from light and heavy infantry through to elephants and camel riders, never did a Persian battle plan try to integrate all the different types of units to their mutual benefit.[26] In fact the very nature of Persian armies prevented a concerted battle plan. Persian royal armies were composed of levies from every province in the empire.[27] These levies would not have had significant military experience and would be conscripted out of necessity. Persian commanders preferred to rely primarily on the troops they knew best: the Persians and their immediate neighbours.

Ferrill describes the problems of the Persian army best, though he generalises without providing any specific supporting evidence:

> the national army was not a tactically cohesive force. Although it was a tactically integrated army in the sense that Persians used infantry, cavalry and skirmishers in coordination on the field of battle, it consisted of ethnic and regional levies that retained their local, tactical organization. Obviously the resultant mixture was not always tactically harmonious. Again, however, the Greeks benefited, especially when Philip and Alexander learned how to combine the forces of the Macedonians and their allies in a tactically unified army in which every element was familiar with the style of fighting of the units up and down the line of battle.[28]

Most of the soldiers did not fight as professionals. Limited previous training coupled with little time to enact training regimes before battle meant that the quality of individual units varied considerably. The fighting efficiency of the army relied on the core of professional Persian troops and the Royal Bodyguard. Some of the other units would have been experienced and used to war, but many others would have joined the army through compulsion rather than experience or choice. The nature of these troops as levies also suggests a large, but ineffective army. The battle of Pharsalus between Caesar and Pompey aptly demonstrates the superiority of veteran troops against raw recruits pressed into service, even when outnumbered four or five to one.[29]

Moreover, the Persian Empire never sought to impose a single cultural identity onto conquered populations with the result that subsequent military levies of non-Persians were armed in the traditional local style.[30] If a Persian royal army fought in Asia Minor, then it would contain more hoplites from Ionia, but if it was required to attack the Scythians, then Bactrian cavalry would predominate. Without a permanent standing army in constant use, as in Neo-Assyria, the Persians had to rely on untried assortments of regional troops, much to their tactical detriment.

The Persians themselves realised the deficiency in their armies when they fought the Greek hoplites, to the extent that they began to employ Greek hoplites as mercenaries in greater number than before.[31] Briant is probably right that Greek accounts exaggerate the martial deficiencies of Persian armies and overemphasise their reliance on hoplite mercenaries.[32] Nonetheless, the repeated defeats of the Persian army at the hands of armies reliant on a core of heavy infantry utilised in close-quarter combat show that these martial deficiencies were real even if exaggerated.

If the Greek historians are right that mercenary hoplites always fought in the front ranks of Persian armies, this is perhaps more to do with the fact that dead mercenaries cost nothing, and less to do with Persian acceptance of Greek superiority. Nevertheless, mercenaries, in particular Greek hoplites, were employed in great numbers in an attempt to escape from a reliance on untried conscripted levies and to increase the number of heavy infantry in the army. In the fourth century the Persians even experimented with training their own unit of hoplites, the so-called Cardaces.[33]

In battle the Persian archers, on horse and foot, would bombard the enemy for a long period of time. This barrage of missiles was intended to disrupt the formation of the enemy and cause enough confusion that a charge of infantry and cavalry would precipitate the victory using their superior numbers to overwhelm the enemy. This is similar to the tactics used by the Neo-Assyrians. The Persian military system simply continued the style of warfare used for centuries in Mesopotamia. And this is the very basic use of combined arms: missiles followed up by close-quarter assaults of both heavy infantry and cavalry together.

Against light or undisciplined infantry this tactic proved very successful. However, when the Persians came up against opposing armies that were superior in one or more styles of warfare, or who could not be broken by missiles and a

76 The hoplite revolution in Greece

cavalry charge, they did not know how to adapt to win. The Persian army was tactically deficient and ultimately defeated because it did not utilise the principle of combined arms in using each unit in the most tactically efficient way: cavalry as missile troops and for close combat in combination, missile infantry as a support arm, and crucially heavy infantry as the main thrust of the army. Instead they relied almost exclusively on an extensive missile barrage.

The Persian Wars: the mirage of the hoplite's superiority

The Persian army involved a degree of combined arms, using missiles, cavalry, and infantry together in battle, but the level of tactical integration to get the best out of each unit type was minimal. When the Persian forces came up against the Greek hoplites for the first time at Marathon, the Eastern lack of heavy infantry contributed greatly to their defeat.

Sources

The best source for the Persian Wars is Herodotus. It is the only written account that gives full details of the conflict as a whole, with a focus on the battles themselves. Herodotus is also the only near contemporary account. Diodorus gives a brief history of the wars but rarely provides any specifics of the battles that are not already supplied by Herodotus. Plutarch in various *Lives* adds some information, but he is rarely concerned with the details of battles and so is of little concern here. All these sources are Greek and obviously present events in a biased way in favour of the victors. Without a Persian perspective it is difficult, perhaps impossible, to thoroughly distance any historical interpretation from the Greek ideal.

The problem with all of the extant sources is that they never provide a focus on the tactical aspects of battles. Instead the specific units arrayed for battle and their commanders are enumerated with only a brief outline of their armament and battlefield position. This problem is amplified by the considerable hoplite focus of the writers of fifth-century Greek history. Even though Herodotus interviewed survivors and eyewitnesses, he was still writing in the Classical period when the hoplite phalanx was the preeminent formation of heavy infantry.

On account of this overriding concern for hoplites and their superiority, it is difficult to examine the importance, or often even the existence, of other types of soldier in Greek armies. This is exactly what is important in order to determine the extent of the use of combined arms in battle. Despite these problems it is possible to find enough information to make relatively secure conclusions about combined arms in the Persian Wars.

Persian armies exposed without using combined arms properly – Marathon

The battle of Marathon has proved considerably difficult for scholars to reconstruct based primarily on Herodotus' account and the topography of the battlefield.[34] The details of the battle as provided by Herodotus and the other sources obviously give all the credit to the Greeks. All our sources are Greek and seek to magnify their victory. Certainly the troop totals on each side have been altered accordingly and probably some of the specifics of the conflict have also. The main details of the encounter we can accept as fact, but the minutiae of individual involvements are perhaps more uncertain. In order to examine the tactics used by each army in the battle – the main concern here – it is important first to discuss the make-up of the armies.

The Persian expeditionary force took a little longer than a year to assemble.[35] It was perhaps four times smaller than the force assembled by Xerxes ten years later. If his army ranged from 250,000 to 400,000 men, then the force under the command of Datis and Artaphernes in the Aegean in 490 will have numbered anywhere from a very conservative 20,000 to the 90,000 mentioned in the epigram attributed to Simonides.[36] Herodotus does not give a total for the army but states (6.95) that the Persian fleet numbered 600 ships, and Hammond estimates it may have totalled as many as 1,000.[37] Unfortunately, Herodotus does not specify the type of ships in the fleet and so we do not know how many transports and how many triremes there were. Whatever the exact number, the whole force had to have been large enough to besiege and capture a number of islands in the Aegean, not least the whole of Eretria where, according to Herodotus (6.101) both sides suffered many casualties, and still have enough men left to expect to defeat Athens.[38]

There are no reliable numbers provided for the Persian army, either infantry or cavalry, so any calculations are very rough estimates. Although Herodotus' numbers for Xerxes' expedition to Greece are notoriously exaggerated, he lists 80,000 cavalry alongside 1.7 million infantry.[39] Both numbers are too large but the relative strengths may be reliable. There we see a ratio of 20:1 of infantry to cavalry. If the Persians at Marathon had only 20,000 infantry, then we can propose a cavalry force of 1,000.

It is possible that the Persians fielded the rowers and men from the navy to fight in the army. These would have been equipped as light troops, except for the few marines, limiting their effectiveness against hoplites. Hammond is right that the Persians were landlubbers,[40] but Herodotus is explicit that the army contained men from all the Persians' subject states. Many of the ships were supplied by maritime states, such as those from Phoenicia, and it is likely that many of the soldiers were from the same areas. This was not a royal army led by the king himself and so did not require large contingents from the eastern subjects. Moreover, Datis enlisted troops from all the islands in the Aegean as tribute (Herodotus, 6.99). These men must have been Ionian Greeks comfortable with rowing a trireme and presumably also a few hoplites fighting as marines or infantry.

If we assume 200 men as the crew for a trireme, and that the Persian fleet contained over 200 warships, the Persians had at least 40,000 rowers alone.[41] To believe that all these men sat idle in their ships when the Persian army took the field against the Athenians seems ridiculous. The Persians, not needing the fleet to fight a naval battle after their victory at Lade, would have expected to mobilise many of the rowers as infantry on land in the campaign. At Pylos, as discussed next, Demosthenes successfully created and defended a fortified position in enemy territory using the crews and marines of only five triremes. Rowers certainly could be used in battle with considerable success.[42] In fact, perhaps the rowers fighting as light infantry suggests why the Athenian hoplites, though outnumbered, could inflict such heavy casualties on the Persian battle line.

The Greek force consisted of Athenians and Plataeans. The Plataeans numbered 1,000.[43] Herodotus states they came with every available man. The precise troop totals of the Athenian army are not provided by Herodotus. Pausanias states that the Athenian force was less than 10,000 (4.25.5) and not more than 9,000 (10.20.2). Nepos (*Miltiades* 5) numbers the Athenians at 9,000 and Justin (2.9) totals them at 10,000.

Men must also have been left behind to defend Athens. These were probably the older soldiers and those who were not ready to leave the city at a moment's notice.[44] The Athenians almost certainly had a cavalry force in 490 through those in the *hippeis* class.[45] These men would surely have been taken along to Marathon to fight on terrain chosen by the Persians on account of its suitability for cavalry action.

It is hard to believe that the Athenians did not bring *any* cavalry with them to a battlefield well suited for horses and to oppose an army reliant on its cavalry. That we do not hear about them in the historical accounts is not surprising since the political climate at the time, which focused on democracy overcoming barbarian tyranny, sought to place all the credit for victory on the hoplites alone. This is probably also the reason for Herodotus' omission of the armed slaves in the Greek army.

Herodotus (6.112) states that the Greek hoplites charged with no support from cavalry or archers. Many scholars use this as proof that the Athenian contingent comprised only hoplites. Herodotus does not state this. The charge may well have involved just hoplites, as is discussed next, but he never states there were no cavalry or archers supporting the Athenian army. Moreover, he clarifies his position (6.112) stating that "that was what they imagined". He is referring to the Persians' view that the rush of hoplites appeared like a suicidal charge, but he may mean that the Persians imagined that the Greek attack was conducted without cavalry or infantry support.

Pausanias (1.32.3) states that the Athenians mobilised slaves to support their army. Finley suggests that this is the first instance of the Athenians using freed slaves in battle, as did Pausanias.[46] These slaves can hardly have fought as hoplites and must have been used as supporting light infantry in the battle.[47] Van Wees argues that

> the Athenians went so far as to mobilise their slaves for this battle, so there was surely a levy of all available manpower to meet the threat, as one would expect, including poor citizens who fought with any weapons they could lay their hands on.[48]

The problem is that none of these poor citizens are recorded as fighting in the battle in any source and there is nothing to describe the equipment of the freed slaves. For this study of combined arms, it is necessary to speculate on their battlefield use.

The Athenian freed slaves were buried with the Plataeans, separate from the Athenians.[49] Since the Plataeans were probably buried where they were stationed on the left wing of the Greeks, it seems logical that the slaves also fought on this wing.[50] Slaves and any other light infantry present would have been very useful at keeping the Persian cavalry away from the vulnerable left flank of the phalanx while the hoplites closed down the long distance to the Persian infantry.

In my view, it is in the context of a flank guard that the freed slaves played their part in the battle. The Greeks clearly realised the importance of protecting the flanks of a hoplite phalanx against the larger and cavalry-reliant Persian army. The Greek alliance chose to resist the invasion of Xerxes at Thermopylae partly because the terrain would neutralise Persian numbers and prevent the tactical deployment of their cavalry. The non-hoplites in the Greek army would not have had much to do in the battle once the hoplites came to close quarters with the Persians and this may be why they are ignored in Herodotus' account.

The topography of the battlefield and the preliminaries to the battle have been discussed at length elsewhere and are not of direct concern here. Suffice it to say that the Greek line was drawn up in the foothills protecting their flanks with topographical features, namely a marsh and a hillside.[51] The Persians formed up opposite them at a corresponding angle, undoubtedly hoping their cavalry on their right flank would overcome the obstacles of the wooded foothills and be able to attack the exposed Greek left flank.[52]

As far as we can reconstruct them, the events of the battle were as follows.[53] The Greeks drew up for battle and were opposed by the Persians. The Greeks then cut down trees on the slopes of the hills and constructed log barriers on their flanks to prevent attacks by the Persian cavalry. Whether or not Miltiades did await his own day of command to initiate the attack, a delay almost certainly did occur between the arrival of the Athenians at Marathon and the battle. The Persians were restless and somewhat overconfident on account of the Greek delay, but were probably fearful of more Greek reinforcements arriving from Sparta or elsewhere. Once the Greeks, having strengthened their wings, attacked at dawn, they proceeded hastily to close the distance between themselves and the Persians before the latter's arrows could take their toll.

Once they came to grips with the enemy, the Greeks on the reinforced flanks were victorious and turned inwards to relieve the beleaguered centre. At close quarters the Greek hoplites proved superior to the Persian infantry and forced them to flee headlong towards their ships. After the battle turned in favour of the Greeks, the pursuit of the Persians began in earnest. The Persian army made its way back to the ships as fast as it could. The Greeks chased them over the plain, killing many that were hindered by the large marsh beside the Persian camp.[54] The fighting continued right up to the Persian ships, where two of the Athenian generals and the poet Aeschylus' brother were killed. Only six ships were captured intact on the beach (Herodotus 6.115), but Herodotus does not mention how many escaped.

80 The hoplite revolution in Greece

Herodotus (6.117) lists over 6,400 Persian casualties. Almost all of these must have been among the infantry and the largest proportion was likely those overtaken in the marsh. Although the number seems high compared with the 192 Athenian dead (Herodotus 6.117), in most battles where one side is routed and has to cover much ground to reach safety,[55] casualties are disproportionately high.[56] If the Athenians did have cavalry this would have added to the success of their pursuit of the Persian infantry. Hoplites would normally be outrun easily by the more lightly armoured Persian infantry, even if they did know the terrain better.

Most vessels of the Persian navy left without anything close to their full complement aboard. The rush to escape would have caused such urgency that every ship would have left as soon as it was able. Very few ships were left behind because of this disorderly departure. The 6,400 Persian casualties would account for all the missing men in each ship to the extent that only six ships remained completely unused.[57]

There are a number of points that require further consideration from a combined arms perspective. The first problem is the Greek formation of an extended line with a weakened centre (Herodotus 6.111). Certainly this deployment was adopted in an effort to match the greater length of the Persian battle line. It is also possible that this formation was in part decided on through a concern for the vulnerability of the Greek flanks and rear to the Persian cavalry. A fast and unexpected attack by the Greeks would leave little time for the cavalry to inhibit them and weight of numbers would allow the hoplites to succeed against the Persian infantry, while simultaneously warding off cavalry attacks. Even as many as 2,500 Persian cavalry would have had little impact on 10,000 hoplites attacking at speed. The arrows of the Persians would not have been numerous enough to halt the Greek charge. At Thermopylae it took a number of hours for fewer than 1,000 hoplites to succumb to the missile bombardment of a significantly larger Persian army.[58] All the Persian cavalry could do was fire their arrows into the Greek force until hoplites clashed with the Persian infantry. Once the battle became a melee the Persian cavalry may have joined the conflict until they saw the cause was lost, when they fled.

It is possible that the Persians did not make use of their cavalry in the battle itself. But the cavalry was the principal force in the Persian army and would have been deployed in a large enough number to make it worth the expense and effort of ferrying the horses across the Aegean. The Persians chose to land at Marathon because it was the most suitable place for cavalry action.[59] With this in mind, it is highly unlikely that the cavalry were not used to some extent in the battle. The Stoa Poecile does depict the Persian commanders fighting on horseback and they cannot have been alone.[60] Even in joining the melee a rider would be easily unhorsed by a hoplite.[61] The fact that Herodotus makes no mention of the Persian cavalry in the battle does not prove they were not present, or that their number was small enough to be insignificant.

Burn, among others, uses the absence of the cavalry in Herodotus to suggest that the battle did not commence until the Persians had begun to embark the cavalry on the ships.[62] The evidence for this is circumstantial at best and rests on the speed of the Persian navy's departure and the lack of cavalry mentioned in Herodotus and the few shown on the mural in the Stoa Poecile in Athens. The argument is untenable. If the Persians intended a withdrawal of the whole army they would have been better served strategically to load the cavalry last so that they could use their mobility in the plain to cover the movement of the infantry. Moreover, cavalry would not have been much use in a ship-borne attack on Athens and would have been better served to ride the short distance from Marathon to Athens in order to combine with an infantry assault from the fleet. The cavalry would have been the first soldiers to reach the ships once the Persian army began to be routed and would probably have had time to embark and leave before the rest of the infantry and the pursuing Greek hoplites arrived.

News of the imminent arrival of the Spartan reinforcements may have caused the Persians to assume that the Athenians would not attack. But it did not prompt them to begin the process of loading their army onto the ships in order to leave Marathon. The Persians chose to land at Marathon intending to fight a battle there and they would have remained confident in their ability to defeat the Greek army with or without the Spartan contingent. The fact that the Persian army maintained its position opposite the Greek line proves that they intended to face whatever army the Greeks arrayed against them.

Hammond argues that the cavalry were absent from the fighting because they had not returned from overnight pasture when the Athenians attacked at dawn.[63] He even suggests their absence is the reason that Miltiades initiated the Athenian attack. Burn is right that this takes it too far,[64] but the alternative to Hammond's argument is not that the cavalry were not present at all. In my view, the cavalry were present but played such a small role in the outcome of the battle that the Greek sources simply ignored their contribution.

Shrimpton has argued that the Athenians were stationed opposite the Persians at Plataea because their hoplites were the only ones among the allied Greeks who knew how to fight against cavalry, having learned how to do so at Marathon ten years earlier (cf. Herodotus 6.27).[65] The Persian cavalry must have been present at Marathon to make the Greek deployment at Plataea relevant. The Persians were caught off guard by the Greek attack and this surprise would have led to a delay in the attack of the Persian cavalry, but it does not prove their complete absence from the field. The cavalry were probably stationed on the right flank of the Persian line to make best use of the open spaces.

It is possible that the Persian cavalry prompted the Greek charge by wheeling in front of them while discharging their missiles. It would have been very foolish of the Persians to remain drawn up for battle opposite the Greeks for a number of days without harassing the Greeks with their cavalry. Perhaps it was a daily occurrence, which usually was ignored by the Greeks. These cavalry forays may have been the direct catalyst for the creation of defensive barricades by the Greeks.[66]

Once the Athenians had resolved to attack, perhaps they launched their charge at the moment when the Persian cavalry began to harass them and caught them unawares. Alternatively, Shrimpton may be right when he states that the Persian cavalry were still resting behind the lines when the Greek attack began a little before dawn.⁶⁷ By the time they armed themselves and rode out the Greeks were already well advanced and perhaps already engaged in hand-to-hand combat with the infantry. If this is true, the Persian cavalry had little time to attack. Perhaps the Persians were so surprised that the Greeks were attacking at all, especially without much cavalry support, that their response was slow enough to allow the Greeks to close the distance between the armies quickly without much resistance, thus giving the impression that they ran the whole way.

As Storch has demonstrated, the Greek charge was not prompted by a Persian missile barrage.⁶⁸ Certainly the Persians loosed a considerable number of arrows in the battle. The area around the burial mound on the plain at Marathon revealed a large number of arrows. As outlined previously, archery was the main method of warfare in Persian armies and most of their infantry at Marathon were archers.⁶⁹ All the Persian army principally relied on arrows and must have done so at Marathon, so the number of arrows does not imply the widespread use of cavalry.

Herodotus' account emphasises that Marathon was the first occasion where battle was joined at a run. This is certainly not the case as the distance covered was too great for a fully armed hoplite. The total distance between the armies as given by Herodotus is roughly a mile. Shrimpton estimates that it would have taken the Greeks between 15 and 20 minutes to cover the distance to the Persian line.⁷⁰ Moreover, the standard Persian deployment involved a static shield wall behind which the archers could fire their missiles in relative safety. The static nature of the Persian infantry line allowed the Greeks the freedom to determine when exactly to break out into a run. Although the Olympic Games in Greece included a race conducted in full hoplite armour, a mile was too far for a whole army to cover at a run and maintain order, especially in the dense phalanx formation. What is more likely is that the Greeks covered the distance at the double; a rapid march culminating in a final charge at the run when they were within about a hundred metres of the enemy. It also suggests that the phalanx was not a densely packed close-order formation since any amount of running would create significant gaps in the line.

What may have influenced Herodotus is the overall speed of the Greek advance. A rapid attack would save the Greeks from a long and irritating barrage of missiles from the infantry and the cavalry. The Greeks would have been able to cover in two or three minutes the final 200 yards where they would be under fire from the Persian archers.⁷¹ Even if the Persians were unprepared they would have had time to arm and ready themselves, sending the cavalry to attack the Greeks with their missiles. Storch rightly stresses that Herodotus never explicitly states that the Athenians ran in order to get through the Persian missile bombardment.⁷² That does not prove that there was no missile bombardment, just that it was not the main reason for the Greek tactic. The charge would have drastically reduced the length of time the Greeks were exposed to the Persian missiles.

If the Greek charge was conducted at speed, regardless of how far the soldiers ran, it is likely that the hoplite formation was more open than at first imagined. A hoplite phalanx in close order could not run at any speed without losing formation. If the Greeks attacked at speed at Marathon, the hoplites cannot have overlapped their shield with the soldier next to them. Rather we must understand the Greek army fighting in the open style of battle as suggested by Van Wees.[73] This would also explain the novelty of the speed of the attack at Marathon in the eyes of later Greeks. Classical hoplite phalanxes concerned with maintaining a tight formation were not able to charge at a run, just as the later Macedonians could not.

Combined arms conclusions

At Marathon the Greeks were probably supported by light infantry in the form of freed slaves, and possibly also some cavalry. Nevertheless, the Greeks did not *intend* to use combined arms fully in battle and relied on hoplites alone for the victory, to the extent that the very existence of light infantry and cavalry in the Greek army is denied. The Persians fielded an army that consisted of many types of unit but they were unable to use them all to their best advantage, the main principle of combined arms.[74] The Persian cavalry was present in the battle but rendered ineffective by the Greek tactic of unexpectedly attacking the static Persian battle line at speed. The Greeks were victorious principally because their heavy infantry proved superior in close-quarter situations to any units in the Persian army. Either the Greeks had not yet adopted a classical phalanx close-order formation, or they abandoned it in favour of speed of attack. Once their superiority of numbers was nullified by the extended Greek wings, the predominantly lightly armed Persian army was forced to flee. Neither side used combined arms fully even if the Persians did field different types of unit.[75]

Marathon was a significant victory for the Greeks that prevented Athens and other Greek *poleis* from becoming part of the Persian Empire. The battle was won through superior armament and speed of action rather than an innate superiority of the Greek hoplite over his barbarian opponents. We may never fully understand many of the specific details of the battle itself or the wider campaign, but it is possible to see that combined arms was not used fully by the Greeks or the Persians in the battle even though the plain of Marathon provided suitable terrain to do so. Nevertheless, the success at Marathon of the Greek heavy infantry phalanx exposed the deficiency of the Persian army in heavy infantry. It should have led Xerxes, in his invasion of Greece ten years later, to adapt his army to face such formidable heavy infantry by using combined arms in a more sophisticated fashion, fully integrating all his thousands of soldiers, cavalry, missile troops, and other infantry, in order to neutralise and overcome the Greek hoplites. Instead Xerxes relied on hoplites provided by his Greek subject states to oppose the Greek phalanx, but only in limited numbers and with limited success.

The beginnings of successful combined arms in Greek armies – Plataea

The only battle discussed here in detail in Xerxes' invasion of Greece is the battle of Plataea.[76] Thermopylae was a defensive engagement more like a siege of a

84 *The hoplite revolution in Greece*

static defended position than a pitched battle, and thus did not allow the utilisation of combined arms in full from either side. The later battles of Mycale and Eurymedon were smaller, and similar to Plataea, so the one major battle will suffice as an example of the whole conflict.

At Plataea the many controversies surrounding logistics, route, and personalities are not of concern. Instead the focus is on the military and tactical aspects of the campaign, primarily the battle itself. However, before examining the battle it is necessary to comment on the make-up of Xerxes' army in his invasion of Greece in order to see if it relied on combined arms.[77] For the first time the full Persian Royal Army came up against the largest Greek army ever assembled by the various poleis, which fielded substantial units of missile infantry and cavalry for the first time. As a result, Plataea serves as a perfect starting point to determine the level of combined arms in each army, and exhibits the main differences between the styles of warfare of the east and west.

Xerxes' army

The troop totals given by Herodotus for Xerxes' army are certainly too large. Logistically, it would have been impossible for the Persian Empire to support over 1.7 million men, let alone the innumerable camp followers and attendants. Alexander the Great was able to take an army of over 50,000 men through Asia from Greece, but he still had a number of worries about supplies.[78] The armies of the Successors of Alexander often reached 150,000 men if you include both sides.[79] Certainly, then, Asia Minor and northern Greece were capable of supporting an army of at least 150,000.[80]

While Xerxes was preparing the expedition's army, he had his logistical corps throughout the empire spend four years preparing provisions for his march and storing them in the most fitting places on his route to Greece.[81] It is likely that all the cities and peoples under his sway, especially on his line of march, were instructed to use the four-year grace period to begin storing supplies for his large force, not just the Phoenicians and Egyptians Herodotus mentions (7.25). Therefore, the army did not have to live off the land. Food items could have been prepared, and certain amounts of water could be stored for a while. Xerxes had almost complete naval dominance over Asia Minor and therefore could use his considerable fleet to continuously resupply his army with both water and food.

The Persian logistical corps was very capable. They were able to carve a canal through Mount Athos (Herodotus 7.22.1) wide enough for two triremes side by side (7.24), and build not one, but two bridges of boats across the Hellespont (7.34–36). The Persian Royal Road system and the extensive navy would maintain provisions for the army, and the tales given by Herodotus (7.43) of the army drinking rivers dry are plausible, though somewhat exaggerated, if you include all the horses and other animals alongside the soldiers and non-combatants. All this suggests that Xerxes' expedition was very well prepared and was amply supplied. If the area could support 150,000 living off the land, then it is not inconceivable to see how these preparations allowed for an army of 250,000–300,000.

Xerxes spent over four years assembling his force, so the final total of men, goods, and ships was likely at least four times greater than the normal army that was ready for immediate action.[82] The Persian force at Marathon was probably somewhere between 25,000 and 90,000 men, as discussed previously. This army took just over a year to assemble and was not a royal army involving the bodyguard units. Xerxes' army took over four times as long to gather, suggesting a total of between 100,000 and 360,000 men. In view of this, it seems probable that his expedition numbered somewhere between 200,000 and 300,000 men, including camp followers and aides. The actual fighting force was probably on the lower end of the scale although we cannot be certain. This was still by far the largest army ever fielded in Greece at the time and would have been impressive to all observers.

Herodotus 7.82 states that the infantry force of Xerxes' expedition to Greece was organised into six divisions, each commanded by a senior Persian. The army marched in three columns, one of which was led by Xerxes (Herodotus 7.121). Modern divisions are usually 20,000 men, and this comparison is used by Maurice to arrive at his figure of 150,500 fighting troops in the army.[83] This seems a plausible number to me and maintains a ratio of roughly 10:1 for Herodotus' figures to reality.[84]

The non-combatants accompanying the Persian force were probably very numerous. Herodotus 9.76 states that after Plataea the courtesan of one of the 29 Persian infantry commanders and her attendants was spared by the Spartan commander, Pausanias, because she was the daughter of his guest friend. The fact that one of the relatively junior Persian officers was accompanied at Plataea by a courtesan, and that she had more than one attendant, demonstrates the large number of camp followers in the Persian force. If we follow the list of attendants accompanying Darius III at Issus,[85] Xerxes was followed by a very large retinue. Herodotus 9.82 states that his tent was left behind with Mardonius after Salamis and upon finding it Pausanias ordered Mardonius' chefs to prepare a meal. If we trust Herodotus, Xerxes and his generals enjoyed enormous luxury on campaign with their accompanying families and personal staff perhaps numbering in the hundreds if not thousands.

The exact number of Xerxes' force is impossible to determine for certain but the make-up of his army was similar to other Persian military levies.[86] The Persian units, in particular the Royal Bodyguard units, were very well trained and experienced and were used as the decisive force in battle, as discussed previously. The Persian strength was in cavalry and other missile troops depending on the mass of missiles to weaken the enemy lines. As discussed previously, most of the Persian infantry were lightly armed and reliant on archery and missiles. Other than the Greek hoplites from allied or subject states, only the Persian and Babylonian infantry were heavily armed and even they still used the bow as their principal weapon.[87]

Although Herodotus' army totals for infantry and cavalry are far too large, there is no reason to doubt that many if not all the peoples he mentions (7.61–96) did indeed send levies to Xerxes. The vast majority of Xerxes' army was light infantry and the navy boasted more heavy infantry on board ship than serving in the land army. Even the 10,000 Immortals in the Royal Bodyguard were trained as individual warriors and were expected to excel with the bow first and then the spear.

After the defeat at Salamis, Xerxes allowed Mardonius to select the troops he wanted to remain with him in Greece. Herodotus 8.113 lists the following troops: the Persian Immortals, the Persian spearmen, and the picked Persian cavalry also from the bodyguard units, the Medes, Sacae, Bactrians and Indians, both cavalry and infantry. To these he added personally selected men from the other nations. Herodotus gives the total of 300,000, but Mardonius' army probably numbered between 30,000 and 50,000.[88] These were the best troops on offer in Xerxes' whole army. Yet even in this force Mardonius had only the few Greek contingents for close-quarter heavy infantry. Since, as discussed previously, the Persian style of battle did not utilise heavy infantry, this did not matter to Xerxes or Mardonius. They still expected to be able to rely on their excellent cavalry and sheer volume of missiles for victory.

The Greek army

The Greek force at Plataea is outlined by Herodotus.[89] The totals are 38,700 hoplites and 69,500 light infantry.[90] This is the largest number of light infantry ever listed in a Greek army. Most attention of scholars is given to the Spartan contribution of 5,000 hoplites each accompanied by seven helots and how they were used in the battle.[91] Seventy thousand light infantry is a large number for the Greeks to field if their phalanx consisted of only hoplites. Nevertheless, whether or not Herodotus' numbers are accurate, the Greek phalanx had to fight in a more open style in order to accommodate so many light infantry or, more likely, the light troops were massed together on the flanks.[92] Unless the light troops fought together as a unit separated from their hoplite countrymen, which Herodotus suggests was not the case, the Greek force was much more mixed in nature than is generally assumed.

Infantry

Before the Peloponnesian War, post-Archaic Greek warfare was almost entirely focused on hoplite battles. Virtually all poleis in Greece relied on their hoplites. They very rarely cultivated any other type of soldier.[93] As discussed previously, the evidence for Greek warfare in the seventh and sixth centuries does not show any clear delineation of light infantry from hoplites in battle. There was also no concept of cavalry as an offensive arm in early Greek warfare.

The Persians found Greek hoplites superior to their own heavy infantry and more resistant to archery than any army they had come across before. At the battle of Marathon, the Persian missiles did little damage, not just because the Athenian hoplites ran to cover the final hundred metres when they were in range of the infantry.[94] Even at Thermopylae, where the Greek forces were finished off by a hail of missiles from the Persians (Herodotus 7.225.3), it took thousands of missiles to overcome the few remaining hoplites and Herodotus famously preserves the anecdote that the missiles would be so numerous that they would block out the sun (7.226.2). At Plataea, the Persian missiles did not sufficiently impact the Greek force to prevent their charge or their final victory.[95]

Herodotus (9.62.3–63.2) is clear that the Greek hoplites won at Plataea because of their superior armour and skill in hand-to-hand combat. The battle of Thermopylae (Herodotus 7.207–224) is a good example of the relative strengths of Persian and Greek heavy infantry. At this battle the Greeks were able to hold a fortified position for two days before they were defeated when isolated and outflanked. Cavalry was not able to manoeuvre in the confined terrain and so the Persian attack rested on their infantry. Herodotus is clear that the Greek hoplites were easily able to repel repeated Persian assaults. The most telling event is the defeat of the Immortals (7.211). As discussed previously, this was the best unit of heavy infantry in the Persian army and trained to excel in individual combat both at range with arrows and javelins and at close quarters. Although the Greeks were aided by the fortification walls, clearly the hoplites were abler soldiers in hand-to-hand combat than any Persian heavy infantry forces.[96]

At Thermopylae the weight of Persian numbers only told on the Greeks once the Persians were led around the back of the Greek position, allowing them to attack on more than one front simultaneously (Herodotus 7.225). Even then, had Leonidas not sent home the majority of the allies (Herodotus 7.219.2–220), the Greek hoplites could have held their position for longer, such was their advantage over the Persian army in terrain not suitable for the full deployment of Xerxes' forces, especially cavalry.[97] One of the two reasons given by Herodotus for the Greeks' success against the Immortals is that they could not make use of their great numbers on account of the terrain (7.211.2).

At Cunaxa in 401 the opposing armies were both primarily Persian in style, but Cyrus the Younger's army relied on its core of 10,000 Greek hoplite mercenaries for victory, whereas Artaxerxes' royal army appears to have not had any hoplites, and this lack of heavy infantry was easily exposed.[98] Despite the withdrawal of the rest of Cyrus' army, the Greek phalanx extracted itself from the battlefield without any significant casualties, such was their military dominance.[99] Cunaxa definitively confirmed the superiority of the hoplite phalanx over other Near Eastern heavy infantry but showed that the phalanx had to be supported by cavalry and light infantry, as discussed in more detail in the following chapters.

There was no considered attempt to use combined arms in Greek warfare but it is unlikely that light infantry were excluded from battle.[100] According to Van Wees:

> we know enough to say that great numbers of poor light-armed citizens almost always fought alongside the heavy infantry, and that in various ways cavalry, personal attendants, mercenaries and other "helpers" all played a vital military role in ensuring the success of a campaign, and indeed victory in battle.[101]

As discussed previously, at Marathon there is no definitive evidence that light infantry or cavalry were used alongside hoplites against a Persian army that used some level of combined arms, but we can infer their presence.[102] At Plataea Herodotus is clear that there was one light-armed soldier for every non-Spartan hoplite (9.29.2), and these men were expected to fight (9.30). The actions in the battle of these light infantry troops are not attested anywhere, apart from archers assisting the Megarians (9.22) and that the Spartans and Tegeans stood alone waiting for battle both hoplites and light-armed together (9.61.2). Exactly how the hoplites and light infantry fought in the battles of the Persian Wars is impossible to determine.

Herodotus also records seven helots were stationed with every Spartan. Hunt argues that the Spartan formation in this battle was one hoplite in the front rank followed by seven helot attendants armed as light infantry.[103] Isocrates 6.99 states that at the battle of Dipaea a few years later (c. 471) the Spartans fought in a formation only "one shield deep". As Van Wees states, at both battles

> the Spartans were vastly outnumbered by their opponents, so they may have been forced to adopt the shallowest of hoplite formations in order to match the length of the enemy line, and to rely on a mass mobilisation of helots in order to fill out their ranks.[104]

If this formation was used then the Spartans certainly were not fighting in a phalanx and in fact formed their own version of the Persian shield wall. Hanson argues that the Greeks did not fight in a phalanx during the Persian Wars because they fought against a non-Greek enemy.[105] This is unlikely since the phalanx was used in the fourth century against Persian armies and Herodotus, as Van Wees points out,[106] emphasises the Spartan victory was gained through their own strengths not innovative tactics (9.62–5).

The only unit of light infantry that did apparently fight separately and did have a tactical impact on the outcome of the battle was the Athenian archers. The Greeks were harassed by the Persian missile cavalry and were unable to counterattack until the unit of archers arrived and inflicted casualties on the Persians, most notably the commander Masistius. This unit alone is credited with staving off the cavalry attack. But how this unit, or other forces of light infantry, fought once the full battle raged is impossible to determine.

Nevertheless, that Herodotus records the existence at Plataea of so many lightly armed soldiers suggests that combined arms was used to some degree. There is little evidence for any degree of tactical coordination and once again the use of combined arms tactics may have been an accidental result of fielding light infantry and hoplites rather than specific design. After Marathon and the Persian Wars any contributions of non-hoplites in battles were forgotten. "Within a generation, these non-hoplites had been written out of the picture".[107]

Cavalry

The Persians did not adequately make use of their numbers or superior cavalry,[108] and were unable to adapt to find a way of defeating the Greeks.[109] The Greek army at Marathon, relying on its hoplites, should have been exposed on the flanks to the Persian cavalry, as was the case at Chaeronea at the hands of the Macedonians.[110] At Plataea, the Persian cavalry harassed the Greek army with missiles for an entire day without being able to demoralise or defeat the resilient hoplites.[111] Because the Persian style of warfare favoured using missiles rather than hand-to-hand combat, the Persians were not used to abandoning their bows and charging at close quarters the exposed flanks and rear of the Greek lines before the hoplites could win the inevitable hand-to-hand confrontation.

On one occasion in the battle, a Greek hoplite force was caught in a plain exposed to cavalry attack and suffered significant casualties. The Theban cavalry fighting on the Persian side came across one section of Greek hoplites rushing to join the battle travelling through the plain in a disorganised manner and assaulted them, trampling 600 and forcing the rest back to the safety of Mount Cithaeron. This shows that cavalry could be effective against hoplites if used in the right way. So the Greeks could have been exposed to and defeated by strong cavalry forces if the tactical situation allowed. Unfortunately for the Persians they never managed to achieve this tactical option.

The battle

Before the two opposing forces met at Plataea there was an initial engagement at Erythrae on the slopes of Mount Cithaeron. There the Persian cavalry under Masistius repeatedly attacked the Greek line in order to force them down from their secure defensive position. Herodotus (9.20–3) states that the cavalry attacked in successive squadrons inflicting heavy losses and taunting the Greeks. The Persians fired arrows at the Greeks while wheeling their horses in front of the Greek forces. Each squadron rode up, discharged their missiles and withdrew, to be followed by the next wave.[112] The Persians did not assault the Greeks directly in a hand-to-hand assault. If they had done so they would have been unable to taunt the Greeks or withdraw rapidly to allow the attack of the succeeding squadrons.

Herodotus 9.21.1 does say that they pressed on against the Megarians where the Greek line was most open and vulnerable to cavalry. This must mean where the Persians had the most space to wheel and shoot unheeded by the terrain on the mountain slopes. Masistius was killed after he was thrown to the ground when his horse was shot by a Greek archer (9.22.1–3). Herodotus is clear that the Persians did not notice this had happened until they had moved away since he fell just as they had wheeled about and retired for another charge. These are the tactics of cavalry firing missiles not charging in to fight at hand to hand with infantry.

Once the Persians learned that Masistius was killed, Herodotus states that they launched a massed attack from all the squadrons together in order to recover the body. Such an attack would have involved a cavalry charge at close quarters engaging the Greeks with spears and swords. The battle for Masistius' body was fierce and the Greeks got the upper hand once reinforcements came up. It seems from this that the Persian cavalry was more than capable of engaging infantry at close quarters with some success.

It must be stated that the 300 Athenians, who suffered greatly from the cavalry charge before the arrival of the Greek support, must have been outnumbered.[113] They certainly included all the Greek archers. This explains to some degree the ability of the Persian cavalry to contend for Masistius' body. As soon as the main force of Greek hoplites approached, the Persians were forced to retreat with significant losses. The principal form of attack of the Persian cavalry was to fire missiles while wheeling their horses in front of the enemy line. Only when they were forced into a direct assault, either through the approach of the enemy or to recover a commander's body, did they engage at close quarters. Once they did so against the Greeks they were unable to match the ability of the hoplites in hand-to-hand combat.

At the main battle of Plataea Mardonius stationed the Persians, as his best troops, opposite the Spartans and Tegeans. The other national contingents posted in the front lines, according to Herodotus, were the Medes, the Bactrians, the Indians, the Sacae, and then the Greeks in the Persian army (9.31.1–5). The rest of the units were stationed behind these units. This suggests that Mardonius, even after the lessons of Marathon and Thermopylae, did not consider Greek hoplites to be superior to his Persian infantry. Had he done so, the simplest choice would be to station his allied Greek hoplites opposite the best enemy hoplites, the Spartans. It is possible, though, that the aura of invincibility of the Spartans would have affected the Greek troops but not the Persians.

The Greeks' defensive position on the river Asopus was such that the two armies faced each other for ten days before the final battle was begun.[114] All the time the Persian cavalry continually harassed the Greek lines in an attempt to provoke a battle. Eventually Mardonius decided to attack at dawn. During the night the king of Macedon, Alexander I, who was serving as an advisor to the Persian army, informed the Greeks of this plan. The Spartans decided the Athenians should face the Persians because they had experience fighting them at Marathon. Mardonius was informed of the movements and followed the Spartans, who returned to their previous position opposed still by the Persians. The Persian herald inquiring the cause of Spartan movement was ignored, so Mardonius ordered his cavalry to attack.

On the eleventh day the Persian cavalry launched a larger attack on the Spartans. The Persian cavalry, as horse archers, proved difficult for the Greeks to handle being unable to fight them at close quarters. The Persians also polluted the spring providing the Greeks with water, forcing them to decide to withdraw during the night to the river Oeroe if the rest of the Persians did not attack. Eventually the Greek line moved out to their new position prompting Mardonius to order a rapid general advance at speed and in disorder to try to catch the Greeks as they withdrew.

The Persian cavalry quickly caught and attacked the Spartans, who were hard pressed and so asked the Athenians for assistance, especially for their archers. The Athenians were detained by Greek hoplites fighting on the Persian side. The Persian infantry arrived and joined in the missile bombardment of the Spartans. Herodotus 9.61.3 states that

> many of them [the Spartans] fell in this time, and more by far were wounded, for the Persians had made a barricade of their wicker shields and from the protection of it were shooting many arrows unsparingly.

The Spartans (and Tegeans) withstood the missiles of the Persians and waited for favourable omens before launching an attack.

Once they did attack the Persians stopped firing missiles and fought at close quarters. Eventually the Spartans forced back the Persians once they broke through the wicker shields of the front rank of spearmen. Herodotus states that the Persians fought bravely, though they were less well armed and trained, and greatly inferior in skill. They fought on until the death of Mardonius and his bodyguard even though they were light armed with no armour. The Persians fled to a temporary fort in Theban territory. With the arrival of the Athenians, following their hard-fought defeat of the Boeotian hoplites fighting for the Persians, the Greeks forced an entry into the fort and prompted a general retreat. The rout spread to the rest of the Persian army despite a large number of troops who had not yet been engaged in the battle thanks largely to Artabazus not really wanting to fight. Herodotus states that the cavalry was the only unit of the Persians that was not routed and some units actually covered the line of the Persian retreat.

Combined arms

What we can see at Plataea is that the Persians relied on cavalry and missiles for victory. The cavalry used harassing tactics throughout the battle only engaging once to recover the body of their general. Herodotus gives no indication that the Persian cavalry entered the melee to fight hand to hand once the Greek line closed on the Persian infantry. This may explain why the cavalry escaped the battle relatively unscathed.

When a Persian army fought against an enemy whose line was not broken by the volume of missiles, the Persian infantry was ill equipped for close-quarter combat, and the cavalry unable or unwilling to charge at all. The defensive armour of the Greek hoplites was sufficient to protect them during eleven days of constant missile bombardment with few casualties. The Persians must have been perturbed by the ineffectiveness of the prolonged missile attack but still relied on their superior numbers and traditional tactics for victory.

It is not clear how the many light infantry on the Greek side were used in the battle. They probably fought alongside the hoplites in a more open phalanx formation, as argued by Van Wees, or they may have protected the Greek flanks from the Persian cavalry.[115] However they were used, the victory was won by the superiority of the Greek hoplites in hand-to-hand combat. In fact, the only occasion in the battle where the Persian forces had any success against the Greeks was the resistance of the Thebans against the Athenian hoplites. There Herodotus (9.67) is clear that it was a hard-fought engagement which the Athenians eventually won after killing over 300 of Thebes' best hoplites.

The disorganised nature of the final Persian attack may have indirectly allowed the Greeks the freedom to attack and defeat sections of the Persian army individually rather than face the whole force. This disorganised structure of battle actually had prevented much of the allied Greek army from engaging the enemy. Only the Athenians and Spartans, with the Tegeans, had engaged. Herodotus states that news of the Spartan victory reached the rest of the Greeks "who were by the temple of Hera and had stayed out of the fighting",[116] and they then pushed on to join in the pursuit. It is in this context when the Greek cavalry allied to the Persians defeated a force of hoplites. It is perhaps noteworthy that the only minor victories for the Persian army were achieved through their Greek allies, though this is likely more to do with Herodotus' pro-Greek theme and sources.

Nevertheless, it is clear that the Persian army, just as at Marathon, neglected to use any real form of combined arms and their entire plan rested on the missile barrage sufficiently weakening the Greek lines. When this did not happen the Persians were powerless to defeat the heavily armed hoplites in the close-quarter melee fighting that followed and so the legend of hoplite superiority was confirmed.

Combined arms conclusions

The battles of Marathon, Thermopylae, and Plataea demonstrate the inability of the Persian army to deal with an enemy that was significantly superior at close-quarter combat and resistant to a missile barrage. At both Plataea and Marathon, and also at Mycale (9.102), once the Greek hoplites were able to close on the Persian infantry and break through the shield wall they easily won the battle.

The Persians lacked a reliable heavy infantry force and were unable to adapt their battle plans to make adequate use of their many resources and troop types. The battles of the Persian Wars show that a cavalry force reliant on attacking with missiles at a distance is often unable to win a battle on its own if the accompanying infantry is severely outclassed in the general melee of combat. Had the Persians been able to prevent the Greek hoplites coming to grips with them at close quarters, it is possible that the Persian missiles would have taken their toll. However, the time required would have been lengthy, since at Sphacteria it took over a day for the Athenians to force the Spartan hoplites to surrender despite a huge numerical advantage.[117] Moreover, since the Persian deployment of their infantry involved a static shield wall, the archers and other missile troops were unable to escape any advance by Greek hoplites and so were forced into hand-to-hand combat. The Greeks were able to rely on their heavy infantry always defeating Persian infantry, and the Persians failed to find a way to adapt their battle plan to address this problem, despite having many types of unit in their army including their own allied hoplites.

It is important to note that the only times in any of the battles of the Persian Wars where Greek hoplites were hard pressed by forces of the Persian army was at Plataea where the Thebans fought hard against the Athenians (Herodotus 9.67), and the Theban cavalry rode down the Megarian and Philasian forces (Herodotus 9.69).[118] There were units in the vast armies of the Persians that could have successfully opposed the Greek hoplites and exposed their vulnerable flanks but Persian generals did not alter their battle tactics to make use of them. As a result, the Persian military system was never able to make full use of an integrated system of combined arms despite fielding many different units.

Notes

1 Root (1979); Root (1989); Garrison (2000).
2 See Sekunda (1992); Head (1992); Gabriel (2002); Anglim et al. (2002); Holland (2007). For a list of the Persian troops at Issus as an example of the many types and origins of units see Arrian 3.11.3–7. The Persian army defeated a Carian revolt because of an eventual weight of numbers, not through martial supremacy (Herodotus, 4.119).
3 Herodotus 4.128. Cavalry, especially lightly armoured missile cavalry, once static in close combat was vulnerable to infantry whether light or heavy. Numerous battles throughout history demonstrate this. Perhaps the best is the vulnerability of the French knights once their charge was stopped by the English arrows. Bennett et al. (2005).
4 Herodotus 4.136.
5 For the effectiveness and range of Persian archery see McLeod (1965, 1970, 1972); Blyth (1977).
6 For the cavalry fiefs see Rahe (1980). As Cook states (1983: 102–3), "They had already begun to be granted some years before Darius I came to the throne, and the chariot fiefs may have been something of an anachronism almost from the outset. But until it became usual to make monetary payments in lieu of service, cavalry were certainly to be raised from fiefs".
7 DNb 8h: Kent (1953: 140); Schmitt (1991); Garrison (2000: 134–6).
8 Nimchuk (2002: 63), in discussing the ideological motivation for his minting of Archer coins, states: "This figure is now generally accepted as representing the notion of the Achaemenid king and Achaemenid kingship". See also Root (1979, 1989: 46, 1991). She states (1991: 16) that this figure is "a quintessentially Persian, Achaemenid, manifestation of imperial power".
9 Herodotus (3.39) suggests that Polycrates' force of a thousand bowmen was the reason for his many naval successes. To Herodotus, archery was an important skill even for Greeks.
10 Herodotus 1.214. It is certainly possible that Herodotus has invented this battle and the ensuing death of Cyrus. He is the only source that follows this version of the king's death, although Diodorus (2.44), possibly using the same source as Herodotus or Herodotus himself, states he was captured after a defeat to the Massagetae. Nevertheless, Herodotus thinks it likely enough, as do his Persian sources, that a battle between the Scythians and Persians may well have occurred in this style. The Scythians are described by Herodotus (4.46) as being "accustomed, one and all, to fight on horseback with bows and arrows," emphasising their expertise in archery more than the Persians.
11 Cook (1983: 103).
12 In Herodotus' list of units in Xerxes' army (7.61–81), the Cissians, Hyrcanians, Bactrians, Indians, Arians, Parthians, Chorasmians, Sogdians, Gandarians, Dadicae, Caspians, Sarangians, Pactyans, Utians, Myci, Paricanians, Arabians, Ethiopians and men from the islands of the Persian Gulf all were equipped as infantry archers. The Sacae were armed with bows as well as a large battle-axe. The Libyans, Paphlagonians, Ligyans, Matieni, Mariandynians, Syrians, Phrygians, Mysians, Thracians, Pisidians, Cabalians, Milyans, and Marians were all principally armed as javelin men. Other light infantry, that is, using short spears and small swords like *peltasts*, were the Kolchians, Alarodians, and Saspires. Infantry armed with non-hoplite heavier shields, weapons, or armour were the Moschians and Assyrians. The latter could be called heavy infantry because of their bronze helmets, shields, long swords, and linen corselets. Other than the Greek hoplites collected in Greece, principally from Boeotia, the Lydians were armed in the Greek manner. For the cavalry, the Persians, Medes, Cissians, Indians, Bactrians, Caspians, Paricanians, and Caspeirians were armed as archers. The Arabians were archers on camels and the Libyans used javelins on horseback. Of the marines, the Phoenicians, Cilicians, and Lycians were armed as javelin men, with Persians, Medes, and Sacae acting as archer marines. The Egyptians were armed as heavy

infantry with large shields, boarding spears, and heavy axes. Many other marines were armed as hoplites: Cyprians, Pamphylians, Asiatic Dorians, Carians, Ionians, Pelasgians, Aeolians, and men from the towns on the Hellespont and Bosphorus.

13 Herodotus 9.62 in describing the battle of Plataea provides the best example of the barricade of shields in front of the archers. He also states that when the Spartans charged the barricade, the archers stopped firing missiles and prepared to meet them face-to-face with whatever weapon they had at hand.

14 Cf. Xenophon *Anabasis* 1.9.3–5 who describes the competitive nature of the Persian nobles' education and its focus on the use of the bow and javelin in war, and horse riding in particular.

15 According to Herodotus (7.103–5), Xerxes boasts to Demaratus that in his bodyguard there are Persians who would willingly fight individually against three Greeks together. Demaratus replies that the Spartans are individually a match for any soldier "but fighting together they are the best soldiers in the world". They are encouraged to always remain in formation and this is their advantage (cf. Curtius 3, where Charidemus is chastened for falling out of formation). As we shall see below, a hoplite, and the phalanx in general, is only effective as long as the unit maintains its cohesion. Once it is broken it is vulnerable and easily defeated, as the Romans showed at Pydna (Plutarch, *Aemilius Paullus* 16–22; Livy 44.40–42).

16 It is true that other factors aided the Greeks, such as the narrow confines of the pass that prevented the weight of Persian numbers being decisive and the walls of the fortification. Nevertheless, in this situation the Immortals fought the hoplites on relatively even terms where numbers and other units could not assist the Immortals and they were soundly beaten in hand-to-hand combat.

17 Shrimpton (1980: 29) claims that the Sacae and Persians mentioned by Herodotus were cavalry only using Plataea as his primary example. He seeks to prove the cavalry were involved in the Persian army in the battle. But the cavalry would have disrupted the Persian battle lines if they fought in the middle of the infantry. Moreover, both Persians and Sacae are listed by Herodotus as fighting as marines in Xerxes' navy. They can hardly have done so if they were cavalry. The Scythians in battle with the Persians of Cyrus and Darius used infantry just as much as cavalry in a similar manner to the Persians. Undoubtedly Herodotus is correct that Sacae fought as both infantry and cavalry in the Persian army, and those mentioned at Marathon in the centre of the Persian line were infantry.

18 7.61.1 "the Persians were equipped in this way: they wore on their heads loose caps called tiaras, and on their bodies embroidered sleeved tunics, with scales of iron like the scales of fish in appearance, and trousers on their legs; for shields they had wicker bucklers, with quivers hanging beneath them; they carried short spears, long bows, and reed arrows, and daggers that hung from the girdle by the right thigh". 7.63. "The Assyrians in the army wore on their heads helmets of twisted bronze made in an outlandish fashion not easy to describe. They carried shields and spears and daggers of Egyptian fashion, and also wooden clubs studded with iron, and they wore linen breastplates". 7.64.2. "The Sacae, who are Scythians, had on their heads tall caps, erect and stiff and tapering to a point; they wore trousers, and carried their native bows, and daggers, and also axes which they call 'sagaris'".

19 Head (1992).

20 I noted previously the existence of hoplite mercenaries in the Assyrian army and without doubt early Persian armies also made use of hoplites from subject Hellenic populations such as the Ionian Greek cities of Asia Minor. But as Briant (2002: 783–800) has shown, these hoplites were never implemented into the Persian army in large numbers and until Marathon an enemy force had never comprised entirely hoplites. Even in the Ionian Revolt the rebel armies made use of local Ionian cavalry units. In the decisive battle at Salamis on Cyprus the rebel army was defeated when a significant number of men changed sides, not least the war-chariots from Salamis (Herodotus, 5.112–4).

Without a mobile force to oppose the Persian cavalry the rebel hoplites were easily routed despite the abilities of their heavy armed infantry. The Greeks took more than a century to learn the lesson that even hoplites must be supported by cavalry in order to succeed in an open pitched battle against a mixed army.

21 Herodotus 1.80. It is possible that Croesus' cavalry were heavy cavalry intended for close-quarter combat against the missile cavalry preferred by the Persians, but there is no evidence for this.
22 Herodotus (9.49) notes at the battle of Plataea that the Persian cavalry armed with the bow "were not easy to come to grips with".
23 Cook (1983: 102).
24 Nefedkin (2006).
25 See in particular the battles of the Granicus (Arrian *Anabasis* 1.12–16; Diodorus 17.19–21; Justin 11.6), Issus (Arrian *Anabasis* 2.7–11; Curtius 3.8–11; Diodorus 17.32–34; Justin 11.9) and Gaugamela (Arrian *Anabasis* 3.8–15; Curtius 4.9; Diodorus 17.56–61).
26 Briant (2002: 582) states that "throughout Achaemenid history, the mobilization of a royal army proved to be the rarest exception". More often than not a local levy of troops added to the Satrapal army proved sufficient to overcome rebellions throughout the kingdom. These armies relied on cavalry and missile troops to an even greater extent than the Royal army since the professional units were not present. If the levies were inexperienced, the army relied even more on the core of satrapal troops accompanying the general.
27 For example, Herodotus (7.21) states that Xerxes' army prepared over four years for the invasion of Greece: "some nations provided ships, others formed infantry units; from some cavalry was requisitioned, from others horse-transports and crews; from others, again, triremes for floating bridges, or provisions and naval craft of various kinds". Persian documents detail the system of conscription and the difficulties it placed on landowners. See Briant (2002: 597–602) for a brief analysis of this problem.
28 Ferrill (1986: 83).
29 Caesar, *Civil War* 3.85–99; Cassius Dio 41.52–61; Appian, *Civil Wars* 2.70–82; Plutarch, *Caesar* 42–45; Plutarch, *Pompey* 68–72.
30 Briant (2002).
31 Herodotus (2.163) notes that in Egypt the Pharaoh Apries took battle against Egyptian rebels with 30,000 Carian and Ionian mercenaries. The total is certainly too large a force, but it does show the reliance on foreign mercenaries in Near Eastern kingdoms. Herodotus (3.1) elsewhere states that Cambyses invaded Egypt at the head of an army taken from various subject peoples including Ionian and Aeolian Greeks. In the ensuing battle (3.11) the Greek and Carian mercenaries in the Egyptian army fought valiantly for their employer against the fellow Greeks in the Persian camp.
32 Briant (2002: 783–800).
33 For a detailed discussion of the Cardaces see Tarn (1948: 180–2); Bosworth (1980b: 208); Briant (1999).
34 Many scholars have written on Marathon. The most influential has been Hammond (1968). The best of the more recent books is Krentz (2010). Some of the other works most relevant to our concerns here are: Balcer (1989, 1995); Burn (1962); Cawkwell (2004); Cook (1983); Doenges (1998); Donlan and Thompson (1976, 1979); Evans (1984, 1993); Lloyd (2004); Massaro (1978); Shrimpton (1980). My primary concern here is to examine the battle from a perspective of tactics and the use of combined arms in the battle. Other scholars have debated the merits of various theories concerning all aspects of the battle, such as the route the Athenians took to Marathon, the location of the battle in the plain and the position and size of the Persian fleet in the bay. I will present my interpretation of these problems only where it is important for determining the events of the battle itself.

35 Herodotus (6.95) states that Darius had requisitioned horse transports the year before. Since cavalry was crucial to the Persian military, these vessels would have been first on the list of logistical organisation for the invasion.
36 Hignett (1963: 71) suggests 20,000 for the Persian army; Meyer (1944: 306) favours an even smaller force.
37 Hammond (1968: 32). In my view, many of the Persian infantry could have been the rowers of the warships, therefore reducing the total number of vessels required for the army, which Hammond does not take into account. On troops in triremes, see in particular Coates (1993).
38 Hammond (1968: 32) is right that the Persians cannot have been certain that the other Greek poleis would not come to Athens' aid and had to plan to face an allied force perhaps as large as the one fielded by the Greeks at Plataea.
39 See in particular Head (1985). See for example Munro (1902); Maurice (1930); Plumpe (1938).
40 Hammond (1968: 33).
41 Coates (1993).
42 Thrasyllus armed 5,000 of his rowers as peltasts in the Peloponnesian War (Antiphon 2; Xenophon, *Hellenika* 1.2.1).
43 Herodotus 6.108. Nepos (*Miltiades* 5) and Justin (2.9) both total the Plataeans at 1,000.
44 As Hammond (1968: 34 n. 98) rightly notes there must have been more Athenian hoplites than those at Marathon. Those hoplites that lived in the outlying villages of Attica would have been mobilised to defend the polis but could not have been ready to leave in time for the march to Marathon. Some of them may have joined the Athenian army in the field but most were almost certainly used as the home defence force.
45 Xenophon was a member of the cavalry force in Athens at the end of the fifth century and it is difficult to believe that men such as Xenophon began to serve as cavalry only after the prevalence of hoplite warfare in Greece. Surely cavalrymen, as a class distinction throughout Athenian history, always served as such in war (Bugh 1988). See also Evans (1986). For the social system of cavalry in Athens see Spence (1993).
46 Finley (1980: 99). See also Snodgrass (1999: 79–84 n. 85).
47 Notopoulos (1941); Hunt (1998).
48 Van Wees (2005: 180). Hunt (1998: 26–8) argues that slaves were mobilised but not the free poor. This seems unlikely considering the extraordinary nature of freeing slaves to fight when a significant resource of manpower already existed among the poorer citizens. The use of freed slaves in the Athenian navy at the end of the Peloponnesian War was only instigated because total Athenian manpower was low after the defeat in Sicily.
49 Pausanias 1.32.3.
50 Herodotus 6.111. See Hammond (1968: 30). It is unlikely those burying the Plataeans after the battle would move all the bodies to a new point on the battlefield and the burial mound of the Plataeans must have been located where the majority of the dead Plataeans fell, just as the Athenian burial mound was located at the point where most Athenians fell (Pausanias 1.29.4). If the slaves were buried with the Plataeans on the left wing, either the bodies of the slaves were moved to this location or the majority of them also fell here. In my view the latter is the more likely.
51 For the most detailed discussion of the topography see Hammond (1968: 14–26). Hammond also provides detailed maps of the battlefield (1968: 19–21). His orientation of the Greek line based on the Persians' being parallel to the sea is wrong since the Persians would have orientated their line to match that of the Greeks, which was drawn up cautiously between the two rises in terrain of Mount Agriliki and Mount Kotroni. This would also have allowed the Persian line to keep its camp and ships at its rear for ease of supply.
52 Contrary to Hammond's opinion (1968: 19) the Persian line was not parallel to the sea but was at an angle to it, with the river that runs through the plain to the rear. This

would allow their cavalry freedom of movement in the plain while also allowing easy access to their camp at the other end of the bay.

53 The basis of this reconstruction is Herodotus' account 6.102–117. A number of controversies will be discussed in more detail below to add to this brief summary of the battle.
54 The Persian cavalry, if they were present, were the first to escape, and had time to board the ships and sail away, with or without their horses. The distance covered across the plain would have taken much time for the infantry but very little for the cavalry at the gallop.
55 *Stelai* were put up on the burial mound for the Athenian dead and the names of the individuals inscribed. As Hammond (1968: 14) states, "The *stelai* stood there in the time of Herodotus and Thucydides, so that the number of names could have been checked by anyone". We should accept Herodotus' statement that 192 Athenian hoplites died at Marathon.
56 For tables of proportional battle casualties in ancient battles see Gabriel and Boose (1994: 28).
57 Whether these were warships or transports is rather irrelevant. They were probably whichever ships were closest to the shore or those furthest away from the retreating soldiers, who would board whatever ship was nearest to them.
58 See Blythe (1977) for the effectiveness of Persian archery.
59 Herodotus 6.102.
60 Pausanias 1.15.3 decribes the images on the Stoa.
61 Cf. Herodotus' anecdote (5.111) about the Persian general at Cyprian Salamis in the Ionian revolt who had trained his horse to lash out with its hooves against infantry.
62 Burn (1962). The most recent statement of this idea is Billows (2010).
63 Hammond (1968.
64 Burn (1969: 118–20).
65 Shrimpton (1980: 22–37).
66 The barricades certainly could not have been set up in order to protect the Greek charge. Construction of such an extensive obstacle would have exposed its builders to the whole Persian army and its vast array of missiles. The barricades were intended to protect the Greek army while it was still passively situated opposite the Persian forces.
67 Shrimpton (1980: 35).
68 Storch (2001).
69 See Forsdyke (1919–20).
70 Shrimpton (1980: 26).
71 Donlan and Thompson (1976, 1979).
72 Storch (2001).
73 Van Wees (2005). Herodotus' anecdote (5.111) about a groom and hoplite general together fighting as a team to defeat a Persian cavalryman and his rearing horse suggests the same. That the hoplite's groom was not only present but fighting alongside his master shows that they did not fight in a tight phalanx formation. The groom is not called a hoplite by Herodotus and his actions do not suggest he was armed as such. This event occurred in the land battle of Salamis on Cyprus in the Ionian Revolt. It is very unlikely that styles had changed significantly only five years later at Marathon. The Athenians at Marathon fought in a more open formation perhaps also attended by their grooms. The Spartan hoplites at Plataea were attended by helots (Herodotus 6.28.2), just as at Cyprian Salamis, suggesting that even in 479 the close phalanx formation had not been adopted.
74 Here it is important to note that the process of armies using combined arms is a continuum and that there are different levels of sophistication. In this case the Persian army did use a form of combined arms, by fielding cavalry, missile infantry and heavy infantry separately, but their tactics did not allow for the optimum use of each type of unit in battle. Had the Persians used integrated warfare, the full realisation of combined

98 The hoplite revolution in Greece

arms, the Greek reliance on hoplites should have been exposed, as it was by the integrated army of Philip II at chaeronea (Diodorus 16.85–6).

75 It is possible that the Persian army would have won if they had used combined arms properly opposing the Greek phalanx with heavy infantry, in particular their own hoplites, while using missile infantry and cavalry to harass the flanks and rear of the Greek line. In this case, if the Greek hoplites had been delayed for long enough, the Persian arrows may have caused more casualties among the Greeks and the Persian cavalry could have charged into the vulnerable rear of the Greek line. As discussed previously, at the battle of Malene the very sight of Persian cavalry in the rear prompted the retreat of the phalanx of the Greek rebels (Herodotus 6.29) and the same thing would likely have occurred at Marathon.

76 The main source for the battle is Herodotus. The problems with his account have been discussed previously.

77 The Persian army has been discussed in detail previously.

78 See Engels (1978).

79 See the battle of Ipsus below (Plutarch, *Demetrius* 29).

80 Munro (1902) calculates that 180,000 people are the most that the area of Thrace can supply adequately. Maurice (1930), using water availability, rates of march, and twentieth-century army reports, calculates that Xerxes' fighting force can have been no more than 150,500 with 60,000 non-combatants accompanying the army.

81 Herodotus 7.25.

82 Herodotus 7.20.1.

83 Maurice (1930).

84 As discussed previously, Green (2006: 46–7, 74) proposes a distortion of 10:1 in Greek historians after a misunderstanding of numerical representation.

85 See Athenaeus 13.608 for a list of Darius' equipment.

86 Herodotus 61–96 is the full list of all the troops martialled for the invasion of Greece. See Barkworth (1993).

87 Herodotus 7.61–63.

88 In general, a tenth of Herodotus' numbers often proves to be more accurate for actual troop totals (Green 2006: 46–7, 74).

89 Herodotus 9.28–31. Beloch and others argue that Herodotus' troop totals are based on known figures or rounded estimates. See Beloch (1916: 2.2.74–7); Anderson (1970: 237–9) contra Lazenby (1985: 50–4).

90 He lists in order from the right wing: 10,000 Lacedaimonians accompanied by 35,000 light-armed helots; 1,500 Tegeans, 5,000 Corinthians, 300 Potidaeans, 600 from Orchomenos, 3,000 from Sicyon, 800 from Epidaurus, 1,000 from Troezen, 200 from Lepreum, 400 from Mycenae and Tiryns, 1,000 from Phlius, 300 from Hermion, 600 from Eretria and Styra, 400 from Chalcis, 500 from Ambracia, 800 from Leucas and Anactorium, 200 Palleans, 500 from Aegina, 3,000 from Megara, 600 from Plataea, 8,000 Athenians all hoplites, and another 34,500 light infantry alongside the helots. He also states that 1,800 men surviving from Thespiae were present though not fully armed as hoplites. Herodotus also states that during the ten-day delay at Plataea the Greek force continually increased with new arrivals.

91 Hunt (1997) argues that the helots made up ranks two to eight in the Spartan phalanx behind a line of Spartiates. Cornelius (1973) argues that they made up the final six ranks. If this is true it does show that the classical phalanx full of densely packed hoplites was not yet in use in Sparta. Some scholars argue that the helots were at the battle but did not fight, some that they did fight and some that they are added mistakenly by Herodotus. See Grundy (1901: 443, 501); Munro (1904: 152–3); Macan (1908: 352); How and Wells (1912: 298, 364); Beloch (1916: 2.2.78); Hignett (1963: 438); Green (1970: 266); Burn (1964: 505); Garlan (1988: 169); Barron (1988: 597); Ducat (1990: 158). Welwei (1974: 123) argues that the helots protected the supply lines and acted

as personal attendants. Tritle (2010: 87) argues that many, if not all, hoplites in the Spartan force at Pylos were accompanied by a helot attendant to act as batman, and who "could also serve as light-armed fighters". See also Lazenby (1993: 228). Cawkwell (1983: 385–400) is probably right when he argues that the Perioikoi fought in the Spartan phalanx behind the Spartiates. On the other hand, Cartledge (1979) is certainly incorrect when he dismisses the existence of 35,000 helots at Plataea as a danger to the Spartans since light infantry could easily be used alongside the hoplite phalanx. It is not my concern here to examine the position and use of the helots since we are examining Plataea to determine the cause of the Persian defeat rather than the Greek deployment. I agree with Van Wees (2005: 177–83) that the helots were included in an open phalanx formation interspersed among the hoplites, while others protected the flanks and opposed the Persian cavalry as light infantry.

92 Van Wees (2005: 173–7).
93 Aetolians often produced peltasts, due more to the geography of the region than to a desire to advance warfare techniques (cf. Thucydides 3.94.3–5), but they were never a force in the political climate of Greece (Best 1969). Thrace was on the fringes of the Greek world but even so eventually the importance of Thracian peltasts was adapted into Greek warfare as a whole (Webber 2011). Rhodes produced slingers and siege experts while Crete developed expert archers, but again neither island significantly influenced anything to draw other states away from the traditional hoplite army (Anglim et al. 2002). Thebes is perhaps the only city that was open to branching out its military forces, and traditionally had a strong cavalry force to accompany its hoplite army, but it was not until the fourth century that they actually attempted to utilise both together in harmony in a battle. As discussed below, the use of cavalry at Delium did not stem from a concerted battle plan to combine cavalry and infantry but was the reaction of an alert general to the situation at hand (Thucydides 4.90–96).
94 See earlier full discussion of Marathon.
95 Herodotus 9.24, 9.49, and in particular 9.60–62. For the effectiveness of Persian missiles against a hoplite's armour see Blythe (1977).
96 This is certainly true regardless of whether the Greeks used a phalanx formation at Thermopylae. The walls suggest they did not have to do so, as does the fighting lasting throughout the day (Herodotus 7.210.2). Herodotus states the Greeks used the tactic of a feigned withdrawal to defeat the Persians suggesting a less rigid formation (7.211.3). See Cartledge (2006).
97 How (1923); Starr (1962).
98 The Greek mercenaries were stationed on the right flank protected by a river. To their left were Cyrus and his bodyguard and the rest of the Persian infantry and cavalry. Artaxerxes' army significantly outnumbered Cyrus'. In the battle the Greeks easily routed the Persians opposite them and continued in pursuit. Unfortunately, Cyrus was killed while charging his brother's bodyguard, meaning that the whole campaign was for nothing (Xenophon *Anabasis* 1.8; Plutarch *Artaxerxes* 11). See also: Lee (2007); Lane Fox (2004).
99 On casualties in Greek battles see in particular Krentz (1985b); Rubincam (1991).
100 Van Wees (2005: 61–5) argues that they were present in all Greek conflicts but were ignored in any accounts of the battles except under special circumstances.
101 Van Wees (2005: 61–2).
102 As discussed previously, there is some evidence that light infantry in the form of freed slaves fought at Marathon and it is possible that some Athenian cavalry did also.
103 Hunt (1997).
104 Van Wees (2005: 181–2).
105 Hanson (2000: 211–2).
106 Van Wees (2005: 298 n. 58).

100 *The hoplite revolution in Greece*

107 Van Wees (2005: 180). See also Van Wees (2005: 62); Hunt (1998: 26–8) for the possibilities of a general levy of free poor in Athens. See below for a full discussion of the absence of non-hoplites in accounts of Greek warfare.
108 At Marathon, as discussed previously, there is a debate that the cavalry were present in the battle, in large part because Herodotus does not state explicitly that they were involved in the fighting.
109 The Greeks on the other hand had no qualms about altering their tactics to face the Persians. At the battle of Marathon the Athenians strengthened their wings and lengthened the line, a sensible tactic to use in the face of a large enemy army.
110 Chaeronea: Diodorus, 16.85–86; Polyaenus, 4.2.2; Plutarch, *Alexander* 12 and *Demosthenes* 20. At the battle of Marathon, as discussed previously, the freed Athenian slaves were probably placed on the left flank of the Greek line in order to contain the Persian cavalry.
111 Herodotus 9.49–51. For the resilience of the armour of the Greeks see Blythe (1977).
112 Cf. Herodotus 9.18.1.
113 Cf. Herodotus 9.21.3, 9.23.2.
114 The account of what follows is taken from Herodotus, 9. 19–70; Plutarch, *Aristides* 11–19; Diodorus, 11.30–32.
115 Van Wees (2005).
116 Herodotus 9.69.
117 Sphacteria: Xenophon, *Hellenika* 4.5.11–17; Diodorus 14.91.2; Plutarch, *Agesilaus* 22.2. At Lechaeum (Thucydides 4.26–39), Iphicrates' peltasts were able to defeat Spartan hoplites, but the number of forces involved on each side was small and did not involve archers protected behind a static shield wall.
118 This latter incident marks the key difference between the tactics of Theban (and also Thessalian and Macedonian as discussed below) and Persian cavalry. Persians rely on missiles and charge into close combat only as a last resort, whereas the Theban cavalry charged their opponents and rode them down, according to Herodotus, clearly engaging in hand-to-hand combat. Nefedkin (2006) argues that the tactics of the Persian cavalry changed after the Persian Wars to favour hand-to-hand combat over horse archery.

Section 2
The implementation of combined arms in Greek warfare

4 The Peloponnesian War – combined arms innovation on the battlefield

Before the Peloponnesian War, after Greek hoplite armies had resoundingly defeated the mixed army of the Persians, there was no necessity for the Greeks to change their style of warfare. Because of their success against the Persians, the Greeks wrongly believed that a successful military was built solely on having a very strong heavy infantry division at the expense of other types of units.[1] Even the Persians themselves sought to recover their military prowess by incorporating an increasing number of Greek hoplite mercenaries into their army instead of making the best use of what they already had.

Sources

There are a number of sources for the Peloponnesian War. The fullest and most detailed is that of Thucydides, but his work ends with the events of 411. This is a contemporary historical account focused on providing a detailed description of the events of the war in chronological order. However, the lack of comparative texts means that it is necessary to rely perhaps too heavily on Thucydides. He was an Athenian who was directly involved in the war in Athens until his exile after the battle of Amphipolis in 423, but despite his subsequent estrangement from Athens his account is very Atheno-centric.[2] The very fact that we call the war the Peloponnesian War, the same name as the title of his work, shows the huge influence Thucydides' history has had on modern interpretations of events.[3]

Xenophon in the *Hellenika* began his history of Greece at the point where Thucydides ended. This is the fullest source for the final years of the war. However, most of the battles in the last few years of the war were naval and so not of direct concern here.[4] The fragmentary *Hellenika Oxyrhyncia* also covers the last few years of the war but does not discuss any battles that are of concern here.[5] Diodorus Siculus describes the Peloponnesian War in its entirety but his account often does not discuss battles in many details.[6] Plutarch's various biographies of the individuals involved in the Peloponnesian War add some information but he is rarely concerned with detailed battle descriptions.[7]

It is very difficult to find a Spartan view of the war and virtually impossible to examine the war from the perspectives of other Greek poleis. Nevertheless, I focused on the development of combined arms in land battles in the Peloponnesian War up to the end of the Athenian expedition to Syracuse in 411. For this period, Thucydides' accounts of battles are suitably detailed and reliable enough to enable a reconstruction of tactical developments and practices.[8]

Infantry

Most early fifth-century battles in Greece were fought between hoplites on either side with little concern for other types of soldiers.[9] The mountainous topography of Greece contributed to this by reducing the importance, or impact, of cavalry. It is noticeable that in areas where there was virtually no flat land, such as Aetolia, hoplites were spurned in favour of light-armed peltasts.[10] And in areas where land was more suited to horses, such as Thessaly, Macedonia, and even Boeotia, states did use cavalry in battle alongside hoplites.[11] Other factors led to the eminent position of hoplites in Greek warfare, such as agriculture, democracy, and the lack of imperialistic ideas of warfare, but none of these directly impacts the development of combined arms and so will not be discussed here.[12]

Hoplites were the main infantry deployed by almost every polis, but light infantry featured also. More mountainous areas of Greece, such as Aetolia, fielded a greater proportion of light infantry since the landscape lent itself to that arm. Other states became famous for types of light infantry. Crete was famous for its archers, and Rhodes for its slingers. Slingers, archers, and javelin men fought on Greek battlefields in large numbers, but unfortunately they are largely ignored in our sources, so we have very few details about their deployment, numbers, and tactical usage. We will discuss their uses in battle in the combined arms section that follows.

Cavalry

Most Greek cavalry consisted of lightly armed men with javelins and swords riding small horses. Except for horse-rearing areas of Greece where riding was as natural as running, such as Macedon, Thessaly, and to a lesser extent Boeotia, the skill of riders was not good enough for close combat on a horse. Light cavalry, especially against an army reliant on hoplites, was reserved for scouting, skirmishing, and pursuit.

Aside from Thessaly and Macedon in the north, Boeotia was the one area of Greece where the topography actually suited the use of cavalry, and as a result the Thebans often fielded units of cavalry in battle.

> To fight effectively on horseback required expertise at mounting quickly, riding in formation, wielding the sword or spear and throwing the javelin from horseback – and all without stirrups. All these skills were much easier to acquire for riders. Northern states, such as Macedonia, Thessaly and even Boeotia, possessed large aristocracies with strong horseback-riding

traditions. Indeed, Thessaly and Macedonia rarely mobilized substantial hoplite armies, but were able to recruit nobles, and sometimes also their retainers, for cavalry service.[13]

Thucydides (2.100) discusses the excellence of Macedonian cavalry against the Thracians in 429. He states they were armed with cuirasses and overran all those against whom they charged until they were overwhelmed by the numbers of the enemy. This shows that, just as the Thebans, Macedonian cavalry favoured charging into hand-to-hand conflict rather than relying on missiles as the Persian horsemen did.

Other Greek states had some cavalry but usually "used the cavalry of allies or hired mercenaries".[14] As a result they rarely had enough to use in combined arms tactics in battle. Athens, in particular, made use of its extensive empire and "deliberate policy" to furnish its cavalry forces, since "the countryside did not support a large enough class of rural nobility to field a large cavalry".[15] Towards the end of the Peloponnesian War, Athens even went so far as to provide a partial subsidy for those who would serve as cavalry in the army, giving "a loan for the purchase of a horse, an allowance for the horse's maintenance and reimbursed the value of horses lost in combat".[16] This force of cavalry had to go through regular training regimes and practice battles since they were not natural horsemen like their northern neighbours.[17]

Spence argues that social factors limited the importance of Athenian cavalry.[18] Worley and Gaebel argue that the importance of cavalry in Athens increased during the Peloponnesian War,[19] however, only 30 horsemen were sent on the original Athenian expedition to Sicily despite the Syracusan excellence in cavalry and the open terrain of Sicily suiting cavalry deployment.[20]

Cavalry took a long time to be integrated tactically into the Greek way of war. It is no coincidence that the first instance of cavalry winning a battle against hoplites was an accident, a reaction to the events of the battle rather than a deliberate ploy.[21] The decisive factor at the battle of Delium in 424 (Thucydides 4.90–96), was an unoccupied force of Boeotian cavalry that Pagondas ordered secretly around a hill in the Athenian rear to fall on them unexpectedly (4.96.5). The Athenians feared the arrival of another army and fled in disorder (Figure 4.1). The Theban cavalry turned the retreat into a rout and cut down over a thousand Athenians, 10% of their available hoplite manpower (4.96.8). Delium demonstrates the ability of cavalry not only to pursue a retreating enemy but to deliver victory with a direct charge at exposed flanks or rear.[22] These valuable lessons were not learned in Greece until the disaster at Chaeronea nearly a century later when inflicted on them by the Macedonian cavalry led by Alexander.[23]

As Hunt summarises, for most states "Greek warfare in the classical period was dominated by infantry and not cavalry".[24] The development towards a true system of combined arms did not begin until all types of units were integrated into the original battle plan on an equal level.

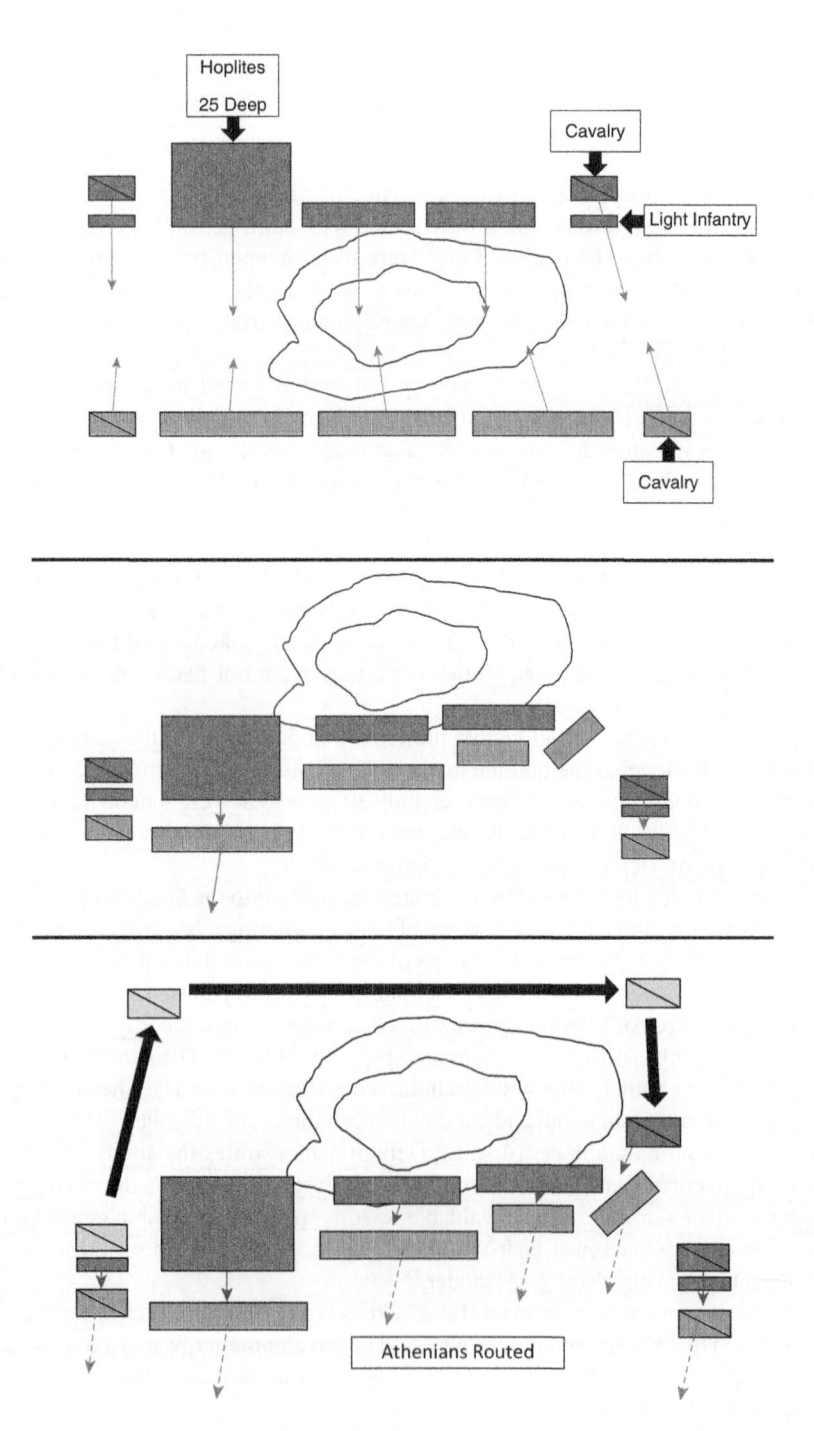

Figure 4.1 Battle map of Delium showing the crucial movement of Pagondas' cavalry around the hill to win the battle

Combined arms

A willingness to experiment with arms and tactics was crucial in the development of combined arms and required a move away from a reliance on the supposed invulnerability of a hoplite phalanx alone.

After the Persian Wars the Greek poleis went back to fighting among themselves in minor conflicts of little importance. But two battles, though not recorded in detail in the sources, suggest that gradually poleis became more used to fielding forces of cavalry and light infantry alongside hoplites. Though we still have no indication of how they fought in battle their acknowledged presence hints at the changes in Greek warfare that began in earnest with the Peloponnesian War.

At the battle of Megara in 458, the Athenians routed the Corinthian army.[25] There is nothing unusual in the actual battle. Though we have no details it was likely hoplites vs. hoplites as normal. However, in their flight a large section of the Corinthian army became trapped in an orchard where the Athenian light infantry killed them all with stones.[26] This proves that light infantry in relatively large numbers fought in Greek battles and were largely tasked with chasing down the defeated enemy. Though battles were still decided by hoplites, light infantry were present in enough numbers that eventually they were incorporated more into the battle tactics.

At the battle of Oinophyta the Athenians under the general Myronides defeated the Thebans.[27] Polyaenus states that by charging with the left wing and wheeling to the right, saying we are victorious on the left, Myronides scared the Thebans into running away.[28] In the same campaign in Boeotia, Myronides persuaded his Athenians to stand and fight by pointing out if they fled how suitable the area was to cavalry and how many horsemen the Thebans had to aid in pursuit.[29] We know so little about this battle it is hard to make any conclusions, but aspects of innovation are clearly apparent. If we can trust Polyaenus' account, the Greeks were used to dealing with cavalry in areas suitable for cavalry attacks and some generals were happy to use tricks to gain victory.

During the Peloponnesian War, as Athens, Sparta, and their allies started to campaign with more frequency in unfamiliar and somewhat inhospitable terrain, Greek generals were forced to use light infantry and cavalry alongside hoplites. As Tritle states, "[s]uch a combination of arms would become more common as the war progressed".[30] Forced somewhat into using other units the Greeks began to develop the tactics necessary for the successful application of combined arms in battle. It was only occasions where hoplites were defeated by light infantry or cavalry, or both, that prompted the Greeks to appreciate the limitations of hoplite armies.

The first step on the road to combined arms in Greece was taken by the Chalcidaeans against the Athenians. This was the battle of Spartolus in 429, the first occasion in the Peloponnesian War where a battle was decided by light infantry.[31] This was a resounding success for lightly armed missile troops in defeating hoplites using hit-and-run tactics and demonstrates the expertise of Thracians in that style of guerrilla warfare.[32] The devastating defeat certainly disheartened the

Athenians but the Chalcidaeans were never important politically in the Peloponnesian War and so the advances towards combined arms seen in this battle were not exploited.

Despite this defeat, the Athenians took many years to fully appreciate the advantages of light infantry alongside the hoplite phalanx. Demosthenes, the principal Athenian general open to experiment with military innovations, suffered a similar defeat at Aegitium in 426 at the hands of the Aetolians (Thucydides 3.97–98) and this prompted him to move away from hoplite only armies.[33] The Aetolians, after losing the city of Aegitium to Demosthenes, retreated to the surrounding hills. The arrival of Aetolian reinforcements prompted them to attack, using missile troops to harass the Athenian hoplites. The peltasts ran down to throw their javelins and fled back uphill again when the Athenians advanced. These hit and run tactics caused a number of casualties and the Athenians fled once the captain of their archers was killed. In their retreat, many of the Athenians were caught in a wood which the Aetolians promptly set alight.

This defeat is often cited as being the education of Demosthenes in demonstrating to him the effectiveness of light infantry against hoplites on unfamiliar or rugged terrain. But this was only the start of his education as a general, as Roisman rightly concludes:

> Demosthenes had other lessons to learn in Aetolia, such as the dangers of overambitious goals and convoluted plans, the inability of a surprise attack to overcome problems of deficient intelligence and manpower, and the commander's duty to be sensitive to the cost of human lives.[34]

Aegitium was a devastating blow to Athenian manpower and Demosthenes rightly did not immediately return to Athens almost certainly for fear of exile.[35] He applied the lessons he learned from this defeat in his subsequent battles in the area and it may have indeed influenced his continued use of light infantry in various military enterprises.[36] But also important to note is that the Athenian force of Demosthenes included a contingent of archers that was sizeable and effective enough to prolong the battle until the unit's commander died. Just as at Plataea, discussed previously, the Athenians now regularly fielded small forces of missile troops to accompany their hoplites in the field. This is a crucial early step on the way to true combined arms in the battle plan. The Athenians realised that there were occasions when missile troops were essential as a complement to hoplites, they just never fielded many of them or included them tactically into the battle plan.

Once the Athenians in particular began to use larger numbers of light infantry in battle, their generals experimented with innovative tactics such as surprise attacks or night raids on the enemy camp. Demosthenes was the first Greek general to begin regularly to use tricks to overcome numerical, strategic, or armament inferiority, while also making use of light infantry alongside hoplites.[37] At the battle of Olpae in 426–425 BCE (Thucydides 3.107–108), he did not expect to defeat the allied Ambraciot and Peloponnesian army without using his own hoplites. But he employed a surprise flanking manoeuvre, involving concealed light infantry and hoplites, in order to overcome the Spartan hoplites' superiority in ability and numbers.

Demosthenes was greatly outnumbered and outflanked by a Peloponnesian and Ambraciot army. Offering battle with his own small hoplite phalanx, he waited until the battle was swinging the way of the Peloponnesians before unleashing a small force of hoplites and light infantry which he had hidden in a wood on his right flank. The shock to the Peloponnesian left flank of an attack from behind, and the death of the Spartan general Eurylochos, was enough to send them into headlong flight. The men of the other Peloponnesian flank, who had won and pursued their opponents, returned to the field to be unexpectedly set upon by the waiting forces of Demosthenes.

Demosthenes was the first Greek general to design a battle plan reliant on a combined arms force, recognising the ability of a mixed infantry force in exposing the weak flanks of a hoplite army. As Tritle states, "[a]t Olpae Demosthenes would not only smash his assembled enemies and so clear his name and record but establish himself as a brilliant tactician, successfully combining lightly and heavily armed troops".[38] This is counter to the theory of Kagan and Viggiano, discussed previously, that Greek generals did not launch flank attacks because they feared weakening their own phalanx. Demosthenes was happy to weaken his phalanx in order to win so easily on the flank, thus negating the deficiency in the main force.

Roisman in contrast argues that "[i]t is questionable whether the light infantry contributed much to the fighting against the heavily armed enemy soldiers after the initial surprise. Their role was too limited to set an example for future generals".[39] Certainly the lesson was not heeded, but to say that the actions of the light infantry were not decisive enough to set an example is severely depreciating Demosthenes' innovative battle plan. The resounding victory over such a superior hoplite force, superior in terms of both number and abilities, perfectly demonstrates the possibilities of combined arms in battle. It was the novelty and shock that contributed to the defeat of the Spartans and that is more important. Demosthenes should be credited with this innovation regardless of the actual amount of fighting done by the light infantry alongside the hoplites.

It is possible that Demosthenes simply adopted the ambush at the suggestion of his Acarnanian allies, but he should still take the plaudits for adapting the plan to an army of light infantry and hoplites on a battlefield. As Roisman concludes, "[w]e should not deny Demosthenes his share of the credit for the victory at Olpae".[40] Demosthenes' other actions in Acarnania did demonstrate that he was an innovative general ahead of his time,[41] despite Roisman's contrary belief.

After the battle of Olpae Demosthenes came to a secret agreement with the new Peloponnesian commander to allow him to withdraw his men unmolested if he did so without the Ambraciots. He then marched out to intercept a relief force of Ambraciots headed for Olpae. His men occupied a hill across the valley from the hill on which the enemy camped. Demosthenes attacked their camp at night with half the army after sending the other half behind the hill to cut off their retreat.

When he attacked they were all still asleep in camp. At the vanguard of his army he placed Messenians with orders to address the Ambraciot sentries in their own dialect so as not to raise suspicion. Those who were not killed in their beds fell into the arms of the other half of Demosthenes' army (Thucydides 3.109–112).

At Idomene, Demosthenes' attack on the enemy army while they were still asleep in camp was one of the first battles in Greek warfare to be conducted entirely at night and Demosthenes relied exclusively on surprise to achieve his victory. His use of local knowledge was indispensable, but perhaps more important was his decision to have his soldiers speak in the dialect of the enemy in order to cause greater consternation.[42] As Roisman states, "Idomene was a triumph, perhaps Demosthenes' greatest".[43] Idomene and Olpae both demonstrate Demosthenes' ability to make use of local knowledge in formulating innovative tactics to overcome tactical or strategic weaknesses.[44]

At the siege of Megara in 424 Demosthenes used a night attack by light infantry as a vanguard to create a bridgehead into the city's long walls, which was quickly consolidated by hoplites (Thucydides, 4.66–8). Although the light infantry did not win the battle, they were instrumental in gaining the upper hand over the defenders. Roisman suggests that this plan may have been created by the Megarian traitors rather than Demosthenes.[45] Nevertheless, the success of the light infantry in creating the bridgehead is notable and innovative.

Demosthenes was not alone in implementing dawn assaults with light infantry, and others did so particularly during sieges. In 423 Brasidas used light infantry as the vanguard for an assault on the city of Torone (Thucydides, 4.110–3). Like Demosthenes at Megara, he secretly had the light infantry enter the city just after dawn to spread panic among the defenders and followed them in, when the main gate was opened, using his hoplites to secure the walls. Whether Brasidas had learned of Demosthenes' earlier attack on Megara is unclear but the similarities between the two sieges are considerable. Brasidas certainly appreciated the possibilities offered by light infantry and used them just as successfully as his Athenian counterpart.[46] Alcibiades' capture of Selymbria in 408 also used the surprise installation of a small force of peltasts at night supported later by hoplites.[47] Clearly the practice became common among the better generals by the end of the war.

Such tactics were not dependent upon the use of combined arms but were easier to accomplish with a mixed army. The speed and quietness of light infantry is perfectly suited for leading a surprise attack on a fortified position, especially at night when the noise of the attack had to be at its least.[48] The security of knowing that they were not expected to hold the captured ground themselves, but to hand it over to more suitable heavy infantry hoplites, gave the light infantry the enthusiasm to pursue their task with vigour. Demosthenes' crushing defeat while leading a full army in a night attack against Syracuse (Thucydides 7.43–4), aptly demonstrates that a small force of light infantry operating independently was not only useful but necessary for this type of night operation. Larger forces would easily fall prey to confusion and the difficulties of coordinated movement at night, especially in unfamiliar territory.

Light infantry also proved very capable of defending a fortified position against hoplites.[49] The number of failed attacks on Aetolia demonstrates that fact.[50] The best example is Demosthenes' defence of Pylos against Spartan assaults from both land and sea (Thucydides 4.3–23) utilising only the rowers from his fleet of five ships and a handful of hoplite marines. Demosthenes planned to create a fortified position in Spartan-occupied territory but he was unable to persuade the other naval commanders of the merits of his plan, perhaps because he was only serving on the expedition as a volunteer at his own request.[51] When a storm forced the whole navy to land at Pylos, the other generals eventually allowed Demosthenes to carry out the construction of an improvised fort, although Thucydides suggests it was because the soldiers themselves were bored and wanted something to do. Once the storm cleared, the rest of the navy sailed on leaving Demosthenes with only the crews from five ships. He was also reinforced by the crews of two Messenian ships.[52]

Demosthenes' success in defending his position against repeated attacks by Spartan hoplites from both land and sea shows the resilience of light infantry in favourable situations, especially when defending a fortified position.[53] This reliance on light infantry was a significant development. For the first time, Demosthenes proved that hoplites were not always required in Greek warfare and, more importantly, were not always successful.

Perhaps the most important use in Classical Greek warfare of light infantry in battle was at Sphacteria, where the Athenians defeated a Spartan hoplite army with only missile troops (Thucydides 4.26–39). This should have been the impetus for further Athenian experiments with alternatives to hoplite only armies during the Peloponnesian War; not least because Athenian hoplites were inferior to Spartans and the numerous states in the Athenian Empire provided access to large numbers of light infantry.

Cleon was the lead general in the Athenian assault on the marooned Spartans on the island of Sphacteria, but he was quick to have Demosthenes join him in command. Thucydides argues that it was contempt for Nicias and the other generals that prompted him to take no Athenians in his expeditionary force. Instead he took men from Lemnos and Imbria, who were at Athens, with some peltasts and 400 archers to join the light infantry of Demosthenes' fleet still at Pylos.[54] Best argues that it was at Demosthenes' insistence that the Athenian force was composed entirely of light infantry.[55]

Demosthenes' first action in the attack on Sphacteria probably was to burn the forest on the island.[56] Once this was achieved Cleon and Demosthenes were so sure of victory that they proposed terms of surrender to the Spartans, which were quickly refused.[57] During the night Demosthenes landed hoplites at two points on the island to quietly overwhelm the Spartan sentry posts. This they achieved easily, catching the Spartans still asleep. Then all the light infantry landed in groups of 200 and harassed the Spartans all day with missiles.[58] The Spartans were forced to retire to the acropolis as the best protection from the missiles. Once some Athenian auxiliaries assailed the Spartans in the fortress from the heights overlooking their position (4.36), the surviving hoplites agreed to surrender after the Athenian generals called a halt to the missile barrage (4.37–8). Of the 420 hoplites on the island, 292 surrendered and the rest were killed (4.38.5).

Roisman goes too far in his efforts to account for Demosthenes' luck at Pylos and Sphacteria stating that "Demosthenes' contribution to the Athenian victory at Pylos, then, has been overestimated".[59] He is right that Demosthenes could not foresee the Spartan response to his creation of a fort at Pylos, but that should not take anything away from its success. Likewise, his defeat of the Spartans on Sphacteria using only light infantry was planned, even if the surrender of the Spartans was not. Whether or not Thucydides minimised Demosthenes' generalship out of enmity or in order to promote luck in his success is somewhat irrelevant. Demosthenes showed innovative generalship in defending his fort with primarily light infantry and in using the same lightly armed soldiers to defeat the Spartans on Sphacteria. Roisman is wrong to lessen his abilities when stating that "Demosthenes demonstrated good but not exceptional or revolutionary generalship at Pylos".[60] He is, however, correct to conclude that "[h]e was successful because he had adequate intelligence, time to plan, some luck and used surprise tactics on a careful and limited basis". Surely these traits themselves demonstrate Demosthenes' innovative generalship. Roisman's monograph after all is focused specifically on Demosthenes' somewhat revolutionary idea to use surprise in almost every battle.

The fact that it took over 10,000 light infantry a whole day to force the 420 hoplites to surrender, having killed only 128 of them, demonstrates just how ineffective missiles were against hoplite armour, as discussed previously. It was still a great coup for Cleon and Demosthenes and their reliance on light infantry, but despite the victory none of the other Athenian commanders were inclined to use peltasts in any significant numbers. Perhaps the Athenians were disheartened by the time and numbers required to achieve victory without hoplites. Before his departure the Athenian Assembly laughed at Cleon's assertion that he would defeat the Spartan hoplites on Sphacteria using only light troops, showing their disdain for the abilities of such troops next to hoplites.[61] It was probably not just the Athenians who were so disparaging of light infantry, and the Greek reliance on hoplites in battle never really went away.

The most talented Spartan general, Brasidas, "[a]s gifted a military commander as the Spartans ever produced", led a Spartan invasion of Athenian territory in the Chalcidice.[62] He was forced to adapt his plans to succeed in Thrace precisely because his army was a combined force in terrain well suited for such armies. Thucydides (5.6) states that Brasidas commanded 2,000 heavy infantry, at least 2,500 light infantry and 300 cavalry. Brasidas' victory at Amphipolis completely expelled the Athenian army from the area, but in the battle most of the fighting was done by the hoplites until the Athenians fled when the cavalry and light infantry came to the fore.[63] This was standard practice in a Greek battle. Though it was a combined arms army, there were no combined arms tactics in the battle. It was Brasidas' use of a surprise attack with hoplites on Cleon's exposed flank that won the victory not any coordinated use of combined arms. Unfortunately for the Spartans, Brasidas died from the wounds he received in the battle. Although Brasidas was hailed as a hero and deified in Amphipolis,[64] the Spartans did not follow up his innovative generalship, just as the Athenians ignored Demosthenes' successes.

Brasidas also demonstrated how to defend against a combined arms attack when deficient in light infantry and cavalry. At Lyncus in 423 Brasidas was abandoned by his ally, Perdiccas, king of Macedon, and left without cavalry (Thucydides, 4.125). Threatened by the Illyrians, who had numerous cavalry and light infantry, though few hoplites if any, Brasidas formed his hoplites into a hollow square and placed his few light infantry inside.[65] His small force successfully beat off the Illyrians, who were surprised at the vigour of their defence and turned instead to attack Perdiccas' Macedonians. As Best rightly conjectures, the departure of most of the Illyrians to deal with the Macedonians is what saved Brasidas, whose men would have become exhausted and easy prey for missiles and cavalry.[66] Nevertheless, his use of the hollow square was a perfect solution to ward off cavalry attacks. Keeping the light infantry inside the square, instead of having them protect his flanks and rear and act as the vanguard, was an interesting decision. It perhaps suggests that he was harassed more by cavalry than missile troops, since a defensive square that maintains formation is almost impossible for cavalry to break.[67] The Ten Thousand Greek mercenaries who retreated from Cunaxa also formed their hoplites into a square on the march through hostile territory since they had few cavalry to protect their flanks.[68]

Hoplites remained the main force used in Greek armies in the Peloponnesian War, but some generals did attempt to use innovative deployments in the phalanx. At Delium the Thebans began experimenting with different tactical dispositions of the phalanx (Thucydides 4.90–96). The formation was drawn up 25 men deep, but this was not the factor that decided the battle. The cavalry was the crucial unit. Thucydides states that the Thebans fielded a combined arms army involving 7,000 heavy infantry, over 10,000 light infantry, 1,000 cavalry, and 500 peltasts. The Athenian army did not have any light infantry apparently but did field a few cavalry. The Theban light infantry and cavalry were placed on the wings of the army and although the army involved different units, the tactical deployment of the army still relied on the hoplite phalanx in the centre. Thucydides states that the terrain prevented the troops on the wings from entering the battle. The Athenians fled when cavalry appeared unexpectedly in their rear while their phalanx engaged with the Theban phalanx.

Thus, it was the use of combined arms that won the battle for Thebes. However, although the combination of cavalry and hoplites together proved successful at Delium, it seems that that was not the original battle plan.[69] It was very much the case of individual initiative on the part of Pagondas.[70] Though this is still a case of combined arms in battle, and the first main one in mainland Greek warfare, the crucial deficiency is that it was not a plan to integrate the cavalry into the tactics of the battle to achieve victory. The Thebans still intended on using their light infantry and cavalry simply as flank guards while deciding the battle through the hoplite phalanx in the centre.

Delium, however, does demonstrate a new willingness to adapt battle tactics among the Thebans, which culminated in the innovations of the later generals

Pelopidas and Epaminondas, as discussed next. Combined arms was used in terms of the deployment and use of different units in the Theban army but the tactical emphasis still favoured a hoplite confrontation. Nonetheless, Delium represents the first large-scale application of combined arms by a Greek polis on the battlefield, and it was the cavalry not the hoplites that decided the result of the battle.

Through Demosthenes, Brasidas, and Pagondas the Greeks had a few excellent commanders who were very comfortable trying to win battles using units other than the hoplite phalanx. However, none of them had any lasting influence on Greek warfare, or even the tactics of their polis. Still Greek warfare remained reliant on hoplites until the successes of Iphicrates and Chabrias in the Corinthian War, over two decades after the death of Demosthenes and three after Brasidas'.

Sicily and the Athenian siege of Syracuse – large-scale combined arms in practice[71]

The failed Athenian expedition to Sicily was a critical event in the Peloponnesian War causing Athens to lose their best general in Demosthenes (among others), thousands of soldiers and an entire navy. It also saw the crucial generalship of a hitherto unimportant Spartan, Gylippus. Like Demosthenes, Brasidas, and Pagondas, military history has largely forgotten Gylippus' contribution to combined arms warfare, but in dealing Athens such a great blow at Syracuse his success is perhaps the greatest of all. The Athenian expedition to Syracuse is the best-case study for combined arms in the Peloponnesian War as it demonstrates well the Athenian army's reliance on hoplites, despite sending reinforcements of other arms, and its inability to cope with the Syracusan combined arms forces reliant on cavalry in terrain well suited to its deployment and well marshalled after Gylippus' arrival.

Sources

The principal source for the expedition is Thucydides. Plutarch also gives some information about a few of the battles in his *Life of Nicias*.[72] Since there is so little information about this campaign elsewhere it is necessary to rely on Thucydides.[73] Fortunately he provides numerous details about the tactics employed in the battles and even comments himself on the crucial final battle of Epipolae.[74]

Early warfare in Sicily

Syracuse was probably the first state in the Greek world in the Classical period to develop an effective combined arms army. The tyrants of Syracuse had developed large armies containing many types of unit. The Syracusan cavalry was experienced in war and probably made up of the aristocrats.[75] The flat plains of Sicily were well suited to cavalry manoeuvres, the city of Gela's lack of a port had led to an emphasis on raising horses, and the Syracusans' Greek heritage led to the usual reliance on a strong core of hoplites.[76] Hippocrates, tyrant of Gela before

The Peloponnesian War – combined arms 115

the more famous Gelon who was also tyrant of Syracuse, also introduced the use of mercenary light infantry in his army to combat native Sicel light infantry in the mountains.[77]

The frequent wars with the cavalry forces of Carthage and the light infantry of the native Sicels influenced the implementation of an army able to cope with a more mobile style of warfare reliant on cavalry and missile troops.[78] The Carthaginians usually fielded large armies of mixed forces reliant on a core of aristocratic cavalry alongside their numerous mercenaries.[79]

At the crucial battle of Himera against Carthage in 480, Gelon had 10,000 mercenaries in his army as a part of 50,000 infantry and 5,000 cavalry.[80] This battle saw the most lauded tyrant of a Sicilian city defeat a large Carthaginian invasion force. Xerxes may have asked the Carthaginians to invade Sicily in the summer of 480 in order to distract the Greek colonies there from aiding Greece during his invasion that same summer.[81] Unfortunately for the invaders, a storm off the coast had denied them their cavalry forces and thus left them at a great disadvantage (Diodorus 11.20–23). In the first engagement with Greek Sicilians outside of the city of Himera the general of the Carthaginian army, Hamilcar, led out his best troops and easily defeated the small force of hoplites who came out to resist them. The loss of the cavalry did not matter as their superior numbers and effective infantry won the day. However, when Gelon suddenly arrived with his army his strong cavalry forces caught the Carthaginians foraging in the countryside without cavalry protection and, according to Diodorus, captured 10,000 prisoners. Gelon then learned from a captured messenger the precise day that a Greek city Selinus was sending cavalry to Hamilcar's camp. Utilising this as a ruse he sent his own cavalry to the Carthaginian camp to pose as the allied cavalry with instructions to find and kill Hamilcar and burn the camp. The rest of the army opposed the Carthaginians while awaiting signs of the burning camp. The infantry of both sides clashed and the battle raged either way until the fires from the camp disheartened the Carthaginians and encouraged the Greeks who pressed on with orders to take no prisoners.

Though the details of the engagement suggest that the battle was fought between infantry forces only, Gelon won because of his superior cavalry and a lack of Carthaginian cavalry forces. His army must also have contained light infantry, as did the Carthaginian, and so Himera is the first large-scale battle in the Greek world where combined arms was fully used. Unfortunately, there is not enough to reconstruct the tactical details, but it is likely that the light infantry in the Greek army fought on the flanks of the hoplites with the cavalry seemingly engaged in the ruse. However, in my view it is unlikely that Gelon sent all his cavalry to the Carthaginian camp. I doubt the force Hamilcar expected from his allies was as many as 5,000 as that would be a huge amount for one small Greek city to send. Moreover, Gelon would have wanted to retain some cavalry to protect his flanks and communication lines, and more importantly aid in the crucial role of chasing down the fleeing enemy after the victory. If this is true, then Gelon did field a truly combined arms army at Himera to great success. However, again the battle likely involved few combined arms tactics merely a hoplite confrontation in the centre loosely supported on the wings by cavalry and light infantry.

At the onset of the Persian Wars, the Greeks sent an embassy asking for aid from Gelon, which was unsuccessful despite his offer to provide 20,000 hoplites, 2,000 cavalry, 2,000 archers, 2,000 slingers, and 2,000 light horsemen. The Greeks turned down his offer because he wanted overall command on either land or sea,[82] but this offer shows just how strong Gelon's army was in being the first to deploy significant numbers of troops in a combined arms style. Unfortunately, there is little detail on the tactical deployment of these Sicilian mixed armies and so it is impossible to assess how much combined arms tactics were used on the battlefield.

Syracuse was unusual in the Greek world because of its willingness and ability to field mixed armies but their example did not influence Greece proper. To the mainland Greeks, and to most modern military historians, Gelon's contribution to warfare was lost in the aftermath of the Greek victory in the Persian Wars and so his use of combined arms never spread across the narrow sea from Sicily to Greece.[83] But in Syracuse Gelon's achievement was such that when Timoleon removed any memories of tyrants the Syracusans preserved alone the statue of Gelon.[84] As Champion summarises, the "large numbers of cavalry and supporting missile troops also show how much more tactically advanced the Sicilians were than their kinsmen in Greece".[85]

The Athenian campaign

The Athenian invasion fleet sent against Syracuse in 415 numbered 134 ships, including the transports, carrying 5,100 hoplites, 480 archers, of whom 80 were Cretan, 700 slingers, 120 peltasts from Megara, and 30 horses on one transport (Thucydides 6.43).[86] This shows that by this time Athens was used to fielding armies that featured relatively high proportions of light infantry. As discussed previously, the Greeks had already begun to utilise light infantry better, though not fully, in their battles. But the notable element missing from a true combined arms force is the small amount of cavalry.

Nicias in his speech before the expedition argued that the Syracusan strength was in cavalry (6.20.4) and that the Athenians should field an army containing many hoplites, but in particular a great number of archers and slingers to counter the enemy cavalry (6.22).[87] The lack of cavalry in the Athenian army demonstrates their reliance on infantry in battle. In open terrain such as on Sicily light infantry was insufficient to contain the Syracusan cavalry, as the Athenians would discover but clearly were unaware of at the time. Thucydides (6.64) makes clear that the Athenians realised their deficiency in cavalry would be a problem and so were forced to trick the Syracusans in order to land safely in Sicily. It seems to have not occurred to the Athenians that they should field more cavalry in order to match the Syracusan strength, rather than rely on allies in Sicily to do so, or they were incapable of fielding their own substantial force (cf. 6.21.1). That they took so many light infantry shows that by 415 Athens had come to appreciate the benefits of such troops alongside hoplites, probably thanks to the exploits of Demosthenes. But considering the strength of the Syracusan cavalry force and the open terrain of Sicily this is a far too inadequate number of horsemen for Athens to field.[88]

The first battle for Syracuse was at Olympeium in 415 (Thucydides 6.67–71; Plutarch, *Nicias* 16). The Athenians were able to land unmolested after fooling the Syracusans and prepared for battle, choosing a narrow location where the Syracusan cavalry could not fight effectively.[89] The Syracusans had no choice but to send in their hoplites against the Athenian phalanx, stationing the cavalry and light infantry on the wings as usual. The engagement began with the light infantry skirmishing between the two armies. Then the hoplite phalanx of either side came to close quarters. Eventually the greater skill and experience of the Athenian hoplites sent the Syracusans into retreat.

After the battle the Athenian generals decided to use the oncoming winter to send for a strong cavalry force either from Athens or its allies (6.74.2). Thucydides (6.71.2) states that it did not seem possible to continue the war without such forces, again showing the Athenian oversight in not bringing cavalry to begin with. Clearly, on arrival in Sicily the generals saw first-hand that the region was so suited to cavalry that their strategy on relying on light infantry was now going to fail.

Perhaps the biggest strategic blunder of the Athenians was to abandon their hard won and advantageous position next to Syracuse at Olympeium and move camp first to Naxos on Sicily and then to Catana (6.88.3–5, cf. 7.42.3). The next summer (414) Athens sent cavalry reinforcements to the sum of 250 horsemen without horses and 30 horse archers (6.94.4).[90] With this cavalry, once horses were procured, the Athenian army would be able to engage the Syracusans with a combined arms army. However, they would still be deficient in using cavalry inexperienced in fighting in terrain that favoured cavalry manoeuvres and against an enemy who had horsemen of excellent quality.

The next conflict between the two sides was the first battle of Epipolae. This place was a flat hill overlooking the city of Syracuse and both sides realised its strategic importance (Thucydides 6.96–7). The Athenians managed to steal a march on the Syracusans and seized the heights first while the enemy were holding a review of the troops. The Syracusan response was to send soldiers against the Athenians as they were available and having to cover over three miles of ground. As a result, the Syracusan units attacked individually and were easily beaten back by the Athenians. We have no details as to whether this engagement involved the use of combined arms. Since the Syracusan army attacked piecemeal it is likely that the Athenian hoplites alone were enough to win the day.

Straight after the battle the Athenians received around 400 allied cavalry, bringing their total horsemen to 650 (6.98.1).[91] Now secure in their ability to sufficiently counter the Syracusan cavalry the Athenians began construction of a wall to circumvallate the city. Syracuse sent out its whole army but pulled back the infantry for fear of defeat on account of their disorder. The cavalry remained and harassed the Athenians until a force of hoplites and the Athenian cavalry drove them away (Thucydides 6.98.3–4). This action by the Syracusans shows that their combined arms army was deficient in the quality of their hoplites in opposing the experienced Athenian phalanx. Though their cavalry was superior the combined arms army could only gain victory if the infantry could hold the ground in the centre.

The Syracusans began building a counterwall to intersect the Athenian construction and prevent its completion (6.99). When the Athenians did not come out to stop them most of the Syracusans went back to the city. The Athenians waited until lunchtime and then sent a rapid attack force of 300 chosen hoplites and some light infantry to seize and destroy the Syracusan wall (6.100.1–3). This they did effectively though suffering a number of casualties.

The next day the Syracusans began another counterwall and again the Athenians sallied to destroy it. The Syracusan forces were beaten back until the same Athenian picked force of 300 men strove to cut off their retreat. The Syracusan cavalry and some of the retreating infantry closed on the Athenians and threw them back in disorder on to the Athenian right wing prompting the retreat of another force of Athenian hoplites. The Athenian general Lamachus came to the aid of this wing with hoplites and archers but was killed when stranded across the river (6.101.1–6). The rest of the Syracusan army came out and succeeded in destroying a large section of the Athenian wall. Other Athenian troops came up and the Syracusans retreated into the city (6.102.1–4).

This engagement demonstrates for the first time the effectiveness of the Syracusan combined arms army. It was the hoplites and cavalry fighting in harmony that forced back the 300 picked Athenian hoplites and right wing. Though Thucydides does not say so we can assume the Syracusan cavalry pressured the exposed flank of the Athenian phalanx with the hoplites pressing frontally. It also shows the Athenian tactics of countering cavalry with light infantry. Instead of sending in their new cavalry force, some of which presumably was on the Athenian right wing, Lamachus led on hoplites and archers with no success and fatally so. This is perhaps the best example in the whole campaign that demonstrates the need to oppose cavalry with cavalry on flat terrain. The Athenians' methods were still ingrained in infantry warfare and paid no heed to how best to utilise cavalry in battle.

After this skirmish, Gylippus, a Spartan general, arrived at Syracuse with a force of 700 marines and sailors, a thousand heavy infantry and light troops from Himera with a hundred cavalry, and a thousand other allies (Thucydides 7.1.4–5). Just as in Athens' expeditionary force, Gylippus, though a Spartan hoplite, brought a combined arms army to integrate into the Syracusan defences. By now even the most hoplite focused Greek polis realised that fighting on certain terrain necessitated fielding a combined arms force.

Gylippus joined with the Syracusan army and offered battle to the Athenians in the open plain of Epipolae but Nicias, now the sole Athenian general, refused to leave the fortification wall. The next day Gylippus again offered battle while also sending a force to take an Athenian fort in secret (7.3.3–4). The Syracusans and the Athenians continued to build their respective walls, with Gylippus continually offering battle on Epipolae. The continued refusal of Nicias to engage with

The Peloponnesian War – combined arms 119

Gylippus demonstrates the Athenian fear of exposure to the combined arms army of the Syracusans. In view of the relative unit strengths on each side this fear must have come about through the superiority of the Syracusan cavalry alone.

Eventually the Athenian army decided on an engagement and the two sides met at the second battle of Epipolae (Thucydides 7.5–6). The battle was fought in the confined space between the two fortification walls and did not provide enough room for the Syracusan cavalry to be of use. This is almost certainly why Nicias did offer battle. He found a way to use the terrain to maximise his own strengths in hoplites and light infantry and nullify the enemy's in cavalry, demonstrating his ability as a general and tactician. Without the support of their cavalry the Syracusans fled after sustaining many casualties. Gylippus took all the blame for the defeat for not utilising the cavalry in a combined arms manner and vowed to always use cavalry in the future. Gylippus accepting the battle in the narrow terrain showed how much infantry reliant combat was ingrained in the military minds of the Greeks. Even when he led a combined arms army in a place renowned for its cavalry Gylippus still resorted to the tried and true hoplite phalanx despite such an inferior phalanx as the Syracusans fielded. Gylippus immediately rectified his error, but the error in itself says more about Greek warfare than anything else. Greeks were far too obsessed with hoplites to utilise the other combat arms fully in battle.

Gylippus led out the Syracusans again this time away from the walls onto the plain of Epipolae, stationing the cavalry and missile troops on the right wing in the open spaces. Nicias chose to accept battle despite the terrain advantage for the Syracusan cavalry where before he avoided it. Perhaps he and his men were overly confident from the previous victory. At this battle, the Syracusan cavalry attacked the exposed Athenian flank. They easily routed the hoplites there (presumably after overcoming the small Athenian cavalry first) and the retreat spread to the whole army, which fled behind the fortifications (7.6.1–3).

The Syracusan cavalry now controlled the plains preventing the Athenians from venturing too far from their walls (7.11.4). Once again the Syracusan cavalry proved decisive in defeating the Athenians and Gylippus used combined arms successfully. This is the first battle in Greek warfare where a Greek general deliberately planned a battle to rely for victory over hoplites on an assault of cavalry alone with hoplites only in support by pressuring the centre of the line. This is the crucial step since Delium in the adoption of combined arms by planning from the outset to make the best use of each type of unit in harmony.

After his defeat Nicias wrote to Athens demanding reinforcements or withdrawal (7.10–15). The Athenians sent their best general Demosthenes and another general Eurymedon (7.16.2). Demosthenes left Athens with 1,200 hoplites and a large number of light infantry (7.20.2) without waiting for the expected 1,300 Thracian peltasts (7.27.1).

Before Demosthenes' forces arrived Gylippus planned for a combined naval and land attack (7.21–4). The navy would attack the Athenians in the Great Harbour while Gylippus would attack the three Athenian forts around Plemmyrium. The naval engagement went badly for the Syracusans but Gylippus succeeded in taking all three Athenian forts largely because the defenders were watching the sea battle and were caught by surprise. According to Thucydides, the capture of the forts was the first and foremost reason for the subsequent destruction of the Athenian army, denying them the full control of the harbour and denuding them of many provisions. Though this is not a combined arms battle, it is one of the earliest examples in Greek warfare of something much more complicated: a combined operations attack. Successfully integrating and timing separate attacks on land and at sea was very difficult to do in the ancient world, which is why such campaigns are so rare. This shows just how good an innovative general Gylippus was.

Gylippus launched another combined attack on land and sea after the Syracusans refitted their ships to aid them in battle by strengthening their prows for head-on collisions, something alien to Athenian naval combat (7.36). The ships set out again in the Great Harbour while Gylippus and the Syracusan troops from Olympeium attacked the Athenian fortifications from both sides. Each engagement was a stalemate and the Syracusans waited a day before another attack. This headed the same way until a Syracusan contrivance to move the market to the sea shore and refresh the troops for another unexpected attack in the afternoon. This worked well, catching the tired Athenians unprepared and ill-equipped, and the Syracusans won their first naval victory (7.37–41).

Eventually Demosthenes and Eurymedon arrived with 5,000 hoplites, and a large number of light infantry.[92] Demosthenes soon after his arrival correctly determined that whoever controlled Epipolae would control the city (7.42–4). He tried to take the Syracusan wall with siege engines and attacks at various points but all his efforts came to nothing. Demosthenes then decided to reverse Athenian fortunes with a full-scale night attack on the Syracusan camp and counterwall.[93] Demosthenes' initial attack was successful routing various Syracusan forces and capturing sections of the wall, but as the Athenians pressed on their ranks became disordered. In the darkness the Athenians could not tell friend from foe and so called out their password to everyone. The Syracusans were coming on in formation and, armed with the password, easily overcame the Athenian survivors. Some of the Athenians even began attacking each other confused by the dialects of their allies. The next morning the Syracusan cavalry mopped up the remaining Athenians.

Unfortunately, Thucydides does not provide any information on the troop dispositions and make-up of the Athenian army. In view of his previous successes in capturing cities with light infantry at night in my view it is likely that the Athenian advance forces were peltasts closely followed by picked hoplites who could keep up. This advance of light infantry would help to explain along with the confusion of darkness why the Athenian army was turned back easily at the onset of the Syracusan hoplites once the fighting came to close quarters.

After this disaster Demosthenes argued for going home to save the army and fleet in order to use them both against the Spartans at Decelea (7.47–50). Nicias argued they should stay because the Syracusans were in a difficult financial state and therefore likely to succumb at any moment. Demosthenes argued that it was a strategic necessity to abandon the siege and withdraw into another area where the

The Peloponnesian War – combined arms 121

troops could live off the land free from the Syracusan cavalry. Nicias' argument won until the Syracusans received reinforcements from Sicily and the Peloponnese. The Athenians decided to leave but an eclipse of the moon persuaded the soldiers and Nicias to stay longer.

Gylippus and the Syracusans planned another combined attack on land and sea and the navy practised for a few days (7.51–3). The attack in the harbour went well and the Syracusans succeeded in killing the Athenian general Eurymedon. Gylippus took troops to the harbour side to cut off and capture the Athenian sailors but was forced back by Tyrrhenians fighting for Athens. The Syracusans were encouraged after this engagement that their navy could match the Athenian.

The Athenians decided that their position was untenable and determined to make a final push for command of the sea by manning the ships with troops from the army, and if they failed, to retreat en masse across land after burning the fleet (7.60). The Syracusans noticed what was happening and prepared for the upcoming sea battle (7.65). Some soldiers prepared to capture beached Athenian sailors and the rest of the army sailed out against the Athenians. The battle was hard fought but the Syracusans eventually forced the Athenians to fall back (7.70–71).

Demosthenes argued that they should try to force a way out with the fleet again since they still held an advantage in numbers, but the sailors refused despairing after the defeat (7.72–4). They all then agreed to retreat overland and set about preparing to do so. The Syracusan general Hermocrates tricked the Athenians out of escaping at night by sending news that the roads were blocked. The Athenians then stayed an extra day to pack up their belongings before heading out. This delay gave the Syracusans time to set up guards at all the likely routes of escape for the Athenians and almost certainly doomed the whole Athenian army.

The demoralised Athenian army set off marching in a hollow square of hoplites with the baggage and light infantry inside. This was the formation that had served Brasidas well in Thrace, but his enemy had abandoned the pursuit. The Syracusans were never going to let the Athenians escape so easily. The Syracusan cavalry and missile troops constantly harassed the Athenian force causing numerous casualties. Demosthenes and Nicias then changed the route of the march and headed off secretly at night but the forces of the two generals became separated. Gylippus and the Syracusans overcame Demosthenes first surrounding and harassing his men with cavalry attacks and missile barrages. Demosthenes was forced to surrender while Nicias continued his retreat. Eventually the Syracusans caught up with Nicias' force too and harassed his march in the same fashion achieving the same result of the surrender of the army. Demosthenes and Nicias were killed, contrary to Gylippus' desire, and the rest of the Athenian army was put to work in the stone quarries (7.78–86).

Combined arms

The Athenian disaster at Syracuse is the perfect example of the difficulties of opposing a combined arms army when lacking in one arm, in this case cavalry. The Syracusan cavalry first used guerrilla tactics to harass the Athenians while they were building the wall to cut off the city. Their control of the countryside limited the actions and foraging of the Athenians. Although led by an experienced Spartan general it was the ability of the Syracusan cavalry that defeated the Athenians and eventually led to the defeat of the whole Athenian expedition. This was perhaps a more important development than the victories of either Demosthenes or Brasidas, and the final third battle of Epipolae demonstrates well the vulnerability of the exposed flank of a hoplite phalanx to a cavalry charge.

This was the first implementation of a tactical plan to utilise cavalry to win a battle against hoplites, a crucial development of combined arms. It also shows that even a Spartan schooled in hoplite combat, once shown the way by a prior defeat, was willing to move completely away from standard Greek military principles and use an unfamiliar arm, cavalry, to bring victory. This is especially noteworthy since the Spartans did not even have a significant cavalry force of their own. Gylippus, though almost forgotten as a general in history, proved to be a great innovator and won because he adapted his own tactical plans and training to best utilise local knowledge and expertise at the expense of the hoplite phalanx.

Greek hoplite armies had always fought in the confined spaces of Greece and had rarely been exposed to the difficulties of protecting the flank of a hoplite phalanx on an open battlefield. The Athenian siege of Syracuse demonstrates the ability of some Greek generals to adopt the use of combined arms in certain situations. It is of even more interest because it marks the death of Demosthenes, the first great innovator in combined arms tactics in Greece, at the hands of a well-organised multi-faceted army led by an otherwise unimportant but tactically adaptable Spartan general.

Gylippus' ability to adapt his tactics to the troops and situation at hand led to the resounding successes of the Syracusan army. Even with arguably their greatest general at the helm, the hoplite focused army of the Athenians was unable to cope with an enemy reliant on heavy cavalry, fighting on terrain well suited for horses. The Syracusan victory over Athens showed that even a significantly superior hoplite phalanx, without an adequate force of horsemen to protect the flank, was very vulnerable on an open plain against a strong cavalry force. This is one of the main principles of the system of combined arms, using one unit to protect the weaknesses of the other and to attack the Achilles' heel of the enemy.[94]

The largest disaster for Athens, and setback in the development of combined arms, was the failure of Demosthenes' night attack. In leading the whole army forwards he must have organised the Athenian army according to the principles of combined arms as much as possible with cavalry, light infantry, hoplites, and presumably siege machinery intended to act together against the Syracusan defensive walls. However, the amount of coordination of a combined arms army in a night action was too great for the largely semi-professional Athenian army even under the command of such a gifted general in Demosthenes.

Demosthenes overreached in his efforts to defeat the Syracusans at night. He had demonstrated twice previously the possibilities of a night attack with only light infantry to capture and hold an enemy position, at Idomene and Megara as discussed previously, and he should have stuck with this more limited approach.

To have achieved his objective Demosthenes need not have taken the whole army on this enterprise (7.43.2). It would have been far safer on a night mission to take a smaller force, preferably only Ionians [light infantry], requisite for the task. These could have held their position until daybreak, at which time the remainder of the army could have come up in support. Demosthenes' first and only objective of that night attack should have been to secure a position on the Epipolae from which subsequent attacks could be mounted. In going for a complete victory the very size and composition of his forces produced the scenario for failure.[95]

Demosthenes' execution by the Syracusans after the final Athenian defeat in the harbour of Syracuse robbed Athens of its first military innovator. Demosthenes was undone, as Roisman states so succinctly, by his "fascination with military surprise, his optimism and self-confidence, and his penchant for quick and radical solutions" and he "ignored the lessons of his failures and selectively applied the lessons of his victories".[96] His willingness to try a night attack with a full army shows his ingenuity, but his defeat shows that he lacked the required leadership and communication to make a coordinated mass attack of a combined arms army at night, a feat which was especially difficult in the ancient world.

The Athenian defeat at Syracuse had crucial repercussions for the outcome of the Peloponnesian War and critically weakened the military capabilities of Athens, indirectly contributing to the eventual Athenian defeat. But the battles for the city perfectly demonstrate the benefits of using combined arms in battle, and the deficiencies of hoplite armies. The hoplite phalanx was an excellent formation of heavy infantry in battle, but when exposed on the flanks and rear by cavalry in particular, it was very vulnerable.[97] Yet despite the lessons on Sicily, cavalry still took a long time to be incorporated into the Greek style of warfare and only really came of age after the Macedonian conquest of Greece in the mid-fourth century.

This is even true on Sicily where, despite almost constant warring with Carthage, the Greek armies rarely made use of combined arms. Under the infamous tyrant Dionysius I even the large armies mobilised were heavily reliant on the hoplite phalanx, as were the Carthaginian armies opposed.[98] The Sicilian Greeks also did not heed the lessons of their defeat of Athens and still engaged in hoplite focused warfare despite their local advantages in cavalry.[99]

Perhaps the most significant development in combined arms in the last part of the Peloponnesian War was the complete reorganisation of the Spartan army from hoplites in territorial based regiments, or *lochoi*, to *morai* that were accompanied in battle by organised units of light infantry and cavalry. At the battle of Mantinea in 418, Thucydides 5.67 clearly describes the Spartan army as being organised into separate lochoi of Spartiates (full Spartan citizens) and *perioikoi* (those who literally "lived around" Sparta). By 403 and the Spartan invasion of Attica Xenophon describes the Spartan regiments as morai.[100] The composition of these morai is described in detail by Xenophon in the *Spartan Constitution*. There were six morai of cavalry and hoplites, subdivided into four lochoi, eight *pentekostiai*, and 16 *enomotiai*. Though he states that the army was thus divided by the semi-legendary founder Lycurgus, the terminology used and description given is clearly different from the earlier Spartan army described in Thucydides.

Sekunda has argued, and I agree, that this new reorganisation of the Spartan regimental system was carried out during the Dekelean War in 413 in response to having to leave a permanent Spartan garrison in Attica, and I would add perhaps as a response to Gylippus' victories in Sicily.[101] What is more important to the present discussion is that this proves that by the end of the Peloponnesian War even the most hoplite focused polis, Sparta, fielded combined arms regiments not just a combined arms army. As Sekunda makes clear, each cavalry mora was always attached to one of the hoplite morai to protect its flanks, except in largescale battles when all the cavalry combined was stationed on each flank of the whole phalanx.[102] In fact, it is easier to understand the cavalry as a detachment within the Spartan mora. Each hoplite phalanx had a detachment of cavalry at its disposal wherever it went as a separate entity.[103]

Again, as Sekunda states, this Spartan system is the first concrete example we have in Greek warfare of the divisional concept of separate tactical bodies of troops able to act independently using a combination of types of arms.[104] In this case it is simply cavalry and heavy infantry, the most basic form of combined arms. But it is clear that the Spartans decided that a hoplite phalanx had to be constantly supported by cavalry in order to protect its flanks and to ward off attacks by light infantry. As discussed next, Iphicrates' peltast victory over hoplites at Lechaeum was only achieved because of the mishandling of the Spartan cavalry. Dionysius I of Syracuse also used a divisional system in an attack on the camp of the Carthaginians in 405.[105]

This is a crucial development in combined arms. Even the hoplite focused state of Sparta realised that cavalry was essential in safeguarding the hoplites and allowing the phalanx to be at its best in battle secure in the knowledge that its flanks and rear are protected. True to the maxims of combined arms doctrine, each arm protected the weaknesses of the other and made the whole stronger.

It is interesting to note the absence of light infantry in the Spartan system. Athens, as discussed previously, in the invasion of Syracuse relied on large forces of light infantry to safeguard the flanks and rear of the phalanx rather than cavalry. Perhaps the difference in emphasis is that Athens had much more light infantry available than Sparta. Regardless, the Spartan system of mutually supportive cavalry and hoplite *morai* proves that the system of combined arms had well and truly arrived in Greek warfare and saw the end of hoplite only focused battles.

Combined arms conclusions

The Peloponnesian War saw many developments in the use of combined arms in Greece, both in defence and attack. But no state fully realised the great benefits of using combined arms in battle. Demosthenes was the first general in Greece to begin to experiment with the tactics and basic principles of the theory of combined arms, and to develop tactics to overcome an enemy's superiority. "Demosthenes clearly possessed a basic understanding of tactics and recognized that combining different types of troops (peltasts, hoplites, and archers) and the weapons they carried could produce striking results".[106] But even he failed to fully achieve a complete application of combined arms and tried too much too soon in attempting a large-scale night attack at Syracuse.

On the Spartan side the general Brasidas was the foremost innovator, but the innate Spartan military conservatism prevented him having any long-lasting effect on the style of warfare conducted. Likewise, the enormous success of Gylippus on Sicily did not even cement his place as a general of note let alone change the Spartan way of war. However, something happened to prompt the Spartan military system to fundamentally change by 403 into a rudimentary combined arms force always fielding cavalry alongside hoplites even in smaller detachments and garrisons. What or who it was that led to this is less important than the end result.[107] The Spartan army, and presumably the armies of all other Greek poleis, from this point onwards always fielded either cavalry or light infantry or both alongside hoplites. Hoplites remained the principal strike force in Greek armies but by the end of the fifth century they were always supported by combined arms though admittedly in its most basic form. It took other states on the fringes of the Greek world to fully develop and utilise a combined arms army, first Syracuse, as we saw previously, and then Macedon.

Notes

1 This generalised proposal will be examined in more detail in this section.
2 It is not necessary here to delve into the controversies of the historiography of Thucydides. On his work see for example Adcock (1963); Stahl (1966). On other historiographic problems with Thucydides' work see for example Hunter (1973); Hornblower (1991–2008).
3 See for example Cawkwell (1997); Morpeth (2006).
4 See Tuplin (1986); Lee (2009).
5 On this text see in particular Bruce (1967); McKechnie and Kern (1988).
6 On Diodorus' history as a comparison to Thucydides see Green (2006). For Diodorus' sources see Drews (1962).
7 Tracy (1942); Wardman (1971); Stadter (1992).
8 Cobet (1986). On the reliability of Thucydides' battle casualty figures see Rubincam (1991). For Thucydides' description of the battle of Pylos see Wilson (1979) and for the Sicilian expedition in particular see Liebeschutz (1968); Luginbill (1997); Brice (2013).
9 Much has been written about the Greek penchant for hoplite warfare. For a description of hoplites with images see Sekunda (2000). The best analyses of hoplite warfare are Hanson (1989, 1991b, 1999); Van Wees (2000b, 2005); De Souza (2008); Schwartz (2009); Matthew (2012); and most recently Kagan and Viggiano (2013a). For Sparta in particular see Cartledge (1977); Trundle (2001).
10 Best (1969). For the style of warfare practiced in Aetolia as viewed by Messenians at Naupactus see Thucydides 3.94.3–5. For northern Greek uses of light infantry see Griffith (1981); Webber (2011). Though we have very few references to hoplites in Arkadia, another very mountainous region similar to Aetolia, a new inscription details Arkadian hoplite recruitment and training Heinrichs (2015). Similar things may have occurred in Aetolia about which we know nothing.

126 Combined arms in Greek warfare

11 I already noted previously the exploits of the Theban cavalry at Plataea. For Macedonian cavalry see Hammond (1989); Hammond (1998); Moreno Hernandez (2004); and for Thessalian cavalry see Westlake (1935).
12 All these topics and more have been discussed elsewhere. For agriculture see in particular Hanson (1983). For the influence of political ideals on Greek warfare see Salmon (1977); Ridley (1979); Hanson (1989); Bowden (1995); Hanson (1996); Rosivach (2002). For imperialism see Cawkwell (1989); Hanson (2000); Krentz (2002); Christ (2004).
13 Hunt (2007: 134–5).
14 Hunt (2007: 135). He states that "some states, especially in the Peloponnese, which lacked a strong tradition of aristocratic horsemanship did without cavalry in the classical period".
15 Hunt (2007: 135). See also Bugh (1988: 221–3).
16 Hunt (2007: 135).
17 Xenophon, *On the Cavalry Commander* 1.13, 1.18, and especially 3.2–14. See also Worley (1994: 75) and Bugh (1988).
18 Spence (1993).
19 Worley (1994); Gaebel (2002).
20 This campaign is discussed in detail below. Athens was later forced to send more cavalry and procure allies.
21 Before the battle the Athenian general left a body of 300 cavalry in the rear to fall on the Boeotians but the Thebans sent some cavalry to prevent them doing so. On the battle see in particular Lendon (2005: 78–90).
22 As discussed previously the simple appearance of cavalry in the rear of the Greek hoplite phalanx at Malene prompted a wholesale retreat (Herodotus 6.29).
23 Diodorus, 16.85–86; Polyaenus, 4.2.2; Plutarch, *Alexander* 12 and *Demosthenes* 20. This battle will be discussed in detail below. Cavalry featured in other battles but none was as decisive in Greek politics than Chaeronea.
24 Hunt (2007: 119).
25 Thucydides 1.105.2–106; Diodorus 11.79.1–4.
26 Thucydides 1.106.2.
27 Thucydides 1.108.2–3; Diodorus 11.83.1.
28 Polyaenus *Stratagems* 1.35.1.
29 Polyaenus *Stratagems* 1.35.2.
30 Tritle (2010: 53).
31 Thucydides 2.79. The Athenian contingent marching against the Chalcidaeans was 2,000 hoplites and 200 cavalry. The citizens of Spartolus, after receiving reinforcements from Olynthus, sallied out to fight the Athenians. The Chalcidian hoplites were quickly routed but their cavalry and light troops easily routed the Athenian cavalry. After receiving reinforcements of more light infantry from Olynthus the Chalcidian missile infantry attacked the Athenian hoplites using hit and run tactics, falling back when the Athenians charged only to attack again when they fell back. These tactics added to repeated charges by their cavalry caused the Athenians to retreat which turned quickly into a rout. Over 430 Athenian hoplites died along with all of their generals.
32 See Webber (2011).
33 For more on Demosthenes' generalship see in particular Roisman (1993).
34 Roisman (1993: 27).
35 Roisman (1993).
36 See Krentz (2000).
37 For more on the history of surprise in Greek warfare see Sheldon (2012).
38 Tritle (2010: 79).
39 Roisman (1993: 29).
40 Roisman (1993: 29).
41 Lendon (2010: 233) "Thucydides did not much like Demosthenes and subtly belittles his achievements". According to Woodcock (1928: 93–108), Thucydides did not give

credit to Demosthenes for his achievements. Lendon (2010: 236) argues that Thucydides may have lost a relative at the battle of Aegitium and therefore never forgave Demosthenes. Roisman (1993: 11–22) argues otherwise but without being able to suitably disprove Woodcock.

42 Krentz (2000).
43 Roisman (1993: 31).
44 For Olpae and Idomene see Hammond (1936–7).
45 Roisman (1993: 42).
46 For Demosthenes, and Brasidas' use of light infantry in sieges see Best (1969).
47 Xenophon, *Hellenika* 1.3.10; Diodorus, 13.66.4; Plutarch, *Alcibiades* 30.3–10.
48 Xenophon reports that the Thracians north of the Hellespont often attacked their enemy at night *Anabasis* 7.2.22. Herodotus (7.45.1) provides the first instance of a Thracian night attack in 492 when they caused significant losses to Mardonius' Persian army. Nonetheless it took a long time for other Greeks to adopt this practice. Alexander was possibly encouraged to attempt a night attack against Darius at Gaugamela but he reportedly refused to steal his victory (Arrian 3.10.1–3; Plutarch, *Alexander* 31; Curtius 4.13).
49 This is an interesting contrast to the inability of the Persian infantry to capture the fortified position of Thermopylae against hoplites (Herodotus 7.210–225), as discussed previously.
50 The best example of such failed attacks is the battle of Aegitium in 426, as discussed previously (Thucydides 3.97–98).
51 Lendon (2010: 252). Strassler (1990: 113) argues that the Athenian fleet brought tools for this purpose. Thucydides 4.3.1–3 only suggests that Demosthenes planned on raiding Spartan territory and had been given discretion by the Athenians to do so (4.2.4). See also Thucydides 4.8–9. Whether he intended to create a fort or not the fact that he did was a significant advance in innovative generalship. See also Adcock (1947); Holladay (1978); Strassler (1988); Strassler (1990).
52 Thucydides 4.9.1. This would give him a force of around 1,200 men. When Demosthenes asked for assistance from the Athenian navy it came accompanied by ships from Naupactus (4.13.2). Since Naupactus was the city home of the ex-helot Messenians who had asked Demosthenes to attack Aegitium (3.94.3) the arrival of these two Messenian ships could have been in response to a direct request from Demosthenes rather than the simple accident as Thucydides claims. Moreover, Thucydides states that Demosthenes always intended to place a Messenian garrison at Pylos, probably in order to encourage their fellow Messenian helots to revolt from Sparta and come to Pylos for safety and freedom (4.3.1). Best (1969: 23–4) argues well for Demosthenes' friendly Messenian relations and original intentions.
53 Since this is a siege situation rather than a pitched battle it is not of direct concern for our focus on combined arms and so will not be dealt with in detail. The Spartans launched an attack both from land and sea with an experienced hoplite force against the fortified position held by Demosthenes' small band of light infantry and marines. Even the heroic exertions of Brasidas in leading the naval assault on the beach were not enough to dislodge Demosthenes' force and the Spartans were forced to retreat in disorder after a counterattack by the Athenian navy.
54 Thucydides 4.31.1–4. On the Athenian troops and the various problems with Thucydides' account see in particular Wilson (1979: 104–5); Lazenby (2004: 76–7).
55 Best (1969: 21).
56 Thucydides (4.30.2) states that the fire was started accidentally although indicating the more probable event, that Demosthenes must have learned from the loss of so many hoplites in the fire started by the Aetolians at Aegitium. Roisman (1993: 38) disagrees and argues for an accidental fire, but his arguments are all circumstantial. Thucydides mentions that Demosthenes blamed his defeat at Aegitium on the fire (4.30.1). He was too good a general not to notice the advantages for the Spartans of the cover offered by the wood and would have taken steps to remove this significant obstacle to the success

of his plan to defeat hoplites with peltasts alone. Once the smoke cleared Demosthenes could see for himself exactly how many hoplites he had to deal with. See also Woodcock (1928: 101); Stahl (1966: 151); Hunter (1973: 72). For the traditional view of Demosthenes' innovative generalship see for example Kagan (1974).
57 Thucydides, 4.30.4. The terms were relatively lenient offering gentle imprisonment while an agreement was reached to return the Spartans home.
58 Thucydides 4.32.2 states that the light infantry were all the crews of 70 triremes apart from the bottom set of rowers (around 9,000 sailors), 800 archers, 800 javelin men, an unspecified number of Messenian reinforcements and those around Pylos who were not required to garrison the fort, probably around 12,000–15,000 men.
59 Roisman (1993: 40).
60 Roisman (1993: 41).
61 Thucydides, 4.28.5. They may have laughed at Cleon's overconfidence rather than the composition of the army but the fact that they did not think Cleon would succeed with such an army is clear.
62 Tritle (2010: 95). On Brasidas' generalship see in particular Wylie (1992a).
63 Thucydides 5.6–11. The Athenians held the advantage in hoplites and the Athenian general Cleon tried to use that to defeat Brasidas, besieging the city. Brasidas refused Cleon's offer of battle in front of the city. Cleon despaired deciding to withdraw to await expected reinforcements. In marching off Cleon's unprotected right flank passed close to the city. Brasidas took his opportunity and charged out of the city with some of his hoplites. They fell upon the Athenians in disorder with devastating effect. The Athenian left wing fled when attacked by the rest of Brasidas' army that had sallied out of a different gate. Cleon fled and was cut down by the chasing peltasts. Some Athenian hoplites made a stand on a hill until they were overcome by the volume of missiles of Brasidas' peltasts and they too fled. The approaching Athenian reinforcements, led by the historian Thucydides, did not even bother to try to rectify the situation, to the famous historian's personal cost.
64 See Habicht (1970).
65 He placed his youngest hoplites in the front ranks since they were more able to run out and engage the enemy's light infantry. Brasidas stood in the rear line with 300 picked men ready to fight a way through for this slow-moving square. The Illyrians occupied the valley ahead of Brasidas expecting to catch him in the defiles but Brasidas sent 300 picked men to capture the first hill and he successfully led his army after them.
66 Best (1969: 30).
67 The many instances of infantry squares fending off cavalry in the eighteenth and nineteenth centuries show the effectiveness of this tactic. In fact, the German cavalry regiment that successfully charged and broke three French infantry squares at Waterloo was so praised because it was such a rare achievement.
68 Xenophon, *Anabasis* 3.2.36. See Lee (2007). There are numerous other examples of this in the *Anabasis* (for example 3.3.6, 3.4.19). In fact, the Greek mercenaries decided that the square was an inappropriate formation for crossing bridges or narrow gorges. Therefore, they created a more flexible tactical formation where they detailed 600 men in companies of 100 to hold back and then fill the square again once over or through the difficult passage (3.4.19–23). On this spontaneous reorganisation see Aupperle (1996).
69 Lendon (2010: 307) notes that Pagondas' battle plan rested on the depth of the Theban phalanx at 25 ranks.
70 "It is not beyond the bounds of possibility and more probable that the *hipparch* (cavalry commander) of the squadrons on the right, finding his men unengaged because of the topography, used his initiative to counter the threatening development on the Boiotian left by leading the cavalry upstream to a fordable point and behind the hill to make his surprise attack". Hutchinson (2006: 49).
71 For the best and most recent secondary discussions of the campaign see in particular Roisman (1993); Hutchinson (2006); Fields (2008); Champion (2010); Brice (2013).

72 Plutarch's account of the Athenian attack on Sicily may have been influenced by Sicilian historians: Pearson (1987).
73 For Thucydides' use of the Sicilian sources see Bosworth (1992).
74 For Thucydides' battle descriptions with particular reference to Epipolae, see in particular Paul (1987).
75 Gelon was cavalry commander under Hippocrates (Herodotus 7.154). It was Gelon's handling of the aristocratic cavalry at Gela that subdued the mob and allowed him to become tyrant: Champion (2010). Pindar (*Nemean Odes* 9.39.4) records the bravery of a member of the Gelan cavalry in battle against Syracuse. Before the battle of Himera the Syracusan cavalry captured a number of Carthaginian prisoners out foraging gaining complete control of the area (Diodorus 11.21.2).
76 At the battle of Himera it was the Syracusan hoplites who routed the Carthaginian infantry (Diodorus 11.22.3).
77 Polyaenus 5.6. Champion (2010: 30–1).
78 Champion (2010: 30). See also Dunbabin (1948).
79 Polybius (6.52) criticises the later Carthaginian armies for neglecting citizen infantry forces in favour of mercenaries to the detrimental effect of their reliability in battle, though they pay attention to their native cavalry forces also supplemented by mercenaries. Diodorus 11.20 and Herodotus 7.165 both state that the Carthaginians brought an army of 300,000 against Gelon and Syracuse. Green (2006: 46–7, 74) in his commentary to Diodorus suggests that a misinterpretation of numerical representation led to Greek historians overestimating troop totals by a factor of ten, so here 300,000 should be 30,000, a much more likely number for a ship-borne invasion force. Nonetheless, it is clear that the Carthaginian army usually fielded a combined arms army though still reliant on a central heavy infantry force, but not yet hoplites. There is not space in this volume to address the history of combined arms warfare in states outside of Greece.
80 Mercenaries: Diodorus 11.72. Troop totals: Diodorus 11.21.
81 Diodorus 11.1.
82 Herodotus 7.157–162. Athens would not give up command of the navy and Sparta would not relinquish the army. Had either done so our discussion of Greek military history likely would not be so focused on the hoplite phalanx alone. The Greeks won the war with Persia anyway but Gelon's forces and skilled generalship would have perhaps made the victory easier and even if not would have at least introduced true combined arms into Greek warfare a century earlier.
83 The Greeks on hearing news of the victory at Himera were encouraged to continue their resistance against Xerxes' forces in Greece (Diodorus 11.23), but did not take any tactical lessons from it.
84 Plutarch *Timoleon* 23.
85 Champion (2010: 37).
86 Bugh (1986) (cf. 1988: 12 n. 44) argues that these 30 horsemen were heralds to induce other Sicilian cities to join Athens and not as cavalry.
87 Gomme et al. (1970: 257) state that it is noteworthy that Nicias does not intend to transport cavalry and suggest that "it was simply not practicable to transport enough cavalry with their horses to make much difference". Hornblower (1991–2008: 3.357 (6.21.1)) merely remarks that "[i]t is remarkable that Nicias does not actually ask for a large cavalry force, merely for a large infantry force to cope with the cavalry superiority of the enemy".
88 Van Wees 2005: 59.
89 The site was enclosed by houses, trees, and a marsh on one side and by cliffs on the other (6.66.1).
90 See Hornblower (1991–2008: 3.1061–6) for a good discussion of the troop totals of the Athenian army, including an estimate of battle casualties.
91 As Hornblower (1991–2008: 3.527 (6.98.1)) emphasises, even after the reinforcements the Athenian cavalry was still only half the size of the Syracusan force. Diodorus

13.44.1–2 states that 600 cavalry also arrived from Campania, thus making both sides virtually equal in cavalry: see Frederiksen (1968).
92 If this statement is true of the large number of light infantry it explains why Demosthenes did not await the Thracian peltasts as he already had a substantial force of light infantry to bring along.
93 Thucydides (7.44.1) states that this was the only night battle in the war. He is incorrect, but this is the only instance of such a full-scale attack being conducted at night. Its disastrous result for the Athenians is probably the reason for his emphatic statement. See Pritchett (1985: 160–71) for an analysis and list of other Greek night attacks.
94 Xenophon (*On the Cavalry Commander* 4.13–14) stated that it is always preferable to attack the enemy's weak point no matter how hard the task, rather than more dangerously opposing a stronger force.
95 Hutchinson (2006: 153). On the benefits of such an attack launched with only light infantry see above.
96 Roisman (1993: 63).
97 This is similar to the disaster suffered by the Roman legions at Carrhae where the heavy infantry were exposed by repeated attacks of light and heavy cavalry (Cassius Dio 40.20; Plutarch, *Crassus* 23).
98 See Champion (2010). In fact, the political motives and differences between the cavalry and hoplite classes led to great turmoil in Syracuse in particular and the establishment of Dionysius' tyranny.
99 In my view this may be because of the tyrant Dionysius' overreliance on mercenaries, most of whom must have been hoplites and light infantry. The wealth of cavalrymen proved problematic politically and mercenary hoplites were in the most plentiful supply after the Peloponnesian War, hence the famous Ten Thousand signing on to fight for Cyrus the Younger in Asia Minor. It was easier and safer for Dionysius to field armies of hoplites and light infantry than attempt to field substantial forces of cavalry alongside them, let alone allow the cavalry any tactical, and therefore somewhat political, independance in battle. Likewise, the Carthaginians led primarily mercenary armies into Sicily that fielded hoplites to combat the native Greeks' way of war and reduced their cavalry forces lest the Carthaginian citizen population be denuded unnecessarily in wars away from home. The treaty agreed between Dionysius and the Carthaginian general Himilco at the siege of Syracuse in 397 demonstrates the Carthaginian reluctance to commit too many citizen cavalry or officers to the Sicilian Wars. There Himilco secretly agreed to abandon his entire mercenary army on condition that he and his Carthaginian citizen forces could return home safely (Diodorus 14.1–4).
100 Xenophon *Hellenika* 2.4.31.
101 Sekunda (2014a: 49–50). His argument is based on the need for a permanent garrison to feature a mix of full Spartan citizens and perioikoi (50) "to ensure that should some disaster overtake the garrison, as had happened at Sphakteria, the losses would not fall disproportionately on any one district of the city of Sparta". This is certainly true but it does not explain why the Spartans also reorganised their army to give a regimented position of prominence to cavalry alongside hoplites. In my view the successes of Gylippus at Syracuse in 413–411 was the catalyst for this revolutionary change to combined arms organisation. Gylippus openly acknowledged after his initial defeat that it was his misuse of cavalry that brought about the loss. In all his subsequent engagements he gave the excellent Syracusan cavalry free reign to turn the flanks and rear of the Athenian phalanx with the result that the Athenians refused to offer battle lest they be exposed to the cavalry. The news of this tactic must have spread to Sparta not least on Gylippus' return home, and the crucial military lessons likely would not have gone unheeded.

102 Sekunda (2014a: 53–4).
103 So the *mora* of Praxitas stationed at Sicyon had a mora of cavalry led by Pasimachos (Xenophon *Hellenika* 4.4.10), and the Spartan mora defeated at Lechaeum had a mora of cavalry attached, whose absence and improper handling prompted Iphicrates' famous peltast victory as discussed below (Xenophon *Hellenika* 4.5.12).
104 Sekunda (2014a: 56–7).
105 Diodorus 13.109.3.
106 Tritle (2010: 81).
107 It may have been the Dekelean War as Sekunda argues, and it may indeed have been Gylippus' successes at Syracuse. It may have been both together, since they happened around the same time, that finally prompted the Spartans to change.

5 The Corinthian War and Iphicrates

Light infantry integration

The defeat at Syracuse put the Athenians on the back foot, and for the last few years of the Peloponnesian War the significant battles were almost all naval and so not of concern here. It is possible, however, that in the last few years of the war Athens had developed its own force of peltasts so that it did not have to rely on mercenaries.[1] The Athenians, and other Greeks, had learned their lesson that an army had to contain some troops other than hoplites in order to win, and the reliance was on light infantry, who were now plentiful in the Athenian empire and lower classes of Greek poleis.

Needing other troops besides hoplites was especially true on terrain that was disadvantageous to the hoplite phalanx, in particular the wide-open plains of Sicily, as discussed earlier, Asia Minor, and Thessaly. During the Spartan hegemony the Ten Thousand mercenaries of Xenophon and the Spartan army of Agesilaus both were forced to create mixed armies when fighting campaigns in Asia. This need for non-hoplite troops contributed to the growing importance of mercenaries or foreign allied troops in fourth-century armies.[2] The Corinthian War challenged the traditional Greek mindset of battle based on the hoplite phalanx with a new wave of innovations. The prime mover was Iphicrates, who won renown as a commander of light infantry.[3]

Sources

There are few detailed, military-focused accounts of the early fourth century. Most information comes from the various works of Xenophon. His continuance of the historical narrative of Thucydides in the *Hellenika* is by far the fullest source of the history of this period. His account of his own trials in the expedition of Cyrus as detailed in the *Anabasis* provides the earliest first-hand account of a military expedition. His technical treatises, *On Horsemanship* and *On the Cavalry Commander*, provide a number of details about the training and tactics of Greek cavalry. Since there is so little other detailed evidence available for this period specifically concerned with military matters it is necessary to take the evidence of Xenophon on face value despite the associated problems of historiography.[4]

Diodorus also provides an account of the early fourth century and occasionally adds information not in Xenophon, for example concerning Iphicrates' reform of peltasts as discussed next.[5] The fragmentary *Hellenika Oxyrhyncia* also covers this period. The only battle of concern here that it discusses is Sardis in 395.[6]

Infantry

Infantry in Greece remained a combination of hoplites and light infantry ranging from slingers and archers to peltasts and javelin men. But what is crucial after the Peloponnesian War is the integration of light infantry into almost every battle plan and generals seeking victory outside of the clash of hoplites in the phalanx.

At the battle of Munychia in 403, Thrasybulus opposed a hoplite army of Athenian oligarchs and Spartans with a small number of working class Athenian hoplites and a mass of light infantry.[7] Thrasybulus took position on the high ground and forced the enemy phalanx to attack uphill along a small road where they were forced to mass 50 deep. He had the missile troops harass the Spartans over the heads of the Athenian hoplites in front. The missiles caused great casualties among the extended column of the Spartan phalanx and the downhill attack of Thrasybulus' hoplites forced the Spartans into retreat. This tactic of light infantry firing over hoplites and using the advantages of the slope of the hill was new to a Greek battlefield and won the battle for Thrasybulus.[8] The Spartan army fielded few light infantry and suffered greatly as a result.

It is important to note that Thrasybulus' army still relied on its hoplites to form the first line of defence in the battle, however, his tactical flexibility demonstrates that the Greeks were moving away from hoplite phalanx only warfare to one that equally included light infantry. A few days earlier Thrasybulus' small force of 700 men attacked the enemy camp at night catching them asleep and killing many of them (Xenophon, *Hellenika* 2.4.5–7). This is reminiscent of Demosthenes' tactic at Idomene, as discussed previously. Finally, the process of using different troops in combination, while also attempting innovative tactics, was taking root.

Outside of Greece light infantry were vital to the success of an army. Xenophon in his account of the march of the Ten Thousand often mentions light infantry, from slingers through to Thracian peltasts armed with shield and spear.[9] At the outset of the expedition, the various Greek mercenary commanders brought light infantry along with hoplites.[10] The total light infantry of Greek mercenaries was around 2,000 according to Xenophon.[11] These light infantry troops were removed from the Greek hoplites by Cyrus to fight among the similar Persian troops at Cunaxa.[12] On other occasions on the retreat of the Greeks the light infantry fought as one unit rather than commanded by the individual Greek commanders.[13] Clearly the Greeks knew of the tactical importance of light infantry in battle in combination with hoplites.

Yet the original force of light infantry among the Greek mercenaries was not sufficient for their tactical purposes, especially after the defection of the rest of Cyrus' army. Xenophon argued to his fellow commanders that it was a military necessity to furnish a reliable force of cavalry and light infantry, especially slingers, in order to combat the large numbers of Persian missile troops and cavalry.[14] The Greek mercenaries employed 200 Rhodians from the army as slingers, suggesting that these men originally fought as hoplites.[15] It is clear that Xenophon did not believe that an army of only hoplites would make it through Asia Minor safely.[16]

By 401 any force of hoplites was expected to be accompanied by light infantry to protect its flanks on the march and to serve as scouts and attendants. As Best concludes in his review of peltasts among the Ten Thousand, "at the end of the fifth century BC the peltasts were certainly integrated completely as a special fighting body in the Greek armies".[17] The lessons of Demosthenes and Brasidas had taken root and the days of hoplite-only Greek armies had passed.

During the Corinthian War in 378 Chabrias, the Athenian peltast commander, ordered his troops to kneel and await the attack of Agesilaus' hoplites with their spears.[18] Agesilaus, the Spartan general, was so taken aback by the confidence of Chabrias' men that he did not even attempt an attack despite leading Spartan hoplites against light infantry. Seeking to explain this surprising hesitancy of hoplites against peltasts, Best has argued that at this battle Chabrias gave the order to kneel to his hoplite force leaving the peltasts to act as missile troops in support.[19] Parke argued that this is evidence for the implementation of peltasts changing function to act as spear-armed infantry, but this is not certain.[20] Peltasts could have knelt with their javelins until the Spartans came into throwing range and then resumed usual light infantry tactics. This incident is more famous for demonstrating the crumbling aura of Spartan invincibility than for the increased use of peltasts in Greek warfare.[21] It does show that Greek light infantry was well trained in the early fourth century and was perhaps even viewed as equal to hoplites.

The first Greek general to really make full use of light infantry in battle was an Athenian mercenary commander Iphicrates. Iphicrates' army of light infantry is now famous for revolutionising Greek warfare, particularly by defeating a regiment of Spartan hoplites at Lechaeum. Of all the generals included in Polyaenus' *Stratagems*, a work that collects over 900 notable stratagems employed in battle, on campaign, or in politics, Iphicrates receives the most attention. Polyaenus includes no fewer than 63 mentions of stratagems of Iphicrates while of other Greek generals Agesilaus has the next most with 33 (tied with Julius Caesar, the Roman general with the most stratagems included). Alexander the Great receives 32 and Philip II of Macedon only 22. Dionysius of Syracuse is also mentioned 22 times and Antigonus Monophthalmus 21 times. Timotheus receives 17 mentions, and Epaminondas and Chabrias get 15 mentions. A general as great as Hannibal receives only ten mentions, alongside Cyrus the Great of Persia. Eumenes of Cardia, one of the most successful generals in the Hellenistic period, only receives five mentions, and the great Pyrrhus of Epirus only three.

Clearly to the Greeks and Romans Iphicrates was head and shoulders above every other general (almost twice as many mentions) when it came to innovative generalship. Yet our extant histories preserve very few accounts of his battles and campaigns and we are left with a very scant record of his career. Nevertheless, it is clear that Iphicrates was perhaps the foremost innovator of the period in terms of utilising combined arms on a Greek battlefield by integrating light infantry very successfully into his battle tactics.

The Corinthian War and Iphicrates   135

In the Corinthian War under Iphicrates, and his Athenian contemporary Chabrias, light infantry peltasts were armed and used in the same way as before. The only difference is that they were no longer solely from Thrace or Thessaly and could come from any Greek city.[22] Peltasts quickly became the main form of light infantry in an army because of their hybrid nature, as missile infantry who could use their shield and slight armour to fight at close quarters, and consequent usefulness.

The term peltast is important to understand here. In Greek accounts the term usually refers to any light infantry whatever their defensive armament.[23] Literally the term refers to soldiers armed with the small shield, the pelte. When a unit was specifically armed the exact weapon is described, especially archers, and these are usually given their national origin such as Cretan archers and Rhodian slingers, or the Athenian archers we saw fighting at Plataea. So peltasts were usually armed with a shield and therefore used a missile weapon that could be thrown with one hand. Usually these were javelins, but they could have thrown rocks and other missiles also.

But more importantly, the shield allowed the peltast to fight in hand-to-hand combat. Often peltasts were armed with a short sword as a secondary reserve weapon to aid in close combat. Some peltasts may even have been armed with a thrusting spear.[24] This ability to fight at close quarters gave peltasts a great advantage over strictly missile light infantry. Most often they would fight against other light infantry and so their sword and shield were adequate armaments. When fighting with hoplites, importantly only when they were not in a phalanx formation, the peltasts would benefit from a thrusting spear as opposed to a sword to overcome the hoplites' greater armour and weaponry. Usually this was likely in ambushes, chasing routing hoplites, or in a siege.[25]

Nonetheless, peltasts were usually used as missile throwing light infantry when they appear in Greek history before 370. This is an important distinction since in other cultures and in later history light infantry was not always missile troops. An armed mob of peasants, slaves, or sailors would be classed militarily as light infantry but need not throw weapons and could fight with whatever they could find from farming implements such as scythes and pitchforks to axes, knives and spears. However, in Greece light infantry in the age of the hoplite was most often missile troops of some form or another. This is likely because non-missile light infantry had no hope of achieving anything in battle fighting at close quarters with a heavily armed hoplite in a phalanx. As a result, the only way light troops were useful was in throwing missiles from a distance. Nevertheless, the hybrid nature of peltasts as both missile and close combat light infantry meant that they were the most tactically flexible and useful to commanders in battle.

We have already seen a number of examples of light infantry defeating hoplites, most notably at Sphacteria under Demosthenes. Iphicrates' famous routing of the Spartan mora of 600 hoplites with only peltasts at Lechaeum in 390 again demonstrated the vulnerability of hoplites to mobile light infantry, despite the usual Spartan practice of having the youngest hoplites give chase and even after the arrival of a unit of Spartan cavalry.[26] It is this victory more than any other that alerted the Greeks to the restrictions of hoplite-based warfare and the advantages of light infantry largely because the force defeated was of elite Spartan hoplites. Iphicrates' peltasts killed 250 hoplites out of 600 and proved to be more successful in terms of casualties inflicted over time than the 10,000 light infantry who overcame the Spartans at Sphacteria, as discussed previously.

The battle of Lechaeum is often seen as a turning point in Greek military history. It was the first time that an elite Spartan regiment of hoplites was routed (indeed almost annihilated) by a force of light infantry. It demonstrates well the vulnerabilities of a heavy infantry phalanx when isolated and unsupported by other units. Though the main fighting was not strictly a battle between two combined arms forces, the two armies were combined arms in nature and it does reveal crucial aspects of the theory of combined arms.

Iphicrates' force of peltasts, crucially supported at a distance by a unit of hoplites which gave them the security to operate, had free reign to use hit-and-run tactics on the slower Spartan hoplites. The Spartan force consisting of cavalry and hoplites had escorted troops a distance away from Corinth so they could go home to celebrate a festival. The commander Bias decided to turn back to the city when the escort was no longer needed but crucially decided to let the cavalry travel further with the festival goers. This meant that when the Spartan hoplites got back to Corinth they were unsupported. This tactical error by Bias is what allowed Iphicrates to launch the attack with his peltasts. The presence of cavalry may have caused Iphicrates to reconsider since cavalry hold the advantage in speed, range, and close combat abilities over light infantry.

Iphicrates' peltasts attacked down a hill against the unprotected right side of the Spartan phalanx. The heavier armoured Spartan hoplites despite sending out the youngest hoplites to oppose the enemy were unable to get to hand-to-hand combat with the light infantry and thus could not inflict a single casualty. This shows the main strength of any heavy infantry force is in melee combat, but also their biggest weakness is a lack of manoeuvrability. On the other hand, it demonstrates the advantages in speed and range of attack of light infantry, but their disadvantages in close combat. Since Iphicrates' peltasts could escape from the hoplites before they came to close-quarter fighting the hoplites could do no damage. The security offered by the supporting hoplites allowed the peltasts greater freedom to run in close and discharge their missiles knowing that if they did happen to get caught by the Spartan hoplites their own heavy infantry would come and extricate them from the hand-to-hand melee fighting.

When fighting on their own and able to continue to fight at a distance light infantry, or any missile unit, usually always has the upper hand over slower heavy infantry. Once the delayed Spartan cavalry arrived the Spartans expected that the advantage would switch to them. Normally cavalry has the upper hand over light infantry on account of its greater mobility, thus neutralising the main advantage of light infantry. Iphicrates' men were hesitant at the arrival of the horsemen fearing that they might be chased down by the greater speed of the cavalry and at the least that the horsemen would prevent their hit-and-run tactics. However, in this instance the Spartan cavalry did not charge at Iphicrates' peltasts but hugged the flanks of the slow Spartan phalanx even during a counterattack. For whatever reason the Spartan cavalry refused to attack the light infantry and thus became just as exposed to the peltasts' javelins as the hoplites.[27] They even proved incapable of defending the hoplites as they retreated from the onslaught of the peltasts. It was this inaction by the cavalry that doomed the Spartan hoplites not any innovative generalship of Iphicrates in harassing the Spartans with missile troops. That had been a tactic long before, as discussed previously and as best exemplified by Demosthenes at Sphacteria.

This is perhaps the most crucial tactical message taken from Lechaeum. With the cavalry the Spartan army became a combined arms force fielding heavy infantry and cavalry, just as Iphicrates' force was combined arms in fielding light and heavy infantry together. Iphicrates' troops fought correctly in combined arms style with the heavy infantry providing a base of operations for the hit-and-run tactics of the peltasts. The Spartans, however, in no way utilised combined arms when the cavalry refused to attack or even screen a withdrawal. There was no benefit to the Spartans of having cavalry.

Perhaps this more than any other battle in Greek history shows why it took so long to integrate cavalry as an offensive force into Greek armies. The Spartan cavalry were used to supporting the flanks of a hoplite phalanx in battle and then attacking only when pursuing the retreating enemy. So much so that when the tactical situation demanded that they attack in front of the phalanx against an enemy who were far from defeated they were unwilling to do so. This is perhaps why Xenophon is so critical of Spartan cavalry in general.[28] Spartan cavalry may have been always and only used to pursue fleeing troops rather than any of the other tactical uses of light cavalry as screens, scouts, or to ward off light infantry. It was the lack of cavalry action and the initial error of the Spartan commander to return without cavalry support that condemned the Spartan hoplites to destruction not any innovation by Iphicrates, but the victory by Iphicrates' peltasts nevertheless enhanced their general's great reputation.

Iphicrates' later success against the Spartan general Anaxibios outside Abydos in the plain of Cremaste was similarly effective at destroying a large number of soldiers in a hoplite force using light infantry in a surprise attack.[29] Iphicrates laid an ambush in the mountains and attacked the Spartan column from the rear with his 1,200 peltasts. Anaxibios thought Iphicrates had left the area and so was marching in casual formation. Anaxibios and 12 Spartans fought to the death once they realised the rest of the army was too spread out to aid them and the rest of the rearguard of hoplites was cut down in flight along with many from the centre and vanguard of the column.

So Iphicrates at Lechaeum did not do anything new or innovative, he simply made the most of the opportunity presented to him by the tactical errors of the Spartan force. But it is clear that by the Corinthian War it was normal for armies to support the flanks of the hoplite phalanx with units of cavalry or light infantry or both.[30]

As Greek armies learned to protect the flanks of the phalanx with light infantry and cavalry and began to attempt combined arms tactics in battle other forms of infantry developed. The most important are the *hamippoi*. As their name suggests these were infantry who were mobile enough to run alongside cavalry in order to maintain a link to the slower moving heavy infantry phalanx and to support the cavalry when fighting a battle or skirmish. They ran holding onto the tails of the horses or clothes of the rider.³¹ Their use in battle is not well documented in Greek history. They first appear in the army of Gelon of Syracuse in the early fifth century but were likely only in use outside of Greece proper where cavalry was always fielded in greater numbers and with more tactical flexibility and expectations.³² But they start to appear more frequently towards the end of the Peloponnesian War when armies start to integrate light infantry and cavalry regularly.³³

There are no details as to what their armament may have been. They cannot have worn much if any armour as they had to run at speed alongside horses. But they were expected to be able to hold their own in close combat engagements. Though Greek cavalry at this time was light cavalry and normally armed with javelins as missile troops, they could fight at close quarters if necessary. Similarly, the hamippoi were likely armed with javelins like most Greek light infantry but probably also had small swords or clubs to engage in hand-to-hand combat where necessary.

Thessalian light infantry were likely peltasts armed with spears and armour intended to fight in close combat. Sprawski has shown that coinage and other imagery often depicts Thessalian infantry as armed with shields and helmets.³⁴ They also fielded large numbers of traditional Greek light infantry as missile troops, as attested in the extant sources.³⁵ Thessaly was most proud of its cavalry, which was likely the first in Greece to practice heavy cavalry charges in battle. This meant that Thessalian infantry was accustomed to keeping up with the charging horses. They cannot have been armed as hoplites. "A preference for cavalry and peltasts may have worked in the Thessalians' clashes with their neighbours, where this type of fighting was common".³⁶ But later in fighting against the other Greek poleis they had to field hoplites.

It seems the tyrant Jason of Pherae was the first to field large numbers of Thessalian hoplites, and Sprawski suggests that was because he equipped soldiers with his new invention of the *hemithorakion* or half breastplate allowing for a cheaper hoplite panoply.³⁷ According to Sprawski "there may have been two types of light infantry in Thessaly. One type was armed only with javelins and swords; the other type was also armed with a light, round shield", and though he does not specify it here the shield was intended to help in close combat.³⁸

The Sciritae regiment of the Spartan army, if Sekunda is right that they became *hamippoi* after 318, regularly fought in close combat engagements. Diodorus states that the Sciritae was sent to help sections of the hoplite phalanx that were in distress and being composed of select men often turned the battle favourably.³⁹ Xenophon states that guard duty was usually done by the Sciritae, as well as scouting ahead, and that patrols usually carried their spears.⁴⁰ This suggests that the Sciritae, and in my view other *hamippoi* units, were armed with weapons intended for close combat use not missile weapons like javelins. The Macedonian *hamippoi*, discussed in the relevant chapter, always fought in hand-to-hand

The Corinthian War and Iphicrates 139

combat since the Macedonian cavalry was heavy not light and so always engaged in close combat warfare.[41] These troops were lightly armoured not lightly armed, and that is a crucial difference. Though wearing little armour they were elite troops able to fight in a melee and still move rapidly alongside horses.

So by the end of the Peloponnesian War peltasts were missile infantry or close combat light infantry or a hybrid of the two. They also appeared regularly on the Greek battlefield as mercenaries or national levies and began to be used tactically to defend or attack the weaknesses of the hoplite phalanx, the main principle of combined arms warfare. This is the reason that the later Hellenistic tactical manuals describe peltasts as between heavy and light infantry.[42] They could function as either but to a lesser degree in each case.

A revolution in peltast armaments arrived in the 370s. Iphicrates is credited by Diodorus and Nepos with reorganising the equipment of his professional mercenaries.[43] According to these sources his troops were reequipped with the smaller *pelte* instead of the large Greek *aspis*, thus gaining the name peltasts. Their spears were made half as long again or even double the length of the hoplite *dory*. Their swords were also doubled in length. They were given light but sturdy footwear, now termed *Iphicratids*, and linen armour. Diodorus dates these reforms to 374 during Iphicrates' time serving as mercenary general in the Persian invasion of Egypt.

The problem with this information is that it seems to describe a reform of hoplite equipment. This is possibly because of the confusion of Diodorus' and Nepos' source that the reforms involved hoplites. However, none of the equipment is necessarily new to Thracian peltasts, including the long thrusting spear.[44] Most interesting is the omission of the javelin as necessary equipment. All of Iphicrates' subsequent battles suggest that his peltasts were equipped with javelins. In fact, no historical information suggests any change in use or equipment of peltasts in battle. These reforms may just be a fabrication of Diodorus' source to explain the successes of peltasts against hoplites, as Best suggests.[45] However, despite Xenophon (and Polyaenus) ignoring these reforms, Iphicrates' experience in Egypt seems logical as a place and catalyst for such changes as suggested by Diodorus.

I need not go into too much detail here as I agree on most things with Sekunda's recent discussion. But these reforms do have a significant impact on the development of combined arms in Greek warfare. Iphicrates likely equipped his mercenary peltasts with these new armaments, not hoplites. He sought to make his troops more effective against the traditional Egyptian heavy infantry armed with long spears and shields that covered them down to their ankles. It was too expensive to use traditional hoplite arms and so Iphicrates adapted what he had seen elsewhere. Long spears or pikes were used by certain tribes well before Iphicrates, and by the Egyptians themselves, and the pelte shield had been used by peltasts for decades. The longer sword is unclear, but as Anderson suggested this was likely a longer version of the small Spartan style sword, not a doubling of the long Greek one.[46] It is likely that elements of the Persian army had longer swords than the Greeks did, since some Celtic tribes had very long swords, and Iphicrates perhaps just borrowed these for his Greek peltasts.

Iphicrates did not invent any new weapons or armaments; he simply altered the armament of Greek mercenary peltasts by borrowing elements from other units in the Persian army. We know nothing of how, when, and with what success Iphicrates employed these newly armed peltasts. After his withdrawal from Egypt he served as admiral for the Athenians and likely did not use these peltasts on board ships. Because of his lack of major independent command in Greece he was not able to implement his innovations on any large scale, or at least our sources are silent on the subject. Xenophon, our best source for Greek warfare in the 370s and 360s, mentions nothing of Iphicrates' reforms. This is certainly because Iphicrates' campaign in Egypt was out of the scope of his concern in writing the *Hellenika* about Greece only, and the reforms had no impact on affairs in Greece. As problematic as it is to make an argument from silence, Xenophon's silence on any changes to peltast armament anywhere at any time suggests that widescale changes following Iphicrates' reforms did not occur, or at the very least did not occur in enough places to impact the history he describes.

Sekunda, on the contrary, argues that all mentions of peltasts in Greek warfare after Iphicrates' reforms are to Iphicratean style peltasts and that every Greek state retrained their peltasts accordingly.[47] By that he means peltasts armed with long spears. If this is the case this is a huge upheaval in Greek military science and a crucial event that has seemingly escaped mention in our sources. I agree that one of the examples he provides shows peltasts fighting against hoplites, but that does not mean they had to be armed with a long spear. As I argue earlier, peltasts as light infantry could fight in hand-to-hand combat if necessary even before Iphicrates' reforms, just as mediaeval light infantry did. In fact, that is likely the reason peltasts had a shield anyway. Other strictly missile infantry did not have a shield or need one. They always stayed well out of the way of close combat.

At the battle of Kromnos, discussed by Sekunda as his main example,[48] the peltasts are running ahead of the Spartan king, who is leading the main force, when they attack an Arcadian hoplite unit outside of a stockade. But the details do not say how they attacked this unit. In my view it is likely that the peltasts found the Arcadian hoplites on the march, and thus out of formation, and so were trying to attack the exposed hoplites. Perhaps they could attack their exposed right side just as Iphicrates' normal peltasts at Lechaeum, as discussed previously. Xenophon does not say they attacked the hoplites head-on. Moreover, Xenophon goes on to state that the cavalry endeavoured to join in the attack of the peltasts, but the Arcadians did not give way and formed into a compact formation and their counterattack forced the peltasts and cavalry backwards. Even after Archidamus brought up the rest of the Spartan forces the Arcadian hoplites forced the Spartans to withdraw even wounding Archidamus in the process. As Sprawski has shown in the same volume,[49] Xenophon always uses the term peltast to refer to light infantry, so he is likely doing so here also. Just because the peltasts attacked hoplites, does not meant they had to be armed with long spears. In fact, being armed with longer spears would make it harder to run at speed. These peltasts at Kromnos were certainly armed in traditional manner as javelin men with a shield enabling close combat or ranged fighting.

Sekunda uses the evidence from the Hellenistic tactical manuals to argue that peltasts after Iphicrates always fought with long spears.[50] These manuals describe peltasts as between heavy infantry and missile light infantry because their shield is smaller and lighter and their spear shorter. The Macedonian pike should be no less than 8 cubits (12 feet) according to Aelian, and Sekunda takes this to mean that the Iphicratean peltasts spear was 8 cubits. But Aelian is talking about sarissas, the unit of all phalanx infantry after the Macedonian dominance of Philip II and Alexander the Great. Indeed, the peltasts referred to by the tactical authors have more in common with the hypaspists of Alexander than the light infantry peltasts of the early fourth century. The Antigonid peltasts, used by Sekunda as evidence of Iphicratean peltasts, could fight alongside the sarissa phalanx and were elite troops used for special actions. This is exactly the description of Alexander's hypaspists who were far from Iphicratean peltasts and closer to Greek hoplites in armament though crucially not armour. I do not see the direct connection of Iphicrates' reforms to the description of peltasts in the Hellenistic manuals and armies. The military evolution in the third and second centuries was more dependent on Alexander than Iphicrates and thus more likely to represent hypaspists than Iphicratean peltasts who are otherwise unattested in Greek warfare.

Sekunda uses as evidence of a large-scale training regime throughout Greece a fragment of the tactician Hermolytos mentioned in Eustathius recounting four generals teaching a closed shield formation (*synaspismos*).[51] Sekunda's argument rests on the last of these four generals, a certain Charidemus, being a mercenary under Iphicrates' command. This does not prove the formation was for peltasts armed with long spears since the other generals are Lycurgus, Lysander, and Epaminondas who all led hoplites not peltasts. Moreover, the Arcadians and Macedonians taught by Charidemus are famous for rarely if ever fielding their own forces of hoplites, and so of all Greeks their troops would be the ones in need of training even in regular hoplite drill such as the synaspismos manoeuvre.

In my view nothing proves that Iphicrates' reform of his peltasts in Egypt ever led to all Greek peltasts adopting the longer spear, and there is very little evidence that any polis made use of this change except perhaps for Macedon and the famous sarissa. Sekunda and Matthew are likely right that Iphicrates' time in Macedon and Thrace prompted Philip II or an earlier Macedonian king to utilise the sarissa in the phalanx not the hoplite panoply.[52] However, it cannot have been when he was there before his activities in Egypt in 373, as Matthew suggests. Sekunda is likely right that Iphicrates was in Macedon again in 368 and that this is when he was heavily involved in Macedonian royal politics and played host of the future king Philip II.

Iphicrates may not have had much impact directly on contemporary Greek warfare or even made any revolutionary changes in inventing new equipment or employing new tactics. Nevertheless, his many achievements with mercenary peltasts against hoplites certainly furthered the development of combined arms and showed that the era of hoplite only combat was drawing to a close. However, apart from Iphicrates and to a lesser extent his contemporary and colleague Chabrias, there were not many generals who tried to experiment in using other troops instead of hoplites. He was the first general in the Greek world, after Demosthenes, to rely solely on the abilities of peltasts in battle and that is what earned him such a stellar reputation that Polyaenus recorded more of his stratagems than any other ancient commander.

Cavalry

Greek armies by the fourth century had moved away from relying solely on hoplites. Light infantry became a necessary complement to any army in Greece or abroad. However, it still remained for Greek armies to integrate cavalry units fully into their armies. Greek cavalry even in foreign climes was still a light cavalry force intended for scouting, skirmishing, and pursuit only. Heavy cavalry like that of the Macedonians and Thessalians in Greece or the Bactrians and Persians in Asia does not appear in Greek armies until the middle of the fourth century.

The Ten Thousand were forced to form a unit of cavalry to protect them on the march, but it numbered only 50 and contributed little to their successful retreat.[53] In Thrace, the Greeks joined the army of Seuthes in order to receive good pay and provisions before the arrival of winter.[54] After this the Greek light infantry and the cavalry force, now numbering 40, united with Seuthes' Thracian forces in tactical deployments.[55] In his speech arguing for the Greeks to leave Seuthes, Xenophon states that it had been a military necessity for the Greeks to join Seuthes because they had no good force of cavalry or light infantry with which to ward off or capture the enemy when opposed by large numbers of each type of soldier in an open country.[56] He goes on to say that after Seuthes' cavalry joined them they never saw a force of enemy whereas before the local horsemen and light infantry harassed their march preventing the Greeks from sending out foraging parties.[57] Clearly Xenophon realised the importance of having significant numbers of light infantry and cavalry in an army in open terrain.[58]

Best supposes that the inclusion of cavalry and light infantry in the army was the usual Greek practice. He states that Xenophon's argument "implies that contingents of cavalry and peltasts must normally have been fixed components of Greek armies (which was also the case through Asia Minor) and that in Thrace the Greeks were severely handicapped by their absence".[59] It is true that in Thrace it was a military necessity for an army to have cavalry, but his suggestion that it was normal in Greece itself is false. Best believes that the unit of cavalrymen that was formed by the Ten Thousand was sufficient to make their army able to fight in a combined arms system. He ignores the fact that the Greek mercenary army had no accompaniment of cavalry until Xenophon formed this small unit out of necessity, as discussed previously, and that a force of 50 cavalry was insufficient to really do anything on a battlefield except scout and pursue.[60] In his desire to focus on the effectiveness of the peltasts among the Ten Thousand, Best has completely ignored the lack of effective cavalry.

Roy's conclusion is correct that when the Greek force combined with the Thracian army "[i]t had now reached its highest point of structural and tactical efficiency".[61] Best believes Roy is wrong because the tactical combination of the

The Corinthian War and Iphicrates 143

Greek hoplites and peltasts on their march was excellent. However, in none of the battles he discusses does the small unit of cavalry play any significant role, and they could not do so being so few in number.

The Ten Thousand never had a large enough cavalry force to provide them with tactical efficiency. Since their march was principally through mountains this was not a huge problem, and they were able to rely on their force of light infantry. In Thrace, the flat terrain suited cavalry and Xenophon was quick to notice the tactical deficiency of the Greek army.

Greek commanders were beginning to accept the necessity of having cavalry as well as light infantry alongside the hoplites in an army regardless of terrain. Contrary to Best's assertion, significant contingents of cavalry – light, missile, and heavy – were fixed components of Greek armies only outside of Greece in open terrain that suited cavalry manoeuvres. Yet almost every Greek army by the end of the fifth century did feature at least a nominal force of cavalry. Some, such as the Spartan army discussed previously, actually formalised the inclusion of cavalry into the army. But cavalry was still composed of lightly armed horsemen acting as screens and scouts more than engaging in full tactical integration into the battle plan.

Combined arms

Combined arms in the 20 years after the Peloponnesian War developed apace. As discussed previously, the Spartans, and likely others, had introduced permanent units of cavalry to accompany even small regiments of hoplites on the march or in battle. Light infantry had always been part of Greek armies but are rarely recorded, suggesting they had little part to play in the outcome. By the time of the Athenian invasion of Syracuse light infantry, whether peltasts, slingers, or archers, were becoming integral enough to battle outcomes that their presence is described by the written sources. For the most part these units were integrated into the forces deployed but not into the tactics that determined the outcome of the conflict. However, the few examples where light infantry or cavalry did contribute significantly to the victory are numerous enough in this period to show that the use of combined arms was increasing rapidly in Greek battles.

Aside from revealing the Greek acceptance of the need for cavalry and light infantry in an army fighting in Asia, Xenophon and the Ten Thousand provide us with one important tactical innovation in the use of combined arms in battle. In a skirmish with the Kolchians, the Greeks had to cross a wide mountain ridge held by the enemy.[62] They were going to attack in the traditional hoplite phalanx until Xenophon pointed out the vulnerability of this formation to encirclement by the more numerous and lightly armed Kolchians. Instead, the Greeks divided their army into separate units which were to be tactically independent but were to come to the aid of any other unit that required assistance. In this way they could attack over a sufficiently wide front to avoid encirclement and be able to rely on their heavier armed infantry for victory. The army was divided into 80 companies of 100 hoplites and three companies of 600 peltasts and archers. In attack formation the two experienced light-armed companies formed the left and right flanks while the third was in advance of the centre of the line. When the Greeks attacked, their flanking peltasts threatened to outflank the Kolchians who withdrew men from the centre to compensate. The third light company of the Greeks at once ran forward in the centre to occupy the hill, followed by a unit of hoplites. The Kolchians saw that they had been outmanoeuvred and fled.

The formation adopted by the Greek mercenaries was unusual for Greek warfare at the time. There is no other instance of such a deliberate separation of individual hoplite units in battle separated by light infantry. Perhaps the closest is the battle of the Granicus where Alexander's sarissa phalanx crossed the river in its separate battalions loosely connected to each other.[63] However, this plan was adopted only to enable the crossing of a river at a narrow point and they did not intend to fight a battle in such a formation.[64] The tactical organisation used by the Ten Thousand here is very similar to the manipular organisation of the army of Republican Rome.[65] The success of the formation against a less well-armed mass of infantry is clear. The Romans used such a formation to defeat the sarissa phalanx of Perseus at Pydna when the terrain caused the phalanx to lose its cohesion and the Roman maniples were able to penetrate gaps that appeared in the hedge of sarissas with devastating effect.[66]

The Ten Thousand was not the only Greek army to realise the importance of cavalry and light infantry in the army. The Spartan commander in Asia Minor before Agesilaus, Derkyllidas, also incorporated cavalry and peltasts into his army. In his battle formation against Tissaphernes and Pharnabazus, he placed his peltasts and cavalry on the flanks of his hoplite phalanx.[67] This is the basic formation in a system of combined arms, using light infantry and cavalry to protect the vulnerable flanks of the phalanx, and was the standard formation of Greek armies as early as the Persian and Peloponnesian Wars, just as in the Boeotian army's disposition at Delium as discussed previously.[68]

Agesilaus, the Spartan king, in his expedition into Asia Minor quickly discovered that he could not hope to defeat the Persians in the open terrain with an army of hoplites and minimal cavalry support. He sent for levies of cavalry and light troops from the allied cities in the area in order to give himself the varied army required for his expedition.[69] Agesilaus realised that outside of Greece there was a need for the most basic use of combined arms: having cavalry, missile troops, and heavy infantry in the army. Even though he did not often deviate from his battle plan of relying on hoplites for victory, he did incorporate the other types of unit into his army.

At the battle of Paktolos in 395, Agesilaus' mixed army crossed the river and was attacked by a force of cavalry alone. Seeing that the enemy had no infantry Agesilaus ordered an attack led by the cavalry, followed by the peltasts and the youngest hoplites, who could move fastest, and followed finally by the rest of the hoplites.[70] The Persian cavalry held out against the Greek cavalry but were forced to retreat when the peltasts and hoplites came up. This is the first occasion when a Spartan army won a battle through the use and initial attack of cavalry. Even the most traditional of Greek states was forced to adapt its tactics in certain situations reminiscent of the Spartan general Gylippus using cavalry at Syracuse.

All his victories in Asia Minor were won using some form of combined arms, but when Agesilaus returned to Greece to face the threat of the Greek alliance at the battle of Coroneia he reverted to a reliance on hoplites.[71] This is despite Agesilaus' pride at the victory of his cavalry over the Thessalians, a people renowned for their horsemanship.[72] Clearly his pride was not enough to warrant integrating them into his battle plan. Xenophon is clear that both sides fielded a combined arms army at Coroneia with hoplites, light infantry, and cavalry marshalled together.[73] Nevertheless, the battle was primarily fought and decided by the two hoplite phalanxes.

The same is true of the other major engagement of the Corinthian War, the battle of Nemea.[74] Both sides fielded relatively large numbers of light infantry and cavalry,[75] but the battle was decided by the clash of hoplites in the centre. Famously in this case the two battle lines edged to their right and thus each outflanked the other and routed them. The victorious Spartan right wing wheeled to the left after its victory over its direct opponents and attacked the victorious right wing of the enemy in the flank as it returned from pursuing its defeated opposition. There is no mention in the accounts of the battle how the light infantry and cavalry were involved in the fighting only that they were present in large numbers on both sides. This is an important point that warrants emphasis.

By the early fourth century almost every Greek army now fielded all three arms together on the battlefield, with light infantry and cavalry shielding the flanks of the hoplite phalanx in the centre. But it is important to note that this does not mean the Greeks now utilised combined arms, just as the multi-faceted army of the Persians did not. It seems from every conflict in this period that the hoplite phalanxes decided the battle and the light infantry and cavalry did virtually nothing besides skirmishing, scouting, and pursuit of a defeated enemy. They were never integrated fully into the battle plan in order to utilise their specific advantages over hoplites and were just side notes to the hoplite confrontation in the centre. This is still the same as was happening 30 years before at Delium and even earlier likely at Plataea, Marathon, and Himera.[76] Though our sources pay more attention to the presence of light infantry and cavalry on Greek battlefields at the start of the fourth century, there is no evidence that those units were usually integrated into the battle plan.

Best comments that "It is remarkable that horsemen did not play a part in the battle at Koroneia".[77] Best, as discussed previously, is under the misapprehension that the use of cavalry in battle was by then commonplace, whereas it was still alien in Greece.[78] After his campaign in Asia Minor Agesilaus dispensed with his successful combined arms tactics and continued the war in Greece with his battle plans relying on hoplites.[79] This Spartan conservatism eventually contributed to their defeats at the hands of the more innovative Thebans at Leuctra and Mantinea.[80]

Iphicrates' famous victory over the Spartan mora at Lechaeum, as discussed previously, was successful only because the Spartan officers failed to use their supporting cavalry in a combined arms manner therefore allowing Iphicrates' peltasts the freedom to attack at distance without being engaged themselves. Yet the one combined arms tactic demonstrated by Iphicrates was the use of hoplites as a base of operations for light infantry to make them secure in their movements. Thus, Iphicrates' victory was a result of a basic form of combined arms.

Although Greek armies in the fourth century did often field cavalry and light infantry alongside hoplites, the tactics in battle still remained fixed on the hoplite phalanx. Without battle plans that involved all the types of unit in the army acting together in a concerted and mutually beneficial way, the Greeks could not make the best use of a combined arms army.

Combined arms conclusions

Following the Peloponnesian War, Greek generals were confident in adopting different tactics if the situation warranted it. It is this tactical flexibility that allowed the subsequent implementation of integrated warfare. Without it the Greeks would have continued their reliance on the hoplite phalanx. However, in the Greek mind of the early fourth century the use of the tactics of integrated warfare in battle, in this case using hoplites, light infantry and cavalry together, was something that was only important when fighting outside of Greece. To the Greeks, the hoplite was still the bringer of victory in any battle on Greek soil, whether supported by cavalry and light troops on the flanks or not. Since the Spartans were by far the most conservative in adapting their way of war or in adopting new strategies it is not surprising that during the Spartan hegemony Greek warfare remained tactically static.

Notes

1 See Best (1969: 36–46).
2 The history, importance, ethnicity, training and recruitment of mercenaries have all been discussed in detail elsewhere and are not of primary concern here. See Parke (1933); Griffith (1935); Russell (1942); Miller (1984); Whitehead (1991); Krasilnikoff (1992); McKechnie (1994); Yalichev (1997); Trundle (2004).
3 Surprisingly there are no good secondary sources written about Iphicrates despite his importance in fourth-century warfare. The main accounts are of his role as a mercenary in accounts covering mercenaries as a whole. The three best are Best (1969); Parke (1933); and Trundle (2004).
4 Much has been written on the reliability of Xenophon's various works. Of importance here to military discussions are Anderson (1970); Cawkwell (1972); Anderson (1974a); Gray (1979); Nickel (1979); Gray (1980); Tuplin (1986); Dillery (1995); Hutchinson (2000); Lane Fox (2004); Waterfield (2006); Christensen (2006); Lee (2007); Lee (2009); Pascual (2009).
5 On Diodorus' battle descriptions see in particular Hammond (1937); Sinclair (1966); Gray (1980); Westlake (1987); Green (2006).
6 On this work see in particular Bruce (1967); Harding (1987); McKechnie and Kern (1988); Tuplin (2004). See in particular Gray (1979). See also Anderson (1974b); De Voto (1988); Wylie (1992b). This battle is important for Agesilaus' campaign in Asia Minor but adds little to the development of combined arms and so is not dealt with in detail here.
7 Xenophon, *Hellenika* 2.4.13–19; Diodorus 14.33.2–3.

8 As discussed previously the Spartan deployment only one shield deep at Dipaea (Isocrates 6.99) was probably a one-off incident.
9 For a full discussion of Xenophon's varied terminology for light troops and their different uses on the march see Best (1969: 36–78). Roy (1967) argues that the light infantry furnished by the mercenary commanders were local levies not merecenaries. Nevertheless, a number of the Greek commanders saw the importance of bringing light infantry to the expedition alongside their hoplites.
10 Xenophon *Hellenika* 1.2.3, 1.2.6, 1.2.9.
11 Xenophon *Hellenika* 1.2.9. The actual total was nearer 2,300 adding up all the troops brought by each commander. At Babylon the Greek army was counted and Xenophon (1.7.10) lists 2500 light infantry. Parke (1933: 41–2) argues that this number should be accepted despite the discrepancy with the totals given to each commander by Xenophon.
12 Xenophon *Hellenika* 1.8.5, 1.10.3.
13 Xenophon *Hellenika* 4.1.6, 3.4.42–3, 4.8.15–18.
14 Xenophon *Hellenika* 3.3.15–16. Xenophon (3.3.15) bemoans the fact that the Cretan archers and javelin men of the Greeks do not have the range to inflict damage on the Persians.
15 Xenophon *Hellenika* 3.3.20. Cf. 3.3.16.
16 Xenophon *Hellenika* 3.3.12–16.
17 Best (1969: 75).
18 Diodorus 15.32–33; Polyaenus 2.1.2; Nepos, *Chabrias* 1.2.
19 Best (1969).
20 Parke 1933: 81.
21 See for example Parke (1933: 77).
22 See Parke (1933); Griffith (1935); Miller (1984).
23 Xenophon almost always uses peltast to refer to light infantry, unlike Thucydides who differentiates between light-armed psiloi and peltasts (Thucydides 2.79). See Sprawski (2014: 96).
24 Bertosa (2014: 115–20) is the most recent discussion that goes through all the scholarly interpretations as well as the visual and literary evidence. See especially 117: "Abundant representational evidence exists of thrusting-spears used by peltasts on vases of the sixth and fifth centuries BC".
25 See Bertosa (2014: 120).
26 Xenophon, *Hellenika* 4.5.11–17; Diodorus, 14.91; Plutarch, *Agesilaus* 22. On the battle see in particular the various articles in Sekunda and Burliga (2014). The best description of the battle is Konecny (2014), the English translation of Konecny (2001). Iphicrates' previous victory at Phlius in 392 should have been the advanced warning the Spartans needed about his abilities as a peltast commander. Xenophon, *Hellenika* 4.4.15; Diodorus, 14.9.
27 See Konecny (2014: 25–6). Cf. Spence (1993: 144).
28 Xenophon, *Hellenika* 5.2.41.
29 Xenophon, *Hellenika* 4.8.33–9.
30 See below for the level of tactical integration of these units into the battle plan.
31 Jacoby *Frag.Gr.Hist*: 347–50 no. 328 frg .71.
32 Herodotus 7.158.
33 The Boeotians fielded 500 hamippoi paired with 500 cavalry when campaigning around Argos before the battle of Mantinea (Thucydides 5.57.2). Sekunda (2014a: 60–4) argues that a Spartan allied regiment of Arcadian Sciritae consisted of hamippoi and was introduced into the army after this very campaign against the Boeotians.
34 Sprawski (2014).
35 Xenophon *Hellenika* 6.1.9, cf. 6.4.19, 6.5.23; Isocrates 8.118.
36 Sprawski (2014: 110).
37 Sprawski (2014: 110). Pollux *Onomastikon* 1.134 supplies the evidence for Jason's invention. I am not convinced of this argument since the linen cuirass, the *linothorax*,

was already in widespread use by this point, having replaced the expensive and heavy bronze breastplate, and it was hardly much cheaper to make a half cuirass of linen. But it is still an attractive interpretation of Thessaly's sudden output of hoplites in a similar way to Philip II of Macedon's sudden output of a Macedonian phalanx armed with the sarissa and *linothorax* rather than with the expensive traditional hoplite weapons.

38 Sprawski (2014: 104).
39 Diodorus 15.32.1. He may be confusing the Sciritae for elite hoplites but it could be embellishment as Sekunda (2014a: 61–2) argues.
40 Xenophon *Lac. Pol.* 12.4 (camp guards and spears), 13.6 (scouts).
41 The Agrianes javelin men in Alexander the Great's army also linked the cavalry to the slow-moving phalanx and they were always missile troops. However, they are never attested as hamippoi and this is likely Alexander's tactical deployment to create a flexible light infantry link between his pahalnx and the cavalry. The hamippoi who do run alongside the cavalry are close combat troops though lightly armoured.
42 E.g. Asclepiodotus *Tactica* 1.2.
43 Diodorus 15.44.2–4; Nepos, *Iphicrates* 11.1.3–4.
44 The evidence for Thracian peltasts before Iphicrates having a long sword is vague at best but cannot prove conclusively that he introduced them. See Konijnendijk (2014) for previous scholarly interpretations of Iphicrates' reforms and the consequent impact on the battle of Lechaeum. Best (1969: 102–10) gives a full discussion of the reforms to argue that they did not occur at all. Also see Whitehead (1991); McKechnie (1994); Webber (2011); and most recently Bertosa (2014) and especially Sekunda (2014b).
45 Best (1969).
46 Anderson (1970: 130).
47 Sekunda (2014b: 137–41).
48 Sekunda (2014b: 138–9).
49 Sprawski (2014: 96).
50 Sekunda (2014b: 132, 134).
51 Eustathius 13.130–34, 924. Sekunda (2014b: 139–41).
52 Sekunda (2014b: 141–2).
53 Xenophon, *Anabasis* 3.3.19–20.
54 Xenophon, *Anabasis* 7.3.13–14
55 For example, Xenophon, *Anabasis* 7.3.40, 7.3.46.
56 Xenophon, *Anabasis* 7.6.25–27.
57 Xenophon, *Anabasis* 7.6.29.
58 That Xenophon appreciated the military need for cavalry in Thrace should not be surprising considering his own expertise in cavalry as evinced by his publication of two works on horses, *On Horsemanship* and *On the Cavalry Commander*.
59 Best (1969: 75).
60 It is possible that Clearchus' force of mercenaries contained a unit of mostly Thracian cavalry numbering more than 40 horsemen (Xenophon, *Anabasis* 1.5.13). However, this unit is mentioned only once in the *Anabasis* and is not listed in the original force brought by Clearchus (1.2.9). Certainly after the battle of Cunaxa and Clearchus' subsequent murder this force of cavalry was not present or Xenophon would not have stressed the need to create a separate unit of 50 horsemen from among the hoplite mercenaries. See Roy (1967) for Clearchus raising this cavalry from Thrace.
61 Roy (1967: 295).
62 Xenophon *Anabasis* 4.8.9–19.
63 Arrian, *Anabasis* 1.12–16; Diodorus 17.19–21; Plutarch, *Alexander* 16; Justin 11.6. This battle is not one of the case studies used in this study since Issus and Gaugamela serve the same purpose and so the Granicus is not discussed in detail. For good secondary discussions of the battle see in particular Fuller (1960); Davis (1964); Nikolitsis

(1973); Foss (1977); Badian (1976); Hammond (1980b); Devine (1988); McCoy (1989); Bosworth (1989).
64 In fact, Alexander never needed to adopt a separated phalanx formation in battle since his combined arms army always had sufficient flank protection to avoid the encirclement that the Ten Thousand feared. At Gaugamela Alexander also had to attack an army that threatened encirclement but he used a variation of the oblique formation to avoid this (Arrian, *Anabasis* 3.8–15; Curtius 4.9; Diodorus 17. 56–61; Plutarch, *Alexander* 32–33). See below for a full discussion of Gaugamela.
65 See Wheeler (1979); Wheeler (1992). See also Wheeler (2004) for the late empire.
66 Plutarch, *Aemilius Paullus* 16–22; Livy 44.40–42. The causes for the success of the Roman legions against the phalanx is a much debated topic but is unfortunately outside the scope of this study. See Wheeler (1992) in particular. I discuss elsewhere combined arms in the battle of Pydna, as well as that of Cynoscephalae in 197 (Polybius 18.19–26; Livy 33.6–10; Plutarch *Flamininus* 7–8), Wrightson forthcoming.
67 Xenophon, *Hellenika* 3.2.12–20.
68 Thucydides 4.90–96.
69 Xenophon, *Hellenika* 3.4.15.
70 Xenophon, *Hellenika* 3.4.22–4; *Agesilaus* 1.31; Plutarch, *Agesilaus* 10.
71 Xenophon, *Hellenika* 4.3.15–17; *Agesilaus* 11.9–11.
72 Xenophon, *Hellenika* 4.3.4–9. Agesilaus adopted the now normal practice of marching with his hoplites in a hollow square with cavalry in front and behind. When attacked in the rear he sent his vanguard of cavalry to join the battle.
73 Xenophon *Hellenika* 4.3.15.
74 Xenophon *Hellenika* 4.2.15–23. Cf. Diodorus 14.83.1–2.
75 Xenophon *Hellenika* 4.2.16–17.
76 In my view cavalry and light infantry had always been present in number on Greek battlefields but they did nothing of import in the battle and so were usually ignored in our surviving accounts. By the fourth century, thanks to Demosthenes, Brasidas, Thrasybulus, Chabrias, Iphicrates and others, these troops began to take on more prominent roles in battles and so begin to be mentioned in the sources. But crucially they are still not fully combined with hoplites into the battle plan.
77 Best (1969: 85, n. 34).
78 Best (1969: 84–5) is also wrong when he argues that the decisive charge of Herippidas' phalanx that caused the Argives to break was led by peltasts. Xenophon (*Hellenika* 4.3.15–17) makes it clear that it was the phalanx that charged and states that the Argives fled "when they came within spear-thrusting distance". Best is trying to find evidence for Agesilaus' reliance on peltasts when it is clear that the battle of Coroneia was fought almost exclusively by hoplites, just like all the other Spartan battles.
79 Westlake (1986).
80 Leuctra: Plutarch, *Pelopidas* 20–23; Xenophon, *Hellenika* 6.4.8–15; Diodorus 15.53–56. Mantinea: Xenophon, *Hellenika* 7.5.21–27; Diodorus 15.84–87. These two important battles will be discussed in detail in the next section detailing the Theban contributions to combined arms in Greece.

6 The Theban hegemony – the inclusion of heavy cavalry

Thebes eventually became the dominant state in Greece after the Corinthian War and the overthrow of Spartan hegemony. This was achieved thanks largely to their two innovative generals, Pelopidas and Epaminondas, who were both willing to adapt the tactical use of the hoplite phalanx and integrate light infantry and cavalry in battle together.

Sources

The middle of the fourth century is not very well documented in the surviving sources. Xenophon's history, the *Hellenika*, just as Thucydides' account of the Peloponnesian War, is focused almost exclusively on Athens and Sparta. His exclusion of Thebes and Epaminondas in particular is a much debated problem for scholars.[1] Here the reasons for this exclusion are not the concern since it is still possible to reconstruct the tactics of battles from Xenophon's account. Diodorus Siculus' much later account adds a few details but is not concerned with military details.[2] Despite the few sources it is possible to examine the nature of Greek warfare in this period by focusing on the few battles that are described in relative detail. The focus of these sources, in particular Xenophon, is still on hoplites and so it is difficult to examine in detail the tactical uses and importance of light infantry and cavalry, but not impossible.

Infantry

Thebes was the polis in Greece proper that seemed most comfortable with experimenting militarily, as the earlier use of a 25-man deep phalanx in victory at Delium aptly demonstrates.[3] At the battle of Nemea in the Corinthian War the Theban forces reneged on their agreement with their allies and drew up their phalanx exceedingly deep according to Xenophon. Before the battle the allies had been in hot debate concerning the depth of the phalanx to use against the Spartans lest they be outflanked and surrounded and had agreed on 16 men deep.[4] The Theban decision to ignore this agreement and draw up even deeper, as well as Xenophon even mentioning the heated debate of the allies concerning the phalanx depth, suggests that by the 390s it was standard Theban practice to field a deep phalanx but that was unusual for the other Greek poleis and was seen as detrimental to the strength of the overall battle line. Thebes, then, was unusual in often fielding deepened phalanxes and had not yet definitively proven to other Greeks that that was a successful tactic in hoplite battles.

The Theban generals Pelopidas and Epaminondas crucially experimented with battle tactics and deployments together. For the Theban infantry already familiar with stacking the hoplite phalanx to extra depth, a crucial military tactic, it was a simple addition for Pelopidas to introduce the concentration of the 300 members of the Sacred Band into one place on the battlefield to give the stacked phalanx more of a cutting edge.[5]

The Sacred Band was the first professional unit of citizen hoplites equipped and maintained at state expense outside of Sparta and consisted of 150 homosexual pairs of hoplites.[6] This change to professionalism is another hallmark of the fourth century but in itself is not a necessity for the development of combined arms.[7] According to Plutarch, previously the Sacred Band was distributed evenly among the front ranks of the whole phalanx, thus diluting its effectiveness.[8] It was its concentration at the front of one wing of the Theban battle line that brought about the defeat of the Spartans at Leuctra, one of the most important battles in history, and later at Mantinea.[9]

The battle of Leuctra marks the first time that a full Spartan army was defeated in battle through the superiority of the enemy hoplites (Figure 6.1).[10] In conjunction

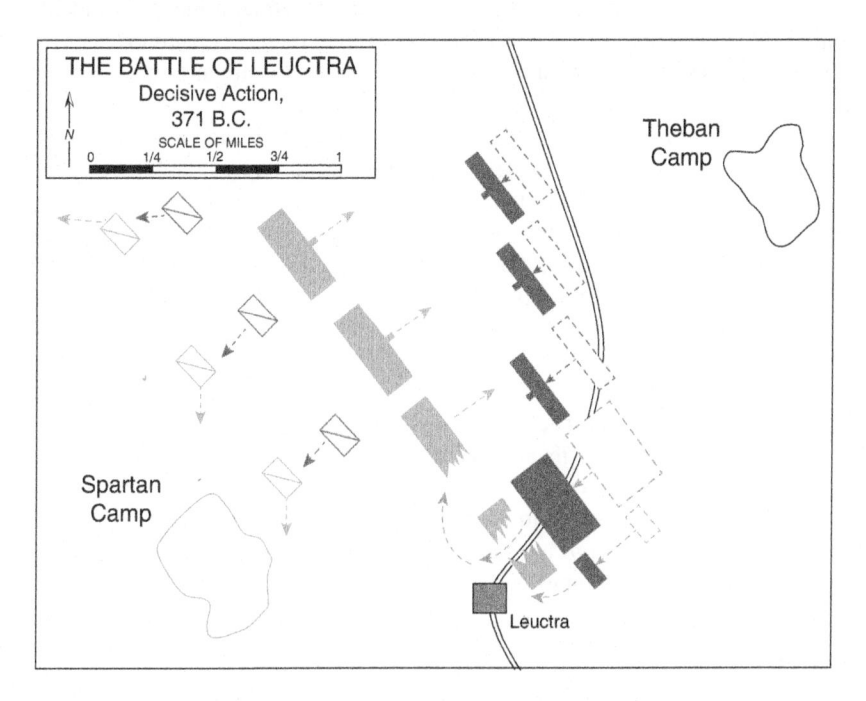

Figure 6.1 Map of Leuctra showing the crucial innovation of the oblique formation and the deep phalanx led by the Sacred Band under Pelopidas

152 *Combined arms in Greek warfare*

with stacking his hoplites 50 ranks deep, Epaminondas' implementation of the oblique formation, where one wing is held back out of the fight, is perhaps the most significant tactical innovation of the period. The Theban army was outnumbered and so Epaminondas created a means of neutralising the Spartan numbers and superior Spartan hoplites. Epaminondas also changed the usual pattern of a hoplite confrontation by directly opposing the elite Spartan troops with his own best forces. Usually each side posted their best troops on their respective right wing with the result that battles often resulted in each side's right winning and then turning to face each other.[11] The oblique formation allowed the Thebans to confront the elite Spartiate hoplites with their own elite Sacred Band at the front of an extra deep phalanx while holding back their weaker troops. Unlike at Nemea previously, the oblique formation prevented the Spartans from outflanking the stacked phalanx of the Thebans or defeating the weaker wing of the army quickly.

Pelopidas' command of the Sacred Band at Leuctra is what precipitated the victory when he charged the Spartans while they were in the process of a formation change, and caught them unawares.[12] Nevertheless, the oblique formation was the foundation that allowed Pelopidas the time and positioning to defeat the previously invincible Spartan hoplites before the rest of the Theban line was defeated.[13] It was such a successful ploy that the Thebans used it effectively again at Mantinea, and Philip and Alexander and the Successors relied on it as the principal tactic of the Macedonian army.[14]

The battle of Mantinea in 362 marks the end of Spartan military dominance, and also the beginning of the end of the era of the hoplite.[15] Epaminondas again relied on the oblique formation that had proved so successful at Leuctra massing his hoplites on his left wing 50 deep. He stationed his cavalry in front and to the side of his refused wing and posted a small force of cavalry and light infantry on a hill overlooking his left wing to prevent the Spartans turning his flank. The Theban cavalry defeated their opposition and the Theban hoplites overcame the Spartans opposite them. Had Epaminondas not been mortally wounded leading the phalanx the defeat of the Spartans would probably have become a rout.[16] His death led the Spartans to claim a victory despite the tactical supremacy of the Theban army. It was a resounding success for the Thebans and proved again the effectiveness of the oblique formation in battle. But Epaminondas' tactical use of the cavalry in front of his refused flank was purely defensive and did not make the best use of the unit's offensive capabilities. The Thebans possessed excellent cavalry, as discussed next, but still did not always use them in an offensive manner in conjunction with their hoplite phalanx and so did not gain full benefit from using combined arms tactics.

The Thebans were the first to increase the depth of the phalanx, use new phalanx tactics and continue to use their effective cavalry. But their dependence on the Sacred Band shows that even the Thebans still relied on hoplites for victory.

Cavalry

In the 370s, Jason of Pherae's army was the first in Greece to have a considerable strength in cavalry as well as hoplites. "In cavalry Thessaly had always been extraordinarily strong, and the very unusual proportion in the army of Jason – not far short of one cavalryman to two hoplites – need occasion no surprise; it rather serves to authenticate the army-list".[17] Macedon's successes were based on the ability of their heavy cavalry but even they did not enjoy a ratio of infantry to cavalry of 2:1.[18] Alexander the Great's battles against Persia often made use of his unit of Thessalian cavalry as equal to the Companions, showing the strengths of the Thessalian horsemen.[19] There are almost no details of Jason's conquests and army, but the fact that even the contemporary Greek commentators paid attention to Jason having more cavalry in battle shows the rising importance of cavalry in Greek warfare. Herodotus does not show similar trepidation at the huge numbers of Persian cavalry because they proved so ineffective in the Persian Wars. Xenophon, by contrast, is almost scared of Jason's forces because at the hands of a good commander cavalry, especially heavy cavalry, now posed a threat to the hoplite phalanx.

Thebes had a great influence on Greek warfare in the first quarter of the fourth century because it was the one main Greek polis that maintained a relatively strong and reliable cavalry force alongside its hoplites.[20] The main Theban general innovative in using combined arms was not the well-known Epaminondas, but his friend Pelopidas.[21] His defeat of the Spartan hoplites at Tegyra may have been the first successful frontal charge by cavalry against a hoplite phalanx in Greek warfare.[22] Plutarch states that Pelopidas ordered up his cavalry from the rear "to attack" while he formed up his 300 hoplites into close order to cut through the outnumbering enemy. Noticeably, Plutarch makes no mention of cavalry after the initial instruction to attack and it is clear Pelopidas was fighting on foot among the phalanx. We cannot conclude for certain that the battle involved a frontal cavalry charge against hoplites. Cavalry may have been used to attack the Spartan flanks, as the Syracusans did to the Athenians 50 years earlier, to assault the Spartan cavalry that presumably was attached to the phalanx, or to prevent the 300 Theban hoplites from being surrounded. Whatever exactly happened tactically, Tegyra was the first battle where the Spartan hoplite army was defeated severely by a significantly inferior force, using cavalry offensively alongside hoplites.[23]

It is this beginning to Theban dominance that has always made Tegyra such an important battle in Greek military history. Nevertheless, after Pelopidas' exploits, for the first-time cavalry came to be viewed as a very effective offensive weapon, even against heavy infantry. Pelopidas' success here was a significant step on the road of the development of combined arms by combining cavalry and hoplites in attack.

Epaminondas was the instigator of the oblique formation in a hoplite battle, with an accompanying cavalry screen, at the battle of Leuctra, as discussed previously. But he never demonstrated any aptitude for using cavalry in an offensive manner to complement the phalanx, and still relied on his hoplites for victory at both Leuctra and Mantinea.[24] This lack of concern for cavalry tactics was probably because both Theban generals, just as most Greeks, fought as hoplites in the phalanx. Unlike Alexander, Philip, and other Macedonian generals, they did not command their armies from horseback, and so may not have appreciated the effectiveness of cavalry.[25]

Combined arms

By 382 even the Spartans were beginning tactically to rely more on cavalry in battle, but still only when in foreign territory using foreign troops. At Olynthus, the Spartan garrison commander Teleutias was supported by Macedonian and Boeotian cavalry.[26] When he drew up for battle he placed the phalanx of hoplites in the centre and the allied cavalry on his right flank. In the battle the Olynthian cavalry eventually routed Teleutias' and the neighbouring infantry fled. A reserve squadron of Teleutias' cavalry charged straight for the city gates causing the victorious Olynthians to try to get there first lest they be stranded outside. This reserve cavalry action turned a certain defeat into a victory.

Here we see the advantages of maintaining a reserve of cavalry, and that the phalanx cannot remain intact if its flanks are turned. However, this combined arms army involving cavalry was only formed because the Macedonian allied troops were expert horsemen and the Olynthian enemy were also experts in mounted warfare. The obvious lessons of combined action using all the types of unit available were still not learned by the Spartans or the other Greek states.

Teleutias' eventual death against the same enemy shows that Greeks were still unfamiliar with how best to manipulate combined arms armies in battle.[27] The Olynthians, on the contrary, demonstrated that they knew well how to utilise a combined force of cavalry, peltasts, and hoplites while also using the terrain to their advantage. Teleutias advanced to Olynthus to remove the crops and was opposed by Olynthian cavalry that had crossed the river to harass him. Teleutias launched his peltasts to fend them off and the Olynthians retreated over the river. The peltasts pursued them across the river only to be cut down by the Olynthian cavalry. Teleutias crossed the river with the rest of the army, ordering the cavalry and peltasts to pursue the Olynthians to the city. Unfortunately, they got too close to the missile towers on the city walls and were forced to retreat. The Olynthians sent out their cavalry and peltasts followed by their hoplites who all pressed the disordered Spartan army. Teleutias was killed along with the majority of his army. Teleutias and his army had pressed the Olynthians too far, but by sending peltasts alone against the Olynthian cavalry he lacked the required application of a combined arms army and paid the ultimate price. On the opposite side, the Olynthians sent out cavalry first to press home the advantage against the disordered Spartans and followed up with light infantry and hoplites to force the issue, lest the cavalry come unstuck fighting against reformed hoplites or light infantry.[28]

Those states that had always fielded cavalry and peltast forces, as well as hoplites, were better able to employ them through years of practice. This native reliance on light infantry and cavalry is one reason why it was the Macedonians who eventually perfected the tactical manipulation of a combined arms army while the Greeks failed to do so.

Perhaps the general who came closest to fully implementing a combined arms system tactically in Greece was Jason of Pherae. Little is known about him, since for the most part Thessaly is excluded from Xenophon's account of Greek history in the *Hellenika*. In the one section in which Xenophon does refer to Jason (6.1),

The Theban hegemony – heavy cavalry 155

he is presented as a successful and feared tyrant. Xenophon states that once he succeeded in setting himself up as *Tagus* of Thessaly,[29] "his cavalry, along with that of his allies, came to more than eight thousand, his hoplites were calculated to be no fewer than twenty thousand, and he had enough peltasts to set against all men; for it is a labour even to count their cities".

Jason, then, had the most powerful army of the day. Even Philip of Macedon's cavalry numbered only 4,000, his phalanx certainly comprised fewer than 20,000 men, and Macedon was not renowned for producing peltasts in significant numbers.[30] Even if we make allowances for exaggeration on the part of Xenophon, Jason certainly had an army with which he could easily have conquered Greece, and more.[31] As Westlake comments in his work on Thessaly,

> [a]t the battles of Nemea and Mantinea, in which an exceptionally large number of combatants were involved, neither side can have exceeded this figure, so that it is remarkable that Jason, backed by military resources of such magnitude, did not at once strike a blow for the hegemony of Greece.[32]

Jason also had 6,000 mercenaries as his personal guard, loyal to him and expertly trained. Xenophon (6.4.8) comments that "he maintained about him many mercenaries, both foot-soldiers and horsemen, these moreover being troops which had been trained to the highest efficiency". With such a large core of professionals his army would have been very capable. From Xenophon we see that Jason trained his whole army rigorously every day and rewarded martial vigour.[33] Clearly his soldiers were very capable and would have been considerably better if he had been given time to continue his methods.

It is unfortunate that we know nothing of Jason's many victories, how he deployed his army, or the specific tactics that he used in battle. He may be considered the first Greek general to consistently and successfully make full use of the theory of combined arms. But we cannot conclude anything since the evidence is so scarce. Jason's assassination prevented almost certain Thessalian domination, since even his inept successors had armies powerful enough to cause significant problems for the other Greek poleis.[34] Had Jason lived his army likely would have been expert enough to allow him to become *Hegemon* of Greece, and perhaps even conquer Persia as he perhaps intended.[35]

Pelopidas' battles against Alexander of Pherae, Jason's successor as the tyrant of Thessaly, showed his abilities at adapting his army and tactics as the situation required. His final crushing victory over Alexander at Cynoscephalae is a prime example of how to win a battle by holding off the enemy's best troops while winning the battle with your own, a key principle of combined arms.[36] Pelopidas' superior Thessalian cavalry routed Alexander's while Alexander's mercenary infantry overcame Pelopidas' Thessalian hoplites while also holding the important strategic hill in the centre of the battlefield. Pelopidas ordered the victorious cavalry to attack Alexander's hoplites while he himself followed behind leading his few but elite Theban hoplites. He easily defeated Alexander's infantry using this combination of cavalry and infantry attacks though we do not know exactly

156 Combined arms in Greek warfare

how this was achieved and whether the cavalry actually charged the Thessalian phalanx. Unfortunately, Pelopidas' martial enthusiasm got the better of him and he was killed trying to slay Alexander, probably preventing further Theban advances in the area of combined arms.

Epaminondas' use of the cavalry screen and the oblique formation are still key components in the development of combined arms. Both serve the defensive aspect in gaining time for the heavy infantry to win the battle, with their flanks protected by the other troops. However, the best tactical use of a combined arms army utilises the offensive power of all the types of units rather than simply relying on one alone for victory. As a result, Pelopidas, not Epaminondas, was the principal Theban innovator when it comes to the use of combined arms by using both cavalry and hoplites as his offence and sometimes together, depending on the situation.[37]

Combined arms conclusions

The resounding defeat of Sparta by Epaminondas at Leuctra and Mantinea proved that warfare had moved on beyond the limited tactics of traditional hoplite battles, but the tactical use of combined arms on the battlefield was still in its infancy, though at least now past the conception stage. Pelopidas' death at Cynoscephalae and Epaminondas' death at Mantinea undoubtedly left a void in the area of innovative Greek generals and once again slowed down the process of developing combined arms. This allowed the mantle to pass to the Macedonians.

Notes

1. See among others Westlake (1975); Gray (1980); Tuplin (1986); Tuplin (1987); Tuplin (1993); Dillery (1995).
2. On Diodorus' battle descriptions see in particular Hammond (1937); Sinclair (1966); Gray (1980); Westlake (1987); Green (2006). Another source is the fragmentary *Hellenika Oxyrhincia* but this does not detail any of the battles of concern here. On this work see in particular Bruce (1967); Harding (1987); McKechnie and Kern (1988); Tuplin (2004).
3. See: Gaebel (2002); Hanson (2010).
4. Initial debate Xenophon *Hellenika* 4.2.13. Cf. 16 deep Xenophon *Hellenika* 4.2.18.
5. See De Voto (1992).
6. Plutarch, *Pelopidas* 18.
7. For the nature of the Sacred Band see Leitao (2002), and for its use in battle see for example De Voto (1992).
8. Plutarch, *Pelopidas* 19.3–4.
9. Leuctra: (Plutarch, *Pelopidas* 20–23; Xenophon, *Hellenika* 6.4.8–15; Diodorus 15.53–56). Mantinea: Xenophon, *Hellenika* 7.5.21–27; Diodorus 15.84–87.
10. For the best recent summary of the battle see Buckler (2013). For innovation see in particular Hanson (1988).
11. The battle of Coroneia between the Spartans and Thebans in 394, is the best example of this where the Thebans won on the right as did Agesilaus and when they turned 90 degrees to face each other the Thebans had to fight back through the Spartan lines to get back to their camp.

12 Plutarch, *Pelopidas* 23. Xenophon, *Hellenika* 6.4.13–15 makes no mention of the formation change or the Sacred Band. He argues that the Spartans were winning the confrontation because they were able to extract the body of the dead king Cleombrotus.
13 Jones (1987: 5–6) argues that it was the greater depth of the Theban phalanx that was so crucial at Leuctra. He does not even note the use of the oblique formation. Perhaps the reference works he used as an expert in the US Civil War summarising earlier warfare practices did not discuss this tactical deployment.
14 Perhaps the most decisive use of the oblique formation was Philip's defeat of the Greeks at Chaeronea where the Thebans succumbed to their own tactic (Diodorus, 16.85–86; Polyaenus, 4.2.2; Plutarch, *Alexander* 12 & *Demosthenes* 20). On the Sacred Band at Chaeronea see Rahe (1981). This battle will be discussed in more detail below. See Hammond (1938).
15 Xenophon, *Hellenika* 7.5.21–27; Diodorus 15.84–87. For secondary discussions of the battle see in particular Woodhouse (1918); Pritchett (1969); Cawkwell (1983); C. Hamilton (1983); C. Hamilton (1991); Singor (2002); Cartledge (2003); Rusch (2011).
16 Had Pelopidas still been alive at Mantinea he likely would have led the Sacred Band, as at Leuctra, leaving Epaminondas safe from harm in the main phalanx. A what if moment of history, but the death within a few years of Thebes' two greatest generals left a huge void that prevented Theban domination of Greece and inhibited further innovations in Greek warfare until Philip II of Macedon arrived 15 years later.
17 Westlake (1935: 108).
18 On the Macedonian cavalry see in particular Hammond (1998). Also see Adcock (1957); Brunt (1963); Milns (1966); Ashley (1998); Moreno Hernandez (2004).
19 This will be discussed below in the section on Alexander.
20 Pascual (2007).
21 See Plutarch, *Pelopidas*. He was schooled in the ways of the hoplite, like all Greeks, and commanded the Sacred Band under Epaminondas at Leuctra, but he was also the first prominent and successful cavalry commander.
22 Plutarch, *Pelopidas* 17. Plutarch suggests he led a frontal assault on the Spartans, but the difficulty for cavalry to break a phalanx formation from the front makes this doubtful. Whatever tactics he did employ, they worked. Plutarch unfortunately does not provide any further details on how the attack began but simply narrates how the two armies joined battle, particularly around the generals of each side, until the Spartan polemarchs were killed. At this point the Spartans opened a way for the Thebans to continue through but Pelopidas instead continued to attack the clumps of enemy hoplites.
23 Diodorus (15.37) in discussing the battle stresses the importance placed on the Theban victory: "For as the Lacedaemonians maintained a garrison of many soldiers in Orchomenus and had drawn up their forces against the Thebans, a stiff battle took place in which the Thebans, attacking twice their number, defeated the Lacedaemonians. Never indeed had such a thing occurred before; it had seemed enough if they won with many against few. The result was that the Thebans swelled with pride, became more and more renowned for their valour, and had manifestly put themselves in a position to compete for the supremacy of Greece".
24 Leuctra: Plutarch, *Pelopidas* 20 & 23; Xenophon, *Hellenika* 6.4; Diodorus, 15.53–56. Mantinea: Xenophon, *Hellenika* 7.5; Diodorus, 15.84–87.
25 On the unusual nature of command from the rear in Macedonian armies see Wrightson (2010).
26 Xenophon, *Hellenika* 5.2.39–43.
27 Xenophon, *Hellenika* 5.3.1–6.
28 This tactic of a supported assault by units in order of speed is very similar to Alexander the Great's methods of attack. Particularly at Gaugamela, Alexander charged into a gap in the enemy line with his cavalry and supported the breach with light infantry and

fast-moving heavy infantry in turn. This allowed the rapid attack to main cohesion and connection to the rest of the battle line.
29 The *Tagus* was the elected federal commander of all the cities in the Thessalian League and commanded all four districts of Thessaly. Herodotus 5.63 refers to the position as king, and Dionysius 5.74 as archon. See Westlake (1935).
30 Lloyd (1996b); Hammond (1998); Ashley (1998). On Macedonian peltasts see Griffith (1981).
31 Xenophon (6.4.32) mentions how Jason's murderers were feted wherever they went in Greece. "By this it was clear how deeply the Greeks feared that Jason would become a tyrant".
32 Westlake (1935: 106–7).
33 Xenophon, *Hellenika* 6.1.6: "And he himself – for I must tell you the truth – is exceedingly strong of body and a lover of toil besides. Indeed, he makes trial every day of the men under him, for in full armour he leads them, both on the parade-ground and whenever he is on a campaign anywhere. And whomsoever among his mercenaries he finds to be weaklings he casts out, but whomsoever he sees to be fond of toil and fond of the dangers of war he rewards, some with double pay, others with triple pay, others even with quadruple pay, and with gifts besides, as well as with care in sickness and magnificence in burial; so that all the mercenaries in his service know that martial prowess assures to them a life of greatest honour and abundance".
34 See for example the Theban intervention in Thessaly against Jason's successor Alexander (Plutarch, *Pelopidas* 31–32; Diodorus 15.80).
35 Westlake (1935: 118) is probably right when he states that "[f]ar too much stress has been laid by historians on the intention of Jason to invade Persia". Jason states that he felt it would be easier to subdue the king of Persia than Greece, as recorded by Xenophon (*Hellenika* 6.1.12), and Isocrates says as much in his letter to Philip (5.119). Jason would certainly have known that he could not have attempted such an expedition without establishing a secure dominion over all the important states in Greece and securing their assistance for the invasion. He may even have had to subdue Macedon before leaving for Persia. But Persia at this time was weak after the King's Peace and would soon be divided by the Satrap's Revolt. Jason's army was certainly strong enough to have conquered Persia had he been able to establish himself in Greece first.
36 Plutarch, *Pelopidas* 31–32; Diodorus, 15.80.
37 Had Pelopidas had overall command against Sparta instead of Epaminondas he may have tried to use combined arms tactics at Leuctra. This is a case of revisionist history, but it was his initiative as the commander of the Sacred Band that won the battle for the Thebans and his earlier victory at Tegyra demonstrated his superior tactical ability.

Section 3
Macedon and integrated warfare

7 Philip II – the sarissa phalanx and heavy cavalry

The Macedonian army after the accession of Philip II was the first in the Greek world to make full use of combined arms in every battle regardless of terrain. This army

> in many ways represented the culmination of classical trends. The Macedonian army was powerful, not only because of the phalangite who replaced the hoplite as the mainstay of the infantry, but also because of the coordinated use of different types of military forces: cavalry of different types, peltasts, slingers and archers. . . . Although Demosthenes claimed that Philip fought in an altogether new and formidable way (Dem. 9.47–52), many of the features of his army were symptomatic of the growing specialization and professionalization of armed forces in the fourth century.[1]

Before Philip the Macedonian army probably comprised light infantry variously armed and a large core of aristocratic heavy cavalry; and mercenaries were probably also used.[2] Philip is criticised by Demosthenes (9.47–52) for instilling into his professional army the discipline and ability to fight year-round. It is this professionalism that allowed Philip's army to become so proficient in battle and expert at the use of combined arms.[3]

Sources

The references to Macedon before Philip are occasional in Greek sources and occur only when they involved the Greeks directly. Perhaps the best sources for Philip's army are the speeches of Demosthenes.[4] These are, however, a very one-sided view of his activities and are not concerned with providing any real military details. The works of Diodorus and Justin are limited in military details and probably both based on a now lost history of Theopompus.[5] Diodorus is the best source for Philip's early battles, of particular concern here Heraclea Lyncestis, as discussed next.

Infantry

When Philip acceded to the throne of Macedon acting as regent for his nephew Amyntas, the young son of the recently deceased king, the kingdom was in a

162 *Macedon and integrated warfare*

terribly insecure position. King Bardylis of Illyria had just won a decisive victory over Philip's predecessor Perdiccas, killing the king along with 4,000 of his soldiers, and had invaded the northern parts of the country.[6] Macedonia even before then was by no means a secure kingdom and there were significant divisions between the northern and southern peoples that had only become worse after the invasion of the country.[7]

Until Philip came to the throne the main strength of the Macedonian army lay with its cavalry of nobles who probably served as a form of feudal dues owed to the king in return for the lands they held, similar to the feudal system that was common throughout Europe in the Middle Ages. The Macedonian infantry were far from being professional natives and may have entirely consisted of hired Greek hoplite mercenaries and local peltasts. Nor was the infantry very numerous and the death of 4,000 in the defeat of Perdiccas must have severely dented the military resources that were available to Philip.

For his first battle in 358 BCE, a year after his accession, when he defeated Bardylis Philip commanded 10,000 infantry and a mere 600 cavalry.[8] Although this would be a relatively large army for a Greek *polis* to put into the field, in terms of later Macedonian manpower this was a small force and was in number only equal to or even less than the opposing force of Illyrians. It is to Philip's credit that he could muster so many men so quickly despite the disastrous casualties suffered only a year previously and his withdrawal of the troops sent to help Amphipolis in their war with Athens, although it was politically necessary to do so in order to deny Athenian help to a rival for the throne, must have been militarily necessary so that they would form the majority of his army. His army may have been bolstered by hired Greek mercenaries, as was the tradition in Macedonia, and by the survivors of the earlier defeat but he may also have simply armed the resident Macedonian peasants. Whatever the origin of his first soldiers was within six years Philip had doubled the size of his army,[9] and in 20 years he commanded a force of 30,000 men, three times larger than the army that he had in 358 BCE.[10]

His successes in annexing neighbouring lands and peoples goes some way to explaining this severe increase in manpower, whether he incorporated the conquered populations into the army or merely used them to work the land, allowing the proper Macedonian citizens to become professional and permanent soldiers. His granting of vast tracts of conquered land to his friends and supporters allowed him to increase the ranks of the noble Companion cavalry from the 600 he had in 358 BCE to over 3,000 by the end of his reign.

Like the Greek hoplite the Macedonians fought in a phalanx formation. The difference is that the Macedonian phalangite was equipped with a new weapon called the sarissa. The sarissa was a long pike between 15 and 18 feet long, although later kings extended the length to as much as 25 feet.[11] The extreme length of the sarissa meant that the sarissas of the first three, four, or five rows of the phalanx would extend beyond the front rank. This extra range of attack gave the phalanx a greater penetrative power making it hard for an attacker with shorter weapons to get within range of the front rank before they themselves were wounded or killed. The numerous lines of spear points that protruded from the front line made the phalanx an impenetrable defensive hedgehog and by advancing with its flanks protected, it became a relentless force.[12]

The fact that the sarissa had to be held by two hands meant that the power that a Macedonian phalangite could put behind his attacking thrust was huge. The hoplite held his spear with one hand and so could only put half the force into his attack as the Macedonian phalangite. This extra power coupled with the extra range meant that the Macedonian sarissa phalanx held significant advantages over the traditional hoplite phalanx and was virtually unstoppable when it advanced.

Not only did the sarissa give the Macedonian phalangite an increased effective range, its protective qualities meant there was less of a need for personal body armour. The long pike could be held aloft by the rear ranks of the phalanx over the heads of the men in front and significantly reduced the chance of missiles penetrating the phalanx without being deflected off-target. This great protection from missiles, and the close order of the formation, meant that the infantry in the phalanx did not need so much protective armour.

Most Macedonian phalangites would have worn a leather thorax as body protection instead of the bronze cuirass of traditional hoplites. This reduced the weight of the body armour by half from around 25 pounds to approximately 10, thus making the Macedonian a far more mobile heavy infantryman. It must be noted, however, that the leather thorax does not have a significantly reduced defensive capacity when compared with the bronze armour and so even when the Macedonian phalangites fought without their sarissas they would still be sufficiently protected. Since the bronze armour that was worn by the Greek hoplites was so expensive, dispensing with the need for it also meant that the poorer Macedonian peasants could now fight in the phalanx in great numbers for a fraction of the expense.

Moreover, the need to hold the sarissa with two hands meant that a reduction in the size of the shield was necessary but also beneficial for mobility. The new smaller shield was only 2 feet in diameter instead of 3 feet and was held in position covering the left half of the body by an arm strap and a neck strap. The left hand protruded from the side of the shield so that the sarissa could be gripped with two hands on the right-hand side.

The Macedonian infantry, then, were protected by a small helmet, greaves and a leather corselet, as well as their small shield that was two feet in diameter. The weight of this armour would probably have been around 12–15 pounds and when compared with the weight of armour of a traditional hoplite of 24–30 pounds the significant weight reduction is obvious. The sarissa itself, as shown by Markle, probably weighed between 12 and 14.5 pounds,[13] whereas the hoplite spear probably weighed just over 2 pounds. Therefore, the whole armaments, including the sarissa, of a Macedonian phalangite would have weighed between 25 and 30 pounds. The full panoply of a hoplite would have weighed between 30 and 35 pounds. Because of the extra weight of the sarissa the Macedonian phalangite had to have lighter armour or he would have been too weighed down to move. The lack of armour and the smaller shield was significant in maintaining the manoeuvrability of the phalanx despite the greater size of the sarissa. Therefore, even with the sarissa the Macedonian phalangite was more lightly armoured than his Greek hoplite opponent with almost half the weight of equipment.

The sarissa phalanx was an invention of the Macedonians, probably by Philip II in or around 359.[14] Philip perhaps borrowed the sarissa from the Thracian Triballians in 339 BCE and adapted it for use by infantry. Philip is recorded as being stabbed through the thigh by a sarissa in a battle with them,[15] perhaps because he was wounded by a sarissa he saw its potential.[16] However, this late date in his reign would mean that he only implemented its use for the battle of Chaeronea and not before.

Recent scholarship argues that Philip, or his predecessor Alexander II, adopted the sarissa from Iphicrates.[17] As discussed previously, Iphicrates implemented a long spear for his infantry when he fought for the Persians in Egypt. He then served Athens in Macedon and was adopted by the Macedonian King Amyntas III as his son. Iphicrates also intervened on behalf of his adopted brothers during a crisis in the Macedonian accession. A fragment of Anaximenes states that a certain Macedonian king named Alexander created a unit of foot companions, *pezhetairoi*, comprising the majority of the infantry.[18] Matthew suggests that the reform mentioned refers to Alexander II implementing the sarissa into the Macedonian phalanx following Iphicrates' successes in the region on behalf of Amyntas. Matthew further argues that it was implementing the sarissa that led to Iphicrates' adoption by Amyntas. If this is when the Macedonians adopted the sarissa, whether under Amyntas III. Alexander II, or Perdiccas III, the military reform did nothing to enhance their fortunes in war.

Alexander II was assassinated, which Greenwalt suggests was because of his sweeping political reforms, but Perdiccas was defeated decisively by the Illyrians.[19] This suggests that the Macedonian military was still far from being as dominant as it became under Philip II. To me that implies that the sarissa was not in use since its implementation likely would have improved the Macedonian infantry enormously as it did for Philip's army. The failure of Xenophon to account to Iphicrates such a significant military innovation despite the author's enthusiasm for and expertise in all things military suggests the pike was never popular in Greece in Xenophon's time.[20] Nevertheless, wherever the idea of the sarissa originated Philip was probably the first to adapt it successfully in battle using combined arms tactics and this is the crucial point.

The various formations that the phalanx could employ, especially the wedge,[21] allowed the phalanx to adapt to most eventualities of terrain or position and to be able to break most, if not all, opposing infantry formations. Even at the battle of Pydna in defeat to the Romans the sarissas of the Macedonians proved unstoppable in a frontal assault.[22] It was only the vagaries of the terrain and some poor generalship that allowed the Romans to get within close range of the phalangites. Once the range was closed the Roman maniples hacked their way into the gaps in the phalanx and ended the phalanx's domination of infantry warfare in the Mediterranean.

Crucially the extra length of the sarissa made the phalanx formation particularly vulnerable on the flanks or in the rear. If attacked in those places the sarissa phalangite had to drop his weapon and draw a short sword since with the long sarissa it took too long a time to adjust the formation to turn to face the direction of the oncoming enemy. This is much more the case than for a hoplite phalanx. Though vulnerable on his right flank and rear a hoplite could turn to face the enemy more quickly simply by raising his spear, and as discussed previously was more than capable of holding his own in a more open melee style of fighting. The sarissa definitively could not be used in one-on-one combat and so was useless in a general melee, a siege, or out of a phalanx formation.

The sarissa phalanx was supplemented by a royal bodyguard unit, the *pezhetairoi* or foot companions (to mirror the horse companions of the heavy cavalry). Though the details of the units in Philip's army are few it seems likely that this bodyguard unit predated Alexander. It is not clear exactly how many men made up the *pezhetairoi* but named as foot companions they likely fought near the king in battle and thus must have been considered an elite unit. With what they were equipped is a problematic discussion. It is likely they were hoplites in light linen armour and with perhaps smaller shields or perhaps they were *hamippoi* thus enabling them to keep up with the king in battle assuming he rode with the cavalry. They functioned as the elite force in the Macedonian army in a similar way to the elite Spartan Sciritae, who were lightly armoured and very mobile but still able to act as heavy infantry tactically.

There has been much debate over the *pezhetairoi* both concerning their origins and their identity.[23] The Athenian orator Demosthenes is the first contemporary source to discuss the *pezhetairoi* in relation to Philip in the second *Olynthiac* passage 17. Here he states: "They (his subjects) are constantly buffeted and wearied and distressed by these expeditions north and south . . . as for his household troops and *pezhetairoi* they have indeed the name of admirable soldiers well grounded in the art of war". Clearly in this passage Demosthenes is drawing a distinction between the professional and loyal elite Macedonian troops and the general mass of his Macedonian soldiers. This suggests that *pezhetairoi* was originally a term used to denote the elite infantry battalion in Philip's army and not the whole phalanx.

The scholiast on the passage of Demosthenes states "Theopompus says that the greatest and strongest chosen from all the Macedonians are the bodyguards of the king and are called the *pezetairoi*".[24] Here again we can see that the *pezhetairoi* were classed as the small elite squadron of Macedonian infantry, likely heavy infantry perhaps hoplites if so praised by Greeks. They are also termed as "spear carriers" showing that they formed the personal bodyguard of the king. This is also seen in another passage that says they are "the guards of the body of Philip",[25] showing the special function of the *pezhetairoi*. It seems, then, that the *pezhetairoi* were the elite Macedonian infantry under Philip and the rest of the phalanx had no specific name.

There is, however, an argument against accepting the definition of Theopompus because of the fragment of Anaximenes. In the fragment Anaximenes credits to an Alexander the creation of both the Companion cavalry and the *pezhetairoi*, who are *the majority* of the Macedonian phalanx.[26] There is much debate between the identity of this King Alexander. Recent scholarship has made a strong case for the early Alexander being Alexander II, but I am in favour of Alexander I.[27]

Whether the Alexander in question is taken to be Alexander I or II, there is still a problem since the *pezhetairoi* under Philip are only his elite bodyguard and not the majority of the phalanx, which would mean a change in terminology had taken place under Philip, or more likely Philip's infantry grew in size that the *pezhetairoi* unit was no longer the majority of his troops. If Alexander is understood to be Alexander III then Anaximines seems to be suggesting that Alexander III created the whole Macedonian army from scratch. This is clearly an impossibility because the *pezhetairoi* are attested fighting under Philip before Alexander was even born. Alexander's elite infantry guard was the hypaspists and the *pezhetairoi* were all the infantry of the phalanx. So perhaps Anaximenes refers to the name change under Alexander.

But the passage came in the first book of Anaximenes' *Philippica*, suggesting that it referred to a king before Philip. Erskine presents all the previous arguments in detail and arrives at the most satisfying conclusion that when taken in context Anaximines was referring to an early Alexander but that the military reforms in organisation were to do with a select body of troops, in my view a royal bodyguard unit, and not with the whole infantry phalanx, thus allowing both passages to be accepted.[28] This is more convincing since we know before Alexander II the Macedonian infantry was so small in number that it was ineffective and ignored by Greek historians and so a bodyguard unit would have been the majority of the infantry. Regardless of which Alexander implemented the *pezhetairoi*, we can conclude that the term *pezhetairoi* in the army of Philip referred to a small body of elite infantry and not to the whole phalanx.

If we believe Demosthenes the majority of the Macedonian phalanx troops were unhappy and disconcerted by constant foreign campaigning whereas the *pezhetairoi* always remained loyal. This also suggests that only a small proportion of the Macedonian phalanx was expertly and professionally drilled, and the majority were perhaps just peasant citizen levies needed to bolster the numbers.[29] At Heraclea Lyncestis, it was likely that only Philip's best infantry, namely the *pezhetairoi*, were the expertly drilled phalangites who broke the front left corner of the Illyrian defensive square as he may not have had time to train sufficiently a phalanx of 10,000 peasants.

The hypaspists, who figured so prominently in the campaigns of Alexander, appear not to have existed in the army of Philip. None of the sources for Philip's reign mention hypaspists and this was undoubtedly a specialist term used for Alexander's elite infantry. The hypaspists are regularly called *doruforoi* "spear carriers" by the Alexander historians, the usual term for bodyguards, and they undoubtedly filled the same role for Alexander as the *pezhetairoi* did for Philip. It seems, then, that Philip's elite body of infantry bodyguards were either renamed as or replaced by the hypaspists under Alexander.

Philip's army also featured a large number of light infantry. We have no descriptions of the proportions of slingers, archers or javelin men, but he had enough to perform the usual tasks of scouting, pursuit and protecting the flanks.

Demosthenes commenting on the nature of the troops that Philip used in fast forced marches says that "you hear of Philip marching wherever he wishes not because he leads a phalanx of hoplites but because he depends on light infantry, cavalry, archers, mercenaries and such troops".[30] It seems that Philip may have depended more on light troops than a phalanx, though Demosthenes could be confusing lighter armoured and more mobile phalangites for light troops in contrast with the heavily armed and slower Greek hoplites with which he was familiar. In Philip's first battle with Onomarchus his troops are not described as carrying sarissas but attacked with javelins (*ekrobolisanto*) according to Polyaenus.[31] This also suggests that the Macedonian phalanx were lightly armed and may even have been a phalanx of light troops, unless they were armed with javelins as well as the traditional hoplite spear that was too big and heavy for accurate throwing from a distance. Whatever the precise armament of the Macedonian phalangites was and regardless of exactly when the sarissa was introduced, Philip's way of war was still primarily based on the traditional heavy infantry phalanx supplemented by cavalry, both light and heavy, and light infantry.

Philip may have begun the training of his army before he became king immediately after his return from acting as a hostage in Thebes in about 365 BCE. His brother Perdiccas III set aside some land for Philip to allow him to begin training soldiers as hoplites.[32] Philip also spent a considerable amount of effort in the training of his men in the hardships of war. He made them march repeatedly with full equipment all day and constantly drilled them on their battle manoeuvres.[33] The many wars that Philip fought during his reign meant that his Macedonian soldiers became extremely experienced as well as being very well drilled and therefore gained in skill and confidence. Philip developed the first large national standing army of native professional soldiers and he trained them to a level of skill and ability that was unmatched in the ancient world until the Roman legions of the late Republic.

By freeing his soldiers from their obligations to work the land and to prepare crops Philip created a large professional standing army that could fight anywhere at any time of the year thus escaping the limitations of a campaign season that revolved around the agricultural seasons. Demosthenes says that for his campaigns there was "no difference between summer or winter".[34] This gave him a significant advantage in the pursuit of his aims of expansion over his more limited opponents and he did not have to worry so much about the loyalty of his troops, as the commanders of standing armies of mercenaries did. Once he had annexed the profitable mines of western Thrace he had more than enough money to pay his troops and to bribe his opponents, especially when it was added to the wealth of raw materials that were already available in Macedon, such as wood and land.

Cavalry

The Macedonians and northern Greeks had always been adept at using cavalry.[35] Cavalry were crucial to the success of the Chalcidaeans at Spartolus,[36] as discussed previously, and the early successes of the Olynthians in their war against

Sparta were entirely due to their cavalry.[37] The flat topography of Macedon lent itself towards horse rearing and the Macedonian aristocratic elites held a long-standing tradition of equestrian excellence both in battle and in hunting. Riding bareback from an early age, as all Greeks did since the solid saddle was not introduced in Europe until the first century BCE, gave the Macedonian cavalry a significant advantage in ability over other Greeks. Most importantly the horsemanship of Macedonian cavalry allowed them to fight in close-combat scenarios as heavy cavalry using lances and swords, rather than acting as light cavalry relying on the javelin. This greatly increased their effectiveness in battle and added to the tactical options of Macedonian commanders.

The Macedonian cavalry was made up of the aristocracy for whom it was an honour to serve alongside the king in battle. Since they fought next to the king, were the class from where officers, generals, and officials came, and served as the members of the royal court this cavalry force was known as the Companion cavalry, companions to the king in battle and in peace time.[38]

The excellence of the Macedonian cavalry was only matched by the Thessalian cavalry. After Philip's annexation of Thessaly after the Third Sacred War, he incorporated Thessalian cavalry into the army at almost an equal level with the Macedonian Companions. The Greek sources are full of praise for the ability of Thessalian cavalry and their addition into his army gave Philip the luxury of two heavy cavalry squadrons in battle so that he could station one on each wing, as Alexander did in all his battles. This allowed him to increase his offensive options as he could launch a deadly heavy cavalry assault on either wing wherever and whenever the enemy line became most exposed.

Philip used cavalry as the main striking force in all his battles. This is perhaps the most crucial development in Greek warfare. While also maintaining forces of light cavalry, as was usual in Greek armies, Philip was able to employ more aggressive and varied tactics in using heavy cavalry as a strike force that was much more mobile than heavy infantry. Philip could use his phalanx to hold the line in the centre while his cavalry attacked on either flank at speed and with great offensive power. Having both cavalry and infantry attacking simultaneously prevents the enemy from knowing where the decisive attack will be and forces them to defend against both attacks equally, hence the ineffective defensive square adopted by Bardylis at Heraclea Lyncestis discussed next. Against Greek hoplites a general knew that any assault was coming from the phalanx alone and could arrange his battle line and tactics accordingly. The uncertainty created by having two different offensive units in an army immediately put the enemy on the back foot, as seen at Chaeronea.

Field artillery

Artillery played only minor roles in the field armies of the ancient world on account of the lack of easily manoeuvrable light machines. There are only a few examples in any of our extant sources from the whole of the ancient world.[39] There must have been other instances of the use of artillery in battle but unfortunately our lack of military-focused sources has denied us any other accounts.[40] Field artillery is an aspect of combined arms that is not a necessity but one which obviously increases the offensive power of missiles. Since missile troops can assume the same role as artillery, and are more mobile, there are few instances of the use of field artillery in the ancient world; their use was reserved for siege warfare.[41]

The first use of artillery in a pitched battle, and perhaps most innovative, was the cause of Philip's defeat by Onomarchus, general of the Phocians in the Third Sacred War.[42] Polyaenus is the only source who provides the details of this battle. He states:

> Onomarchus, drawing up his men in battle order against the Macedonians, occupied a crescent shaped mountain in his rear. After he had concealed stones and stone throwing catapults in the ridges on both sides, he led his forces into the underlying plain. When the Macedonians, coming against them, hurled their javelins, the Phocians pretended to flee into the midst of the mountain. The Macedonians in spirited and quick pursuit pressed against them, but the Phocians by discharging stones from the ridges shattered the Macedonian phalanx. Then Onomarchus signaled the Phocians to turn around and close with the enemy. The Macedonians, with their adversaries attacking them from the rear and throwing stones at them from above, were put to flight and retired with much suffering.[43]

Onomarchus was able to use catapults in this battle only because he had time to secretly deploy them well in advance of Philip's arrival and he was able to bait Philip to come within range. Had Philip attacked from a different direction Onomarchus' catapults would have been ineffective and likely overcome easily.

Artillery had its benefits over missile troops, but its cumbersome nature prevented widespread use. Onomarchus, and Alexander as discussed next, was happy to use artillery when firing from a position where the machines could not easily be attacked or forced to move quickly. Nevertheless, it is clear that fourth-century armies were not averse to using artillery in a battle if it proved beneficial.

Combined arms

In adding a dependable heavy infantry phalanx to Macedon's previous reliance on numerous light infantry and a strong force of heavy cavalry Philip created a truly combined arms army. This was the first of its kind in Greece to make best use of the three basic types of unit, four if you count light and heavy cavalry separately as we should. The variety of tactics Philip could and did use in battle demonstrates conclusively the benefits of combined arms warfare. He could act offensively with his phalanx to oppose other phalanxes, he could charge with his heavy cavalry against any gaps in the enemy line whether against light infantry, cavalry, or perhaps even hoplites if on the flanks, he could use his missile troops to maintain a strong barrage against the enemy battle line, he could defensively protect his flanks with his light infantry and cavalry, and he could hold a defensive position with an impenetrable heavy infantry phalanx.

Contemporary Greek armies fielding different unit types but crucially lacking in heavy cavalry could not perform all of these manoeuvres. The most important one they could not perform was a fast assault with heavy cavalry. And this is the vital point for driving the success of the Macedonian military system for so long. Greek battles decided by hoplites, and especially those won by light infantry missile attacks, could be drawn out affairs. Hoplites simply could not attack fast enough to exploit rare gaps in the enemy line before they closed again. The ability of the Macedonians to attack with heavy cavalry at speed revolutionised Greek warfare.

Ferrill argues that the style of warfare practised in the Near East, involving the integration of cavalry, missile troops and light infantry, developed independently of Greek warfare.[44] He argues that the Greek way of war involving heavy infantry was formed free from any influences from the east, and vice versa, until Philip and Alexander united both styles of battle. This argument is untenable since both sides of the Aegean Sea were well aware of each type of warfare. The Greeks knew of the Persian use of cavalry and missile troops in combination, and the Persian Empire was well aware of the Greek preference for hoplite phalanxes throughout the period when the phalanx was developed.[45] The Neo-Assyrians even incorporated mercenary hoplites into their armies in the late seventh century.

Moreover, Macedon was different from Classical Greek *poleis* in that its traditional style of warfare relied more on cavalry and light infantry than hoplites. In this way Macedon was more eastern than Greek. Philip did newly incorporate a heavy infantry phalanx into his army, perhaps because of his experiences at Thebes, but earlier Macedonian warfare was not directly under the influence of Persia, just as the chariot warfare of Celtic Britain was not directly influenced by the chariot battles of Egypt.[46] The similar styles of warfare reliant on cavalry and light infantry developed relatively independently. The fact that a fully integrated army was not achieved properly in the ancient world until Philip shows, rather, that combined arms had yet to be perfected as separate from diversified arms despite its use throughout Mesopotamian history.

Philip was the first general to marshal an integrated army that was interdependent rather than fielding a large army of varied, but uncoordinated, units in the Persian style. He did so not because fourth-century Greece rediscovered the eastern style of warfare but rather through the creation of a truly national standing army incorporating, and integrating, all the different units available and already used in Greece. As Archer Jones aptly summarised:

> the Macedonian tactical method blended the Greek and Persian systems by depending heavily on cavalry but substituting in the line Greek heavy infantry for Persian light infantry. The reliance on cavalry had its origin not only in the Persian practice but also in the traditional importance Macedonians had attached to cavalry in a country more suited to the horse.[47]

As Ferrill states, Philip was successful because he was the first to create a "tactically unified army in which every element was familiar with the style of fighting of the units up and down the line of battle".[48]

Philip II's first battle after his accession to the throne of Macedon, at Heraclea Lyncestis in 358, confirms his use of combined arms in battle and the importance of the heavy cavalry charge.[49] His resounding victory demonstrated for the first time that a heavy cavalry unit pre-determined to work in tandem with a heavy infantry phalanx could prove very effective offensively on a large scale. King Bardylis of Illyria, fearing an attack on his flanks by the superior Macedonian cavalry, formed his infantry into a defensive square with his best troops in the centre ready to face the expected frontal assault of the Macedonians. Philip noticed the weakness of the Illyrian formation at the corners where the centre met with the flank and drew up his troops accordingly. He used the oblique formation adopted from the Thebans placing his best infantry, the *pezhetairoi*, at the right of his formation opposite the left corner of the Illyrians while refusing his centre and left wing. Philip's cavalry attacked the right flank and rear of the Illyrians while he crushed the corner on the left with his infantry. Eventually his attack forced the corner to crumple and the Illyrians fled with many of them being cut down by the cavalry in their retreat.

This is a significant development from the protective use of cavalry as a screen as used by Epaminondas at Mantinea, and an important addition to the oblique formation. Attacking with both cavalry and heavy infantry on the right flank allowed Philip to be doubly offensive while still affording protection to the weaker flanks of his infantry held back in the oblique formation. The speed and devastating impact of the heavy cavalry assault usually meant that the battle was decided before the refused flank of the army ever came into contact with the enemy line. Nevertheless, it still took many years for Philip's successors to complete the process of perfecting combined arms.

Philip's final battle against Onomarchus at the Crocus Field shows how far the Macedonian military machine had advanced the system of combined arms in his reign.[50] Philip still used his phalanx as his main weapon but in this case he protected it with missile infantry while the heavy cavalry units of the Macedonians and his Thessalian allies pounded Onomarchus' flanks. It was a crushing victory and, although sparse, the accounts suggest this was because of the prowess of the heavy cavalry. Philip continued to develop his army during his campaigns in Thrace so that by the time he defeated the Greeks at Chaeronea his army was experienced in and effective at the use of combined arms.[51]

Chaeronea – Macedonian combined arms vs. Greek diverse units[52]

Chaeronea was the battle that established Macedonian hegemony over Greece. It also demonstrated the superiority of Philip II's professional and multi-faceted army over the traditional Greek army reliant on a large phalanx of hoplites supported by small forces of light infantry and cavalry. As a case study it aptly

172 *Macedon and integrated warfare*

demonstrates the advantages of a sophisticated use of combined arms in battle and marks the beginning of the decline of hoplite-based armies.

Sources

The main sources for the battle are Diodorus, Plutarch in his biographies of Demosthenes and Alexander, and Polyaenus.[53] Polyaenus gives the only account of the tactical details of the battle and is the only source to mention the feigned withdrawal. As a result, most of this reconstruction follows Polyaenus with details added from the other sources.

The battle

Philip advanced into Boeotia to confront the army of confederated Greek *poleis* led by Athens and Thebes. The two armies met on the plain in front of the city of Chaeronea. The Macedonian army totalled more than 30,000 infantry and 2,000 cavalry.[54] The Greeks probably fielded a similar force, but no source provides detailed numbers.[55] Diodorus (16.85.6) states that Philip held the advantage in numbers and generalship. The Greeks had drawn up their battle line on an angle, probably so that they had an escape route through the mountains behind them. The Theban Sacred Band was placed on the Greek right wing by the river Cephisus, the traditional place for the elite infantry. The Athenians were stationed on the left flank protected by foothills and the citadel of Chaeronea. Philip drew up his forces at an angle to the Greek line. His right wing, led personally by him, was closest to the Athenians and his left, where Alexander was with the heavy cavalry, was refused. Philip had posted his light infantry and missile troops on his right flank in the foothills to prevent a flanking manoeuvre (Figure 7.1). This oblique starting formation of Philip mirrored the Theban battle line at Leuctra and Mantinea except that the left wing was refused instead of the right. This is the same formation Philip used in his first battle at Heraclea Lyncestis and became the standard deployment for Macedonian armies of the fourth century.

Philip advanced on the Macedonian right but Alexander remained stationary on the left. The sarissa phalanx held the Greek hoplites in place, protected by light infantry on the flank, and then pretended to withdraw back up the hill. The Athenians thought that the Macedonians were retreating and pressed forwards at speed and without direct concern for maintaining formation. The Sacred Band remained where they were unwilling to expose their flank resting on the river in the face of Alexander's cavalry, with the result that the Greek line was stretched and their formation disrupted. Alexander then attacked the Sacred Band leading the Companion cavalry. Philip, once his retreating phalanx had got onto a slight rise in the ground, attacked the disordered Athenian hoplites and broke them easily. The whole Greek line broke and fled, except for the Sacred Band who fought to the last man.

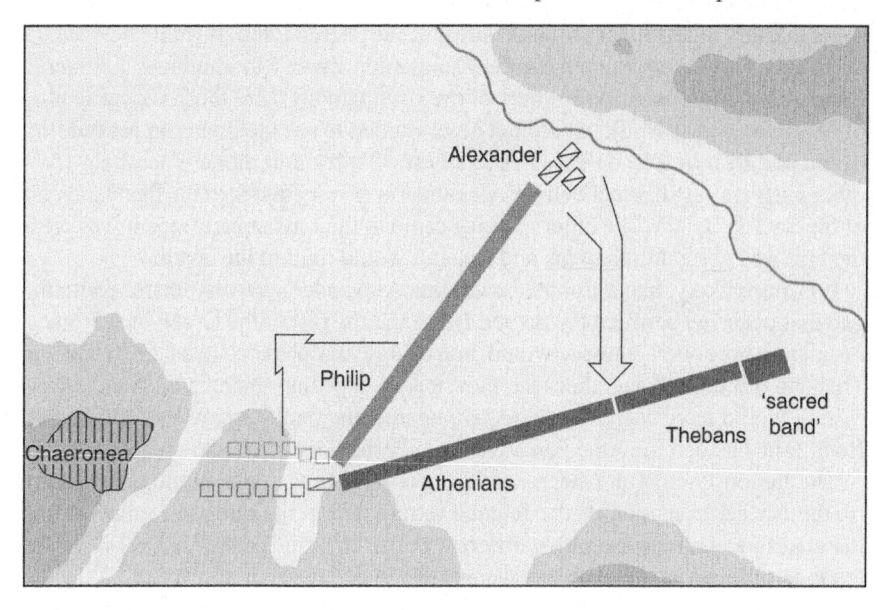

Figure 7.1 The battle of Chaeronea showing the Macedonian oblique formation and the withdrawal up the hill of Philip's phalanx followed by Alexander's charge into the resultant gap

Combined arms

Polyaenus (4.2.2) details the feigned withdrawal as a key stratagem of Philip. This must have been done in order to create an opening for the heavy cavalry to charge into the exposed flanks of the Greek phalanx and force the victory. It is not clear whether Alexander exploited a gap that had been created by the extension of the Greek line, or whether he merely attacked them head on. Diodorus (16.86.3) states that Alexander was the first to break the Greek line, and Plutarch (*Alexander* 9.2) states that he is said to have been the first to assault the Sacred Band, but neither state that he attacked them frontally.

Markle (1978) argues that Philip never armed his infantry with the sarissa and that the sarissa heads excavated at Chaeronea were used by the cavalry against the renowned Sacred Band. Thus, when Plutarch (*Pelopidas* 18.5) records that the Sacred Band did not lose a battle until Chaeronea, and that when Philip, surveying the dead there, was amazed at the bodies of the Thebans mixed with the Macedonian sarissas, it was the sarissas of the cavalry. This would explain how Alexander could break the formation of the Sacred Band by a frontal assault, if that is what he did.[56] However, the practicalities of the use of the cavalry sarissa in a frontal charge at the gallop are disputed.[57] Plutarch may have assumed that the Companion cavalry used sarissas just as the heavy infantry did or more likely some infantry aided in Alexander's defeat of the Sacred Band. It would be difficult and likely very costly in men for the Companion cavalry to eliminate the Sacred Band alone. Moreover, the soldiers of the Companions were the aristocratic elite of Macedon and so Philip would not have wanted to see the flower of his nobility decimated in trying to defeat Greece's best infantry unit alone when help from other units was available. I believe Alexander's cavalry attacked the flank and rear of the Sacred Band while other infantry came to their assistance once it was clear the unit was not going to break and run and would fight to the death.

It is more likely than a frontal assault that Alexander's cavalry charged into the gap that occurred between the Sacred Band and the rest of the Greek line. Horses, no matter how well trained, would not charge the phalanx head on,[58] and the Thebans did not advance because they feared exposing their flank. Alexander's assault would have been more effective against the flanks and rear of the Sacred Band. The haste of the Athenian advance split the Greek line and created the gap.

The famous victory at Chaeronea was due to Philip's novel battle plan relying on the perfect execution of the feigned retreat within the oblique formation and the effective combination of his different units. The pretend withdrawal is one of the most difficult manoeuvres to accomplish in the chaos of an ancient battle and Philip's reliance on it when drawn up en echelon, and its perfect execution here, shows both his own tactical genius and the superb training of the Macedonian army.

The tactics of a feigned withdrawal and the oblique battle line were not vital to the use of combined arms; rather they were the demonstration of tactics that could be used to allow the principles of combined arms to succeed. The annihilation of the Sacred Band by the Macedonian cavalry finally ended the hoplite era in Greece and forced the advanced use of combined arms in warfare. The battle of Chaeronea, then, is a watershed moment in demonstrating the superiority of integrated warfare in battle.

Combined arms conclusions

Philip had inherited a shattered army but within a year had built an army capable of decisively defeating the victorious Illyrians. He went on to train a highly skilful and professional standing army of Macedonian phalangites who were trained in the use of the spear and the sarissa, rather than just a small squadron of elite bodyguards as had been the custom before. The sarissa was Philip's primary innovation and coupled with his use of innovative and decisive tactics, of an oblique battle line and the feigned withdrawal, this made his phalanx of lightly armed phalangites unbeatable. But crucially he also integrated light and heavy cavalry and light infantry into his army and into his battle plans. He established a truly combined arms army where every type of unit was required to protect the vulnerabilities of the other.

Philip's creation of the heavy infantry sarissa phalanx and its perfect integration with the traditional heavy cavalry made Macedon's previously disrespected military the best in Greece. These two units added to an army's normal forces of light infantry and light cavalry made for a very varied military system. None of the units was as effective on its own, but when combined together in integrated warfare they were almost unbeatable with the advantages of each nullifying the others' weaknesses.

Philip also implemented tactics that got the best out of his army on the battlefield and exposed the vulnerabilities of the enemy. The Macedonian army was well trained and able to execute a very difficult tactical manoeuvre at Chaeronea, retreating uphill while in formation and in the face of the enemy. But it was the effectiveness of the Macedonian heavy cavalry, led by Alexander, charging into the gap in the Greek line that precipitated the defeat. This is the same tactic used by Alexander in all of his battles against the Persians, using tactical manoeuvring to create a gap in the enemy line and then launching the heavy cavalry into that gap. At Chaeronea it was the combination of the discipline and steadiness of the heavy infantry phalanx and the offensive rapid attack of the heavy cavalry that was so effective. Philip's army perfectly executed a battle plan reliant on using a simple form of combined arms to devastating effect: heavy infantry and heavy cavalry in perfect combination.

Notes

1 Hunt (2007: 145–6).
2 On early Macedonia see in particular Edson (1970); Hammond (1989) and Borza (1990). See also Ellis (1980); Griffith (1981); Noguera Borel (1999); and the various papers in Roisman and Worthington (2010).
3 For secondary accounts of the army of Philip II see Adcock (1957); Andronikos et al. (1992); Ashley (1998); Hammond (1994); Worthington (2008).
4 See Davies (1949); Wooten (2008).
5 On Diodorus and Theopompus see in particular Shrimpton (1991). See also Hammond (1937); Martin (1981); Martin (1982). On Justin see Heckel and Yardley (1997). On Diodorus' battle descriptions see in particular Hammond (1937); Sinclair (1966); Gray (1980); Westlake (1987); Green (2006).
6 Diodorus 16.2.5.
7 See Ellis (1980).
8 Diodorus 16.4.3. It is likely that a large proportion of the 4,000 troops who died with Perdiccas were from the noble cavalry.
9 Diodorus 16.35.4.
10 Diodorus 16.74.5.
11 Theophrastus *Hist. Pl.* 3.12.2 states that the length of the longest Macedonian sarissa was 12 cubits (or 18 feet), and Asclepiodotus *Tact.* 5.1 states that the shortest was 10 cubits (or 15 feet) long. See Andronikos (1970: 91–107) and Hammond (1980a: 53–63). See also Mixter (1992).
12 Philip's implementation of the sarissa, while important in allowing a cheaper and more effective phalanx, was only a change in armament and the Macedonian phalanx still remained a heavy infantry unit. Therefore, its use is irrelevant to the general process of combined arms which does not require a heavy infantry unit to be specifically armed. I have discussed the sarissa phalanx in detail elsewhere Wrightson (2010); Wrightson (forthcoming). For secondary accounts of the Macedonian phalanx see in particular Adcock (1957); Hammond (1980a); Griffith (1981); Markle (1982); Ashley (1998); Noguera Borel (1999); Heckel (2005); and especially Matthew (2015).
13 Markle (1977: 324).

176 *Macedon and integrated warfare*

14 On Philip's use of the sarissa see Andronikos (1970); Markle (1977); Markle (1978); Hammond (1980a); Mixter (1992); Noguera Borel (1999).
15 Pseudo-Demosthenes 11.22.
16 Markle includes a detailed discussion on the wound and whether it was received from his own men or from the enemy: Markle (1978: 481–2).
17 Sekunda (2014b); Matthew (2015: 1–46).
18 Anaximines *FGrHist* 72 F 4.
19 Greenwalt (2017). See also Greenwalt (2007) and the discussion in King (2018: 107–10).
20 For a discussion of the merits of the argument for Iphicrates' influence on Philip see Griffith (1981) as well as works cited previously.
21 See Devine (1983).
22 Plutarch, *Aemilius Paullus* 16–22; Livy 44.40–42.
23 See Erskine (1989: 385 n. 1) for a short bibliography of studies on the subject and for a detailed analysis of the ancient sources concerning *pezhetairoi*.
24 *Scholia in Demosthenes* 2.17 = Theopompus *FGrHist.* 115 F 348.
25 *Etymologicum Magnum* 699.50–51.
26 Anaximenes *FGrHist* 72 F 4.
27 On Alexander II see Develin (1985); Bosworth (2010); Matthew (2015: 1–46); Greenwalt (2017). For Alexander I see Brunt (1976). The arguments for Alexander I are too complex to lay out here, and I intend to do so elsewhere, but in brief Alexander I was a long reigning monarch (495–450) who annexed Greek colonies on the coast of Macedonia. He also witnessed firsthand the Greek hoplites defeat the Persian army at Plataea and the domination of the hoplite on the battlefield. For him to expand his kingdom without a useful infantry core would be almost impossible, especially in taking cities defended by hoplites. As a successful king he needed a bodyguard unit and so created a phalanx of foot companions to mirror the aristocratic cavalry Companions. Perhaps these foot companions were from the Greek elites in the newly annexed colonies such as Methoni who would be familiar with service as a hoplite. Reames argues that Alexander the Great's best friend Hephaistion was likely from a Greek colony such as this. Moreover, the wide array of exquisite armour and weapons excavated from Archontiko show that some men in the court of the king were infantry armed like hoplites.
28 Erskine (1989: 388–92).
29 This is important for the discussion on at what time Philip trained the whole phalanx in the use of the sarissa.
30 Demosthenes *Philippica* 9.49.
31 Polyaenus 2.38.2. Also see later on a specific analysis of the battle.
32 Diodorus 16.2.2–4; Plutarch *Life of Pelopidas* 26; Justin 7.5; Aeschines 2.26ff.
33 Diodorus 16.3: "After altering for the better the military units and equipping the men appropriately with weapons of war he held continuous manoeuvres under arms and training exercises under combat conditions". Polyaenus 4.2.10: "He made them take up their arms and march often three hundred stades carrying helmet, shield, greaves, sarissa, and in addition to their arms rations and all equipment for day-to-day living".
34 Demosthenes 9.50.
35 For Macedonian cavalry before Philip see Hammond (1998).
36 Thucydides 2.79.
37 As discussed previously, the main victories were both at Olynthus, in 382 and 381, where the Spartan army of Teleutias was routed. Xenophon, *Hellenika* 5.2–3. The Olynthians did use peltasts, cavalry, and hoplites in conjunction, but it is clear their main attack force was the cavalry. On each occasion the Olynthians attacked the Spartans with whatever units they had at hand rather than planning a coordinated assault with all three arms.

38 On the Companions as an institution and in war see especially Heckel (2016: 243–64).
39 Since there are so few instances of field artillery being used in a pitched battle, as opposed to sieges, it is not necessary to enter into a critical analysis of the sources.
40 Marsden (1969: 164–8) outlines all the instances in the Greek world.
41 Marsden (1969: 164–8) notes that there were no mobile catapults until the introduction of the *carrobalista* in 100 CE. See Keyser (1994) for Philip and Alexander's use of artillery.
42 Diodorus 16.34; Polyaenus 2.38.2.
43 Translated by Krentz and Wheeler (1994).
44 Ferrill (1986: 175).
45 See for example Herodotus 7.9.2, where the Persians comment on the stupidity of the Greek way of waging war. See also Hanson (2001: 60).
46 See Griffith (1981) in particular on the influence of light infantry on Macedonian warfare.
47 A. Jones (1987: 21).
48 Ferrill (1986: 83).
49 Diodorus, 16.4–8; Frontinus, *Strategemata* 2.3.2.
50 Diodorus, 16.35.3–6; Pausanias, 10.2.3; Strabo, 9.5.14; Philo Judaeus in Eusebius, *Praeparatio Evangelica* 8.14.33. The sources differ about their accounts of events but it is clear that the battle took place on a wide plain by the sea. Philip perhaps used the same tactics as at Chaeronea and crushed the wing by the sea while holding the other wing back. Whatever tactics he used he soundly defeated the Phocians because of his significant cavalry superiority. The retreating Phocians swam out to reach their allied navy under the Athenian Chares that was anchored nearby but many drowned before they reached him. All the sources agree that the casualty figures were high: over 6,000 troops of the Phocian army were killed and 3,000 taken prisoner. Onomarchus himself died, although the sources disagree on how, and after his death the Phocian cause permanently went into decline. For Philip's campaigns in Thessaly and the Sacred War see Ehrhardt (1967); Markle (1974); Martin (1982); Buckler (1989).
51 Diodorus, 16.85–86; Polyaenus, 4.2.2; Plutarch, *Alexander* 12 and *Demosthenes* 20. There is only one detailed account of the battle from Polyaenus, who is the only source to mention the feigned withdrawal, though others gloss over the actual events. For Philip in Thrace see Badian (1983); Adams (1997).
52 For secondary discussions of the battle see Hammond (1938); Adcock (1957); Rahe (1981); Ashley (1998); Buckler and Beck (2008). For the battle in the context of the other battles of the Macedonians see Pietrykowski (2009).
53 Diodorus 16.86; Polyaenus, 4.2.2; Plutarch, *Alexander* 9.2; *Demosthenes* 20.
54 Diodorus 16.85.5.
55 For the view that the Greeks had the greater numbers see Hammond (1938).
56 See Rahe (1981).
57 On the sarissa in the Macedonian army see in particular Andronikos (1970); Markle (1977); Hammond (1980a); Mixter (1992); Devine (1996); Noguera Borel (1999); Sekunda (2001); Heckel (2005). On the cavalry sarissa in particular see Markle (1978); Manti (1983); Manti (1994); Connolly (2000).
58 Heckel et al. (2010).

8 Alexander the Great – linking the heavy cavalry and the phalanx

Alexander the Great is arguably the most famous general of the ancient world. Alongside Julius Caesar and Hannibal, his name is synonymous with success in war. But as others have argued elsewhere,[1] Alexander inherited from his father the best and most experienced army in the world. He did not make any revolutionary changes in armament like his father, or even in implementing new tactics like his father. His reputation comes from the fact that he perfected the use of integrated warfare and never lost a battle. He introduced a slight adjustment to the deployment of unit types in the Macedonian battle line and fully integrated into his army and battle plans multiple types of unit that he picked up on his campaigns. It is this expertise of command of a truly combined arms army that sets Alexander apart from other generals of his or any era.

Sources

The main histories of Alexander – Curtius Rufus, Diodorus, Arrian, Plutarch, and Justin – are all primarily concerned with Alexander's exploits.[2] As a result they rarely provide details about the individual units in his army. Arrian is by far the author most concerned with military matters, and was a soldier himself, but even he focuses his battle description on Alexander at the expense of the rest of the army.[3] For the fourth century none of the primary historical sources survives, and so it is necessary to determine the underlying sources of the extant accounts. For Philip this is probably Theopompus. For Alexander there are the lost histories of Callisthenes, Cleitarchus, Ptolemy, and Aristobulus.[4]

Infantry

Alexander inherited his father's very experienced and successful army. At its core was the sarissa phalanx and the heavy Companion cavalry. Light infantry and light cavalry rounded out the whole army. In his early years as king Alexander made very few changes to the army and relied on the generals and officers of his father. But as Alexander moved further east in his conquest of Persia, he encountered and incorporated into his own army many different forces and types of units. Thus, when discussing Alexander's army, it is important to draw a temporal line between his time fighting in Greece and his campaign in Asia as the one force was different from the other.

In Greece Alexander's infantry force was very much that of his father. The sarissa phalanx was the mainstay of the battle line, closely supported by the bodyguard unit and light infantry. Alexander's heavy infantry seems to have contained three main divisions, *pezhetairoi*, hypaspists, and *asthetairoi* according to the ancient sources.

One key change under Alexander was the change in terminology for the bodyguards. Before Philip had created and trained a large professional Macedonian phalanx, the *pezhetairoi* were the elite division in the infantry and the only professional soldiers. Under Alexander the term *pezhetairoi* no longer seems to refer to an elite bodyguard; this role has been taken over by the hypaspists. Instead it is taken to refer to the whole phalanx. As Erskine has shown the passage of Theopompus cited previously refers to the function of the *pezhetairoi* as bodyguards in the imperfect tense suggesting that they no longer fulfilled that role when he was writing his account. Arrian is the only historian to use the term *pezhetairoi* in relation to the infantry of Alexander III. It only occurs three times on its own,[5] and "in no case does Arrian say what the term refers to".[6] The term *pezhetairoi* was given to the battalions of the main sarissa phalanx that were not otherwise designated as *asthetairoi*. Alexander then created a new unit of bodyguards, or more likely renamed the old one, the hypaspists and the royal hypaspists.[7]

Under Alexander the *pezhetairoi* were not the elite troops of the infantry bodyguard but were not the whole of the phalanx either. From the first instance in Arrian of the use of *pezhetairoi* it seems that they were an elite body of phalangites only second in preference to the hypaspists.[8] The first instance also shows that the *pezhetairoi* were an elite section of the phalanx taken by Alexander when some of the phalanx was left behind. In the second instance Alexander could not have been leading the whole phalanx but did have all the *pezhetairoi*.[9] Their closeness to Alexander in the first two instances shows that they were of a high status. In the third instance their position in the order of troops shows that they were second in importance among the infantry after the royal *agema* of hypaspists.[10]

The *pezhetairoi* under Alexander did not serve as his bodyguards, as this function was taken over by the hypaspists. Since the *pezhetairoi* were the loyal bodyguard of Philip Alexander may have wanted to create his own bodyguard that was especially loyal to him and him alone. The problems over his succession also suggest that not all of the army were behind him to begin with. Because of this he removed from the *pezhetairoi* their special function of the king's bodyguard, but he let them keep their name and their status as the elite troops of the phalanx.[11]

The *asthetairoi* do not appear in any other source except Arrian and here only six times.[12] Many translators assume the word is a mistake for *pezhetairoi* and amend the text accordingly. This is possible in the first four instances but in the last, 7.11.3, the term occurs alongside *pezhetairoi* and having the latter mentioned twice is unintelligible. In none of the instances does the term refer to the whole phalanx of infantry but rather to one or more battalions.[13] Heckel has shown that these battalions were the ones that always fought closest to the king in battle but were not necessarily the best.[14] I see no reason to disagree with this view and indeed it serves to explain how the term *pezhetairoi* refers to only a part of the phalanx rather than the whole infantry. The few appearances of the name in the sources, like the lack of references to the *pezhetairoi*, can be explained adequately by the fact that they were an individual unit and therefore merely a reference to their commander would indicate their presence. Perdiccas' battalion fought closest to Alexander at the Granicus and Coenus' did so at Issus and was first into the breach at Tyre where it is described as being *asthetairoi*. These two battalions were both *asthetairoi* and anyone hearing the battalions of these two commanders mentioned would know that.

The *asthetairoi* may also have been armed with shield and spear instead of sarissa.[15] They are always stationed next to the hypaspists who fought in this way. Equipment differences rather than closeness to the king perhaps better explains why Alexander would create Persian *asthetairoi*. But it would reduce the Macedonian phalanx's advantage in being armed with the sarissa. If the Macedonian *asthetairoi* were notable enough to have a special designation, then this alone would explain why Alexander would want Persian ones. He meant he would replace Macedonian units serving next to the king with Persian ones. Moreover, the Greek of Arrian with the use of *alloi* suggests that the indication of Persian *asthetairoi* is a qualification to the statement about Persian *pezhetairoi* just as the Royal Persian agema is a part of the Persian Companion cavalry. If he made a wholly Persian phalanx of *pezhetairoi* then those closest to the king would also be *asthetairoi* to truly mirror the Macedonian part of the army.

Since the *asthetairoi* fought close to Alexander in campaigns in rough terrain or in sieges where the hoplite spear would have been preferable to the sarissa, perhaps these were the units like the hypaspists that were regularly experienced in using both sets of armament rather than only using hoplite equipment.[16] Alexander likely did not want to bring from Macedon two sets of weapons for his whole phalanx and could not have had hoplite shields built while on campaign in enough numbers to furnish his whole phalanx. Therefore, it is likely that only the *asthetairoi* among the phalanx battalions were doubly equipped and therefore the ones always selected to lead the attack alongside the hypaspists in sieges or on other instances that required hoplite weapons instead of the long and unwieldy sarissa.

The hypaspists did not exist under Philip, or at least there is no surviving reference to them in the sources for his reign. Anson suggests that they were in place under Philip and fought at the right of his line at Heraclea Lyncestis,[17] but that role was actually performed by the *pezhetairoi*. Milns suggests that the hypaspists were created by Philip "at some time after 356 BC".[18] and that he named them hypaspists as a euphemism, instead of calling them a bodyguard and thus imitating a tyrant, but there is no clear evidence to support his argument. If the *pezhetairoi* remained Philip's elite troops throughout his reign, there was no need for him to create or rename them hypaspists unless the term *pezhetairoi* had been given to another unit. As discussed previously, the term *pezhetairoi* did not necessarily refer to the whole phalanx under Alexander. It seems unlikely, then, that the hypaspists were created by Philip.

Alexander the Great – heavy cavalry   181

The hypaspists were the infantry bodyguards of Alexander. Plutarch, Diodorus, Curtius, and Justin all refer to them as such, *doruforoi, somatophylakes, armigeri*, or *custodes corporis*. They were his most loyal troops and were the only ones to remain loyal to him at the mutiny at Opis.[19] Many of the Successor kings also created a unit of elite bodyguards called either hypaspists or *argyraspids*.[20] Moreover, they were the elite troops of Alexander's infantry. They always took the prime position at the right of the phalanx in his battles and were the first to assault the walls in his sieges. Anson has shown that the term hypaspist was used in Euripides to refer to a position of great honour and in Arrian 1.5.2 to refer to the troops that the Agrianian king sent to Alexander, "his hypaspists, which were the finest and best armed troops he possessed".[21] It is also clear that the hypaspists were men chosen from the phalanx for their excellence.[22] Hypaspists, then, were the elite infantry and the foot bodyguard of Alexander. They had the same role under Alexander as the *pezhetairoi* had under Philip.

They were 3,000 elite soldiers selected as the best from the regular phalanx battalions. Unlike the phalanx regiments which were composed of soldiers from the same region of Macedon, the hypaspists had no local affiliation but were a mix of everywhere. Their loyalty was to the king, and they were usually positioned nearer to his person in battle than the regular phalanx battalions. Their speed of movement and mobility came from their linen thorax, in contrast with the heavy bronze cuirass of the traditional hoplite, and perhaps a lighter shield. Their recruitment from among the best troops of the phalanx meant that they were the fittest and most experienced adding to this mobility. Alongside the Agrianes javelin men, the hypaspists were the troops sent by Alexander on any difficult or speedy missions.

A smaller elite unit within the hypaspists was the royal hypaspists or *agema*. This force comprised young aristocrats who had graduated from the institution of the king's Pages.[23] The Pages were aristocratic youths who served the king directly all the time in guarding him as he slept, bringing him his horse and accompanying him when hunting or if necessary in battle. Once they graduated from this they joined the regular army in an aristocratic unit, either the royal hypaspists or the royal agema in the Companion cavalry though Heckel demonstrates that there is no evidence for the latter.[24] This system of Pages to infantry *agema* to position of command was the aristocratic training regime to take youths through to experienced officers and generals. The Pages, like all Macedonian aristocrats, did everything on horseback but needed to serve as infantry in order to be able to lead an infantry battalion in the future. Senior infantry officers fought on horseback but "did their time" serving on foot in the royal hypaspists first lest they alienate the common infantryman they commanded who trudged everywhere all the time.[25] Unlike the rest of the hypaspists, who were common soldiers selected from the masses of the phalanx, the noble background of the royal hypaspists gave them a higher level of distinction. They were the infantry unit that always accompanied the king's person in battle whether he fought on horseback or on foot.

In battle the royal hypaspists were stationed next to the Companion cavalry while the regular hypaspists stationed next to them were expected to maintain a link between the cavalry and the phalanx. The royal hypaspists functioned as *hamippoi* who could keep pace with the Companion cavalry but fight in close combat well enough to hold the battle line together until the slow-moving phalanx could arrive to press home the victory.[26] Though they ran alongside the Companion cavalry the royal hypaspists, just as regular hypaspists, were armed as hoplites.[27] Since this unit was made up of young nobles, this was also the opportunity for individuals to make their name by conspicuous action close to the king's person in battle. It is through this proximity to the king in battle armed with shields that the unit is also known as bodyguards. When in Illyria the royal hypaspists rode ahead and dismounted to fight alongside the Companion cavalry Arrian terms them *somatophylakes*, bodyguards.[28] All officers of the Macedonian cavalry and infantry regiments in Alexander's army first served in this unit until they gained sufficient experience or admiration to be promoted.

The best example of the royal hypaspists acting as *hamippoi* and seeking renown is in Curtius' account of the death of Lysimachus' brother Philip:

> After this Alexander left the phalanx behind and advanced with the cavalry to suppress the rebels. [34] At first the men somehow coped with the road, which was steep and obstructed with rocks, but soon the horses suffered exhaustion as well as worn hooves. Most could not keep up, and the line became progressively thinner as the excessive effort crushed their sense of shame, as often happens. [35] But the king, frequently changing horses, pressed the retreating enemy relentlessly. The young noblemen who formed his usual retinue had given up the chase, all except Philip, the brother of Lysimachus, who was in the early stages of manhood and, as was readily apparent, was a person of rare qualities. [36] Incredibly, Philip kept up with the king on foot although Alexander rode for 500 stades. Lysimachus made him frequent offers of his horse, but Philip could not be induced to leave the king, even though he was wearing a cuirass and carrying weapons. [37] On reaching a wood in which the barbarians had hidden, this same young man put up a remarkable fight and gave protection to his king when engaged in hand-to-hand combat with the enemy [38] but, after the barbarians scattered in flight and left the forest, that vital spark which had kept him going in the heat of the fight deserted him. Sweat poured suddenly from all his limbs and he leaned against the nearest tree, [39] but even that failed to hold him up; the king took him in his arms, where he collapsed and died.[29]

Clearly Philip was running alongside Alexander's horse armed as a hoplite in order to protect the king during combat. Wearing a cuirass, he was not armed as a light infantry peltast. He ran for so long at such speed he expired after his task in protecting Alexander was completed.

As a result of their speed of movement, the hypaspists were often thought to be light infantry in comparison with the heavy infantry of the sarissa phalanx.[30] Their superior training and abilities, their speed, and their proven loyalty meant that Alexander took the hypaspists with him on his rapid marches or into the most difficult terrain when he needed mobile but heavy infantry.³¹ The hypaspist corps should be distinguished from a hoplite phalanx because they did not fight in a rigid phalanx formation.³² They were often used in sieges as the main assault force since they were Alexander's best heavy infantry unit.³³ Hypaspists were the ideal unit for Alexander to take with him everywhere because they were armed as heavy infantry and they were well trained enough to be able to keep pace with the light infantry and cavalry.

The hypaspists probably used the hoplite panoply in pitched battles although they were also trained in the use of the heavier sarissa.³⁴ Their very name, which means "shield bearer", suggests that their most important weapon was their shield. From the position of the hypaspists as the protective flank guard of the phalanx and their role of acting as a link between the cavalry and the infantry they must have been armed with the spear and larger hoplite shield instead of with the sarissa. The sarissa-armed phalanx would have been vulnerable on its right side where the phalangite was not protected by his shield. In sieges both the phalangites (perhaps only those from the *asthetairoi* battalions) and the hypaspists fought with the panoply of a hoplite alongside the cavalry.

In his invasion of the Thracians at the Shipka Pass, Alexander is recorded by Arrian as telling his hoplites to lie under their shields.³⁵ This must mean hypaspists as the pass was too narrow for the whole phalanx to deploy and Alexander likely relied on his elite troops. At Alexander's last battle, the Hydaspes, the hypaspists likely used the sarissa to attack the elephants.³⁶ The hypaspists were soldiers taken from the regular sarissa phalanx battalions. The hypaspist, then, was trained in the use of both the spear and the sarissa.

The term *argyraspids*, or Silver Shields, is used to describe a unit of elite Macedonian infantry in the period of the Successors. It also appears in Arrian after Alexander returns to the Indus and receives a consignment of silver armour. In Arrian the term then replaces the hypaspists. It seems logical, then, that the *argyraspids* were the same unit as the hypaspists but renamed once they received their shields embossed with silver in India. Both units are 3,000 men strong and both are clearly the elite of the infantry. Lock has argued that they were a different unit,³⁷ but this view has been rightly condemned, most notably by Anson.³⁸

As he marched into Asia Alexander added to his army any unit that he thought would be useful. Almost any type of soldier that was in use at the time featured somewhere in Alexander's battle line. But more importantly Alexander incorporated units of expert light infantry into the army that he sometimes relied on in his most difficult engagements. Like many Greek armies he fielded contingents of Cretan archers. But his most famous and most utilised light infantry unit was the Agrianes javelin men.

These expert light infantrymen were javelin throwers from a Thracian tribe that allied with Alexander during his invasion of that region in his first campaign.³⁹ These javelin men from the upper Strymon valley are attested 50 times in Arrian and are "used on almost every occasion which called for rapid movement on difficult terrain".⁴⁰ They were Alexander's most trusted light infantry unit and he used them in almost every engagement that required his elite or fast-moving soldiers.

At the battle of Gaugamela, it was the use of the Agrianes as the link between the hypaspists and the phalanx that prevented a catastrophic hole appearing in Alexander's battle line. Alexander made great use of his light infantry units in all his battles as part of his integrated system of combined arms warfare.[41]

Alexander's infantry featured every type of unit but still relied on the sarissa phalanx for its main foundation. The various units of light infantry were used as flank guards and vanguards. The elite Agrianes were Alexander's *hamippoi* often charging alongside the fast attacks of the cavalry. The hypaspists were a mobile heavy infantry force and the heavy infantry sarissa phalanx, the *pezhetairoi* and *asthetairoi*, held the centre of the line. These heavy infantry forces were the best infantry units of their day but it was their use in combination with the cavalry that brought Alexander so many victories.

Cavalry

The main offensive unit of Alexander's army was the Macedonian Companion cavalry. This unit functioned as heavy cavalry and relied on hand-to-hand combat rather than missiles in battle.[42] Its form and function was not much different from Philip's Companion cavalry. Made up of eight squadrons of Macedonians recruited on a regional basis this was the elite cavalry unit in the army. Armed with a lance and shield they were heavy cavalry who used the shock of a charge to gain the advantage in battle.

Among the Companion cavalry was the unit that fought immediately alongside and was led by the king. This was known as the royal squadron, and later the *agema*. It is not clear at all who the soldiers were who fought in this unit. Heckel states that there is no evidence they were aristocrats who had graduated from the Pages, but there is no evidence to their identity at all. They may have been an elite unit featuring soldiers chosen from among the other Companion squadrons or they may have been nobles only. Whoever they were they always fought next to the king in battle and thus accompanying Alexander were always in the thick of the fighting.

Equal in importance tactically as heavy cavalry was a unit of Thessalian cavalry that had served in the Macedonian army since the time of Philip II. Alexander usually placed this unit on an equal footing with the Companions, as the battles of Issus and Gaugamela show, as the left wing offensive flank guard to mirror the positioning of the Companions on the right.[43]

Alexander also made use of his other cavalry units ranging from light-armed scouts to allied cavalry.[44] There were scout units of light cavalry attached to the Companions known as *prodromoi*. A named and important unit of light cavalry was the Paeonians. The army also featured a unit of light cavalry armed with lances called the *sarissaphoroi*. These were light cavalry able to engage in a melee if necessary and thus were a good link between missile light cavalry and the heavy Companions and Thessalians. As he advanced into Asia Alexander also used barbarian missile cavalry from javelin armed to horse archers.

Alexander the Great – heavy cavalry

The best example of the varied nature and tactical usage of Alexander's cavalry forces is the battle of the Granicus.[45] The Persians lined the bank of the river with their excellent cavalry and placed their infantry behind. Arrian states that Alexander used an oblique advance. He began by sending forward just to the right of the centre of his line a vanguard of a squadron of Companion cavalry and a force of light cavalry comprising the Paeonians and prodromoi with one unit of infantry in support. This force was by no means strong enough to win any engagement with the elite Persian cavalry on the banks, especially when disadvantaged by attacking uphill. Rather it was Alexander's tactical ploy to draw the Persian forces down from the bank into the river and thus expose their flanks to a counterattack. This is exactly what transpired. The initial force took heavy casualties but did their job and Alexander's counterattack with the Companion cavalry on the edge of the right wing charging into the Persian flank added to the advance of the phalanx and hypaspists in the centre caused the Persians to flee. The subsequent battle with the Persian infantry was then simply a concern with mopping up the remnants of the force with a combined assault of infantry and cavalry.

In this battle, the first in his invasion of Asia, Alexander made integrated use of both light and heavy cavalry together as well as infantry as *hamippoi* and the oblique formation perfected by his father. The tactical reliance on foreign units in crucial roles shows Alexander's ability to make use of every unit according to its merits regardless of origin or national biases. Alexander's army was fully integrated and made the best use of every type of cavalry unit available fulfilling the main principle of combined arms warfare.

Artillery

The only other occasions in our period of interest where artillery was used in battle were by Alexander. The first was to cover his withdrawal against the Illyrians.[46] Alexander was forced to withdraw his army over a river to engage the enemy on the other side. To cover his army, he led the archers and Agrianes javelin men to keep the enemy at a distance. When he realised that he needed more firepower he "set up his engines on the bank and ordered every kind of missile to be discharged from them at furthest range" and succeeded in covering his army's withdrawal.

The second was to cover his crossing of the river Jaxartes in Sogdiana against the Scythians.[47] There, the casualties inflicted and the impression of the weapons caused the Scythians to flee. The great range of the missiles, as described by Arrian, suggests the machines were set up on the bank. Since they were intended to only support the crossing until Alexander could land his archers ahead of his other units, the machines would not need to have been taken across the river themselves. Remaining on the bank they could fire over the heads of Alexander's soldiers until the beachhead was established well enough for the archers and Agrianes to take over the missile bombardment. On both occasions Alexander used artillery to cover the difficult and lengthy crossing of a river in the face of enemy fire. He needed to force back the enemy using missiles to screen his river crossing and artillery had a greater range and power than missile troops. He also needed a way to screen the crossing of his missile infantry so they in turn could screen the crossing of the rest of the army. Outside of siege warfare, it seems that this was the usual use of artillery in battle in Greek warfare.

Clearly Alexander had artillery in his army while on campaign, but most of his battles were fought in an offensive manner without giving him the time, or perhaps need, to deploy static artillery to aid his attack. Against the Persians such static artillery would have been vulnerable to the enemy cavalry, since at Gaugamela his baggage was raided behind the main Macedonian battle line.[48] At the Granicus he did not need to create time for a crossing since the river was shallow enough to allow his army to march over.[49] He perhaps also feared that the Persian cavalry would disrupt his formation if he took time to set up the artillery. At Issus he fought the battle as soon as his army arrived at the river Pinarus and so he had no time, or need, to deploy his artillery train, which must have been left behind because of the speed of his march.[50]

Combined arms

Alexander continued using his father's tactics, which had become standard practice in the professional Macedonian army. Moreover, the Macedonian army was now practiced at using combined arms in battle and achieved a great level of tactical integration of units. For the first time an army practised the most sophisticated level of combined arms, integrated warfare. As Hammond states:

> The remarkable feature of the European army which Alexander inherited from his father and led into Asia was its composite nature and the specialized expertise of each part. Alexander had at his disposal almost every known variety of cavalry and infantry, heavy or light, regular or irregular, as well as experts in siegecraft, artillery, road making, bridge-building, surveying and so on. Each unit was the best of its kind, properly equipped and highly trained.[51]

Although he was undoubtedly a great general, Alexander advanced the cause of combined arms in two crucial ways:[52] the complete integration into the army of every type of useful foreign unit[53] and the use of the hypaspists as a link between the slow attack of the sarissa phalanx and the rapid charge of the heavy cavalry units.

Alexander's first military innovation was not so important in helping win his battles, but it laid the foundation for the future developments of combined arms under his Successors. This was the integration of many types of unit into the Macedonian army. Before Alexander conquered the Persian Empire, Macedonian military forces consisted primarily of the Macedonians themselves, although Philip did make use of mercenaries and allied troops.[54] After Alexander's many conquests, foreign units had to be incorporated in order to maintain his empire.[55]

Arrian describes the enrolling of Persians into the Macedonian phalanx.[56] In each basic section of this mixed phalanx 12 Persian troops are sandwiched between four Macedonian junior officers.[57] This phalanx composition may never have been implemented since we have no other evidence for its existence after Alexander, however, it does show Alexander was willing to experiment with foreign soldiers in the army. The foreign troops Alexander primarily used were missile and light infantry and cavalry.[58] As discussed next, Alexander made great use of his light infantry units in all his battles as part of his integrated warfare system.[59] Dio Chrysostom records an anecdote that Diogenes the Cynic philosopher on meeting Alexander stated that he had to travel with "his Macedonian phalanx, his Thessalian cavalry, Thracians, Paeonians, and many others" but he (Diogenes) could go anywhere alone.[60] This passage highlights the most important non-Macedonian troops in Alexander's army, the Thessalian cavalry viewed as equals of the Companions, the Thracians of whom the most important were the Agrianes, and the Paeonians, a squadron of light cavalry scouts. But Alexander had to lead all these units together in order to maintain his success because his army relied on combined arms so much.

One of the best examples of the level of training and discipline in all of Alexander's units, as well as the effectiveness of his light infantry, is his campaign in Thrace at the start of his reign. In that campaign Alexander found himself trapped between two large armies, one in a city and the other on the heights behind. Alexander could not fight both at the same time. He had to deal with one without being attacked by the other. He decided to surprise the enemy on the hills in his rear by having his army calmly execute numerous drill manoeuvres. He drew up his phalanx and cavalry wings, and presumably his light infantry also, on the plain below the heights and had the whole force silently carry out many different drill exercises in full view of the Illyrians. The Illyrians came down to watch. The whole force fled as soon as Alexander's army moved to engage them. According to Arrian they were surprised and in awe of the expertise of the Macedonian army.[61]

Contrary to popular belief it was not just the drills of the phalanx that drew the admiration of the Illyrians, but the expertise of the whole army. Above everything else this shows the level of combined arms in use in the Macedonian army. The coordinated movements of all the different units in the army[62] was so well done in silence that it was deemed so unusual that it was terrifying to the locals.

The next engagement in the campaign also shows Alexander's ability in leading the combined arms army in difficult operations, in this case making a fighting withdrawal over a river. The Illyrians were on a hill on Alexander's line of march away from the city. According to Arrian, Alexander's location had hills on one side and a river on the other so that to cross the river his rear would be exposed to those in the hills.[63] To extricate the Illyrians from commanding the heights Alexander sent a force of heavy cavalry and mounted royal hypaspists against them with orders for half of the hypaspists to engage the enemy on foot alongside the cavalry if they stood their ground.[64] The Illyrians moved to hills on either side. Alexander rode up to the hill previously occupied by the Illyrians in order to observe the enemy while he sent the archers and Agrianes across the river to screen the crossing of the regular hypaspists and the phalanx. When the enemy charged against the rear, Alexander personally counterattacked and the phalanx turned to threaten to trap the Illyrians between the two Macedonian forces. The Illyrians fled and Alexander shielded the crossing of his rearguard with missiles from artillery on the bank and from the archers midstream.[65]

This engagement is a triumph of Alexander's generalship and his use of combined arms to achieve his objective. He used each unit in the best way so that in combination his army crossed the river in the face of the enemy without suffering a single casualty. A flying force of cavalry and mounted elite infantry gained Alexander the strategically important command of the heights. He screened the crossing of his slow phalanx with the light infantry, and for one of the few times in his campaign made use of artillery also. When the enemy did attack he threatened to trap them between cavalry and the phalanx forcing their retreat. Every type of unit in his army had a job to do and was required to do it properly. Without adequate missile troops he could not have screened his crossing. Without cavalry he could not move fast enough to take the initiative of occupying important terrain. Without heavy infantry he could not threaten a strong counterattack, and without elite infantry capable of riding horses well he could not support his rapid advance force of cavalry with *hamippoi*. Even his artillery was needed here to increase the range and effectiveness of his covering missile barrage. The whole army worked in harmony perfectly.

Alexander finally defeated the Illyrians once both armies had come together by assaulting their undefended camp at night after they thought he had retreated in panic following his withdrawal over the river.[66] Alexander recrossed the river at night and took with him a flying column consisting of the Agrianes and the archers, the hypaspists, and two phalanx battalions likely the *asthetairoi*.[67] The Agrianes and the archers attacked first so unexpectedly that they found some of the Illyrians still in their beds. In such a rapid advance in secret at night Alexander only brought his best units, the more reliable light infantry, his elite hypaspists, and two battalions of the phalanx that were used to rough terrain.[68] He did not bring cavalry likely lest the horses give away his position. Though not a fully combined arms attack it demonstrates the effectiveness and necessity of Alexander's light infantry.

Alexander's second innovation was the most important for combined arms. Because the battle plan under Alexander used a rapid charge of heavy cavalry to press for victory, usually on the right flank, this often left a hole in the battle line next to the slow-moving sarissa phalanx where the enemy could expose and attack the weak flanks of the phalanx. The hypaspists, a unit of heavy infantry who were not armed with the sarissa and could move at a faster speed while still maintaining excellence in close-combat fighting, were used, and maybe even created, by Alexander to bridge this gap.

The battles of Issus and Gaugamela are the best examples of this.[69] In both battles we can see the elite nature of the hypaspists and their role as the link between the phalanx and the cavalry. They attacked with Alexander at a rapid pace and protected the exposed right flank of the phalanx. They were positioned on the right of the phalanx and were used by Alexander, along with the Companion cavalry, as the cutting edge of the attack. This gave the cavalry the freedom to attack wherever the enemy was weak, while allowing the phalanx to continue to advance slowly, without having to worry about its flanks. It was a vital addition to the Macedonian army in the advancement of combined arms and allowed cavalry and infantry to attack in the way that they were best suited without needing to worry about a counterattack.

Alexander used the oblique formation in both battles. It is not specifically mentioned in any source concerning Issus but it was his best tactical option in the circumstances. At Gaugamela Alexander used the oblique formation coupled with the placement of a reserve phalanx of Greek allies in the rear.[70] His positioning of the attack on the right flank is reminiscent of Philip's tactics at Heraclea Lyncestis. After Philip's successes at Heraclea and Chaeronea, the oblique formation became the standard battlefield deployment of Macedonian armies and was used often by Alexander and his Successors.

At his final large-scale battle, the Hydaspes, Alexander did not use the oblique formation.[71] His first assault with heavy cavalry was on the right flank as usual but there is no indication that his centre and left were refused, and indeed this would have been unnecessary since the Indians were not intending to attack. Porus, the Indian king opposing Alexander's crossing of the river Hydaspes, had sent an advance attack force of chariots and cavalry but they were easily routed by Alexander. Porus had drawn up his main army in defensive formation to await Alexander's attack.

Porus had his infantry placed either behind or between the elephants and his cavalry were on his flanks. Alexander advanced with his phalanx in his centre screened by light missile troops. He placed his cavalry on his right wing opposite the main force of Porus' cavalry. The Indian cavalry on their right redeployed to their left wing so that their cavalry numbers were equal to Alexander's on that side. Coenus led a battalion of the Companions around the Indian line while Alexander attacked with his cavalry on the right. The outmatched Indian cavalry was quickly and easily pushed back into the infantry and the elephants thus disrupting the Indian formation. The Macedonian phalanx advanced towards the Indian lines in the centre. They used their sarissas in conjunction with the missile troops and eventually inflicted enough damage on the elephants and infantry that they fled.

Arrian states that the Macedonian phalangites were given orders "not to take part in the action until they observed the enemy's phalanx of infantry and their cavalry thrown into confusion by his (Alexander's) own cavalry force".[72] Here, then, Alexander used his phalangites as his shock troops instead of his cavalry to bring victory. Still the first assault was with the cavalry. Unlike his other engagements in Persia Alexander did not have to face a strong cavalry force. The mainstay of the Indian line was the elephants against which the heavy cavalry was not effective. As a result, Alexander adapted his battle tactics to make full use of the extra length of the sarissa and the depth of the phalanx to push back the disrupted Indian line until it fled.

The hypaspists do not seem to have fought as an elite body of infantry forming a link between the phalanx and the cavalry. The defensive formation of the Indians meant that they did not need to do so and the small number of regular phalangites likely had to be increased by the hypaspists fighting in the phalanx alongside them. Porus fielded 30,000 infantry, 4,000 cavalry, and a significant number of elephants. Alexander had separated his army into three divisions in order to confuse Porus as to where he was going to cross the river thus severely depleting his offensive force.[73] In his lead group, the one with which he fought Porus, there were approximately 10,000 infantry, of which about 3,000 were hypaspists and the same number were phalangites, and 5,000 cavalry. This is a very small army compared with Alexander's other battles. The phalangites, though superior in every way to the Indian troops, were outnumbered 10 to 1 so the hypaspists were required to join the phalanx lowering the odds to only 5 to 1. Since the Indians were in a defensive stance no flank guard was required.

Rather than have a small phalanx armed with the sarissa and one armed with spear and shield in traditional hypaspist style, Alexander may have armed hypaspists with sarissas also. Diodorus states "they used their sarissas to good effect against the Indians stationed beside the elephants".[74] But Arrian states that Alexander "gave a signal for the infantry to lock shields concentrate into the most compact mass possible and advance the phalanx"[75] and Plutarch states that "the battle was fought at close quarters".[76] Both these passages seem to suggest that Alexander's infantrymen were armed with spears and shields, whereas Diodorus, and Curtius, seems to suggest that they used sarissas. It is likely that the different sources refer to the different units in Alexander's army, the phalanx with sarissas and the hypaspists with spears and shields. It is possible that at first the phalanx was armed with sarissas but when these broke or became impaled in a body the phalangites switched to swords or even the axes that Curtius mentions. This battle appears from all the sources to have descended into complete carnage once the Macedonians engaged at close quarters with the elephants.

Combined arms conclusions

Alexander made use of all his different types of units in the best way as each situation demanded. He always fielded every type of unit in his army but the specific uses of each unit depended upon the engagement at hand. Normally he employed the oblique formation holding back his left wing while he attacked in person on the right. The left wing was protected by Thessalian heavy cavalry supported by an assortment of allied or mercenary light cavalry and infantry. In my view the Greek mercenary hoplites likely mirrored the hypaspists in linking the sarissa phalanx with the cavalry on the left wing, though this is not seen in the sources. This left wing at Issus and Gaugamela fought a defensive action to maintain integrity for long enough to let Alexander win on the other flank. In the centre was the sarissa phalanx. The right wing had the hypaspists protecting the immediate flank of the phalanx, the Agrianes and perhaps other light infantry acting as hamippoi, the strike force of Companion cavalry, and then a flank guard of allied and mercenary light cavalry and infantry. At Issus and Gaugamela it was the movement of this flank guard that created the gap for Alexander's decisive charge.

At the Granicus and the Hydaspes, and the use of a rearguard at Gaugamela, Alexander altered his tactics and deployment according to the terrain or the enemy battle line but still organised the army along the same basic structure. Alexander always used a combination of different units and troop types for victory and in doing so established the best example of combined arms warfare in the Greek world at its greatest realisation: integrated warfare.

Issus and Gaugamela: integrated warfare in action

Alexander fought four main battles in his campaign against Persia, but Issus and Gaugamela are the two that best allow for a detailed examination of his use of combined arms. At each, Alexander's tactics were almost identical demonstrating the standard formation and actions of the Macedonian army in utilising combined arms in battle, as shown in the battles of Paraetacene and Gabiene below.

Sources

Our sources for the battles are the Alexander histories of Arrian, Diodorus, Curtius, and Justin, and the biography of Plutarch.[77] Arrian is the only author that provides a full description of the military details, rather than focusing on the actions of Alexander. Even so, at Gaugamela Arrian confuses the details of the specific events of the battle, as discussed next. Nevertheless, from these sources it is possible to reconstruct a relatively reliable version of the events of each battle.

Issus[78]

Alexander advanced into Cilicia in pursuit of Darius after he had subdued the cities on the coast of Asia Minor. Darius decided against advice to wait for Alexander in the wide-open plains of Coele Assyria[79] and advanced behind him through the Syrian Gates to cut off his supply lines.[80] Alexander turned back, and the two forces met at the narrow plain of Issus.

Arrian and Curtius are clear that the battle of Issus was fought across a river and that the Persians were relying on the cavalry situated on their right wing.[81] Diodorus states that the Macedonian cavalry was drawn up in front of the line but there is no evidence for this.[82] It is not clear which river was the river Pinarus that is mentioned in the sources as the place of the battle and it is also possible that Arrian's account of the banks as being precipitous is because of his confusion with the river bank at the Granicus.[83]

Darius was stationed in the centre of his line with the two forces of Greek hoplite mercenaries lining the bank on either side. Next to these were the better units of Persian infantry called the Cardaces, but these were probably only light infantry.[84] The Persian cavalry was on the right wing by the sea where the terrain was the most open and suitable for a cavalry charge in numbers. In the foothills on the other side of the river Darius had left a small force of light infantry and cavalry in order to threaten Alexander's right flank.

Alexander countered the Persian formation by placing all the allied and mercenary cavalry on his left wing under the command of Parmenion, while he led the Companion cavalry against the Persian left. Next to Alexander were the hypaspists and the sarissa phalanx followed behind and to their left, opposite the Persian mercenary Greek infantry. Alexander advanced obliquely hoping to hold back his left wing under Parmenion and prevent it from being overcome by the numerically superior Persian cavalry. The Persian force in the foothills was neutralised by a small force of light infantry and cavalry allowing Alexander the freedom to advance against the main Persian army.

Arrian states that the river bank up which the Macedonians had to fight was precipitous in many places and was in places reinforced by Persian defences.[85] As the Macedonian phalanx advanced across the river its formation was disrupted because of the blockades. The Greek mercenaries took advantage of this situation, able to use their shields and shorter spears to get inside the long sarissas of the Macedonians, and the fight for the banks was fierce.

The Persian cavalry on the Macedonian left wing charged at Parmenion's force thus overcoming Alexander's oblique formation. The Macedonian left under Parmenion managed to hold the Persian cavalry for a time, largely on account of the excellence of the Thessalian cavalry. Alexander launched his heavy Companion cavalry in a rapid charge against the Cardaces on the right. After routing them he turned to attack Darius in the centre.[86] The king's flight caused the Persian line to disintegrate and the whole army to retreat in disorder, despite the gains of the Greek mercenaries in the centre and the cavalry on the Persian right wing.

The success of the Greek mercenaries against the Macedonian phalanx seems to have almost tipped the balance of the battle towards the Persians. Arrian states that 120 Macedonians of note died in this part of the battle.[87] Probably other not so notable Macedonians also died demonstrating the vulnerability of a divided and disorganised phalanx. The arrival of Alexander on the flank and rear of the Greeks caused them to retreat thus saving the phalanx from probable defeat.

Alexander likely adopted the oblique attack that his father Philip had used at Chaeronea. Although it is not specifically mentioned in any source that he held back his left wing, this seems to have been the best tactic for him to use. By refusing his left he would delay the Persian cavalry, albeit briefly, from overcoming his flank and give time for his right to win. Alexander's positioning of the attack on the right flank is reminiscent of the tactics at Chaeronea, Granicus, and subsequently at Gaugamela. The break in the Macedonian phalanx that occurred in the centre, although adequately explained by the uneven nature of the terrain, is even more understandable if the left flank and centre of the Macedonians were to hold back while the oblique right flank attacked rapidly. The terrain caused some parts of the phalanx to move more slowly than normal making it harder to maintain an unbroken line next to the fast-moving hypaspists and so a gap appeared.

Combined arms

Alexander's army fully integrated all the types of unit available into the battle plan. At Issus, just as at Chaeronea, it was the effective combination of heavy cavalry and heavy infantry acting together that won the battle. The light infantry did little at Issus except for the crucial role of neutralising the Persian force in the foothills. Nevertheless, it is clear that Alexander's army was well trained and completely reliant on using heavy cavalry and infantry together. In fact, had the cavalry of Parmenion not fended off the Persian cavalry and Alexander's attack with the Companions not routed the Persian left wing the Macedonian heavy infantry may well have been defeated by the Greek hoplites opposing them. Individually the units in Alexander's army were not that much better than the Persians, but the collective whole was far superior. The battle of Gaugamela aptly demonstrates that.

Gaugamela[88]

Alexander after subduing the rest of Phoenicia and Egypt followed Darius into Mesopotamia and Darius met him with a massive army on the vast plain of Gaugamela, chosen to enable the Persian numbers to overwhelm Alexander's much smaller force. The sources for the battle of Gaugamela all state that the Persian line was significantly longer than the Macedonian on both sides.[89] Alexander drew both his wings back to compensate and placed the Greek allied infantry in his rear as a last line of defence, in order to prevent encirclement and to fill any gaps that may appear in the phalanx. Darius had levelled the plain so that his scythed chariots could attack anywhere along the Macedonian line and may have dug holes to hinder a Macedonian cavalry charge, but this would also hinder his own.[90]

Initially the Macedonian army was severely outflanked, so much so that Alexander on the right was opposite Darius in the centre of the Persian line. Darius intended this so as to rely on overwhelming numerical superiority, and his best cavalry, to counter the known ploy of Alexander, used so well at Issus, in leading a personal charge on the right. Darius hoped to tempt Alexander into a charge against a force so large that he would be overcome. Instead Alexander edged his whole line to the right so that his right flank extended beyond the flattened area and beyond the Persian centre.[91]

Darius could not let Alexander continue to advance like that and so destroy his tactical advantage. Darius sent a strong cavalry squadron of 3,000 to the Persian left to try to get around Alexander's line. This included 1,000 Bactrian horsemen who, alongside the Saca Scythian cavalry, were the best heavy cavalry unit in the Persian army. The forerunners of the Seleucid Cataphracts, both horse and rider were heavily armoured in chainmail and the riders armed with swords, lances, axes, and bows

To counter this move Alexander sent a few hundred mercenary light cavalry to attack the Persians and hold them in place. After the retreat of Alexander's initial force, either forced or planned, Alexander sent in more and better troops of 1,100

194 Macedon and integrated warfare

allied Thracian light cavalry and 6,700 veteran mercenary infantry. To reinforce their cavalry Darius' wing commander Bessus led in around 8,000 more armoured heavy cavalry of Bactrians and Saca. This conflict stretched on for a while with repeated assaults by Bessus' cavalry against the lighter Macedonian cavalry and infantry but the Macedonian line held.

Darius also launched his scythed chariots at the Macedonian lines. One hundred chariots went directly against Alexander's Companion cavalry on the right wing but the Agrianes, Alexander's javelin men, were stationed in front of the cavalry as a screen for just this eventuality. They easily overcame the chariots with their expert missile attacks. Fifty more chariots attacked Parmenion's Thessalian cavalry on the left flank where the missiles of the Macedonian light infantry were similarly disruptive. Fifty chariots apparently attacked the phalanx in the centre of the Macedonian line. The sources state that until they were overcome in the rear of the Macedonian lines these Persian scythed chariots caused carnage among the phalanx even removing limbs of the phalangites. Although stated by the sources, it is unlikely that the phalanx opened its ranks to let through the chariots.[92] This would be a disastrous move for such a tightly packed formation exposing their vulnerable sides to the scythes on the chariot. Moreover, horses would not be able to attack a phalanx frontally on account of the bristling hedge of sarissas. What the sources probably refer to instead is that the light infantry and hypaspists parted to make room for the chariots with the intention of attacking them with missiles as they passed through.

Darius called a halt and general advance for the whole Persian army in seeing Bessus' cavalry engaged on the left. In doing so a gap formed between the centre of the Persian line and Bessus' cavalry. Alexander then led the Companion cavalry supported by the Agrianes and the hypaspists to attack the weak spot caused by the extension of the Persian line. The more mobile heavy infantry force, the hypaspists, acted as the strong link between the slow-moving phalanx and the fast attack of Alexander's cavalry preventing a gap from occurring in the Macedonian line. The javelin men were Alexander's most experienced and trusted light infantry and were better able to link the fast attack of the cavalry with the advance of the hypaspists. Alexander's initial charge caused chaos in the Persian ranks but he was on the point of becoming surrounded when the Agrianes arrived to maintain the link. The hypaspists and then the phalanx in turn engaged the enemy opposite and gained the upper hand. On the other wing the Persian cavalry vastly outnumbered Alexander's second-in-command, Philip's old general Parmenion, and some of the Persians managed to get to the Macedonian baggage train a few miles behind the battle.

Arrian incorrectly states that the Persian cavalry went through a gap in the Macedonian line, whereas Diodorus, Curtius, and Plutarch all say that the cavalry went around the left flank. If a gap had formed in the Macedonian phalanx it would have been a disaster and the phalangites would have been exposed and vulnerable, as they were at Issus. Moreover, the Greek infantry were placed behind the main Macedonian line just for this eventuality. It is unlikely Alexander or any of his experienced commanders would allow such a gap to occur. And if it did they would have rushed reinforcements to plug the hole, just as happened at the battle of Issus. At that battle a break in the Macedonian line occurred on account of the rough terrain in ascending a river bank. The commander of that section of the phalanx, Ptolemy son of Seleucus, rushed personally to plug the gap and he and at least 120 Macedonians died in the hotly contested struggle. It is almost impossible to believe that Alexander's officers would allow a similar gap to occur at Gaugamela and not do anything about it, especially considering the prior positioning of the Greek mercenaries.

Alexander personally led the Companion cavalry through the gap in the Persian left wing. He then wheeled slightly to launch a direct attack on Darius' bodyguard in the centre of the Persian line. Darius apparently fled after his chariot driver was killed by Alexander's own spear. This may be an added layer of personal heroism for Alexander and Darius, but it is likely Darius did not just run away as soon as Alexander attacked as he was a successful general before Alexander. Nevertheless, his flight caused the centre of the army to flee and the retreat spread to the whole Persian line. Parmenion on the Macedonian left wing was hardly managing to hold the outflanking Persians when his opponents retreated along with the rest of the Persian army. The Persians who attacked the Macedonian baggage in the rear also retreated once the result of the rest of the battle became obvious.

Alexander once again used the oblique attack extending his line to the right in order to draw out the Persians and create a weak point in their line. This is exactly the same tactic that Epaminondas used at Leuctra 40 years previously only here Alexander was facing a much larger army and primarily used his cavalry to attack the gap. The placement of a reserve phalanx is similar to the defensive square that Bardylis adopted at Heraclea Lyncestis only Alexander went on the offensive and thus won the battle before he could suffer the same fate as the king of Illyria, encirclement and collapse.

Combined arms

Alexander was forced to make full use of all his units in order to overcome such a numerical disadvantage. Alexander used a tactical deployment to prevent an outflanking manoeuvre. He advanced slowly in order to maintain his formation and edged obliquely to the right to escape the levelled ground. He used his light infantry and missile troops to overcome the Persian chariots in particular and used his light cavalry as a flexible force to aid any part of the line where his units were hard-pressed. His heavy infantry phalanx was the glue in the line advancing slowly at an angle to hold down and attack the majority of Darius' army. The hypaspists, a more mobile heavy infantry unit, protected the phalanx's flank and linked it to the heavy cavalry both before and after Alexander's charge into the Persian lines. In this battle the Agrianes also ran next to the hypaspists to allow extra flexibility in maintaining the intact battle line when advancing at great speed.

On his right flank where the Persians expected to gain superiority and nullify the Companion cavalry Alexander used expertly his various units and types of mercenary cavalry and infantry to continue a holding action and make the decisive gap for Alexander's personal charge. Where Darius intended to wreak havoc with his scythed chariots Alexander ordered his light infantry to make gaps and overcome the horses and drivers with missiles. The phalanx itself was invulnerable to a frontal attack by scythed chariots if it maintained its formation, hence its slow and methodical advance.

Alexander's whole plan was reliant on an offensive use of heavy cavalry charging at speed into a weak point in the enemy line. When the Persians tried to overcome his right flank Alexander sent reinforcements into the fight to at least match the enemy. In fact, it was Alexander's decision to reinforce this skirmish that led to the creation of the gap in Darius' battle line. All of Alexander's units worked together to overcome the numerically superior army of Darius and to nullify Darius' own battle plans.

We can also see the elite nature of the hypaspists and their role as the link between the phalanx and the cavalry. They attacked with Alexander at a rapid pace and protected the exposed right flank of the phalanx while supporting the cavalry as the weight behind the cutting edge of the attack. This gave the cavalry the freedom to attack wherever the enemy was weak, while allowing his phalanx to continue to advance slowly, without having to worry about its flanks. It was a vital addition to the Macedonian army in the advancement of combined arms and allowed cavalry and infantry to attack in the way that they were best suited without needing to worry about a vulnerable break in the battle line.

Alexander used the oblique formation by extending his line to the right in order to draw out the Persians and create a weak point in their line. This tactic had become standard practice in the Macedonian armies of Philip and it continued to feature in the battles of the Successors. Darius set up his battle line so as to prevent Alexander's expected charge on the right flank. Yet it was Alexander's clever manoeuvring by edging his army to the right that foiled Darius' plans and created the very gap and charge that Darius was trying to prevent.

Since every type of unit available was in Alexander's army at Gaugamela, and was used in a system of combined arms, this battle marks the best example of the complete integration of combined arms warfare in the Greek world in allowing an army outnumbered 5 to 1, and fighting on terrain that benefited the enemy, to win such a defining victory. However, Alexander did not make use of elephants in his army, as his Successors did, and this unit, if deployed, still had to be utilised in integrated warfare, as discussed next. Nevertheless, since the elephant never featured in Greek warfare until after Alexander's victory over the Persian Empire the Macedonian army of Alexander did make use of every unit available in a system of integrated warfare, the final realisation of combined arms.

Combined arms conclusions

Alexander inherited an experienced army expert and practised in using combined arms in battle. With two small adjustments to the tactics and deployment of the army Alexander perfected a greater implementation of combined arms using every available unit in the ideal way. The oblique formation gave Alexander time to engineer a gap in the enemy line, often using light infantry and light cavalry to expand an initial skirmish into a battle. He then charged on the right flank with the Companion cavalry closely supported by mobile elite infantry units, the Agrianes and the hypaspists. The slow but impenetrable sarissa phalanx held the centre of the line, and another strong force of light and heavy cavalry held the left of the line. The same system was repeated in all of Alexander's battles but this repetitive process made it difficult to counter given the experience and familiarity built into the soldiers and officers in the army. Such was the success of this system that all the Successors of Alexander and most Hellenistic generals adopted the exact same tactics and deployment.

Alexander had laid down the groundwork for the integrated armies of the Successors and had demonstrated to subsequent generals how to employ the system of combined arms at its greatest level of sophistication, integrated warfare. Such was his success that all the generals of Macedonian style armies that followed sought to emulate him with generally limited success. Unfortunately, not many of these generals proved as successful as their illustrious predecessor. Plutarch provides the anecdote that, "Demades, after Alexander had died, likened the Macedonian army to the blinded Cyclops".[93]

Notes

1 Most notably Gabriel (2010).
2 For Curtius see Atkinson (1975); Atkinson (1980); Gunderson (1982); Hammond (1983); Currie (1990); Heckel (1994); Atkinson (1994). For Plutarch see Tracy (1942); Wardman (1955); Hamilton (1969); Wardman (1971); Stadter (1992). For Diodorus see Drews (1962); Hamilton (1977); Hammond (1983). For Justin see Hammond (1983); Heckel and Yardley (1997). For Persian sources see Brunt (1962).
3 See Harrer (1916); Schepens (1971); Bosworth (1980b); Ameling (1984); Bosworth (1988); De Voto (1993). On Arrian's military descriptions see Milns (1978).
4 On these lost histories see Hamilton (1961); Drews (1962); Atkinson (1963); Welles (1963); Hamilton (1977); Hammond (1983); Devine (1994); Guthrie (1999).
5 There are five other occurrences but they shall be discussed in relation to the *asthetairoi*. See Bosworth (1973).
6 Erskine (1989: 392).
7 On the hypaspists and their armament, training, and function see in particular Milns (1967); Milns (1971); Ellis (1975); Anson (1981); Anson (1985); Foulon (1996a and 1996b); Heckel (2005); Sekunda (2010); Heckel (2012); Heckel (2013); Heckel (2016: 270–4).
8 Arrian *Anabasis* 1.28.3. Alexander leads his phalanx in an assault on a small hill in front of the city. He likely did not have his whole phalanx with him and the terrain would have hindered the whole phalanx deploying effectively.
9 Arrian *Anabasis* 7.2.1. Alexander meets with Diogenes the Cynic and halts before him with the hypaspists and *pezhetairoi*. He did not bring the whole phalanx, all 9,000 soldiers.
10 Arrian *Anabasis* 7.11.3. In the mutiny at Opis Alexander is threatening to replace each unit of the army in turn with Persians and that they will have the same names: "An *agema* called Persian, and Persian *pezhetairoi*, and *asthetairoi* also, and a Persian battalion of silver shields".
11 See Erskine (1989: 392–3).

198 Macedon and integrated warfare

12 Arrian 2.23.2; 4.23.1; 5.22.6; 6.6.1; 6.21.3; 7.11.3.
13 For detailed discussion of the term see Bosworth (1973).
14 Heckel and Jones (2006: 31–2); especially Heckel (2009); and recently Heckel (2016: 266–8).
15 Anson (2010) argues that they had stars on their shields. See Heckel (2016: 268).
16 Heckel (2016: 268).
17 Anson (1985: 246–8).
18 Milns (1971: 186), and see Milns (1967: 509–12).
19 Arrian 7.8.3.
20 See later for argyraspids.
21 Anson (1985: 247).
22 See Tarn (1948: 140).
23 On the Pages and Royal hypaspists and bodyguards see Heckel (2016: 245–9).
24 Heckel (2016: 256). Contra see Reames (2010: 190) that the Pages served in either the infantry or cavalry *agema*.
25 See Wrightson (2010) for infantry officers riding horses in battle and commanding from the rear.
26 On Royal hypaspists as hamippoi see Heckel (2012).
27 Peucestas at the siege of the Malli was a Royal hypaspists who use his hoplite shield to cover Alexander's wounded body against a shower of missiles and gained much fame as a result Arrian *Anabasis* 6.10.2; Diodorus 17.99.4; Curtius 9.5.14–7.1.
28 See below for a discussion of this campaign. See also Heckel (2012: 19) and note 18.
29 Curtius 8.2.33–9. Trans. Yardley. As quoted in Heckel (2012: 18).
30 See Tarn (1948) for the fullest argument as to why the hypaspists were not heavy infantry.
31 Bosworth (1989: 259–60). A good example is Alexander's attack on the Susian Gates: Polyaenus 4.3.27.
32 The hypaspists always were the link between the right flank of heavy cavalry and the infantry phalanx in the battles of Alexander. Their position as a mobile link advancing with the cavalry at speed when they charged forwards, suggests that the hypaspists may not always have been able to stay in a tight formation. If they were armed with sarissas, breaking formation would have been disastrous.
33 The best example is leading the assault into the breach at the siege of Tyre (Arrian, *Anabasis* 2.23.2).
34 Heckel (2005).
35 Arrian *Anabasis* 1.1.9: Alexander stated "to his hoplites that whenever the carts tumbled down the slope, those who were on level ground and could break formation were to part right and left, leaving an avenue for the carts, those caught in the narrows were to crouch close together; and some were actually to fall to the ground and link their shields closely together so that when the carts came over them they were likely to bound over them". The Macedonian phalangites could be armed with the hoplite panoply, and they are even described here as hoplites specifically. However, this passage likely only refers to the hypaspists.
36 Diodorus 17.88.2.
37 Lock (1977: 373–8).
38 Anson (1981: 117–20).
39 The Agrianes were in the army of Philip: Bosworth (1989: 12).
40 Bosworth (1989: 263).
41 See for example at Issus: Arrian *Anabasis* 2.9.2–4. It is not necessary to outline all of the different light infantry units in Alexander's army. Suffice it to say that he used all unit types from archers to javelin men and they were fully integrated into his battle plans, the most important concern for this study of combined arms. See especially English (2009: 67–92).

42 For secondary discussions of Alexander's cavalry see Hamilton (1956); Brunt (1963); Milns (1966); Daniel (1992); Ashley (1998).
43 Issus (Arrian *Anabasis* 2.7–11; Curtius 3.8–11; Diodorus 17.32–34; Justin 11.9) and Gaugamela (Arrian *Anabasis* 3.8–15; Curtius 4.9; Diodorus 17.56–61), cf. Arrian *Anabasis* 3.15.3. These battles are discussed in detail below. On Alexander's use of the Thessalian cavalry see Strootman (2012).
44 The best example is Alexander's troop dispositions at Gaugamela (Arrian *Anabasis* 3.11.8–12.5).
45 Arrian *Anabasis* 1.12.8–17.1; Diodorus 17.19–21; Plutarch *Life of Alexander* 16; Justin 11.6.10–15. Cf. Polyaenus *Strat.* 4.3.16. Fuller (1960: 147–54); Davis (1964: 34–44); Nikolitsis (1973); Badian and Foss (1977); Hammond (1980b); Devine (1988).
46 Arrian, *Anabasis* 1.6.8. His war against the Taulantians and Illyrians lasted a few days and involved a number of conflicts.
47 Arrian, *Anabasis* 4.4.4. Curtius (7.9) states that Alexander placed his artillery on rafts in the middle of the river.
48 Arrian *Anabasis* 3.14.5–6; Curtius 4.9; Diodorus 17.59.5–8.
49 Arrian, *Anabasis* 1.12–16; Diodorus 17.19–21; Plutarch, *Alexander* 16; Justin 11.6.
50 Arrian *Anabasis* 2.7–11; Curtius 3.8–11; Diodorus 17.32–34; Justin 11.9.
51 Hammond (1981: 33).
52 There is much scholarship on the army of Philip and Alexander. The best analyses are Adcock (1957); Fuller (1960); Milns (1976); Bosworth (1989); Ashley (1998).
53 The elephant and the chariot are the two notable exceptions. Elephants were integrated by the Succesors of Alexander. Chariots were almost obsolete, though some of the Successors and the later Hellenistic kings did make use of them.
54 Hammond (1991); Ashley (1998).
55 Hammond (1996). See also Bosworth (1980a); Bosworth (1989); Bosworth (1994).
56 Arrian 7.23.3–4. This unit is called a *dekas*, originally consisting of ten men but increased to 16. It is commanded by a *dekadarches* who fights in the front rank. Behind him is a man on double pay, called a *dimoirites*, and behind him is a ten-stater man who gets more than the average soldier but less than the *dimoirites*. Another ten-stater man is at the back.
57 Bosworth (1989) argues that these were missile troops but that would nullify the effectiveness of a pike phalanx and the mobility of missile troops.
58 Some light infantry may have been Macedonian but there is little evidence. Perhaps the javelin men of Balaccrus at Gaugamela were such troops (Arrian, *Anabasis* 3.12.3, 3.13.5). See Badian (1965).
59 See for example at Issus: Arrian *Anabasis* 2.9.2–4. It is not necessary to outline all of the different light infantry units in Alexander's army. Suffice it to say that he used all unit types from archers to javelin men and they were fully integrated into his battle plans—the most important concern for this study of combined arms.
60 Dio Chrysostom 4.8.
61 Arrian *Anabasis* 1.5.11–1.6.4. The Illyrians, just as the Thracians, usually relied on light infantry and had very little training or organisation in battle. See Wilkes (1992). I have discussed this campaign and Alexander's use of surprise elsewhere: Wrightson (2015a).
62 Though Arrian only mentions the phalanx and 200 cavalry on either wing other forces must have been present too. For a commander of Alexander's experience, he would have brought some light infantry also since the army he opposed had cavalry, javelin men and slingers as well as hoplites, in other words it was a combined arms army. Although he intended it Alexander cannot have been entirely certain that the army's manoeuvres would scare away the Illyrians before they fought a battle. He must have prepared for an engagement and so would have needed some light infantry to oppose the large force of Illyrian missile troops.

63 Arrian *Anabasis* 1.5.12.
64 This shows that the Royal hypaspists were capable horsemen, as was to be expected since they were aristocrats well practiced in riding from childhood, and here fought as *hamippoi* alongside horsemen.
65 Arrian *Anabasis* 1.6.5–8.
66 Arrian *Anabasis* 1.6.9–11. For Alexander's campaign in Illyria Hammond (1974); Hammond (1977).
67 The battalions of Coenus and Perdiccas. As discussed previously the *asthetairoi* fought closest to Alexander and were distinct battalions.
68 As Heckel (2016: 266–8) has shown these two battlaions were from Upper Macedonia, a region that was hilly and very similar topographically to Illyria.
69 Issus (Arrian *Anabasis* 2.7–11; Curtius 3.8–11; Diodorus 17.32–34; Justin 11.9) and Gaugamela (Arrian *Anabasis* 3.8–15; Curtius 4.9; Diodorus 17.56–61).
70 Arrian, *Anabasis* 3.12.
71 Arrian 5.11–18; Plutarch *Life of Alexander* 60; Diodorus 17.87–88; Curtius 8.13–14; Polyaenus 4.3.22.
72 Arrian *Anabasis* 5.16.3.
73 Arrian *Anabasis* 5.9.2. For a detailed analysis of the numbers and units in each group see Fuller (1960: 186–7), although he is confused about the phalanx commanders.
74 Diodorus 17.88.2.
75 Arrian *Anabasis* 5.17.7.
76 Plutarch *Life of Alexander* 60.11.
77 Arrian *Anabasis* 2.7–11; Curtius, 3.8.27–3.11; Plutarch, *Life of Alexander* 20; Justin, 11.9.1–10; Diodorus, 17.32–34.
78 For secondary discussions of the battle see in particular Murison (1972); Devine (1985a); Devine (1985b); Hammond (1992); English (2011). For the fullest critical source discussion see Bosworth (1980b: 285–313). For the battle in the context of the other battles of the Macedonians see Pietrykowski (2009).
79 Arrian *Anabasis* 2.6.
80 Arrian *Anabasis* 2.7.1.
81 Arrian *Anabasis* 2.7.1; Curtius 8.13–15.
82 Diodorus 17.33.1. In fact, Diodorus suggests that Alexander kept the phalanx in reserve behind the cavalry. He has probably confused Issus with the deployment of the Persians at the Granicus. Or his sources noted that Alexander sent out scouting cavalry while still marching to the battlefield and he thought it was the battle deployment.
83 Arrian *Anabasis* 2.10.1. See Devine (1980); Hammond (1992). See also Bosworth (1980b: 203–4).
84 The Cardaces were infantry placed on either side of the Greek mercenaries and are said by Arrian to be hoplites. This is unlikely due to the placement of archers in front of their line, which would have been unnecessary and disadvantageous for a hoplite phalanx. For a detailed discussion of the Cardaces see in particular Tarn (1948: 180–2); Bosworth (1980b: 208).
85 Arrian *Anabasis* 2.10.1.
86 Most of the vulgate sources focus on this event (Diodorus 59.8; Curtius 15.1–2). Alexander's personal prowess is contrasted with the cowardly actions of Darius in Arrian (*Anabasis* 2.11.4). The famous Alexander Mosaic found in a house in Pompeii emphasises the later fascination with Alexander's heroic attack on Darius: see Cohen (1997).
87 Arrian *Anabasis* 2.10.7.
88 Large portions of my description here have been published in a paper in Spanish, Wrightson (2018). For a detailed discussion of the battle see Griffith (1947); Marsden (1964); Cawkwell (1965); Devine (1975); Welwei (1979); Devine (1986); Charles (2008); English (2011). For the battle in the context of the other battles of the Macedonians see Pietrykowski (2009) and Ray 2012.

89 Arrian, *Anabasis* 3.8–15; Curtius, 4.9.9–10 and 12–16; Diodorus, 17.56.61; Plutarch, *Life of Alexander* 32–33. See Devine (1989a).
90 Arrian, *Anabasis* 3.13.3; Polyaen. *Stratagems* 4.3.6, 17.
91 Arrian, *Anabasis* 3.13.1–2, 3.14.1–2.
92 See in particular Heckel et al. (2010).
93 Plutarch, *Galba* 1.4.

9 The Successors – war elephants and integrated warfare

The developments to combined arms warfare that the Successor generals themselves made were the continuing advancement of integrating the different styles of unit incorporated by Alexander.[1] The two generals who did this well were the two most successful of the period: Eumenes and Antigonus.[2] The most important tactical advance in this period was the use of elephants in battle.[3] Elephants do not have to be incorporated into an army in order to achieve integrated warfare in battle, but if they are mustered in an army the battle plan should integrate them tactically in the best way possible according to the general principles of combined arms warfare.

The most successful tactical use of elephants in combined arms warfare was achieved at the battle of Ipsus, and so this is the terminal point for this study. At this battle in 301 the principal last remaining Successor generals fought for supremacy.[4] The battle reveals the usual adoption of Alexander's traditional Macedonian tactics of the oblique formation and integrated warfare in offence and defence. However, the clear development was the effective use of elephants.[5] By 301 the Macedonian style armies of the Successor kingdoms had successfully managed to tactically incorporate all styles of unit available in the army and each unit was at its peak level of martial efficiency.

In this section it is not necessary to divide our examination into infantry and cavalry since at the end of the fourth century all armies used combined arms at a great level of tactical integration of heavy and light infantry and cavalry. Moreover, all of the Successor armies fielded versions of the units that were in Alexander's army, heavy and light cavalry of various forms and ethnicities, light infantry or peltasts, javelin men and archers, the sarissa phalanx and hypaspists. Instead of on individual units or armament differences the focus is on the final developments of combined arms in the fourth century and the perfection of integrated warfare.

Sources

The evidence for warfare in the late fourth century comes almost exclusively from Diodorus.[6] "No historian of Classical Greek or early Hellenistic history can avoid using Diodorus Siculus as a source, and for some periods he is even the most important one. Such is the case for the years after Alexander the Great's death".[7]

Plutarch's various *Lives* add occasional details but are more concerned with the actions of individuals rather than battles.[8] Just as for the histories of Philip and Alexander, it is important to establish the earlier source of both Plutarch and Diodorus. For the Successors this is usually taken to be Hieronymus of Cardia.[9] In view of the few sources available, scholars cannot discount any piece of information that is relevant.

Combined arms

Eumenes' battle at the Hellespont against Craterus and Neoptolemus in 321 demonstrates the level of integrated warfare that was now standard in Greek armies.[10] It also showed Eumenes' ability to formulate a battle plan to neutralise the strengths of the enemy; a principal aspect of combined arms. He placed light cavalry on one wing supported by a defensive screen of elephants in order to draw off and delay the enemy's heavy cavalry. His own heavy cavalry then attacked on the other wing in strength at the same time as his phalanx in the centre. On this occasion his tactics resulted in both enemy generals being killed, one by his own hand, and the superior enemy phalanx was forced to retreat since it no longer enjoyed the protection of any cavalry.

Eumenes' use of light cavalry and elephants as a defensive screen against heavy cavalry was the key innovation of combined arms here. Previously light and heavy cavalry usually fought against units of a similar armament. In Alexander's battles the Persian heavy cavalry was opposed by the Companions or the Thessalians and the light cavalry by Alexander's allied light horsemen.[11] The advantage of light cavalry over heavy was its greater speed. With space to manoeuvre light cavalry could neutralise the effectiveness of heavier units by avoiding close combat while threatening to counterattack on the flanks or rear if the opportunity presented. This often meant that heavy cavalry was unable to disengage from lighter horsemen lest they expose their own battle line to a flank attack, but were at the same time unable to come to hand-to-hand combat and make use of their superior fighting ability.

This battle also demonstrates the best use of elephants in battle, as a static flank screen for cavalry.[12] Elephants were able to hold a flank defensively, especially against cavalry unused to pachyderms.[13] Elephants could be used offensively in battle in a thundering heavy charge, especially against units that were unfamiliar with the large animals. But this was always a dangerous option since the death of the lead elephant or the constant goading of enemy weapons could cause the herd to run amok and charge at friendly forces instead.

Macedonian generals were normally reluctant to use elephants offensively because of the possibility that they could be goaded into turning on their own troops.[14] Pyrrhus' victory over the Romans at Asculum, where his elephants tore through the infantry legions, demonstrates the effectiveness of elephants against an infantry armed with swords rather than spears.[15] But Pyrrhus was successful for the most part because of the Roman soldiers' fear of the unfamiliar beasts.[16] At the final battle of the campaign at Beneventum Pyrrhus' elephants were initially successful against the Roman legions until they fell afoul of the Romans' anti-elephant devices.[17] The defeat of his elephant charge cost Pyrrhus the battle.

Pyrrhus' defeat demonstrates that elephants are most effective against an enemy that has not seen them before. Once the enemy devises plans to deal with elephants, pachyderms alone cannot bring victory. In general elephants are much more effective against cavalry than infantry, since horses that are unused to elephants are terrified of them. Alexander devised a ruse to enable his army to cross the Hydaspes secretly since he feared that Porus' elephants would scare his horses and prevent them crossing on rafts and landing successfully.[18] The victories of Pyrrhus over the Romans at Heraclea and Antiochus over the Galatians,[19] were both a result of sending elephants against cavalry. However, both kings fought against an enemy that was unused to elephants, and so could rely on the psychological effect of an elephant charge to disrupt the enemy formation and precipitate a rout. Generals who were used to pachyderms could effectively counter any offensive thrust of elephants, whether in battle or in a siege, reducing the offensive effectiveness of elephants in war.

Numerous other examples demonstrate the perils of using elephants in battle. At the battle of the Hydaspes, Porus, the Indian king, stationed elephants across the front of his whole battle line, intermingled with light infantry.[20] This was intended to prevent the Macedonian phalanx reaching his inferior infantry and to break up the phalanx. Instead the Macedonians were able to use their sarissas to goad the elephants into turning on their own army causing significant carnage. In 312, Demetrius intended to win the battle of Gaza, against Ptolemy and Seleucus, using his elephants to defeat the phalanx.[21] Unfortunately for Demetrius, Ptolemy wanted to capture the animals and devised easily movable chains of iron spikes to trap the elephants in position. This device proved so successful that Ptolemy was able to capture all 43 of Demetrius' elephants before they could do any damage and seeing this all of Demetrius' army fled.[22]

As a screen on a flank the elephants could be left as an immovable obstacle taking up a lot of space on the battlefield and thus ensuring that it took longer for enemy cavalry to outflank the battle line. Having to ride clean around the elephants, especially when stationed on a refused flank as part of the oblique formation, the cavalry could not close on the enemy fast enough to impact the early stages of a battle. By the time a force got past the elephants the battle was usually won elsewhere along the line.

The other advantage of using elephants in this way was to maintain the threat of destructive offensive power if the opportunity arose. A charge of elephants was a devastating event if harnessed properly. The enemy commander could not just leave his flank exposed to an elephant force just in case they attacked. The flank screen kept the elephants from disrupting friendly formations and attacks while utilising the tactical benefit of a sizeable and threatening force on the wings of an army.

Passing over other instances of creative generalship of Eumenes and Antigonus, or other generals, as irrelevant to the development of combined arms,[23] I shall move on to the battles of Paraetacene and Gabiene in order to examine in more detail the early uses of elephants in fourth-century battles.[24] In these two battles Eumenes and Antigonus faced each other.

Paraetacene

The battles of Paraetacene and Gabiene mark the pinnacle of combined arms in the armies of the Successors. At each battle both opposing armies were very large and fully integrated tactically using all the types of unit available in the late fourth century. As a result, each battle is a perfect case study for the state of combined arms in Greek warfare after Alexander.[25]

Eumenes and Antigonus were the most successful generals of Alexander's Successors.[26] At Paraetacene each general had different strengths and planned on using them in the battle.[27] Eumenes had more elephants and a superior phalanx reliant on a core of veterans of Alexander. Eumenes intended to use the elephants, with light troops, as a screen on his left wing opposite Antigonus' elite cavalry, while he used his heavy cavalry and superior phalanx to defeat Antigonus elsewhere. This was the plan he used at the Hellespont and the same oblique formation used by Alexander complete with an offensive heavy cavalry charge on the right wing to decide the battle.

Eumenes drew up his line as follows from the left: light cavalry fronted by elephants and light infantry, the veteran phalanx with elephants in front, heavy cavalry with an advance guard of squadrons of Eumenes' slaves or pages, and reserve squadrons of cavalry at an angle on the flank. This wing was fronted by 40 elephants at intervals. Antigonus, drawing up his battle in oblique formation all fronted by his elephants, wanted his elite cavalry on his right wing to win before his inferior phalanx succumbed to Eumenes' veterans or his left wing fell to Eumenes' superior cavalry. He drew up most of his light cavalry on his left flank, especially his horse archers, with orders to wheel about firing missiles and to avoid directly engaging with Eumenes' cavalry. Antigonus' line was as follows from the left: light cavalry, the phalanx, heavy cavalry with an advance and rearguard of light cavalry troops of Antigonus' slaves, and the 30 best elephants in an echelon line.

In the battle itself Peithon, the commander of Antigonus' left wing, insubordinately attacked first and engaged Eumenes' right wing relying on his cavalry's numerical superiority. This was the complete opposite of the oblique formation that Antigonus intended in holding the left wing back. Peithon's manoeuvrability did great damage until Eumenes counterattacked with light cavalry and light infantry redeployed from the left wing and routed Peithon's troops all the way to the foothills. At almost the same time the two phalanxes met in the centre where Eumenes' veteran troops won, overcoming the numerically superior troops of Antigonus. Unfortunately, Eumenes' phalanx in the joy of their victory advanced too far becoming disconnected from the static flank screen of elephants and cavalry. Antigonus counterattacked through this gap between Eumenes' phalanx and left wing routing the surprised and isolated cavalry behind the elephant screen. Eumenes was unable to save the situation on that flank immediately since all his army had chased the fleeing enemy too far and the fighting concluded with Eumenes' forces victorious in the centre and on the right wing, and Antigonus winning on the left wing. Both sides rallied their troops for a second confrontation, but they broke off from an attack since it was the middle of the night by the time they were reorganised to fight again. Although victorious, Eumenes' veteran soldiers refused to leave their baggage train unattended and left the field, while Antigonus forced his men to encamp on the field and thus claim the victory.[28]

Combined arms

At Paraetacene both generals relied on the traditional Macedonian oblique formation for victory, as used by Philip and Alexander. Each army was drawn up with right wing advanced and left wing held back. Unfortunately for Antigonus, Peithon's insubordination almost cost him the battle, just as Peucestas' cost Eumenes at Gabiene later, completely destroying the oblique formation. Because of Peithon's unplanned attack, until his personal last ditch charge, Antigonus was completely outgeneraled and his soldiers were outperformed. Antigonus' personal charge robbed Eumenes of a deserved victory and rescued a draw. He expertly exploited the inflexibility of Eumenes' battle line in order to attack the exposed flanks caused by a gap in the line. This tactic is identical to that used so successfully by Alexander at Gaugamela. The devastating gap in Eumenes' line resulted from the static use of his elephants, which were unable to move rapidly to cut off Antigonus' charge and maintain contact with the advancing phalanx.

Though Diodorus does not say so, this must have resulted from a tactical error on the part of Eumenes' left flank commander Eudamus. He commanded light cavalry as well as elephants and so had troops mobile enough to maintain contact with the rest of the battle line. Moreover, the phalanx in the centre could hardly have moved forwards at significant speed while holding sarissas and fighting the enemy. Eudamus should have been able to prevent a gap occurring in the line. In fact, that should have been his main tactical goal in commanding a defensive flank formation. Perhaps he did not want to abandon the protection of the foothills, or perhaps he was disconcerted by Eumenes commandeering some of his troops to rescue the right flank. Whatever the reason, Eudamus' inability to do his job and maintain the cohesion of the battle line cost the army a decisive victory.

Eumenes perfectly employed the principles of combined arms by attacking with his best troops while using the others to hold off the enemy. Antigonus' plan intended to do the same but was foiled by Peithon's insubordinate actions. Eumenes was ultimately unsuccessful because he allowed his left flank guard to become detached from the centre and thus did not neutralise Antigonus' best unit of heavy cavalry, the other main principle of combined arms. Antigonus staved off defeat by exploiting a hole in Eumenes' battle line with a devastating charge of heavy cavalry, just as Alexander at Gaugamela. Both generals knew how to play to their army's strength and attack the enemy's weakness, and the result was a costly draw.

Gabiene

At Gabiene Antigonus made similar plans.[29] Antigonus put cavalry on the wings and the phalanx in the centre, with the whole line fronted by elephants and interspersed light infantry. However, Eumenes, as the chief military innovator among the Successors, experimented with a different tactical deployment. Eumenes stationed his best cavalry on his left wing opposite Antigonus' better cavalry, just as Epamimondas had done at Leuctra. Eumenes also drew up his elephants *en echelon* to the left of the wing as a flank guard, just as at Paraetacene. His phalanx was stationed in the centre again, with the right wing consisting of his weaker cavalry and the rest of his elephants. Eumenes intended to hold back his weak right wing until the battle was decided by his superior cavalry on the left. Antigonus intended to overwhelm Eumenes' elite left wing. So both commanders made use of an oblique formation, Antigonus according to the usual Macedonian manner of advanced right and refused left. Eumenes switched around the angle of the formation to advance his left. He was determined to personally oppose Antigonus and his best troops similar to his victory at the Hellespont against Craterus. Unfortunately for Eumenes, he did not use the elephants properly and in fact they hamstrung his battle plan.

The battle began when the elephants and cavalry engaged on Eumenes' left. Antigonus took advantage of the cloud of dust raised by the battle to send a detachment of light cavalry to capture the baggage train of Eumenes' army.[30] At the same time, again hidden by the dust, Antigonus personally led his heavy cavalry to attack the flank of Eumenes' heavy cavalry. Eumenes' cavalry commander, Peucestas, was frightened into retreat by the horsemen charging unexpectedly out of the dust cloud and took with him almost a third of Eumenes' elite cavalry. Eumenes stayed with the rest of his loyal cavalry fighting fiercely although isolated. In a desperate attempt to save the battle Eumenes attacked with his flank guard of elephants but since they were drawn up at an angle each elephant was introduced to the action one by one, thus losing all the advantage of their numerical superiority. Despairing, Eumenes withdrew his remaining cavalry round to his right wing to join his troops that had been held back in order to attempt to turn Antigonus' flank. In the centre Eumenes' veteran phalanx routed the troops opposite it and then rolled up Antigonus' phalanx from its now exposed flank.[31] Overpowered in cavalry on both wings Eumenes tried to rally Peucestas' retreated squadron but they refused to rejoin the battle. Eumenes was forced to retreat with his remaining cavalry severely outnumbered. His victorious phalanx, now left without cavalry support, formed a defensive square and gradually withdrew from the field.

Once again both generals adopted the standard Macedonian tactic of the oblique formation, but as a variation Eumenes held back his right wing instead of the left. Eumenes' plan to overwhelm the superior units of the enemy right flank is reminiscent of Epaminondas' success against the Spartans at Leuctra, as discussed previously. Antigonus' use of the dust cloud to shield his cavalry manoeuvres shows the importance of a general adapting to the situation at hand and taking advantage of the terrain and the environment.

Antigonus used everything he could think of to claim the victory. It was the capture of their camp that caused the surrender of Eumenes' unbeaten veteran infantry phalanx and it led to Eumenes' eventual execution, when the veterans handed him over to Antigonus. If Antigonus had not captured the camp, Eumenes would have had enough troops available to him to continue the war, and his phalanx would probably still have carried on routing its opponents. Eumenes was undermined by Peucestas' cowardly flight, just as Antigonus was by Peithon's insubordination at Paraetacene. Unfortunately, Eumenes' valiant attempt to rescue the situation was denied by his lack of control over his troops unlike Antigonus' personal charge at Paraetacene.

Combined arms

Both Paraetacene and Gabiene were virtual stalemates, showing just how evenly matched Eumenes and Antigonus were as generals. Both battles demonstrate the standard training and tactics of Macedonian style armies and the successful integration of different units into a battle plan. Both generals were the best exponents of the system of combined arms as it had been developed by the Macedonians and were the best generals of their generation behind Alexander. However, neither got the most out of their elephants. In fact, Eumenes lost both battles because of his overreliance on elephants alongside incompetent subordinate officers.

The normal use of elephants in battle was primarily as flank guards held in echelon, as part of the oblique formation. This is the tactic used by both Antigonus and Eumenes at the battles of Paraetacene and Gabiene. Elephants used as a defensive flank screen serves to add an extra defensive element to the battle formation but does not make sufficient use of the offensive power of elephants.

> As a screen from behind which to charge with one's cavalry, elephants had proved useful at Paraitakene and Gabiene . . . but as an attacking force in themselves, elephants were effective in ancient warfare only against enemies who had not encountered them before and were overawed by their size and strength.[32]

Eumenes' fate at Gabiene demonstrates that it was very difficult to change the tactical deployment or use of elephants during battle.[33] Eumenes sought to kill Antigonus and end the war and so decided to charge with his elephants instead of holding them back defensively. Since they had already been drawn up en echelon in the customary flank guard, Eumenes' elephants arrived into the attack at intervals, thus minimising their impact.[34] The elephant-on-elephant battle that ensued went well for Eumenes until his lead elephant was killed. Despite enjoying a numerical superiority in elephants, once the lead animal fell the others behind turned to flee. Elephants are by nature herd animals and always follow their leader.[35]

Eumenes' attempt to use the elephants offensively was made more difficult since a number of his elephants had lost their mahouts in a previous skirmish with Antigonus.[36] As Kistler describes,

> [i]t takes some weeks for an elephant to trust and obey a new mahout, as is commonly known among elephant trainers. These beasts could still stand on the right wing to hinder the enemy horses from a direct charge, carrying new riders, but they were ineffective for any offensive duties without their trusted mahouts.[37]

Gabiene demonstrates that it is easy to defeat a force of elephants by killing the lead animal or forcing it to flee. Only if a commander can ensure the continued advance of the lead elephant will the others fight. This is the one large drawback of using elephants offensively and is the main reason why they were usually used in a defensive manner.

The one confusing aspect of the use of elephants by Hellenistic generals, as seen at Paraetacene and Gabiene, was the preferred option to deploy the elephants in the centre of the battle line directly in front of the phalanx. Porus' defeat at the Hydaspes demonstrated the ineffectiveness of elephants against a sarissa phalanx disciplined enough to face the beasts and use sarissas to blind them or kill their mahouts.[38] Moreover, the elephants would disrupt the formation of the phalanx and reduce its effectiveness at opposing the enemy infantry. Yet even at Ipsus both sides deployed elephants in front of their phalanx.[39] Perhaps Kistler is right when he states that, faced with Lysimachus' 100 elephants in the centre, "Antigonus had no choice but to put his seventy-five beasts in front of his infantry, lest his own men panic".[40] Certainly the sight of a hundred elephants charging would frighten even the most disciplined army. But there is no evidence that such an elephant charge did take place at Paraetacene or Gabiene, or even Ipsus. It is not clear at all what the elephants in the centre actually did in the battle. They did not disrupt either phalanx and we do not hear of an elephant on elephant battle. In fact there are no examples anywhere of elephants charging Hellenistic infantry phalanxes directly as Bosworth summarises adeptly:

> There is no evidence of the beasts attacking enemy infantry, as Porus' elephants had done at the Hydaspes. Perhaps the dangers of their being wounded in the eyes or trunk were too acute. . . . Accordingly, elephants tended to be used against each other or to keep cavalry at bay. Their usefulness was limited, but they clearly had a mystique, a psychological advantage for their army.[41]

So if not use them in the centre to attack the phalanx why place them there at all if the flank guard against cavalry was more important tactically? Tarn suggests that it was the very frightening experience of facing elephants at the Hydaspes that prompted Seleucus to exchange territory in India for 500 war elephants.[42] Had Antigonus adopted Ptolemy's method of caltrops to defend against an elephant charge at Ipsus, he could have used his elephants elsewhere with much more effectiveness. Armies unused to elephants were vulnerable to them but cavalry whose horses grew up around elephants,[43] and infantry who had opposed the animals before, were able to easily counter offensive actions of elephants.

Perhaps the elephants in the centre were intended as a deterrent against the break-up of the phalanx and usually simply fired missiles at the phalanx rather than charge it. Perhaps our sources simply do not record the attack of the elephants on the phalanx in the centre because such an attack was never a decisive factor in an engagement. Perhaps the elephants in the centre engaged each other while the two phalanxes fought on either side of the animals like turrets in a castle's ramparts. Nevertheless, there must have been some sound tactical reason to deploy elephants in the centre in front of the phalanx if all the Successors did so regularly, we are just unable to determine what that was.

Ipsus

The battle of Ipsus marks the culmination of the developments of combined arms in Greek warfare and the final application of integrated warfare on the battlefield.[44] The battle of Ipsus is described in few sources. Diodorus' account does not survive except for a few fragments and so we are left with the brief descriptions of Plutarch and Appian.[45] Neither author is focused on the military details of the battle, both more concerned with the actions of Demetrius, in not returning to save his father, and Antigonus, in refusing to leave the field until his son returned. As a result, only the bare facts of the battle are discernible from Plutarch, but enough to enable an analysis of the innovative use of elephants, the prime concern here.

Cassander, Lysimachus, and Seleucus opposed Demetrius and Antigonus.[46] The Antigonids had 70,000 infantry, 10,000 cavalry, and 75 elephants, and the allies had 64,000 infantry,[47] 10,500 cavalry,[48] and 120 chariots,[49] but significantly more elephants – to the sum of 400.[50] Both sides used the standard deployment of elephants along the front of the whole line mixed in with peltasts and missile troops. However, Seleucus remained behind the allied line with a reserve force of hundreds of elephants.[51] It seems that neither side adopted the oblique formation, which is unusual, but it could simply be that our sources do not mention it.

A skirmish of the elephants and light troops along the whole line began the battle while the cavalry of each side engaged one another on each wing. This was standard beginning to most battles with each side probing for a weakness along the enemy lines and endeavouring to win the cavalry battle on one flank to enable outflanking of the phalanx in the centre. Demetrius routed the cavalry on the allied left and pursued them too far.[52] Seleucus deployed his elephant reserve to block Demetrius and hold him fast. Seleucus then instead of charging the Antigonid phalanx, which was now unprotected by cavalry, threatened to do so in order to encourage the infantry to change sides. Lysimachus then sent more missile troops to the centre, while he continued the cavalry battle on the right. The missile troops in the centre were so numerous that their volleys forced the Antigonid phalanx to retreat in disorder. Antigonus died fighting in the phalanx, and to the end believed Demetrius would ride in and save the day.

Combined arms

At Ipsus both armies fielded varied units that were fully integrated into the battle plan. The allied army's strength lay in its huge force of elephants. As a result, the generals had to ensure they got the best use out of these animals in order to make the most of their advantage. As discussed previously, the previous use of elephants in battle was as a static flank guard to shield the phalanx. However, the main problem with this deployment was that the slow elephants could not be moved if and when the phalanx advanced beyond the protection they afforded to the flank. At Ipsus the allies had enough elephants to post them opposite Antigonus' animals and still keep hundreds for use elsewhere. It is Seleucus' use of these other elephants as a screen against Demetrius' isolated cavalry that was the catalyst of Antigonus' defeat.

Tarn argued that Seleucus planned this all along.[53] He may have ordered his son Antiochus, commanding the left wing cavalry of the allies, to fall back at the assault of Demetrius in order to draw him away from the battle so that Seleucus could deploy his elephants to block his return.[54] There is no evidence for this in the sources but these are in general lacking in detail and Seleucus' speed of action in successfully redeploying so many slow-moving elephants is more understandable if it was pre-planned. The tactic of the fake retreat was used by Seleucid armies at the later battle of Elasa suggesting that it was a favourite tactic of Seleucus and his successors.[55]

At Ipsus, Seleucus' trap for Demetrius shows that the best use for elephants is as a flank screen against heavy cavalry, as long as their immovability does not expose the flank of the phalanx. Heavy cavalry, used to close-quarter combat, are largely ineffective against elephants. Without missiles or sarissas to harass and turn the elephants, or kill their mahouts, they could achieve little success. It was Demetrius' inability to return to the battle that cost Antigonus both the victory and his life.[56]

Fuller mistakenly believes that the adoption of war elephants as a "shock arm" was the "greatest innovation of all" in Hellenistic warfare.[57] Ducrey even goes so far as to blame the demise of Macedonian cavalry on the increased reliance on war elephants:

> After the death of Alexander, the cavalry gradually lost its importance as a tactical arm. There are a number of reasons for this: one was the growing weight and size of the phalanx, increasingly monolithic and apparently invincible; another, the appearance and widespread use of the war elephant. Like the cavalry and chariots, the elephants were regarded as a mobile unit, capable of a number of maneuvers, including surprise attacks and, above all, encirclement.[58]

212 *Macedon and integrated warfare*

This is certainly going too far. The Successor kingdoms could not produce elephants in significant numbers to replace cavalry. Elephants rarely breed in captivity, even with today's methods of artificial insemination.[59] With the exception of Egypt's elephant capture programme,[60] and the Seleucid Empire's limited breeding programme at Apamea,[61] Hellenistic kingdoms had to rely upon captured elephants, and once those used by Alexander's immediate Successors died, very few were found to replace them. The demise of the heavy cavalry in the third century has nothing at all to do with the use of war elephants, and much to do with the overreliance on the sarissa phalanx and the depletion of the supply of horses and those experienced with riding them in battle.[62]

The allied generals' execution of the battle plan at Ipsus was perfect in its use of combined arms, employing elephants, infantry, cavalry, and missile troops in harmony to attack the enemy's weaknesses while eliminating their own. Ipsus demonstrated the final phase in the perfection of integrated warfare, getting the best use out of elephants as a defensive screen and only the threat of offensive action. It is clear that "At Ipsus, the elephants played a decisive role",[63] and Gaebel is perhaps right when he argues that the battle of Ipsus was "the greatest achievement of war elephants in Hellenistic military history".[64]

Combined arms conclusions

Elephants briefly transformed warfare in the Hellenistic world, but it took time for generals to understand how best to make use of the animals and to overcome their deficiencies, an integral part of the theory of combined arms. Alexander never had to integrate elephants into his army and it was developing the most effective tactical use of these animals that delayed integrated warfare in the armies of Alexander's Successors. The fully integrated army of the later fourth century had to make the best use of elephants, as a counter to heavy cavalry charges without exposing the other units. Once elephants were integrated completely and usefully into the battle plan Macedonian style armies engaged fully in integrated warfare. It was not until the battle of Ipsus that the allied generals got the best out of every unit, including elephants, while simultaneously protecting the weaknesses of each. Ipsus then is the battle that reveals the effectiveness of integrated warfare in the Greek world and is the culmination of all the developments in combined arms that had occurred before.

Notes

1 Bar Kochva (1976: 203) is right that the achievements in battle tactics of Hellenistic generals are often ignored by scholars in favour of Philip II and Alexander.
2 There is really only one book for each general that deals with their military abilities in detail. Eumenes: Anson (2004). Antigonus: Billows (1990); Devine (1985c, 1985d) provides a good discussion of the two main battles between Eumenes and Antigonus. See also Wrightson (2015b), which is an earlier version of this chapter.
3 The various wars of the tyrants of Syracuse during the fourth century, Dionysius I, Dionysius II, Dion, Timoleon, and Agathocles, were all fought using combined arms.

As discussed previously, the armies of Syracusan tyrants had always been adept at using combined arms since the mountains inland led to a need for light infantry, which the local Sicel population specialised in producing, and the plains produced large amounts of reliable cavalry. This added to the normal need for Greek colonies to rely on hoplites. Because the latter tyrants fought Carthage, which always fielded armies that fought in a combined arms style, the Sicilian armies were forced to mimic their component parts and tactics. In fact, the Carthaginians also adopted Greek hoplite armaments for their heavy infantry in order to better match the close-combat abilities of the Greek hoplites. But none of these battles reveal any new developments in the continuum of combined arms, and certainly did not involve any elephants, and so are not discussed in detail here. The Carthaginians used chariots extensively, but not successfully, and this is a backwards looking note on the development of combined arms. I hope in the future to write in more detail on combined arms in non-Greek armies including Carthage.

4 Plutarch, *Demetrius* 28–29; Appian, *Syrian Wars* 55.
5 See in particular, Scullard (1974). Also see Kistler (2007); Nossov & Dennis (2008).
6 For Diodorus see Drews (1962); Hamilton (1977); Hammond (1983); Devine (1985c); Devine (1985d); Landucci Gattinoni (2008).
7 Meeus (2009).
8 For Plutarch see Tracy (1942); Wardman (1955); Hamilton (1969); Wardman (1971); Stadter (1992).
9 See in particular Hornblower (1981).
10 Diodorus, 18.29–32; Plutarch, *Eumenes* 7.
11 At Gaugamela for example Alexander opposed the Scythian horse archers with his allied cavalry rather than the Thessalians or the Companions (Arrian *Anabasis* 3.13.3–4).
12 For the standard use of elephants see for example Bar Kochva (1976: 77).
13 Bar Kochva (1976: 137) states that elephants usually panic horses even if they are used to elephants.
14 There are many instances of this exact thing happening in battle. The most devastating was in the army of Polyperchon at the siege of Megalopolis where the elephants ran amok after their feet had become impaled upon caltrops (Diodorus 18.71.2–3).
15 Plutarch, *Pyrrhus* 21; Dionysius of Halicarnassus 20.1–3; Zonaras 8.5; Orosius 4.1.19–23.
16 Plutarch, *Pyrrhus* 21.7.
17 Plutarch, *Pyrrhus* 24–25; Dionysius of Halicarnassus 20.10–11; Orosius 4.2.3–6.
18 Arrian Anabasis 5.10.2–3.
19 Heraclea: Plutarch, *Pyrrhus* 16–17; Zonaras 8.3; Orosius 4.1.8–15. Galatians: Lucian, *Zeuxis* 8–12.
20 Arrian, *Anabasis* 5.8–19; Curtius 8.13–14; Diodorus 17.87–89; Plutarch *Alexander* 60–62. Discussed in detail previously.
21 Diodorus 19.80–84; Plutarch, *Demetrius* 5.
22 Kistler (2007: 61) summarises the effectiveness of this device well. "Because elephants are heavy, they cannot simply jump up to free themselves from traps holding two feet: normally they only lift one foot at a time. When two feet are impaled, an elephant is trapped in place. The screaming of the wounded elephants caused the unharmed pachyderms to flee, disrupting Demetrius' own cavalry horses. Ptolemy sent his archers and javelin throwers forward to kill the mahouts, clearly intending to capture, and not kill, the elephants. Seeing this major setback, and fearing that their horses might step on more of these traps, Demetrius' cavalry fled the field, and his infantry joined them in full flight".
23 For the various strategies of the two generals see Polyaenus 4.8.1–5 and 4.6.1–20.
24 Paraetacene: Diodorus 19.26–31. Gabiene: Diodorus 19.39–43; Plutarch, *Eumenes* 16.
25 The main source for these battles is Diodorus. Plutarch's life of *Eumenes* briefly discusses the battle of Gabiene but not in much detail. As a result, the following

214 *Macedon and integrated warfare*

      reconstructions are based on Diodorus and ultimately on his source the eyewitness testimony of Hieronymus of Cardia. See Hornblower (1981).
26 See Anson (2004); Billows (1990).
27 Diodorus 19.26–31. The most concise secondary discussion of the battle is Devine (1985c). For the battle in the context of the other battles of the Successors see Pietrykowski (2009).
28 The preoccupation of his phalanx with their baggage should have been a warning to Eumenes that he needed to curtail the growing insubordinate independence of Alexander's veterans as a destabilising factor in his army. Unfortunately for him he did nothing and the phalanx sent Eumenes to his death in return for the return of their baggage and camp followers captured by Antigonus at Gabiene.
29 Diodorus, 19.39–43; Plutarch, *Eumenes* 16. The most concise secondary discussion of the battle is Devine (1985d). For the battle in the context of the other battles of the Successors see Pietrykowski (2009).
30 Cf. Polyaenus 4.6.13.
31 Devine (1985d) says that they must have used a wedge, which may be true, but his reconstruction makes the wedge far too big to be able to function with any speed or manoeuvrability.
32 Billows (1990: 127).
33 This is an important fact to bear in mind when examining Seleucus' deployment of his elephant reserve at Ipsus, as discussed below.
34 Diodorus 19.42.
35 Scullard (1974).
36 Diodorus 19.39.
37 Kistler (2007: 51). See also Kruse (1972: 76).
38 Arrian, *Anabasis* 5.8–19; Curtius 8.13–14; Diodorus 17.87–89; Plutarch *Alexander* 60–62. For full discussions of the battle see Hamilton (1956); Devine (1987).
39 Plutarch *Demetrius* 28–29; Appian, *Syrian Wars* 55.
40 Kistler (2007: 66).
41 Bosworth (2002: 166–7).
42 Plutarch *Alexander* 62; Strabo 15.2–9, 16.2–10. Tarn (1975: 94). See also Tarn (1940).
43 It is for this reason that the Seleucid Empire set up the national cavalry training facility at Apamea in Syria alongside the elephants (Strabo 16.2.10).
44 Still the best analysis of the battle is Bar Kochva (1976: 105–10). For the battle in the context of the other battles of the Successors see Pietrykowski (2009).
45 Plutarch *Demetrius* 28–9; Appian, *Syrian Wars* 55.
46 Diodorus 21.1.2.
47 Bar Kochva (1976: 82) argues that of this force the 20,000 brought by Seleucus were predominantly light infantry.
48 Bar Kochva (1976: 247 n. 11) argues that this is a textual corruption and the allied cavalry total should be 15,000.
49 These chariots probably did not feature in the battle. Seleucus unsuccessfully used chariots against Demetrius shortly before the battle of Ipsus (Plutarch, *Demetrius* 48.2).
50 Plutarch *Demetrius* 28.3. Seleucus, after a failed invasion of India, gave up a significant amount of territory to the Indian king Chandragupta in exchange for 500 elephants (Plutarch *Alexander* 62; Strabo 15.2–9, 16.2–10). Seleucus brought most of these with him to Ipsus. Diodorus 20.113.4 states that Seleucus brought through Cappadocia 480 elephants, 12,000 cavalry, 20,000 infantry, and over 100 chariots, and these figures fit well into the allied troops totals given by Plutarch. Bar Kochva (1976: 76) suggests that Seleucus lost 20 elephants in crossing through Cappadocia and afterwards another 80 were unfit for battle. Ipsus then is the only battle in Greek warfare where so many elephants were deployed.

51 Tarn (1940). Bar Kochva (1976): 108 argues that there was no elephant reserve behind the army.
52 Plutarch, *Demetrius* 29.3.
53 Tarn (1940: 87 n. 1); Tarn (1975: 68–9).
54 Bar Kochva (1976: 109–10) argues that the terrain behind the allied battle line at Ipsus was such that it took significant effort and time for Seleucus to post enough elephants to prevent Demetrius' return. As a result it must have been a pre-planned tactic induced by a fake retreat of Antiochus' cavalry. Since Antiochus was Seleucus' son the two commanders could easily have organised this together. Bar Kochva (1976: 109) also suggests Demetrius may have been attempting to capture the allied baggage camp after routing Antiochus' cavalry.
55 For this battle see Bar Kochva (1976: 184–200). It is only described in I Maccabees 9.1–22 but this account does not mention the fake withdrawal which Bar Kochva believes occurred. Bar Kochva believes that surprise tactics were commonly used in other Seleucid battles, in particular Cyrrhestica (Plutarch, *Demetrius* 48–49. See Bar Kochva 1976: 111–6); against Molon (Polybius 5.48.17–54. See Bar Kochva 1976: 117–23); and against the Galatians (Lucian, *Zeuxis* 9). In every case the ancient source for the battle, just as at Ipsus, does not specifically describe such tactics.
56 Plutarch, *Demetrius* 29.
57 Fuller (1945: 32).
58 Ducrey (1986: 183).
59 Kistler (2007: 68–9).
60 Casson (1993).
61 Bar Kochva (1976: 79) argues that the Seleucid elephants in Apamea, and those used in battle, were nearly all bulls and so could not produce a large new herd.
62 Wrightson forthcoming.
63 Kistler (2007: 67).
64 Gaebel (2002: 226).

Conclusion – Greece, Persia, and Macedon
The success of combined arms and integrated warfare

Combined arms is the best way of tactically ensuring victory in battle in the ancient world and today. Using the model of combined arms warfare, it is possible to analyse comparatively the tactical efficiency of armies throughout history and through this lens assess the effects of culture and society on warfare. For the Greeks it is possible to lay a foundation for examining why warfare remained so static for so long and to see how this affected the development of Greek history and culture. For any historical analysis of warfare, the level of application of combined arms can serve as a perfect comparative tool for determining the relative strengths, weaknesses, and stage of advanced military training in the warfare of each society or culture.

The main difference between early uses of a combined arms system, such as the Assyrians, and that of the later Macedonians can be explained by the evolution of the effectiveness of each type of unit. For example, the Assyrian spearmen did not maintain a formation when in contact with the enemy: After battle was joined, the infantry confrontation became just another melee. By contrast the Macedonian sarissa phalanx was so successful precisely because it was able to stay in formation under any circumstances in battle. It was this unbroken front that terrified opponents, since it was so unusually well executed. Even the phalanx proved ineffective when the formation was disrupted by terrain or the enemy's tactics.[1]

The Assyrian heavy cavalry were the same in that when they charged the enemy they did not necessarily do so in a specific tactical organisation. The Companion cavalry of Alexander and Philip, as well as the Thessalian cavalry, usually charged in a diamond or wedge formation.[2] They remained grouped in this fashion until they had broken the opposing battle lines, when they spread out to attack the disordered enemy. The concept of chariot warfare, popular in the east from which early cavalry warfare developed, almost precludes any attack formation. Chariots cannot stay too close together or the horses and wheels will affect the other vehicles. The impact of chariots is better achieved when charging into the enemy on their own thereby causing widespread damage all along the line. It is this lack of cohesiveness that allowed Alexander's light infantry to easily overcome Darius' chariots at Gaugamela and Porus' at the Hydaspes.

Two of the principal questions that arise from our discussion of the historical development of combined arms are (1) why was the Persian Empire not as successful as the other conquest empire of Macedon; and (2) why did the warfare of the Greeks make little use of varied units until the late fifth century.

Persian kings were able to call on many types of soldier to serve in their armies to the extent that there was no type of unit excluded. Yet despite the numerous logistical and organisational advantages, the Persian army and battle plan rarely made full use of combined arms. Certainly a reliance on traditional Persian armaments, the bow and arrow, led to the subordination of other units, but this alone cannot fully explain the comparative lack of tactical efficiency. We must seek other explanations.

Neo-Assyria was able to utilise very effectively the disparate units taken from the various states in its Empire, most of which were the very same states as in the later Persian Empire. From the little evidence we have of Neo-Assyrian battles, the core of Assyrian troops, namely a heavy cavalry (or chariotry) force supported by heavily armoured bowmen and spearmen, fought alongside other levies of spearmen, bowmen, cavalry, and chariots. Neo-Assyria was able to make use of combined arms for a large part because the national troops represented the different types of unit. The auxiliary units were not drastically different from the national troops and so could easily be integrated into the existing military system. The Assyrians did not have to incorporate elephants, or any distinctly "foreign" unit. From the beginning Neo-Assyria used a system of combined arms, missile and heavy cavalry and missile and heavy infantry fighting together, but still overly reliant on archery as the principal method of fighting battles. As a result, the tactics employed by their generals did not have to change significantly in order to make use of the new units.

Tactical innovations significantly influenced the use of combined arms, as the previous chapters have shown. In Neo-Assyria the battle tactics remained constant, relying on massed archery supported by effective heavy infantry followed up by heavy cavalry assaults. Persia inherited this tactical battle plan but abandoned the use of large numbers of heavy infantry in favour of more missile troops and preferred to utilise cavalry as missile troops too rather than as shock troops, at least until the late fifth century. In the east the honorific unit was the cavalry, both as horse archers and as an assault force of heavy armed horses and men. We have no evidence of any battles in the Persian Empire faced with other tactics before the wars with Greece.

Persian armies expected to win by bombarding the enemy with so many arrows that they were too weak to survive the final close-quarter assault. As soon as they faced an enemy whose tactical abilities allowed them to overcome numerical inferiority or to withstand a large missile barrage, the Persians were unable to adapt their plans to win. As Lacey writes:

> Persia's generals designed and trained its army to defeat armies that fought like it. It relied on the coordinated action of its combined arms-centered on massed archery-to inflict sufficient losses to shatter an enemy's cohesion.[3]

The infantry, protected by wicker shields stuck in the ground, and cavalry loosed their arrows until the formation of the enemy began to disintegrate. At that point the Persian infantry and cavalry charged into close-quarter fighting. Since the Greek hoplites were not very vulnerable to missiles, and attacked the enemy lines hand to hand, the Persian military system was ineffective. Moreover, the generals could not adapt the battle plan to succeed in this new style of warfare.

Persia attempted to solve the problem of facing hoplites, after their crushing defeat against the Greeks, by incorporating mercenary hoplites into their army instead of creating their own force. This meant that they never managed to create a national cohesiveness to this mixed army. However, this was a result of the Persian military system itself. Persian armies always fielded units levied from all the disparate cultures in the Empire. India sent elephants, Scythia horse archers, Egypt spearmen, and the Greek poleis hoplites. Persia did not need to reorganise their national units because they made such extensive use of foreign contingents. The idea of a national army of Persian troops fighting in different fighting styles was a completely foreign one.

As is usual in any empire, the units from the conquering nation were the most important. Persia fell into the same trap. They continued to view the Persian units as the best and their tactics did not incorporate all the other foreign units to the same level. The problems for the Persians, as opposed to the Macedonians, was that their method of winning battles was to rely on weight of numbers and missiles for victory rather than tactical superiority and they proved unable to adapt fast enough.

By contrast, battles in Greece were decided by a direct infantry charge all along the line. The battle was decided at close quarters and usually in a short space of time. This tactical deployment ensured that there was little time for archery to take effect on an opposing army before joining in hand-to-hand combat. Moreover, in this style of warfare the goal was not to annihilate the enemy army in one engagement, but to force them to retreat as quickly as possible. One of the most successful ways to achieve this was to kill, capture, or rout the enemy king or general. More often than not an army will retreat if its leader does so or is removed from the battle. Alexander's personal charge against Darius at Issus aptly proves this tendency.[4] Western armies were designed to fit into this tactical framework. In most cases the heavily armed and armoured infantryman was the preeminent soldier, who did all the hard work in the front lines. In some states, such as Thessaly and Macedon and occasionally Boeotia, the final decisive assault was delivered by a heavy cavalry force instead.

In the heartland of Greece (central and southern Greece), battles before the Peloponnesian War were often instigated to decide a dispute over territory or an assumed insult. However, once these traditional Greek poleis began to expand their interests outside of the local area, whether through forced invasion or voluntary involvement in external politics, they encountered other styles of warfare. In the mountainous regions of Greece light infantry were the most common. In the flat areas of Thessaly and Macedon cavalry were preeminent. The hoplite focused armies of the principal Greek poleis had to learn to adapt to the new methods of warfare when fighting in alien environments. Yet it took many years for the Greeks to utilise the benefits of a diverse, integrated army in any battle regardless

Conclusion – Greece, Persia, and Macedon

of terrain. To the Spartans at least, warfare in mainland Greece should always remain centred on the hoplite phalanx whereas a diverse army was required in the east, as Agesilaus' different campaign armies in Asia and the Corinthian War demonstrate. It is this reluctance of Athens and Sparta to field combined arms armies everywhere that marks out Greek warfare as tactically static when compared with Macedon in particular.

The two different styles of warfare, massed archery intended to annihilate the enemy over time in Persian battles, and rapid, decisive attacks at close quarters intended to force the enemy into retreat in Greek conflicts, required different applications of combined arms. The latter style allowed more of the general principles of combined arms to be utilised, namely employing each type of unit in the most effective way to mutually support the others. But in Greece the preeminence of the hoplite was rarely disputed until the end of the Peloponnesian War when cavalry and light infantry finally became essential parts of the Greek army, though still subordinate to the hoplite.

Macedon was fortunate to be situated between these two schools of warfare, east and west. To Macedon, having observed centuries of Greek successes, an army without a strong core of heavy infantry (hoplites) in phalanx formation would be unsuccessful. The advantages of this unit in close combat were evident and the Thebans had begun to perfect specific tactics to maximise its effectiveness. In the east the Persian Empire relied on cavalry and missile troops for victory. Arrows fired en masse would soften the enemy's resolve to allow the spearmen and heavy cavalry to precipitate the rout. Macedon itself had always used a core of aristocratic heavy cavalry as the main unit in battle accompanied by lightly armed pastoral peasants. Once Philip II, perhaps following developments of an earlier king, had enough money to be able to furnish and train a heavy infantry phalanx to a professional standard, he was able to combine the eastern reliance on cavalry with the western heavy infantry. Philip's army was able to use the phalanx to hold the enemy in position fighting at close quarters, while the heavy cavalry directly attacked the weak points of the opposing formation, or the enemy king or general. Philip could not call on many missile troops to add to this battle plan. Alexander, however, made great use of archers and javelin men to harass the enemy line with missiles while the phalanx and cavalry manoeuvred into position, thus completely combining the eastern and western styles of warfare.

In Macedon, after the creation of the sarissa phalanx using local peasants, the national standing army always constituted the lower-class phalanx (led by aristocratic officers) and the aristocratic cavalry together. This allowed for mutual respect and a coordination of goals that was lacking in armies utilising mercenaries on a large scale. Persia never furnished a national body of heavy infantry that was the ideological equal of the cavalry and archers. Even the 10,000 elite Immortals, often used as heavy infantry in close-quarter combat, were archers first and spearmen second. Persia was let down because their existing national army was not able to oppose an army using combined arms effectively, in particular one reliant on an elite heavy infantry phalanx working in close conjunction with heavy cavalry.

Macedon was able to integrate other units into the army alongside the Macedonian units, and to adapt the battle tactics accordingly. Alexander relied heavily on the Thessalian cavalry and the Agrianes javelin men as support troops for the phalanx, hypaspists, and the Companions. The Persians also used auxiliaries to supplement their national troops, but did not apply the same degree of tactical flexibility as the Macedonians. It is this tactical flexibility that is necessary in order to employ integrated warfare. In fact, the use of combined arms can improve tactical flexibility once it is implemented but cannot be fully realised until that flexibility exists in the first place.

In most cases where combined arms was used successfully based on a national army, the lack of maintenance of the national units led to the fall of the empire. The Neo-Assyrian Empire collapsed from internal wars that resulted, to a large degree, from the national army becoming too reliant on its foreign parts. Macedon similarly was defeated by Rome not least because the national Companion cavalry was replaced with less effective allied contingents.[5] The repeated examples of the collapse of a conquest empire that was previously successful at using a form of combined arms, demonstrate the necessity of maintaining national control. As soon as the national units become supplanted by foreign units, the empire cannot be preserved.

The system of combined arms is best practiced when a state can furnish all the types of unit independently, and develop tactics that make appropriate use of each unit. However, in practice few nations have the resources or inclination to be able to produce every type of unit available. As a result, mercenaries or foreign auxiliaries must be used. Once the proportion of alien units is significantly greater than that of the national units, state control over the army is eroded and consequently so is the army's effectiveness.

Perhaps the best lesson we can draw from the history of combined arms in Greece is that without a concerted effort to maintain a large degree of national influence over the different and most important units in the army, especially without also developing new battle tactics, the army becomes less able to implement the system successfully.

Combined arms warfare can be seen in some form throughout the history of Greek warfare, in this case from Homer to Alexander's Sucessors. But there is a sliding scale of effectiveness for combined arms, from two types of unit together to every type of unit. It was a gradual process in Greece for combined arms to come to involve every type of unit available together in mutually supportive roles. The overemphasis on the hoplite limited the full integration of light infantry and cavalry for centuries. Since so few states in mainland Greece produced heavy cavalry, Greek battles rarely ever witnessed heavy cavalry charges and thus preserved the preeminence of the heavy infantry phalanx. It was not until the Peloponnesian War when Greeks fought in different locales that light infantry and heavy cavalry forces began to inflict defeats on hoplites. Thus began the century of change to integrated warfare culminating in the expert armies of Philip II, Alexander the Great and the Successors.

Conclusion – Greece, Persia, and Macedon

The greatest armies of their time, and perhaps of the ancient world as a whole, the Macedonian forces of the mid- to late fourth century were entirely reliant on integrated warfare. The sarissa phalanx revolutionised the Greek battlefield, but only when fielded alongside effective heavy and light cavalry and light infantry. On its own it was even more vulnerable on the flanks and rear than a hoplite phalanx, but together with supporting units it was unstoppable. Similarly, without the assistance of a reliable and sizeable heavy infantry force the expert Macedonian Companion cavalry had never before enabled kings of Macedon to conquer their neighbours, let alone all of Greece and Asia. Alongside each other the sarissa phalanx and the Companion cavalry proved almost unbeatable. Without the expert implementation of combined arms as integrated warfare Alexander's army would not have won such great fame in conquering Asia at such a numerical disadvantage and Western history would be decidedly different today.

Notes

1. The best examples of this are the Macedonian defeats at the hands of the Roman legions at the battles of Cynoscephalae (Polybius 18.19–26; Livy 33.6–10; Plutarch *Flamininus* 7–8) and Pydna (Plutarch, *Aemilius Paullus* 16–22; Livy 44.40–42).
2. Devine (1983).
3. Lacey (2012: 50).
4. The best example in all pre-gunpowder warfare is King Harold II's death at the battle of Hastings in 1066. In fact, Hastings serves as a very good example of the importance of the general in battle Bennett et al. (2005). It also shows the use of combined arms in the Norman army of William the Conqueror: Jones (1987: 109–13). The Saxons on the hilltop were relatively secure against the assaults of the Norman cavalry. The Normans began to become discouraged and almost precipitated a headlong retreat when someone shouted that Duke William had been killed. It was only when he took off his helmet to reveal himself to his soldiers that they were encouraged to continue the fight. The confidence the Normans then enjoyed after seeing their leader prompted overconfidence in some Saxons who foolishly chased the Norman cavalry down the hill thus breaking their strong formation. On the other side the Saxon army retreated only when they saw that their king, Harold II, had been killed in the fighting. Harold's death prompted the Saxon rout just as the rumoured death of William almost led to a Norman one.
5. Wrightson (forthcoming).

Bibliography

Greece, Macedon, Persia and general warfare

Adams, W. L. 1997. "Philip and the Thracian Frontier," in *Actes 2e Symposium International des études thraciennes. Thrace ancienne*, vol. 1. Komotini: 81–8.

Adcock, F. E. 1947. "EPITEIXISMOS in the Archidamian War," *CR* 61: 2–7.

———. 1957. *The Greek and Macedonian Art of War*. Berkeley and Los Angeles: California University Press.

———. 1963. *Thucydides and His History*. Cambridge and New York: Cambridge University Press.

Ahlberg, G. 1971. *Fighting on Land and Sea in Greek Geometric Art*. Stockholm: Swedish Institute in Athens.

Ameling, W. 1984. "L. Flavius Arrianus Neos Xenophon," *Epigraphica Anatolia* 4: 119–22.

Anderson, J. K. 1965. "Homeric, British and Cyreniac chariots," *AJA* 69: 349–52.

———. 1970. *Military Practice and Theory in the Age of Xenophon*. Berkeley and Los Angeles: University of California Press.

———. 1974a. *Xenophon*. London: Duckworth.

———. 1974b. "The Battle of Sardis in 395 B.C.," *CSCA* 7: 27–53.

———. 1975. "Greek Chariot-Borne and Mounted Infantry," *AJA* 79: 175–87.

———. 1991. "Hoplite Weapons and Defensive Arms," in Hanson 1991b: 15–37.

Andronikos, M. 1970. "Sarissa," *BCH* 94: 91–107.

Andronikos, M., M. B. Hatzopoulos, M. Sakellariou, and L. D. Loukopoulos. 1992. *Philip of Macedon*. Athens: Ekdotike Athenon.

Anglim, S., P. G. Jestice, R. S. Rice, S. M. Rusch, and J. Serrati. 2002. *Fighting Techniques of the Ancient World 3000 BC–AD 500: Equipment, Combat Skills and Tactics*. New York: St. Martin's Press.

Anson, E. M. 1981. "Alexander's Hypaspists and the Argyraspids," *Historia* 30: 117–20.

———. 1985. "The Hypaspists: Macedonia's Professional Citizen-Soldiers," *Historia* 34: 246–8.

———. 2004. *Eumenes of Cardia: A Greek Among Macedonians*. Boston: Brill.

———. 2010. "The Asthetairoi: Macedonia's Hoplites," in E. Carney and D. Ogden, eds. *Philip II and Alexander the Great: Father and Son, Lives and Afterlives*. Oxford and New York: Oxford University Press.

Anthony, D. W. 1995. "Birth of the Chariot," *Archaeology* 48.2: 36–41.

Arnold, R. J. 2012. *Performance Metrics for the Program Executive Office for Integrated Warfare Systems 1.0 and 2.0*. E-book.

Ashley, J.R. 1998. *The Macedonian Empire: The Era of Warfare Under Philip II and Alexander the Great, 359–323 BC*. Jefferson, NC: McFarland.
Atkinson, J.E. 1963. "Primary Sources and the Alexanderreich," *Acta Classica* 6: 125–37.
———. 1975. "Curtius Rufus' Historiae Alexandri and the Principate," in *Acta Conventus 'Eirene'* Amsterdam: 363–7.
———. 1980. *A Commentary on Q. Curtius Rufus' Historiae Alexandri Magni. Books 3 and 4*. Amsterdam: J.C. Gieben.
———. 1994. *A Commentary on Q. Curtius Rufus' Historiae Alexandri Magni. Books 5 to 7.2*. Amsterdam: J.C. Gieben.
Aupperle, K.E. 1996. "Spontaneous Organizational Reconfiguration: A Historical Example Based on Xenophon's *Anabasis*," *Organization Science* 7: 445–60.
Badian, E. 1958. "Alexander the Great and the Creation of an Empire," *History Today* 8: 369–76; 494–502.
———. 1965. "Orientals in Alexander's Army," *JHS* 85: 160–1.
———, ed. 1976. *Alexandre le grand: Image et realite*. Entretiens Hardt 22. Geneva: Fondation Hardt.
———. 1983. "Philip II and Thrace," *Pulpudeva* 4: 51–71.
Badian, E. and Foss. 1977. "The Battle of the Granicus: A New Look," in *Ancient Macedonia ii*. Thessaloniki: Institute for Balkan Studies: 271–93.
Balcer, J.M. 1989. "The Persian Wars Against Greece: A Reassessment," *Historia* 38: 127–43.
———. 1995. *The Persian Conquest of the Greeks 545–450 BC*. Konstanz: Universitätsverlag Konstanz.
Bar Kochva, B. 1976. *The Seleucid Army*. Cambridge: Cambridge University Press.
Bardunias, P.M., and F.E. Ray Jr. 2016. *Hoplites at War: A Comprehensive Analysis of Heavy Infantry Combat in the Greek World, 750–100 BCE*. Jefferson, NC: McFarland.
Barkworth, P.R. 1993. "The Organization of Xerxes' Army," *IA* 27: 149–67.
Barron, J. 1988. "The Liberation of Greece," in J. Boardman, N. Hammond, D. Lewis, and M. Ostwald, eds. *The Cambridge Ancient History* IV. New York: Palgrave Macmillan: 592–622.
Bell, D.A. 2007. *The First Total War: Napoleon's Europe and the Birth of Warfare as We Know It*. Boston: Houghton Mifflin.
Beloch, K.J. 1916. *Griechische Geschichte*. Stassburg: K.J. Trübner.
Bennett, M.J., P. Jestice, J. Bradbury, K. DeVries, and I. Dickie. 2005. *Fighting Techniques of the Medieval World: Equipment, Combat Skills and Tactics*. New York: Thomas Dunne Books.
Bertosa, B. 2014. "Peltast Equipment and the Battle of Lechaeum," in Sekunda and Burliga 2014: 113–25.
Best, J.G.P. 1969. *Thracian Peltasts and Their Influence on Greek Warfare*. Groningen: Wolters-Noordhoff.
Billows, R.A. 1990. *Antigonos the One-Eyed and the Creation of the Hellenistic State*. Berkeley and Los Angeles: UCP.
———. 2010. *Marathon: How One Battle Changed Western Civilization*. New York and London: Duckworth.
Blythe, P.H. 1977. "The Effectiveness of Greek Armour Against Arrows in the Persian War (490–479 B.C.): An Interdisciplinary Enquiry," Diss. University of Reading.
Boardman, J., ed. 1994. *Cambridge Ancient History: Plates to Volumes V and VI, the Fifth to the Fourth Centuries BC*. Cambridge: Cambridge University Press.

Boardman, J., N. Hammond, D. Lewis, and M. Ostwald, eds. 1988. *The Cambridge Ancient History* IV. New York: Palgrave Macmillan.
Borza, E.N. 1990. *In the Shadow of Olympus: The Emergence of Macedon*. Princeton: Princeton University Press.
Bosworth, A.B. 1973. "ASQETAIROI," *CQ* 23: 245–53.
———. 1980a. "Alexander and the Iranians," *JHS* 100: 1–21.
———. 1980b. *A Historical Commentary on Arrian's History of Alexander*. vol. 1. Oxford: Clarendon Press.
———. 1988. *From Arrian to Alexander: Studies in Historical Interpretation*. Oxford: Clarendon Press.
———. 1989. *Conquest and Empire. The Reign of Alexander the Great*. Cambridge: CUP.
———. 1992. "Athens' First Intervention in Sicily: Thucydides and the Sicilian Tradition," *CQ* 42: 46–55.
———. 1994. "Alexander the Great, Part 2: Greece and the Conquered Territories," *CAH* V: 846–75.
———. 2002. *The Legacy of Alexander. Politics, Warfare and Propaganda Under the Successors*. Oxford: OUP.
———. 2010. "The Argeads and the Phalanx," in E. Carney and D. Ogden, eds. *Philip II and Alexander the Great: Father and Son, Lives and Afterlives*. Oxford: OUP: 91–102.
Bowden, H. 1995. "Hoplites and Homer: Warfare and Hero Cult and the Ideology of the Polis," in J. Rich and G. Shipley, eds. *War and Society in the Greek World*. London: Routledge: 45–63.
Bradeen, D. 1974. *The Athenian Agora XVII: The Athenian Councillors*. Princeton: Princeton University Press.
Briant, P. 1999. "The Achaemenid Empire," in K. Raaflaub and N. Rosenstein, eds. *War and Society in the Ancient and Medieval Worlds*. Cambridge, MA and London: Harvard University Press: 105–28.
———. 2002. *The Persian Empire from Cyrus to Alexander*. Winona Lake, NY: Eisenbrauns.
Brice, L. 2013. "The Athenian Expedition to Sicily," in Campbell and Tritle 2013: 621–41.
Bruce, I.A.F. 1967. *An Historical Commentary on the 'Hellenica Oxyrhynchia'*. Cambridge: Cambridge University Press.
Brunt, P.A. 1962. "Persian Accounts of Alexander's Campaigns," *CQ* 12: 141–55.
———. 1963. "Alexander's Macedonian Cavalry," *JHS* 83: 27–46.
———. 1976. "Anaximines and King Alexander I of Macedon," *JHS* 96: 150–3.
Buckler, J. 1989. *Philip II and the Sacred War*. Supplements to Mnemosyne 109. Leiden: Brill.
———. 2013. "Epaminondas at Leuctra, 371 B.C.," in Campbell and Tritle 2013: 657–70.
Buckler, J., and H. Beck. 2008. *Central Greece and the Politics of Power in the Fourth Century BC*. Cambridge: Cambridge University Press.
Bugh, G.R. 1986. "The Athenian Cavalry in the Sicilian Expedition: Some Notes on Thucydides 6.43," in R.I. Curtis, ed. *Studia Pompeiana et Classica in Honor of Wilhelmina F. Jashemski*. New Rochelle, NY: A.D. Caratzas.
———. 1988. *The Horsemen of Athens*. Princeton: Princeton University Press.
Burn, A.R. 1962. *Persia and the Greeks. The Defence of the West 546–478 BC*. London: Edward Arnold.
———. 1964. *Alexander the Great and the Hellenistic World*. London: English Universities Press.

———. 1969. "Hammond on Marathon: A Few Notes," *The Journal of Hellenic Studies* 89: 118–20.
Campbell, B. and L. Tritle, eds. 2013. *The Oxford Handbook of Warfare in the Classical World*. Oxford: Oxford University Press.
Cartledge, P.A. 1977. "Hoplites and Heroes: Sparta's Contribution to the Technique of Ancient Warfare," *JHS* 97: 11–27.
———. 1979. *Sparta and Lakonia*. Boston: Routledge.
———. 2003. *The Spartans: The World of the Warrior-Heroes of Ancient Greece, from Utopia to Crisis and Collapse*. Woodstock, NY: Overlook Press.
———. 2006. *Thermopylae: The Battle That Changed the World*. New York: Overlook Press.
Casson, L. 1993. "Ptolemy II and the Hunting of African Elephants," *TAPA* 123: 247–60.
Cawkwell, G.L. 1965. "Gaugamela Reconsidered," *CR* 15: 203–5.
———. 1972. *Xenophon: The Persian Expedition*. Harmondsworth: Penguin Books.
———. 1983. "The Decline of Sparta," *CQ* 33: 385–400.
———. 1989. "Orthodoxy and Hoplites," *CQ* 39: 375–89.
———. 1997. *Thucydides and the Peloponnesian War*. London: Routledge.
———. 2004. *The Greek Wars. The Failure of Persia*. Oxford: Oxford University Press.
Champion, J. 2010. *Tyrants of Syracuse: War in Ancient Sicily: Vol 1: 480–367 BC*. Barnsley: Pen and Sword.
Charles, M.B. 2008. "Alexander, Elephants and Gaugamela," *Mouseion*, Series III 8: 9–23.
Christ, M.R. 2004. "Draft Evasion Onstage and Offstage in Classical Athens," *CQ* 54: 33–57.
Christensen, P. 2006. "Xenophon's *Cyropaedia* and Military Reform in Sparta," *JHS* 126: 47–65.
Citino, R.M. 1999. *The Path to Blitzkrieg: Doctrine and Training in the German Army, 1920–1939*. Boulder: Lynne Rienner.
Coates, J.F. 1993. "Carrying Troops in Triremes," in J.T. Shaw, ed. *The Trireme Project, Operational Experience 1987–1990, Lessons Learnt*. Oxford: Oxbow: 78–81.
Cobet, J. 1986. "Herodotus and Thucydides on War," in I.S. Moxon, J.D. Smart, and A.J. Woodman, eds. *Past Perspectives: Studies in Greek and Roman Historical Writing*. Cambridge: Cambridge University Press: 1–18.
Cohen, A. 1997. *The Alexander Mosaic: Stories of Victory and Defeat*. Cambridge: Cambridge University Press.
Commager, H.S. 1995. *The Blue and the Gray*. New York: Harper Collins.
Connolly, P. 2000. "Experiments with the Sarissa – The Macedonian Pike and Cavalry Lance – A Functional View," *JRMES* 11: 103–12.
Connor, W.R. 1988. "Early Greek Land Warfare as Symbolic Expression," *Past and Present* 119: 3–29.
Cook, J.M. 1983. *The Persian Empire*. New York: Shocken Books.
Cornelius, F. 1973. "Pausanias," *Historia* 22: 502–4.
Cotterell, A. 2005. *Chariot: From Chariot to Tank, the Astounding Rise and Fall of the World's First War Machine*. New York: Overlook.
Crouwel, J. 1981. *Chariots and Other Means of Land Transport in Bronze Age Greece*. Amsterdam: Allard Pierson.
Currie, H. MacL. 1990. "Quintus Curtius Rufus: The Historian as Novelist?" in *Groningen Colloquia on the Novel* 3. Groningen: Egbert Forsten: 63–77.

226 Bibliography

Daniel, T. 1992. "The *taxeis* of Alexander and the Change to Chiliarchies, the Companion Cavalry and the Change to Hipparchies: A Brief Assessment," *AncW* 23: 43–57.

Davies, G.A. 1949. *Demosthenes: Philippics I, II, III with Introduction and Notes*. Cambridge, MA: Harvard University Press.

Davis, E.W. 1964. "The Persian Battle Plan at the Granicus," *James Sprunt Studies in History and Political Science* 46: 34–44.

Desborough, V.R. d'A. 1972. *The Greek Dark Ages*. London: Ernest Benn.

De Souza, P., ed. 2008. *The Ancient World at War*. London: Thames & Hudson.

Develin, R. 1985. "Anaximenes (F GR HIST 72) F4," *Historia* 34: 493–6.

Devine, A.M. 1975. "Grand Tactics at Guagamela," *Phoenix* 29: 374–85.

———. 1980. "The Location of the Battle of Issus," *LCM* 5: 3–10.

———. 1983. "EMBALON: A Study in Tactical Terminology," *Phoenix* 37: 201–17.

———. 1985a. "Grand Tactics at the Battle of Issus," *AncW* 12: 39–59.

———. 1985b. "The Strategies of Alexander the Great and Darius III in the Issus Campaign (333BC)," *AncW* 12: 25–38.

———. 1985c. "Diodorus' Account of the Battle of Paraitacene (317 B.C.)," *Ancient World* 12: 75–86.

———. 1985d. "Diodorus' Account of the Battle of Gabiene," *Ancient World* 12: 87–96.

———. 1986. "The Battle of Guagamela: A Tactical and Source Critical Study," *AncW* 13: 87–115.

———. 1987. "The Battle of the Hydaspes: A Tactical and Source-Critical Study," *AncW* 16: 91–113.

———. 1988. "The Pawn-Sacrifice at the Battle of the Granicus: The Origins of a Favorite Stratagem of Alexander the Great," *AncW* 18: 3–20.

———. 1989a. "The Macedonian Army at Gaugamela: Its Strength and the Length of Its Battle Line," *AncW* 19: 77–80.

———. 1989b. "The Generalship of Ptolemy I and Demetrius Poliorcetes at the Battle of Gaza (312 BC)," *AncW* 19: 29–36.

———. 1994. "Alexander's Propaganda Machine: Callisthenes as the Ultimate Source for Arrian, *Anabasis* 1–3," in I. Worthington, ed. *Ventures into Greek History*. Oxford: Clarendon: 89–104.

———. 1996. "The Short Sarissa Again," *AncW* 27: 52–3.

De Voto, J.G. 1988. "Agesilaos and Tissaphernes Near Sardis in 395 B.C.," *Hermes* 116: 41–53.

———. 1992. "The Theban Sacred Band," *AncW* 23: 3–19.

———. 1993. *Flavius Arrianus*. Chicago: Ares.

Dillery, J. 1995. *Xenophon and the History of His Times*. London and New York: Routledge.

Doenges, N.A. 1998. "The Campaign and Battle of Marathon," *Historia* 47: 1–17.

Domaradzki, M. 1977. "Shields with Metal Fittings in the Eastern Celtic Region," *Przegla,d Archeologiczny* 25: 53–97.

Donlan, W. 1970. "Archilochus, Strabo, and the Lelantine War," *TAPA* 101: 131–42.

Donlan, W., and J. Thompson. 1976. "The Charge at Marathon, Herod. 6.112," *CJ* 71: 339–43.

———. 1979. "The Charge at Marathon Again," *CW* 72: 419–20.

Drews, R. 1962. "Diodorus and His Sources," *AJP* 83: 383–92.

———. 1993. *The End of the Bronze Age: Changes in Warfare and the Catastrophe ca. 1200 BC*. Princeton: Princeton University Press.

Driessen, J., and C. Macdonald. 1984. "Some Military Aspects of the Aegean in the Late Fifteenth and Early Fourteenth Centuries B.C.," *The Annual of the British School at Athens* 79: 49–74.

Ducat, J. 1990. *Les Hilotes*. Paris: École Française d'Athènes/De Boccard.
Ducrey, P. 1986. *Warfare in Ancient Greece*. New York: Schocken Books.
Dunbabin, T.J. 1948. *The Western Greeks: The History of Sicily and South Italy from the Foundation of the Greek Colonies to 480 BC*. Oxford: Clarendon Press.
Echols, E. C. (1949–50). "The Ancient Slinger," *Classical Weekly* 43: 227–230.
Edson, C. 1970. "Early Macedonia," in *Ancient Macedonia*. vol. 1. Thessaloniki: Institute for Balkan Studies: 17–44.
Ehrhardt, C. 1967. "Two Notes on Philip of Macedon's First Interventions in Thessaly," *CQ* 17: 296–301.
Ellis, J.R. 1975. "Alexander's Hypaspists Again," *Historia* 24: 617–18.
———. 1980. "The Unification of Macedonia," in Hatzopoulos and Loukopoulos: 36–47.
Engels, D.W. 1978. *Alexander the Great and the Logistics of the Macedonian Army*. Berkeley and Los Angeles: UCP.
English, S. 2009. *The Army of Alexander the Great*. Barnsley: Pen and Sword.
———. 2011. *The Field Campaigns of Alexander the Great*. Barnsley: Pen and Sword.
Erskine, A. 1989. "The pezetairoi of Philip II and Alexander III," *Historia* 38: 385–94.
Euben, J.P. 1986. "The Battle of Salamis and the Origins of Political Theory," *Political Theory* 14: 359–90.
Evans, J.A.S. 1984. "Herodotus and Marathon," *Florilegium* 6: 1–27.
———. 1986. "Cavalry About the Time of the Persian Wars: A Speculative Essay," *CJ* 82: 97–106.
———. 1993. "Herodotus and the Battle of Marathon," *Historia* 42: 279–307.
Everson, T. 2004. *Warfare in Ancient Greece. Arms and Armour from the Heroes of Homer to Alexander the Great*. Stroud: Sutton.
Ferrill, A. 1986. *The Origins of War: From the Stone Age to Alexander the Great*. New York: Thames and Hudson.
Fields, N. 2008. *Syracuse 415–413 BC: Destruction of the Athenian Imperial Fleet*. Oxford: Osprey.
Finley, M. I. 1980. *Ancient Slavery and Modern Ideology*. London: Chatto and Windus.
Forrest, J. 1999. *The History of Morris Dancing, 1458–1750*. Toronto: University of Toronto Press.
Forsdyke, E.J. 1919–20. "Some Arrow-Heads from the Battlefield of Marathon," *Proceedings of the Society of Antiquaries* 2.32: 146–57.
Förster, S., and J. Nagler. 1997. *On the Road to Total War: The American Civil War and the German Wars of Unification, 1861–1871*. Cambridge: Cambridge University Press.
Foss, C. 1977. "The Battle of the Granicus: A New Look," in *Ancient Macedonia* ii. Thessaloniki: Institute for Balkan Studies: 495–502.
Foulon, E. 1996a. "La garde a pied, corps d'elite de la phalange hellenistique," *BAGB* 1: 17–31.
———. 1996b. "Hypaspistes, Peltastes, Chrysaspides, Argyraspides, Chalcaspides," *REA* 98: 53–63.
Foxhall, L. 2013. "Can we see the 'Hoplite Revolution' on the Ground? Archaeological Landscapes, Material Culture, and Social Status in Early Greece," in Kagan and Viggiano 2013a: 194–221.
Frederiksen, M.W. 1968. "Campanian Cavalry: A Question of Origins," *Dialoghi di archaeologia* 2: 3–31.
Fuller, J.F.C. 1945. *The Influence of Armament on History from the Dawn of Classical Warfare to the End of the Second World War*. New York: C. Scribner's and sons.
———. 1960. *The Generalship of Alexander the Great*. London: Rutgers.
Gabriel, R.A. 2002. *The Great Armies of Antiquity*. Westport: Greenwood.

———. 2010. *Philip II of Macedonia: Greater Than Alexander*. Washington, DC: Potomac.
Gabriel, R.A., and D.W. Boose Jr. 1994. *The Great Battles of Antiquity*. Westport: Greenwood.
Gaebel, R. 2002. *Cavalry Operations in the Ancient Greek World*. Norman, OK: University of Oklahoma Press.
Gardiner-Garden, J.R. 1987. "Dareios' Scythian Expedition and Its Aftermath," *Klio* 69: 326–50.
Garlan, Y. 1976. *War in the Ancient World*. trans. J. Lloyd. New York: W.W. Norton & Company.
———. 1988. *Slavery in Ancient Greece*. trans. J. Lloyd. Ithaca, NY: Cornell University Press.
Garrison, M.B. 2000. "Achaemenid Iconography as Evidenced by Glyptic Art: Subject Matter, Social Function, Audience and Diffusion," in C. Uehlinger, ed. *Images as Media: Sources for the Cultural History of the Near East and the Eastern Mediterranean (1st Millennium B.C.E.)*. Fribourg: Fribourg University Press: 115–63.
Glover, R.F. 1944. "The Elephant in Ancient War," *CJ* 39: 257–69.
———. 1948. "The Tactical Handling of the Elephant," *G&R* 17: 1–11.
Gomme, A.W., A. Andrewes, and K.J. Dover. 1970. *A Historical Commentary of Thucydides. Volume IV: Books V 25 – VII*. Oxford: Clarendon Press.
Gray, V.J. 1979. "Two Different Approaches to the Battle of Sardis in 395 B.C.: Xenophon *Hellenica* 3.4.20–24 and *Hellenica Oxyrhynchia* 11(6). 4–6," *CSCA* 12: 183–200.
———. 1980. "The Years 375 to 371 BC: A Case Study in the Reliability of Diodorus Siculus and Xenophon," *CQ* 30: 306–26.
Green, P. 1970. *Xerxes at Salamis*. New York: Praeger.
———. 2006. *Diodorus Siculus, Books 11–12.37.1: Greek History 480–431 B.C., The Alternative Version/Diodorus Siculus: Translated with an Introduction and Commentary*. Austin: University of Texas Press.
Greenhalgh, P.A.L. 1973. *Early Greek Warfare: Horsemen and Chariots in the Homeric and Archaic Ages*. Cambridge: Cambridge University Press.
———. 1982. "The Homeric Therapon and Opaon and Their Historical Implications," *BICS* 29: 81–90.
Greenwalt, B. 2007. "The Development of a Middle Class in Macedonia," *Ancient Macedonia* 7: 89–90.
———. 2017. "Alexander II of Macedon," in T. Howe, S. Müller, and R. Stoneman, eds. *Ancient Historiography on War and Empire*. Oxford: Oxbow: 80–91.
Griffith, G. 1935. *The Mercenaries of the Hellenistic World*. Cambridge: Cambridge University Press.
———. 1947. "Alexander's generalship at Guagamela," *JHS* 67: 77–89.
———. 1981. "Peltast and the Origins of the Macedonian Phalanx," in H. Dell, ed. *Ancient Macedonian Studies in Honour of Charles F. Edson*. Thessaloniki: Institute for Balkan Studies: 161–7.
Grundy, G.B. 1901. *The Great Persian War*. London: John Murray.
Gunderson, L. 1982. "Quintus Curtius Rufus: On His Historical Methods in the *Historiae Alexandri*," in Adams and Borza: 177–96.
Guthrie, W.P. 1999. "Persian Army Strengths in Arrian-Ptolemy," *AncW* 30: 117–28.
Habicht, C. 1970. *Gottmenschentum und griechische Stadte*. Munich: Beck.
Hale, J.R. 2013. "Not Patriots, Not Farmers, Not Amateurs: Greek Soldiers of Fortune and the Origins of Hoplite Warfare," in Kagan and Viggiano 2013a: 176–93.

Hall, J.M. 2007. *A History of the Archaic Greek World: ca. 1200–479 BCE.* Malden: Blackwell.

Hamel, D. 1998. *Athenian Generals: Military Authority in the Classical Period.* Leiden: Brill.

Hamilton, C.D. 1983. "The Generalship of King Agesilaus of Sparta," *AncW* 8: 119–27.

———. 1991. *Agesilaus and the Failure of Spartan Hegemony.* Ithaca, NY: Cornell University Press.

Hamilton, J.R. 1956. "The Cavalry Battle at the Hydaspes," *JHS* 76: 26–31.

———. 1961. "Cleitarchus and Aristobulus," *Historia* 10: 448–58.

———. 1969. *Plutarch, Alexander: A Commentary.* Oxford: Oxford University Press.

———. 1977. "Cleitarchus and Diodorus 17," in K. Kinzl, ed. *Greece and the Ancient Mediterranean in History and Prehistory. Studies Presented to Fritz Schachermeyr.* Berlin: De Gruyter: 126–46.

Hammond, N.G.L. 1936–7. "The Campaigns in Amphilochia During the Archidamian War," *BSA* 37: 128–40.

———. 1937. "Diodorus's Narrative of the Sacred War and the Chronological Problems of 357–352 B.C.," *Journal of Hellenic Studies* 57: 44–77.

———. 1938. "The Two Battles of Chaeronea: 338 BC and 86 BC.," *Klio* 31: 186–218.

———. 1968. "The Campaign and the Battle of Marathon," *The Journal of Hellenic Studies* 88: 13–57.

———. 1974. "Alexander's Campaign in Illyria," *JHS* 94: 66–87.

———. 1977. "The Campaign of Alexander Against Cleitus and Glaucias," in *Ancient Macedonia II.* Thessaloniki: Institute for Balkan Studies: 503–9.

———. 1980a. "Training in the Use of the Sarissa and its Effect in Battle 359–333," *Antichthon* 14: 53–63.

———. 1980b. "The Battle of the Granicus River," *JHS* 100: 73–88.

———. 1981. *Alexander the Great: King, Commander and Statesman.* London: Bloomsbury.

———. 1983. *Three Historians of Alexander the Great: The So-Called Vulgate Authors, Diodorus, Justin and Curtius.* Cambridge: Cambridge University Press.

———. 1989. *The Macedonian State. Origins, Institutions and History.* Oxford: Clarendon.

———. 1991. "The Various Guards of Philip II and Alexander III," *Historia* 40: 396–418.

———. 1992. "Alexander's Charge at the Battle of Issus in 333 B.C.," *Historia* 41: 395–406.

———. 1994. *Philip of Macedon.* Baltimore: Johns Hopkins University Press.

———. 1996. "Alexander's Non-European Troops and Ptolemy I's Use of Such Troops," *BASP* 33: 99–109.

———. 1998. "Cavalry Recruited in Macedonia Down to 322 B.C.," *Historia* 47: 404–25.

Hanson, V.D. 1983. *Warfare and Agriculture in Classical Greece.* Pisa: Giardini Editori.

———. 1988. "Epameinondas, the Battle of Leuktra (371 BC) and the 'revolution' in Greek Battle Tactics," *CA* 7: 190–207.

———. 1989. *The Western Way of War: Infantry Battle in Classical Greece.* New York: Alfred A. Knopf.

———. 1991a. "Hoplite Technology in Phalanx Battle," in Hanson 1991b: 63–84.

———, ed. 1991b. *Hoplites: The Classical Greek Battle Experience.* London and New York: Routledge.

———. 1996. "Hoplites into Democrats: The Changing Ideology of Athenian Infantry," in J. Ober and C. Hedrick, eds. *Demokratia.* Princeton: Princeton University Press: 289–312.

———. 1999. *The Wars of the Ancient Greeks: And the Invention of Western Military Culture*. London: Cassell.

———. 2000. "Hoplite Battle as Ancient Greek Warfare: When, Where and Why?" in H. van Wees, ed. *War and Violence in Ancient Greece*. London: Duckworth and the Classical Press of Wales: 201–32.

———. 2001. *Carnage and Culture: Landmark Battles in the Rise of Western Power*. New York: W. W. Norton & Company.

———. 2007. "The Modern Historiography of Ancient Warfare," in Sabin, Van Wees, and Whitby: 3–21.

———. 2010. *Makers of Ancient Strategy from the Persian Wars to the Fall of Rome*. Princeton: Princeton University Press.

———. 2013. "The Hoplite Narrative," in Kagan and Viggiano 2013a: 256–76.

Harding, P. 1987. "The Authorship of the *Hellenika Oxyrhynchia*," *The Ancient History Bulletin* 1: 101–4.

Harrer, G. A. 1916. "Was Arrian Governor of Syria?" *CP* 11: 338–9.

Hatzopoulos, M., and L. Loukopoulos, eds. 1981. *Philip of Macedon*. London: Heinemann.

Head, D. 1985. "Xerxes' Army in Greece, 480–479 B.C.," *Slingshot* 181: 12–20.

———. 1992. *The Achaemenid Persian Army*. Stockport: Montvert.

Heckel, W. 1994. "Notes on Q. Curtius Rufus' History of Alexander," *Acta Classica* 37: 67–78.

———. 2005. "Synaspismos, Sarissas and Wagons," *Acta Classica* 48: 189–94.

———. 2009. "The *Asthetairoi*: A Closer Look," in P. Wheatley and R. Hannah, eds. *Alexander and His Successors: Essays from the Antipodes*. Claremont, CA: Regina Books: 99–117.

———. 2012. "The Royal Hypaspists in Battle: Macedonian *hamippoi*," *AHB* 26: 15–20.

———. 2013. "The Three Thousand: Alexander's Infantry Guard," in Campbell and Tritle 2013: 162–78.

———. 2016. *Alexander's Marshals: A Study of the Makedonian Aristocracy and the Politics of Military Leadership*. London: Routledge.

Heckel, W., and R. Jones. 2006. *Macedonian Warrior: Alexander's elite infantryman*. Oxford: Osprey.

Heckel, W., C. Willekes, and G. Wrightson. 2010. "Scythed Chariots at Gaugamela," in E. Carney and D. Ogden, eds. *Philip II and Alexander the Great: Father and Son, Lives and Afterlives*. Oxford: Oxford University Press: 103–13.

Heckel, W., and J. Yardley. 1997. *Justin: Epitome of The Philippic History of Pompeius Trogus: Volume I: Books 11–12: Alexander the Great*. Oxford: OUP.

Heinrichs, J. 2015. "Military Integration in Late Archaic Arkadia: New Evidence from a Bronze Pinax (ca. 500 BC) of the Lykaion," in W. Heckel, S. Mueller, and G. Wrightson, eds. *The Many Faces of War in the Ancient World*. Cambridge: Cambridge Scholars Press.

Herbert, P. H. 1988. *Deciding What Has to Be Done: General William E. DePuy and the 1976 Edition of FM 100–5, Operations*. Fort Leavenworth: US Army Command and General Staff College.

Hicks, M. 1998. *Warwick the Kingmaker*. London: Blackwell.

Hignett, C. 1963. *Xerxes' Invasion of Greece*. Oxford: Clarendon Press.

Hijmans, B. J. 1976. "Archers in the *Iliad*," in *Festoen, Fetschrift A. Zadoks-Josephus Jitta*. Groningen: Bussum: 343–52.

Hoddinott, R. F. 1981. *The Thracians*. London: Thames and Hudson.

Holland, T. 2007. *Persian Fire: The First World Empire, Battle for the West*. London: Little Brown.
Holladay, A. J. 1978. "Athenian Strategy in the Archidamian War," *Historia* 27: 399–427.
Hooker, J. T. 1976. *Mycenaean Greece*. London: Routledge.
Horden, P., and N. Purcell. 2000. *The Corrupting Sea: A Study of Mediterranean History*. Oxford: Blackwell.
Hornblower, J. 1981. *Hieronymus of Cardia*. Oxford: Clarendon.
———. 1991–2008. *A Commentary on Thucydides*. 3 vols. Oxford: Oxford University Press.
———. 2007. "Warfare in Ancient Literature: The Paradox of War," in Sabin, Van Wees, and Whitby: 22–53.
House, J. M. 1984. *Toward Combined Arms Warfare: A Survey of 20th-Century Tactics, Doctrine, and Organization*. Lawrence, KA: Combat Studies Institute.
———. 2001. *Combined Arms Warfare in the Twentieth Century*. Lawrence, KS: Kansas University Press.
How, W. W. 1923. "Arms, Tactics and Strategy in the Persian War," *JHS* 43: 117–32.
How, W. W., and J. Wells. 1912. *A Commentary on Herodotus*. vol. 2. Oxford: Clarendon.
Hunt, P. 1997. "The Helots at the Battle of Plataea," *Historia* 46: 129–44.
———. 1998. *Slaves, Warfare and Ideology in the Greek Historians*. Cambridge: Cambridge University Press.
———. 2007. "Military Forces," in Sabin, Van Wees, and Whitby: 108–46.
Hunter, V. 1973. *Thucydides the Artful Reporter*. Toronto: Hakkert.
Hurwit, J. M. 2002. "Reading the Chigi Vase," *Hesperia* 71: 1–22.
Hutchinson, G. 2000. *Xenophon and the Art of Command*. London: Greenhill.
———. 2006. *Attrition: Aspects of Command in the Peloponnesian War*. Stroud: Spellmount.
Jones, A. 1987. *The Art of War in the Western World*. Chicago: University of Illinois Press.
Jordan, B. 1975. *The Athenian Navy in the Classical Period*. Berkeley and Los Angeles: UCP.
Kagan, D. 1974. *The Archidamian War*. Ithaca, NY: Cornell University Press.
Kagan, D., and G. F. Viggiano, eds. 2013a. *Men of Bronze*. Princeton and Oxford: Princeton University Press.
———. 2013b. "Introduction," in D. Kagan and G. F. Viggiano 2013a: xi–xxi.
———. 2013c. "The Hoplite debate" in D. Kagan and G. F. Viggiano 2013a: 1–56.
Karasulas, A. 2004. *Mounted Archers of the Steppe 600 BC – AD 1300*. Oxford: Osprey.
Karunanithy, D. 2013. *The Macedonian War Machine 359–281 BC*. Barnsley: Pen and Sword.
Kent, R. G. 1953. *Old Persian: Grammar, Texts, Lexicon*. New Haven: American Oriental Society.
Keyser, P. T. 1994. "The Use of Artillery by Philip II and Alexander the Great," *AncW* 25: 27–59.
Kienast, D. 1973. *Philip II von Makedonien und das Reich der Achaimeniden*. Munich: W. Fink.
King, C. 2018. *Ancient Macedonia*. London: Routledge.
Kirk, G. S. 1968. "War and the Warrior in the Homeric Poems," in J-P. Vernant, ed. *Problemes de la guerre en Grece Ancienne*. Paris: La Haye Mouton: 93–117.
———. 1985. *The Iliad: A Commentary vol. 1: Books I–IV*. Cambridge: Cambridge University Press.
Kistler, J. M. 2007. *War Elephants*. Lincoln: University of Nebraska Press.

Kochly, H., and W. Rustow, eds. 1885. "de Re Strategica," in *Griechische Kriegschriftsteller*. vol. 2. Leipzig: W. Engelmann.

Konecny, A. 2001. "Κατεκοφεν την μοραν Ιφικρατης. Das gefecht bei Lechaion im Fruhsommer 390 v. Chr.," *Chiron* 31: 79–127.

———. 2014. "Κατέκοψεν τὴν μόραν 'Ιφικράτης.' The Battle of Lechaeum, Early Summer, 390 BC," in Sekunda and Burliga 2014: 7–48.

Konijnendijk, R. 2014. "Iphikrates the Innovator and the Historiography of Lechaeum," in Sekunda and Burliga 2014: 84–94.

Korfmann, M. 1973. "The Sling as a Weapon," *Scientific American* 229: 34–42.

Krasilnikoff, J.A. 1992. "Aegean Mercenaries in the Fourth to Second Centuries BC: A Study in Payment, Plunder and Logistics of Ancient Greek Armies," *C&M* 43: 23–36.

Krentz, P. 1985a. "The Nature of Hoplite Battle," *Classical Antiquity* 4: 50–61.

———. 1985b. "Casualties in Hoplite Battles," *GRBS* 26: 13–20.

———. 1994. "Continuing the *Othismos* on *Othismos*," *AHB* 8: 45–9.

———. 2000. "Deception in Archaic and Classical Greek Warfare," in H. van Wees, ed. *War and Violence in Ancient Greece*. London: Duckworth and the Classical Press of Wales: 167–200.

———. 2002. "Fighting by the Rules: The Invention of the Hoplite *Agon*," *Hesperia* 71: 23–39.

———. 2010. *The Battle of Marathon*. New Haven and London: Yale University Press.

———. 2013. "Hoplite Hell: How Hoplites Fought," in D. Kagan and G.F. Viggiano 2013a: 134–56.

Krentz, P., and E.L. Wheeler, eds. 1994. *Polyaenus, Stratagems of War*. Chicago: Ares.

Kretchik, W.E. 2011. *U.S. Army Doctrine: From the American Revolution to the War on Terror*. Lawrence: University Press of Kansas.

Kroll, J.H. 1977. "An Archive of the Athenian Cavalry," *Hesperia* 46: 83–140.

Kruse, G. 1972. *Trunk Call*. London: Elek Books.

Lacey, J. 2012. "The Persian Fallacy," *Military History Magazine:* 42–52.

Landucci Gattinoni, F. 2008. *Diodoro Siculo: Biblioteca storica: libro XVIII: commento storico. Storia. Ricerche*. Milan: Vita e Pensiero.

Lane Fox, R.J., ed. 2004. *The Long March: Xenophon's Anabasis, Old and New*. New Haven: Yale University Press.

Latacz, J. 1977. *Kampfparanese, Kampfdarstellung und Kampfwirkichkeit in der Ilias, bei Kallinos und Tyrtaios*. Munich: Beck.

Lazenby, J.F. 1985. *The Spartan Army*. Warminster: Aris and Phillips.

———. 1993. *The Defence of Greece: 490–479 B.C.* Warminster: Aris and Phillips.

———. 2004. *The Peloponnesian War. A Military Study*. London: Routledge.

Lazenby, J.F., and D. Whitehead. 1996. "The Myth of the Hoplite's Hoplon," *CQ* 46: 27–33.

Lee, J.W.I. 2007. *A Greek Army on the March: Soldiers and Survival in Xenophon's Anabasis*. Cambridge: Cambridge University Press.

———. 2009. "Land Warfare in Xenophon's Hellenika," in R. Strassler, ed. *The Landmark Xenophon's Hellenika*. New York: Pantheon: 391–4.

Leitao, D. 2002. "The Legend of the Sacred Band," in M.C. Nussbaum and J. Sihvola, eds. *The Sleep of Reason: Experience and Sexual Ethics in Ancient Greece and Rome*. Chicago: University of Chicago Press: 143–69.

Lendon, J.E. 2005. *Soldiers and Ghosts: A History of Battle in Classical Antiquity*. New Haven: Yale University Press.

———. 2010. *Song of Wrath: The Peloponnesian War Begins*. New York: Basic Books.

Liebeschutz, J.H.W.G. 1968. "Thucydides and the Sicilian Expedition," *Historia* 17: 289–306.

Lind, W. 1985. *Maneuver Warfare Handbook*. Boulder: Westview Press.

Lissarrague, F. 1990. *L'Autre guerrier. Archers, peltastes, cavaliers dans l'imagerie attique*. Paris and Rome: Éditions de la Découverte – École française de Rome.

Littauer, M.A. 1972. "The Military Use of the Chariot in the Aegean in the Late Bronze Age," *AJA* 76: 145–57.

Littauer, M.A. and J.H. Crouwel. 1985. *Chariots and Related Equipment from the Tomb of Tut'ankhamun*. Oxford: Griffith Institute.

Lloyd, A.B., ed. 1996a. *Battle in Antiquity*. London: Duckworth.

———. 1996b. "Philip and Alexander the Great: The Moulding of Macedon's Army," in Lloyd 1996a: 169–98.

———. 2004. *Marathon: The Crucial Battle That Created Western Democracy*. London: Souvenir Press.

Lock R. 1977. "The Origins of the Argyraspids," *Historia* 26: 373–8.

Lonsdale, D.J. 2004. *Alexander the Great, Killer of Men*. New York: Constable.

———. 2007. *Alexander the Great: Lessons in Strategy (Strategy and History)*. London: Routledge.

Lorimer, H.L. 1947. "The Hoplite Phalanx with Special Reference to the Poems of Archilochus and Tyrtaeus," *ABSA* 42: 76–138.

———. 1950. *Homer and the Monuments*. London: Palgrave Macmillan.

Luginbill, R.D. 1997. "Thucydides' Evaluation of the Sicilian Expedition: 2.65.11," *AncW* 28: 127–32.

Luraghi, N. 2006. "Traders, Pirates, Warriors: The Proto-History of Greek Mercenary Soldiers in the Eastern Mediterranean," *Phoenix* 60: 21–47.

Macan, R.W. 1908. *Herodotus 7–9*. vol. 2. London: Palgrave Macmillan.

Manti, P.A. 1983. "The Cavalry Sarissa," *AncW* 8: 73–80.

———. 1994. "The Macedonian Sarissa, Again," *AncW* 25: 77–91.

Markle, M.M. 1974. "The Strategy of Philip in 346 B.C.," *CQ* 24.2: 253–68.

———. 1977. "The Macedonian Sarissa, Spear and Related Armor," *AJA* 81: 323–9.

———. 1978. "Use of the Sarissa by Philip and Alexander of Macedon," *AJA* 82: 483–97.

Markle, M.M. 1982. "Macedonian Arms and Tactics under Alexander the Great," in B. Barr-Sharrar and E. Borza eds. Macedonia and Greece in Late Classical and Early Hellenistic Times Washington, D.C.: National Gallery of Art, 87–111.

Marsden, E.W. 1964. *The Campaign of Gaugamela*. Liverpool: Liverpool University Press.

———. 1969. *Greek and Roman Artillery I: Historical Development*. Oxford: Clarendon.

Martin, T.R. 1981. "Diodorus on Philip II and Thessaly in the 350's B.C.," *Classical Philology* 76: 188–201.

———. 1982. "A Phantom Fragment of Theopompous and Philip II's First Campaign in Thessaly," *Harvard Studies in Classical Philology* 86: 55–78.

Massaro, V. 1978. "Herodotus' Account of the Battle of Marathon and the Pin the Stoa Poikile," *AC* 47: 458–75.

Matloff, M. 1969. *American Military History*. Washington, DC: Office of the Chief of Military History, US Army.

Matthew, C.A. 2012. *A Storm of Spears: Understanding the Greek Hoplite at War*. Barnsley: Pen and Sword.

———. 2015. *An Invincible Beast: Understanding the Hellenistic Pike Phalanx in Action*. Barnsley: Pen and Sword.

Maurice, F. 1930. "The Size of the Army of Xerxes in the Invasion of Greece 480 B.C.," *JHS* 50: 210–35.

McCoy, W.J. 1989. "Memnon of Rhodes at the Granicus," *AJPh* 110: 413–33.

McKechnie, P. 1994. "Greek Mercenary Troops and Their Equipment," *Historia* 43: 297–305.
McKechnie, P., and S. J. Kern. 1988. *Hellenica Oxyrhynchia*. Warminster: Aris & Phillips.
McLeod, W. 1965. "The Range of the Ancient Bow," *Phoenix* 19: 1–14.
———. 1970. "The Bowshot at Marathon," *JHS* 90: 197–8.
———. 1972. "The Range of the Ancient Bow. Addenda," *Phoenix* 26: 78–82.
Meeus, A. 2009. "Review of *Franca Landucci Gattinoni, Diodoro Siculo: Biblioteca storica: libro XVIII: commento storico. Storia. Ricerche. Milan 2008*," *Bryn Mawr Classical Review* 2009-3-45.
Meyer, E. 1944. *Geschichte des Altertums* iv I. Stuttgart: Cotta.
Miller, H. F. 1984. "The Practical and Economic Background to the Greek Mercenary Explosion," *G&R* 2nd ser. 31: 153–60.
Milns, R. D. 1966. "Alexander's Macedonian Cavalry and Diodorus xvii. 17. 4," *JHS* 86: 167–8.
———. 1967. "Philip II and the Hypaspists," *Historia* 16: 509–12.
———. 1971. "The Hypaspists of Alexander III – Some Problems," *Historia* 20: 186–95.
———. 1976. "The Army of Alexander the Great," in *Entretiens Hardt* 22. Geneva: Fondation Hardt: 87–136.
———. 1978. "Arrian's Accuracy in Troop Details: A Note," *Historia* 27: 374–378.
Mixter, J. R. 1992. "The Length of the Macedonian Sarissa During the Reigns of Philip II and Alexander the Great," *AncW* 23: 21–9.
Moorey, P.R.S. 1986. "The Emergence of the Light, Horse-Drawn Chariot in the Near-East c. 2000–1500 B.C.," *World Archaeology* 18.2: 196–215.
Moreno Hernández, J. J. 2004. "La Caballería macedonia: teoría y práctica," *Gladius* 24: 109–22.
Morpeth, N. 2006. *Thucydides' War: Accounting for the Faces of Battle*. Hildesheim: Georg Olms.
Muir, R. 2000. *Tactics and the Experience of Battle in the Age of Napoleon*. London: Yale University Press.
Munro, J.A.H. 1902. "Some Observations on the Persian Wars," *JHS* 22: 294–332.
———. 1904. "Some Observations on the Persian Wars (Continued)," *JHS* 24: 144–65.
Murison, C. 1972. "Darius III and the Battle of Issus," *Historia* 21: 399–423.
Murray W., and P. R. Mansoor, eds. 2012. *Hybrid Warfare: Fighting Complex Opponents from the Ancient World to the Present*. New York: Cambridge University Press.
Myres, J. L. 1933. "The Amathus Bowl," *JHS* 53: 25–39.
Nardo, D. 2008. *Science, Technology, and Warfare of Ancient Mesopotamia*. Detroit: Lucent Books.
Nefedkin, A. K. 2001. *Chariotry of the Ancient Greeks (Sixteenth – First Centuries BC)*. St. Petersburg: Peterburgskoe Vostokovedenie.
———. 2004. "On the Origin of the Scythed Chariots," *Historia* 53: 369–78.
———. 2006. "The Tactical Development of Achaemenid Cavalry," *Gladius* 26: 5–18.
———. 2009. "On the Origin of Greek Cavalry Shields in the Hellenistic Period," *Klio* 91: 356–66.
Nickel, R. 1979. *Xenophon*. Darmstadt: Erträge der Forschung, Bd: 111.
Nikolitsis, N. 1973. *The Battle of the Granicus*. Stockholm: Swedish Institute in Athens.
Nimchuk, C. L. 2002. "The 'Archers' of Darius: Coinage or Tokens of Royal Esteem?" *Ars Orientalis* 32 *Medes and Persians: Reflections on Elusive Empires*: 55–79.
Noble, D. 1990. "Assyrian Chariotry and Cavalry," *SAAB* 4 1: 61–8.

Noguera Borel, A. 1999. "L'evolution de la phalange macedonienne: le cas de la sarisse," in*Ancient Macedonia: Sixth International Symposium* at Thessalonica: Institute for Balkan Studies. Vol. II: 39–50.

Nossov, K., and P. Dennis. 2008. *War Elephants*. Oxford: Osprey.

Notopoulos, J.A. 1941. "The Slaves at the Battle of Marathon," *AJPh* 62: 352–4.

Ober. 1991. "Hoplites and Obstacles," in Hanson 1991b: 173–96.

Oorthuys, J. 2007. "Combined Arms: Agricola's Naval and Land Campaign," *Ancient Warfare* 1: 20–4.

Pagden, A., and J.W.I. Lee. 2008. *Worlds at War: The 2,500-Year Struggle Between East and West*. New York: OUP.

Parke, H.W. 1933. *Greek Mercenary Soldiers*. Oxford: Oxford Univesity Press.

Pascual, J. 2007. "Theban Victory at Haliartos (395 B.C.)," *Gladius* 27: 39–66.

———. 2009. "Xenophon and the Chronology of the War on Land from 393 to 386 BC," *CQ* n.s. 59: 75–90.

Paul, G.M. 1987. "Two Battles in Thucydides," *EMC* 31: 307–13.

Pearson, L. 1987. *The Greek Historians of the West*. Atlanta: Scholars Press.

Pederson, R.B. 1998. "A Study of Combined Arms Warfare by Alexander the Great," MA Dissertation, Fort Leavenworth, Kansas.

———. 2015. *A Study of Combined Arms Warfare by Alexander the Great*. Fort Leavenworth, KS: US Army Command and General Staff College and Penny Hill Press.

Pietrykowski, J. 2009. *Great Battles of the Hellenistic World*. Barnsley: Pen and Sword.

Plumpe, J.C. 1938. "Cyrus the Younger and the Size of Xerxes' Army," *CJ* 33: 422–5.

Ponting, C. 2004. *The Crimean War: The Truth Behind the Myth*. London: Chatto & Windus.

Poss, J.M. 2011. Behind the Shield-Wall: The Experience of Combat in Late Anglo-Saxon England. MA Thesis. Clemson University.

Power, T., and R. Tremain. 1988. *Total War: What It Is, How It Got That Way*. New York: William Morrow and Company.

Pritchett, W.K. 1969. "The Battles of Mantineia (418, 362 and 207 B.C.)," in *Studies in Ancient Greek Topography, Part II (Battlefields)*. Berkeley: Cambridge University Press: 37–72.

———. 1971–91. *The Greek State at War. Part I*. 1971. *Part II*. 1974. *Part III: Religion*. 1979. *Part IV*. 1985. *Part V*. 1991. Berkeley and Los Angeles: Cambridge University Press.

Rahe, P.A. 1980. "The Military Situation in Western Asia on the Eve of Cunaxa," *AJP* 101: 79–96.

———. 1981. "The Annihilation of the Sacred Band at Chaeronea," *AJA* 85: 84–7.

Ranstorp, M., and M. Normark, eds. 2009. *Unconventional Weapons and International Terrorism: Challenges and New Approaches*. New York: Routledge.

Ray, F.E. 2012. *Greek and Macedonian Land Battles of the 4th Century B.C.: A History and Analysis of 187 Engagements*. Jefferson, NC: McFarland.

Reames, J. 2010. "The Cult of Hephaestion," in P. Cartledge and F. Greenland, eds. *Responses to Oliver Stone's* Alexander*: Film, History, and Cultural Studies*. Madison, WI: University of Wisconsin Press.

Ridley, R.T. 1979. "The Hoplite as Citizen: Athenian Military Institutions in Their Social Context," *AC* 48: 508–48.

Roisman, J. 1993. *The General Demosthenes and His Use of Military Surprise. Historia Einzelschriften* 78. Stuttgart: Franz Steiner Verlag.

Roisman. J., and I. Worthington, eds. 2010. *A Companion to Ancient Macedonia*. Oxford: Blackwell.

Root, M. C. 1979. *The King and Kingship in Achaemenid Art: Essays on the Creation of an Iconography of Empire*. Leiden: Brill.

———. 1989. "The Persian Archer at Persepolis: Aspects of Chronology, Style and Symbolism," *Revue des etudes anciennes* 91: 33–50.

———. 1991. "From the Heart: Powerful Persianisms in the Art of the Western Empire," in H. Sancisi-Weerdenburg and A. Kuhrt, eds. *Asia Minor and Egypt: Old Cultures in a New Empire*. Leiden: Brill: 1–29.

Rosivach, V. J. 2002. "*Zeugitai* and hoplites," *AHB* 16: 33–43.

Roth, J. P. 2007. "War," in Sabin, Van Wees, and Whitby: 368–98.

Roy, J. 1967. "The Mercenaries of Cyrus," *Historia* 16: 287–323.

Royle, T. 2000. *Crimea: The Great Crimean War, 1854–1856*. New York: St. Martins.

Rubincam, C. 1991. "Casualty Figures in the Battle Descriptions of Thucydides," *TAPhA* 121: 181–98.

Runciman, W. G. 1998. "Greek Hoplites, Warrior Culture and Indirect Bias," *Journal of the Royal Anthropological Institute* 4: 731–51.

Rusch, S. 2011. *Sparta at War: Strategy, Tactics and Campaigns, 550–362 BC*. London: Frontline Books.

Russell, A. G. 1942. "The Greek as a Mercenary Soldier," *G&R* 11: 103–12.

Sabin, P. 2009. *Lost Battles: Reconstructing the Great Clashes of the Ancient World*. London: Hambledon Continuum.

Sabin, P., H. van Wees, and M. Whitby, eds. 2007. *The Cambridge History of Greek and Roman Warfare*. vol. 1. Cambridge: Cambridge University Press.

Salmon, J. 1977. "Political Hoplites?" *JHS* 97: 84–101.

Sampson, G. 2008. *The Defeat of Rome in the East: Crassus, the Parthians, and the Disastrous Battle of Carrhae, 53 BC*. Havertown, PA: Casemate.

Schepens, G. 1971. "Arrian's View of His Task as Alexander Historian," *Anc. Soc.* 2: 254–68.

Schmitt, D. B. 1991. *The Bihistun Inscriptions of Darius the Great, Old Persian Text. Corpus Inscriptionum Iranicarum Part 1, vol. 1, Texts 1*. London: Lund.

Schwartz, A. 2009. *Reinstating the Hoplite: Arms, Armour and Phalanx Fighting in Archaic and Classical Greece*. Stuttgart: Franz Steiner Verlag.

———. 2013. "Large Weapons, Small Greeks: Te Practical Limitations of Hoplite Weapons and Equipment," in Kagan and Viggiano 2013a: 157–75.

Scullard, H. H. 1974. *The Elephant in the Greek and Roman World*. Ithaca, NY: Cornell University Press.

Sekunda, N. V. 1992. *The Persian Army 560–330*. London: Osprey.

———. 2000. *The Greek Hoplite, 480–323 bc*. London: Osprey.

———. 2001. "The Sarissa," *Acta Universitatis Lodziensis, Folia Archaeologica* 23: 13–41.

———. 2010. "The Macedonian Army," in J. Roisman and I. Worthington 2010: 446–71.

———. 2014a. "The Composition of the Lakedaimonian Mora at Lechaeum," in Sekunda and Burliga 2014: 49–65.

———. 2014b. "The Chronology of the Iphicratean Peltast Reform," in Sekunda and Burliga 2014: 126–44.

Sekunda, N. V., and B. Burliga, eds. 2014. *Iphicrates, Peltasts and Lechaeum*. Gdansk: Foundation for the Development of Gdańsk University.

Shay, J. 1994. *Achilles in Vietnam: Combat Trauma and the Undoing of Character*. New York: Scribner.

Shay, J., J. McCain, and M. Cleland. 2003. *Odysseus in America: Combat Trauma and the Trials of Homecoming*. New York: Scribner.

Sheldon, R. 2012. *Ambush: Surprise Attack in Ancient Greek Warfare*. London: Frontline Books.
Shrimpton, G. 1980. "The Persian Cavalry at Marathon," *Phoenix* 34: 20–37.
———. 1991. *Theopompus the Historian*. Montreal and Kingston: McGill Queens University Press.
Sinclair, R. K. 1966. "Diodorus Siculus and Fighting in Relays," *CQ* n.s. 16: 249–55.
Singor, H. 1991. "Nine Against Troy: On Epic *phalanges, promachoi*, and an Old Structure in the Story of the *Iliad*," *Mnemosyne* 44: 17–62.
———. 2002. "The Spartan Army at Mantinea and Its Organisation in the Fifth Century B.C.," in W. Jongman and M. Kleijwegt, eds. *After the Past: Essays in Ancient History in Honour of H. W. Pleket*. Leiden: Brill: 235–84.
Snodgrass, A. M. 1964. *Early Greek Armour and Weapons from the End of the Bronze Age to 600 BC*. Edinburgh: Edinburgh University Press.
———. 1965. "The Hoplite Reform in History," *JHS* 85: 110–22.
———. 1999. *Arms and Armour of the Greeks*. Baltimore: Johns Hopkins University Press.
———. 2013. "Setting the Frame chronologically," in Kagan and Viggiano 2013a: 85–94.
Spalinger, A. J. 2003. "The Battle of Kadesh: The Chariot Frieze at Abydos," *Aegypten und Levante* 13: 163–99.
Spence, I. G. 1993. *The Cavalry of Classical Greece. A Social and Military History with Particular Reference to Athens*. Oxford: Clarendon.
Spiller, R. J. 1992. *Combined Arms in Battle Since 1939*. Leavenworth: US Army Command and General Staff College Press.
Sprawski, S. "Peltasts in Thessaly," in Sekunda and Burliga 2014: 95–112.
Stadter, P. J. 1992. *Plutarch and the Historical Tradition*. London: Routledge.
Stahl, H.-P. 1966. *Thucydides*. Munich: C. H. Beck.
Starr, C. G. 1962. "Why Did the Greeks Defeat the Persians?" *PP* 17: 321–9.
Storch, R. H. 2001. "The Silence Is Deafening: Persian Arrows Did Not Inspire the Greek Charge at Marathon," *Acta Archaeologica Academiae Scientiarum Hungaricae* 41: 381–94.
Strassler, R. B. 1988. "The Harbor at Pylos, 425 B.C.," *JHS* 108: 198–203.
———. 1990. "The Opening of the Pylos Campaign," *JHS* 110: 110–25.
Strootman, R. 2012. "Alexander's Thessalian Cavalry," *Talanta* 42/43: 51–67.
Sulimirski, T. 1952. "Les Archers à cheval, cavalerie légère des anciens," *Revue Internationale d'Histoire Militaire* 3: 447–61.
Sutherland, C. 2001. "Archery in the Homeric Epics," *Classics Ireland* 8: 111–20.
Syme, R. 1988. "The Cadusians in History and Fiction," *JHS* 108: 137–50.
Tarn, W. W. 1940. "Two Notes on Seleucid History: 1. Seleucus' 500 Elephants," *JHS* 60: 84–9.
———. 1948. *Alexander the Great*. 2 vols. Cambridge: Cambridge University Press.
———. 1975. *Hellenistic Military and Naval Developments*. Chicago: Ares.
Tracy, H. L. 1942. "Notes on Plutarch's Biographical Method," *CJ* 37: 213–21.
Tritle, L. A. 2000. *From Melos to My Lai: A Study in Violence, Culture and Social Survival*. New York and London: Routledge.
———. 2010. *A New History of the Peloponnesian War*. Oxford: Blackwell.
Trundle, M. 2001. "The Spartan Revolution: Hoplite Warfare in the Later Archaic Period," *War & Society* 19: 1–17.
———. 2004. *Greek Mercenaries: From the Late Archaic Period to Alexander*. London and New York: Routledge.
Tuplin, C. 1986. "Military Engagements in Xenophon's *Hellenica*," in I. S. Moxon, J. D. Smart, and A. J. Woodman, eds. *Past Perspectives: Studies in Greek and Roman Historical Writing*. Cambridge: Cambridge University Press: 37–66.

———. 1987. "The Leuctra Campaign: Some Outstanding Problems," *Klio* 69: 72–107.

———. 1993. *The Failings of Empire*, Stuttgart: Franz Steiner Verlag.

———, ed. 2004. *Xenophon and His World. Papers from a Conference Hold in Liverpool in July 1999*. Historia Einzelschrift 172. Stuttgart: Franz Steiner Verlag.

US Army. 1990. *Army Regulation 600–82, U.S. Army Regimental System*. Washington, DC: Headquarters Department of the Army.

———. 1992a. *Field Manual 71–123, Tactics and Techniques for Combined Arms Heavy Forces: Armored Brigade. Battalion/Task Force and Company/Team*. Washington, DC: Headquarters Department of the Army.

———. 1992b. *Field Manual 21–150, Combatives*. Washington, DC: Headquarters Department of the Army.

———. 1993. *Field Manual 100–5: Operations*. Washington, DC: Headquarters Department of the Army.

US Department of Defense. 2001. *JP 3–0, Doctrine for Joint Operations*. Washington, DC: US Government Printing Office.

———. 2005. *Dictionary of Military and Associated Terms*. Washington, DC: US Government Printing Office.

Van Wees, H. 1986. "Leaders of Men? Military Organisation in the Iliad," *The Classical Quarterly* 36: 285–303.

———. 1988. 'Kings in combat: battles and heroes in the *Iliad*," *CQ* 38: 1–24.

———. 1992. *Status Warriors: War, Violence and Society in Homer and History*. Amsterdam: J.C. Geiben.

———. 1994. "The Homeric Way of War: The 'Iliad' and the Hoplite Phalanx I and II," *Greece and Rome* 41: I 1–18; II 131–55.

———. 1997. "Homeric Warfare," in I. Morris and B. Powell, eds. *A New Companion to Homer*. Leiden: Brill: 668–693.

———. 2000a. "The Development of the Hoplite Phalanx: Iconography and Reality in the 7th Century," in H. van Wees, ed. *War and Violence in Ancient Greece*. London: Duckworth: 125–66.

———, ed. 2000b. *War and Violence in Ancient Greece*. London: Duckworth.

———. 2005. *Greek Warfare: Myths and Realities*. London: Duckworth.

———. 2013. "Farmers and hoplites: Models of Historical Development," in Kagan and Viggiano 2013a: 222–55.

Viggiano, G.F. 2013. "The Hoplite Revolution and the Rise of the Polis," in Kagan and Viggiano 2013a: 112–33.

Vigors, P.D. 1888. "Slings and Sling-Stones," *Journal of the Royal Historical & Archaeological Association of Ireland* 4th ser. 8: 357–66.

Wardman, A.E. 1955. "Plutarch and Alexander," *CQ* 5: 96–107.

———. 1971. "Plutarch's Methods in the *Lives*," *CQ* 21: 254–61.

Waterfield, R. 2006. *Xenophon's Retreat: Greece, Persia and the End of the Golden Age*. London: Faber and Faber.

Webber, C. 2011. *The Gods of Battle: The Thracians at War, 1500 BC – 150 AD*. Barnsley: Pen and Sword.

Webster, T.B.L. 1972. *Potter and Patron in Classical Athens*. London: Methuen.

Welles, C.B. 1963. "The Reliability of Ptolemy as an Historian," in *Miscellanea di studi alessandrini in memoria di A. Rostagni*. Turin: 101–16.

Welwei, K.W. 1974. *Unfreie im antiken Kriegsdienst*. Stuttgart: Franz Steiner Verlag.

———. 1979. "Der Kampf um das makedonische Lager bei Gaugamela," *RhM* 122: 222–8.

Westlake, H.D. 1935. *Thessaly in the Fourth Century BC*. London: Methuen.

———. 1975. "Xenophon and Epaminondas," *GRBS* 16: 23–40.
———. 1986. "The Spartan Intervention in Asia 400–397 B.C.," *Historia* 35: 405–26.
———. 1987. "Diodorus and the Expedition of Cyrus," *Phoenix* 41: 241–54.
Wheeler, E. L. 1979. "The Legion as Phalanx," *Chiron* 9: 303–18.
———. 1992. "Legion vs. Phalanx: The Credibility of Polybius 18.28–32," paper delivered at the 124th Annual Meeting of the *American Philological Association*, New Orleans, 27–30 December 1992.
———. 2001. "Firepower: Missile Weapons and the 'face of battle'," in E. Dabrowa, ed. *Roman Military Studies*. Crakow: Jagiellonian University Press: 169–84.
———. 2004. "The Legion as Phalanx in the Late Empire (I)," in Y. Le Bohec and C. Wolff, eds. *L'armee romaine de Diocletien a Valentinien Ier*. Paris: Le Bohec: 309–58.
Whitehead, D. 1991. "Who Equipped Mercenary Troops in Classical Greece?" *Historia* 40: 105–13.
Wilkes, J. 1992. *The Illyrians*. Cambridge, MA: s.
Wilson, J. B. 1979. *Pylos 425 B.C.: A Historical and Topographical Study of Thucydides' Account of the Campaign*. Warminster: Aris and Phillips.
Wisdom, S. 2001. *Gladiators: 100 BC-AD 200*. Oxford: Osprey.
Woodcock, E. C. 1928. "Demosthenes, Son of Alcisthenes," *HSCP* 39: 93–108.
Woodhouse, W. J. 1918. *The Campaign of Mantineia in 418 BC*. Oxford: Clarendon.
Wooten, C. 2008. *A Commentary on Demosthenes' Philippic I: With Rhetorical Analyses of Philippics II and III*. Oxford: Oxford University Press.
Worley, L. J. 1994. *Hippeis. The Cavalry of Ancient Greece*. Oxford: Westview Press.
Worthington, I. 2008. *Philip II of Macedonia*. New Haven: Yale University Press.
Wrightson, G. 2010. "The Nature of Command in the Macedonian Sarissa Phalanx," *AHB* 24: 71–92.
———. 2015a. "'Surprise, Surprise': The Tactical Response of Alexander to Guerilla Warfare and Fighting in Difficult Terrain," *The Ancient World* 46.2: 162–79.
———. 2015b. "Macedonian Armies and the Perfection of Combined Arms," in T. Howe, E. Garvin, and G. Wrightson, eds. *Greece, Macedon and Persia: Studies in the Social, Political and Military Consequences of Conquest Societies in Honour of Waldemar Heckel* Oxford: Oxbow: 59–68.
———. 2018. "La batalla de Gaugamela y el empleo de 'armas combinadas'," *Desperta Ferro Historia antigua y medieval* 47 (May): 14–22.
———. Forthcoming. "Size Matters: Notes on Using Combined Arms Alongside the Hellenistic Sarissa Phalanx and the Problem of Lengthening the Sarissa," in *Ancient World*.
Wylie, G. 1992a. "Brasidas: Great Commander or Whiz-Kid?" *QUCC* ser. 2, 41: 75–96.
———. 1992b. "Agesilaus and the Battle of Sardis," *Klio* 74: 118–30.
Yalichev, S. 1997. *Mercenaries of the Ancient World*. London: Constable.

Index

Abydos 137; *see also* Cremaste, battle of
Acarnania, Acarnanian(s) 109
Achaea 30
Achaemenids 27, 72, 93, 95
Achilles 35–7, 122
Aegean Sea 18, 77, 80, 170
Aegitium, battle of 108, 127
Aelian 141
Aetolia, Aetolians 14, 27, 99, 104, 108, 111, 125, 127
Africa(n) 22–4
Agamemnon 35, 37
Agathocles 212
Agesilaus 132, 134, 144, 145–6, 149, 156, 219
Agincourt, battle of 29, 44
Agrianes (Agrianians) 8, 20, 148, 181, 183–5, 187–8, 191, 194–5, 197–8, 220
Alcaeus 55–6, 67
Alcibiades 110
Alexander I (king of Macedon) 90, 166, 176
Alexander II (king of Macedon) 164, 166, 176
Alexander III (the Great) 1, 3, 7, 10, 17, 20, 22–3, 25–6, 28–30, 33, 55, 70, 74, 84, 90, 105, 127, 134, 141, 144, 148–9, 152–3, 157, 165, 166, 168–70, 172–5, 177–206, 208, 211–14, 216, 218–21
Alexander of Pherae 155–6, 158
Alexander Mosaic 200
Amathus, 54; Amathus Bowl 54, 59, 61, 63
Ambracia, Ambraciots 98, 108–10
Amiens, WW2 battle of 11
Amphipolis, battle of 103, 112–13, 162
Amyntas III (king of Macedon) 164
Amyntas IV (king of Macedon) 161
Anakreon 55
Anaxibios 137

Anaximenes 164–6
Antigonus Monophthalmus 24, 28–30, 134, 202, 204–11, 212, 214
Antiochus I of Seleucid Empire 211, 215
Antiochus III of Seleucid Empire 23, 29, 204
Apamea 212, 214–15
Arabia, Arabian(s) 93
Arcadia, Arcadians 140–1, 147
Archaic 15, 36–9, 41, 43, 45–6, 55–6, 59, 62–3, 67–8, 86
Archers, archery 18–19, 22–3, 27–9, 37–8, 42–3, 45, 47, 53–4, 56–7, 59, 63, 67, 70–3, 75, 78, 82, 85–6, 88–90, 92, 93–4, 97, 99–100, 104, 108, 111, 116, 118, 125, 128n58, 133, 135, 143, 161, 166–7, 185, 188, 198–200, 202, 217–19
Archidamus 140
Archilochos 45, 55–6, 67
Argive(s), Argos 147, 149
argyraspids 17, 181, 183, 198
Aristobulus 178
Arrian (not including citations) 33, 178–83, 185, 187, 189–92, 194, 197, 199–200
Artaphernes 77
Artaxerxes II 87, 99
artillery 6–7, 11, 26, 30, 168–9, 177, 185–6, 188, 199
Asclepiodotus 28, 148, 175
Asculum, battle of 203
Asia, Asians, Asiatic 44, 54, 179, 183–6, 219, 221
Asia Minor 75, 84, 94, 130, 132, 134, 142–6, 191
aspis 139
Assyria, Assyrian(s) (Neo-Assyria, Neo-Assyrian(s)) 10, 15, 18, 22, 25, 39,

Index 241

54–5, 63, 69–72, 75, 93, 94, 170, 216, 217, 220
asthetairoi 179–80, 183–4, 188, 197, 200
Athena 37
Athens, Athenian(s) 25, 28–9, 38, 43, 59, 71, 72, 77–83, 86, 88, 90–2, 95–100, 103–8, 110–14, 116–24, 126–30, 132–5, 140, 143, 150, 153, 162, 164–5, 172, 174, 177, 219

Babylon, Babylonia, Babylonian 55, 67, 85, 147
Bactria, Bactrians 75, 86, 90, 93, 142, 193–4
Bardylis, king of Illyrians 162, 168, 171, 195
Barnet, battle of 47
Beneventum, battle of 203
Bessus 194
Bias, Spartan commander 136
bodyguard(s) 69, 71, 73, 75, 85–6, 91, 94, 99, 165–6, 174, 176, 179–82, 195, 198
Boeotia, Boeotian(s) 40, 67, 91, 93, 104–5, 107, 126, 144, 147, 154, 172, 218
Boudicca 29
Brasidas 110, 112–14, 121–2, 125, 127–8, 134, 149
Bronze Age 2, 37
Byzantine Empire 55

Caesar, G. Julius 75, 134, 178
Callinus 56
Callisthenes 178
caltrops 24, 209, 213
Cambyses 70, 95
camels 73–4, 93
Cappadocia 214
Cardaces 75, 95, 191–2, 200
Caria, Carian 93–5
Carrhae, battle of 25, 130
Carthage, Carthaginian(s) 55, 115, 123–4, 129–30, 213
Catana 117
Cataphracts 29, 193
Chabrias 20, 114, 134–5, 141, 149
Chaeronea, battle of 16, 28, 89, 98, 100, 105, 126, 157, 164, 168, 171–5, 177, 189, 192–3
Chalcidaeans 107–8, 126, 167
Chalcidice 112
Chandragupta 214
Chares 177

Charidemus 94, 141
chariots: scythed 22, 23, 193–4, 196
Chigi vase 39, 57, 59
Cilicia 54, 93, 191
Clausewitz, Carl von 2
Clearchus 148
Cleitarchus 178
Cleon 111–12, 128
Cleonymos, king of Sparta 65
Coele Assyria 191
Coenus 180, 189, 200
Companions, Companion cavalry 153, 162, 165, 168, 172–4, 176–8, 180–2, 184–5, 187, 189, 191–5, 197, 203, 213, 216, 220–1; foot companions 164–5, 176 (*see also* pezhetairoi)
Corinth, Corinthian(s) 57, 59–61, 98, 107, 136
Corinthian War 20, 114, 132, 134–5, 137, 145, 150, 219
Coroneia, battle of 145, 149, 156
Crassus, Marcus Licinius 25
Craterus 203, 207
Crecy, battle of 29, 44, 47
Cremaste, battle of 137
Cretan archers 8, 116, 135, 147, 183
Crete, Cretan(s) 67
Crocus Field, battle of 171
Croesus 73, 95
Cunaxa, battle of 87, 113, 133, 148
Curtius Rufus (excluding citations) 178, 181–2, 190–1, 194, 197
Cyaxares, King of Media 59, 71, 73
Cynoscephalae: battle of (197) 149, 221; battle of (364) 155–6
Cyrrhestica, battle of 215
Cyrus the Great 69, 73, 93–4, 134
Cyrus the Younger 87, 99, 130, 132–3

Darius I 70, 72, 93, 94, 96, 98
Darius II 73
Darius III 22, 29, 74, 85, 127, 191–6, 200, 216, 218
Datis 77
Decelea 120
Dekelean War 124, 131
Delium, battle of 28, 99, 105–6, 113–14, 119, 144–5, 150
Demaratus 94
Demetrius I (Demetrius Poliorketes) 24, 30, 204, 210–11, 213–15
Demosthenes, Athenian general 78, 108–14, 117, 119–24, 126–8, 130, 133–5, 137, 142, 149

242 Index

Demosthenes, Athenian orator (excluding citations) 161, 165–7, 172
Derkyllidas 144
Diodorus (excluding citations) 76, 93, 103, 115, 125, 129, 132, 138–9, 146, 150, 156–7, 161, 172, 173, 175, 178, 181, 190–1, 194, 197, 200, 202–3, 206, 210, 213–14
Diomedes 37–8
Dion of Syracuse 212
Dionysius I of Syracuse 123–4, 130, 134, 158, 212
Dionysius II of Syracuse 212
Dipaea, battle of 88, 147
dory 16, 35, 139

Egypt, Egyptian(s) 15–16, 22–3, 53, 55, 67, 70, 72, 84, 93–5, 139–41, 164, 170, 193, 212, 218
Elasa, battle of 211
elephants 7, 21, 23–4, 26, 29–30, 74, 183, 189–90, 196, 199, 202–15, 217–18
enomotia (pl. enomotiai) 123
Epaminondas 114, 134, 141, 150–3, 156–8, 171, 195, 207
Epipolae: 1st battle of 117; 2nd battle of 119; 3rd battle of 114, 119, 122
Epipolae heights 118, 120, 123, 129
Eretria 77, 98
Erythrae 89
Eudamus 206
Eumenes of Cardia 24, 28–30, 134, 202–9, 212, 214
Eumenes of Pergamum 23
Eurylochos 109
Eurymedon, Athenian general 119–21
Eurymedon, battle of 84

Gabiene, battle of 24, 30, 191, 204–9, 213–14
Gaugamela, battle of 22, 28–30, 95, 127, 148–9, 157, 184, 186, 188–93, 195–6, 199–200, 206, 213, 216
Gaza, in Phoenicia, battle of (312) 24, 204
Gela, Gelan(s) 114, 129
Gelon, tyrant of Syracuse and Gela 115–16, 129, 138
(Proto-)Geometric period 36–7, 39
Ghazi 55
Granicus River, battle of 95, 144, 148, 180, 185–6, 191–2, 200
Greek allies or mercenary(ies) 54–5, 63, 66–7, 70, 72, 75, 87, 94, 103, 105, 130; in the army of Darius III 191–2, 200; of Iphicrates 140; serving in the Macedonian army 162, 189, 190–1, 193–5; the Ten Thousand 99, 113, 128, 133, 142, 144
Guerrilla warfare 107, 121
Gylippus 114, 118–22, 124–5, 130–1, 145

Haliartus, battle of 30
Hamilcar 115
hamippoi 138, 147–8, 165, 182, 184–5, 188, 191, 198, 200
Hannibal 134, 178
Hector 35–7, 39
Helen 41
Hellenic 94
Hellenistic 12, 16, 26, 134, 139, 141, 197, 199, 202, 209, 211–12
Hellespont 84, 94, 127
Hellespont, battle of 203, 205, 207
helots (helotes) 61, 68, 86, 88, 97–9, 127
hemithorakion 138
Hera 92
Heraclea, battle of 204, 213
Heraclea Lyncestis, battle of 161, 166, 168, 171–2, 180, 189, 195
Hermocrates 121
Herodotus (excluding citations) 15–6, 45, 59, 61, 67–74, 76–82, 84–100, 127, 129, 153, 158
Himera, battle of 115, 129, 145
Himera, city on Sicily 115, 118
Himilco 130
Hippocrates, tyrant of Gela 114, 129
Histiaeus 74
Hittite Empire, Hittites 22, 69
Homer, Homeric 1–2, 10, 22, 33–45, 47, 51, 55–6, 58–60, 63, 67, 220
Homoioi 17
hoplite(s) 1–3, 10, 15–7, 19–20, 27–9, 35–43, 45–68, 70, 72, 74–83, 85–100, 103–30, 132–57, 161–5, 167–72, 174, 176, 180–3, 190–1, 193, 198–200, 213, 218–21
hoplitodromos, (athletic running race in full armour) 50
hoplon 16, 35–6, 42–3, 46, 48, 53, 72
horse archers, archery 21–2, 25, 40, 73, 100, 117, 184, 205, 213, 217–18
Hundred Years' War 47
Hydaspes River 189, 204; battle of 30, 183, 189, 191, 204, 209, 216

Index 243

hypaspists 17, 20, 55, 141, 166, 179–86, 188, 190, 192, 194–8, 202, 220; Royal hypaspists (agema) 179–2, 184, 187, 197–8, 200
Hyrcania, Hyrcanians 93

Idomene, battle of 110, 122, 127, 133
Illyria, Illyrians 28, 113, 128, 162, 164, 166, 171, 174, 182, 185, 187–8, 195, 199–200
Imbria 111
Immortals 17, 28, 69, 71–2, 86–7, 94, 219
India, Indian(s) 22–4, 66, 86, 90, 93, 183, 189–90, 204, 209, 214, 218
Indus river 183
Inessa, battle of 30
Ionia, Ionian(s) 54–5, 72, 75, 77, 94–5, 97, 123
Iphicrates 14–15, 17, 20–1, 23–4, 27–9, 100, 114, 124, 131–2, 134–7, 139–41, 145–9, 164, 176
Iphicratids 139
Ipsus, battle of 1, 28, 30, 98, 202, 209–12, 214–15
Issus, battle of 29, 85, 93, 95, 148, 180, 184, 186, 188–91, 193–5, 198–200, 218

Jason of Pherae 138, 147, 152–5, 158
javelin men 8, 18, 19–20, 22, 63, 93, 104, 128, 133, 140, 147–8, 166, 181, 183, 185, 194, 198–9, 202, 219–20; *see also* Agrianes (Agrianians)
Jaxartes river 185
Justin (excluding citations) 41, 78, 96, 161, 175, 178, 181, 191, 197

knight, mediaeval 29, 43, 47, 52, 93
Knossos 66
Kolchians 93, 143–4
Kromnos, battle of 140

Lade, battle of 77
Lechaeum, battle of 20, 27–8, 100, 124, 131, 134–7, 140, 145, 148
legion(s), legionary (Roman) 15, 43, 63, 130, 149, 167, 203–4, 221
Lemnos 111
Leuctra, battle of 17, 145, 149, 151–3, 156–8, 172, 195, 207
Levant 22
linothorax 147–8
lochos (pl. lochoi) 123

Lycia, Lycians (Lykia) 93
Lycurgus 123, 141
Lydia, Lydians 73, 93
Lyncus, battle of 113
Lysander 30, 141
Lysimachus 182, 209–10

Macedon(ia), Macedonian(s) 3, 10, 15–16, 27–30, 69, 74, 83, 89, 100, 104–5, 113, 123, 126, 138–9, 141–2, 148, 152–4, 156–8, 161–84, 186–200, 202–4, 206–8, 211–12, 216, 218, 220–1
Machanidas 30
Magnesia ad Sipylum, battle of 23, 29
Malene, battle of 74, 98, 126
Malli, Mallian(s) 198
maniple(s) 144, 164
Mantinea: battle of (207 BCE) 30; battle of (362 BCE) 145, 149, 151–3, 156–7, 171–2; battle of (418 BCE) 123, 147, 155
Marathon, battle of 49, 72, 76–83, 85–6, 88–90, 92, 94–100, 145
Mardonius 25, 70, 85–6, 90–1, 127
Masistius 88–90
Massagetae 71, 93
Media, Median 59, 70–2
mediaeval 4, 16, 28, 44, 47, 51–2, 56, 58, 62, 66, 140
Mediterranean Sea 19, 23, 55–6, 60, 63, 164
Megalopolis, battle of (331) 16, 28; siege of (316) 24, 213
Megara, Megarian(s) 98, 116
Megara: battle of (458) 107; siege of (424) 110, 122
Menelaus 35–7
mercenaries 55–6, 59, 95, 115, 129–30, 132, 134, 139, 141, 146, 148, 155, 158, 161–2, 167, 170, 218–20; *see also* Greek allies or mercenary(ies)
Mesopotamia, Mesopotamian 3, 43, 69, 75, 170, 193
Messenia, Messenian(s) 27, 59, 110–1, 125, 127–8
Messenian Wars 59
Methoni 176
Minoan 66
Mora (pl. Morai) 123–4, 131, 135, 145
Mount Athos 84
Mount Cithaeron 89
Munychia, battle of 133
Mycale, battle of 71, 84, 92

Mycenae, Mycenaean(s) 19, 22, 34, 36–40, 42, 45, 53, 98
Myronides 107

Naupactus 27, 125, 127
Naxos on Sicily 117
Near Eastern 27, 56, 60, 87, 95
Nemea, battle of 145, 150, 152, 155
Neoptolemus 203
Nepos, Cornelius (excluding citations) 78, 96, 139
Nestor 39
Nicias 29, 111, 116, 118–21, 129

Odysseus 37, 41
Oinophyta, battle of 107
Olpae, battle of 108–10, 127
Olympeium 117, 120
Olympeium, battle of 117
Olympic Games 82
Olynthus, Olynthian(s) 126, 154, 176
Onomarchus 167, 169, 171, 177
Opis mutiny 181, 197

Paeonians 184–5, 187
Pages 181, 184, 198, 205
Pagondas 105–6, 113–14, 128
Paktolos, battle of 144
Paraetacene, battle of 24, 28–30, 191, 204–9, 213
Paris 35–8
Parmenion 192–5
Parthia, Parthian(s) 14, 24, 93
Patroclus 35
Pausanias, Roman author (excluding citations) 78, 97
Pausanias, Spartan king 85
Peithon 205–6, 208
Pelopidas 114, 150–3, 155–8
Peloponnese Peloponnesian(s) 108–9, 121, 126
Peloponnesian War 1, 20, 25, 30, 34, 62, 86, 96, 103–5, 107–8, 111, 113–14, 123–4, 130, 132–3, 138–9, 143–4, 146, 150, 218–20
peltasts 17, 19–20, 27–9, 93, 96, 99–100, 104, 108, 110–13, 116, 119–20, 124–5, 128, 130–44, 146–9, 154–5, 158, 161–2, 176, 182, 202, 210
pelte 19, 74, 135, 139
pentekostia (pl. pentekostiai) 123
Perdiccas, general of Alexander 180, 200

Perdiccas II, king of Macedon 113
Perdiccas III, king of Macedon 162, 164, 167, 175
Perseus, king of Macedon 144
Persia, Persian 3, 6, 12, 14–19, 25, 27–8, 30, 41, 68–100, 103, 105, 127, 129, 133–4, 139–40, 142, 144–5, 147, 153, 155, 158, 164, 170, 175–8, 180, 185–7, 189, 191–7, 200, 203, 217–20
Persian Empire (of the Achaemenids) 2, 23, 27, 69, 75, 83–4, 170, 186, 196, 216–19
Persian Wars 56, 61, 76, 88, 92, 100, 107, 116, 144, 153
Peucestas 198, 206–8
pezhetairoi 164–6, 171, 176, 179–81, 184, 197
phalanx, phalangites 14, 16, 21, 23, 26, 51, 53, 55, 62, 82, 154, 162, 174, 187, 219–20; Classical Greek hoplite 1, 3, 15–17, 28–9, 35–6, 39–43, 45–6, 48, 51–6, 58–67, 74, 76, 79, 82–3, 86–8, 91, 94, 97–9, 107–9, 113–14, 117–19, 122–4, 126, 128–30, 132–3, 135–9, 143–6, 149–57, 163, 167, 170, 173, 183, 200, 219–21; Macedonian style 10, 15–17, 28–30, 141, 144, 148–9, 161–76, 178–200, 202–12, 214, 216, 219, 221
Pharnabazus 144
Pharsalus, battle of 75
Philip II of Macedon 3, 10, 26, 28, 74, 98, 134, 141, 148, 152–3, 155, 157–8, 161–2, 164–81, 184, 186, 189, 192, 194, 196, 198–9, 203, 206, 212, 216, 219–20
Philip brother of Lysimachus 182
Philoctetes 37
Phocis, Phocians 169, 177
Phoenicia, Phoenician 54, 77, 84, 93, 193
Pinarus river 186, 191
Pisidia, Pisidians 93
Plataea, battle of 15, 61, 68, 70, 73, 81, 83–92, 94–9, 108, 126, 145, 176
Plataea, Plataean(s) 78–9, 96, 98
Plemmyrium 119
Plutarch (excluding citations) 14–5, 33, 76, 103, 114, 129, 151, 153, 157, 172–3, 178, 181, 190–1, 194, 197, 203, 210, 213–14
Poitiers, battle of 29, 44, 47
polis (pl. poleis) 1–3, 9, 27, 40–1, 43, 61, 83–4, 86, 96, 103–4, 107, 114, 118,

124–5, 132, 138, 141, 150–1, 153, 155, 162, 170, 172, 218
Polyaenus (excluding citations) 107, 134, 139, 142, 167, 169, 172–3, 177
Polyperchon 24, 213
Pompeii 200
Pompey, Gnaeus Pompeius Magnus 75
Porus 22, 29–30, 189–90, 204, 209, 216
Priam 36, 41
prodromoi 184–5
Ptolemaic (Egypt) 24
Ptolemy, son of Seleucus 195
Ptolemy I Soter 24, 178, 204, 209, 213
Pydna 94, 144, 149, 164, 221
Pylos 99, 111–12, 127–8; battle of 77, 125
Pyrrhic dancing 50, 52–3, 65–6
Pyrrhus of Epirus 134, 203–4

rhipsaspia 55–6, 67
Rhodes, Rhodian(s) 19, 99, 104
Rome, Romans 4, 15–16, 23, 25–6, 28–30, 43, 53, 55, 63, 94, 130, 134, 144, 149, 164, 167, 203–4, 220–1

Saca, Sacae 72, 86, 90, 93–4, 193–4
Sacred Band (Theban) 17, 151–2, 156–8, 172–4
Salamis, battle of (480) 85–6
Salamis in Cyprus, battle of (497) 94, 97
sarissa 15–17, 24, 141, 144, 148, 162–5, 167, 172–80, 182–4, 186, 188–90, 192, 194, 197–8, 202, 204, 206, 209, 211–12, 216, 219, 221
sarissaphoroi 184
Satrapal 95
Satrapal Revolt 158
Sciritae 138, 147–8, 165
scutum 53
Scythia, Scythian(s) 25, 59, 70–1, 73, 75, 93–4, 185, 193, 213, 218
secutor 53
Seleucid(s) 12, 23–4, 29, 193, 211–12, 214–15
Seleucus 30, 195, 204, 209–11, 214–15
Selymbria, siege of 110
Sennacherib 54, 70
Seuthes 142
Shipka Pass, battle of 183
Sicel(s) 115, 213
Sicily, Sicilian(s) 29, 55, 96, 105, 114–17, 121, 123–5, 129–30, 132, 213

Simonides 77
slaves 135, 205; freed slaves in Athenian army at Marathon 78–9, 83, 96, 99–100
slingers 18–19, 28–9, 63, 99, 104, 116, 133, 135, 143, 161, 166, 199
Sogdiana, Sogdian(s) 93, 185
Sparta, Spartan(s) 17, 20, 27–8, 39, 43, 58–9, 61, 65, 67, 69, 79, 81, 85–6, 88, 90–2, 94, 97–100, 103, 107, 109, 111–14, 118, 120, 122–5, 127–40, 143–7, 149–54, 156–8, 165, 168, 176, 207, 219
Spartolus, battle of 27, 107, 126, 167
Sphacteria, battle of 28, 92, 100, 111–12, 135–7
Stoa Poecile 80–1, 97
Strymon valley 183
Successors 1, 3, 7, 10, 84, 152, 181, 183, 186, 189, 196–7, 199, 202–3, 205, 207, 210, 212, 214, 220
Sumer(ia), Sumerian(s) 7, 12, 19
Susian Gates 198
Syracuse, Syracusan(s) 29, 104–5, 110, 114, 116–25, 129–32, 134, 138, 143, 153, 212–13
Syria, Syrian(s) 93, 214
Syrian Gates 191

Taulantians 199
Tegea, Tegean(s) 88, 90–1, 98
Tegyra, battle of 153, 158
Teleutias 154, 176
Ten Thousand, The 113, 130, 132–4, 142–4, 149; *see also* mercenaries
Thebes, Theban(s) 17, 20, 30, 89, 91–2, 99–100, 104–5, 107, 113–14, 126, 128, 145, 149–51, 152–3, 155–8, 167, 170–4, 219
Theopompus 161, 165, 175–6, 178–9
Thermopylae: battle of (191) 30; battle of (480) 72, 79–80, 83, 86–7, 90, 92, 99, 127
Thessalian cavalry 74, 100, 126, 142, 152–3, 155, 168, 184, 187, 190, 192, 194, 199, 203, 213, 216, 220
Thessaly, Thessalian(s) 14, 51, 104–5, 132, 135, 138, 145, 148, 154–6, 158, 171, 177, 218
Third Sacred War 168, 177
Thrace, Thracian(s) 20, 28–9, 52, 93, 98–9, 105, 107, 112, 119, 121, 127, 130,

133, 135, 139, 141–3, 148, 164, 167,
  171, 177, 183, 187, 194, 199
Thrasybulus 133, 149
Thrasyllus 96
Thucydides (excluding citations) 29, 33,
  43, 97, 103–5, 111–14, 116–18, 120,
  123–30, 132, 147, 150
Timoleon 116, 212
Timotheus 134
Tissaphernes 144
Torone, battle of 110
Trench, battle of the 59
Triballians 164
trireme 77–8, 84, 95–6, 128
Tyre, siege of 180, 198

Tyrrhenian(s) 121
Tyrtaeus 45, 58, 67

Uruk 73

Varangian Guard 55
Viking(s) 55, 67

Warwick, Earl of, the Kingmaker 47

Xenophon 19, 25, 28, 52, 65, 69, 94, 96,
  103, 123, 127, 130, 132–4, 137–40,
  142–3, 145–50, 153–5, 158, 164
Xerxes 72–3, 77, 79, 83–7, 93–5, 98,
  115, 129

Index of battles

Abydos 137; *see also* Cremaste, battle of
Aegitium, battle of 108, 127
Agincourt, battle of 29, 44
Amiens, WW2 battle of 11
Amphipolis, battle of 103, 112–13, 162
Asculum, battle of 203

Barnet, battle of 47
Beneventum, battle of 203

Carrhae, battle of 25, 130
Chaeronea, battle of 16, 28, 89, 98, 100, 105, 126, 157, 164, 168, 171–5, 177, 189, 192–3
Coroneia, battle of 145, 149, 156
Crecy, battle of 29, 44, 47
Cremaste, battle of 137
Crocus Field, battle of 171
Cunaxa, battle of 87, 113, 133, 148
Cynoscephalae: battle of (197) 149, 221; battle of (364) 155–6
Cyrrhestica, battle of 215

Delium, battle of 28, 99, 105–6, 113–14, 119, 144–5, 150
Dipaea, battle of 88, 147

Elasa, battle of 211
Epipolae: 1st battle of 117; 2nd battle of 119; 3rd battle of 114, 119, 122
Eurymedon, battle of 84

Gabiene, battle of 24, 30, 191, 204–9, 213–14
Gaugamela, battle of 22, 28–30, 95, 127, 148–9, 157, 184, 186, 188–93, 195–6, 199–200, 206, 213, 216
Gaza, in Phoenicia, battle of (312) 24, 204
Granicus River, battle of 95, 144, 148, 180, 185–6, 191–2, 200

Haliartus, battle of 30
Hellespont, battle of 203, 205, 207
Heraclea, battle of 204, 213
Heraclea Lyncestis, battle of 161, 166, 168, 171–2, 180, 189, 195
Himera, battle of 115, 129, 145
Hydaspes river, battle of 30, 183, 189, 191, 204, 209, 216

Idomene, battle of 110, 122, 127, 133
Inessa, battle of 30
Ipsus, battle of 1, 28, 30, 98, 202, 209–12, 214–15
Issus, battle of 29, 85, 93, 95, 148, 180, 184, 186, 188–91, 193–5, 198–200, 218

Kromnos, battle of 140

Lade, battle of 77
Lechaeum, battle of 20, 27–8, 100, 124, 131, 134–7, 140, 145, 148
Leuctra, battle of 17, 145, 149, 151–3, 156–8, 172, 195, 207
Lyncus, battle of 113

Magnesia ad Sipylum, battle of 23, 29
Malene, battle of 74, 98, 126
Mantinea: battle of (207 BCE) 30; battle of (362 BCE) 145, 149, 151–3, 156–7, 171–2; battle of (418 BCE) 123, 147, 155
Marathon, battle of 49, 72, 76–83, 85–6, 88–90, 92, 94–100, 145
Megalopolis: battle of (331) 16, 28; siege of (316) 24, 213
Megara: battle of (458) 107; siege of (424) 110, 122
Munychia, battle of 133
Mycale, battle of 71, 84, 92

Index of battles

Nemea, battle of 145, 150, 152, 155

Oinophyta, battle of 107
Olpae, battle of 108–10, 127
Olympeium, battle of 117

Paktolos, battle of 144
Paraetacene, battle of 24, 28–30, 191, 204–9, 213
Pharsalus, battle of 75
Plataea, battle of 15, 61, 68, 70, 73, 81, 83–92, 94–9, 108, 126, 145, 176
Poitiers, battle of 29, 44, 47
Pylos, battle of 77, 125

Salamis, battle of (480) 85–6
Salamis in Cyprus, battle of (497) 94, 97
Shipka Pass, battle of 183
Spartolus, battle of 27, 107, 126, 167
Sphacteria, battle of 28, 92, 100, 111–12, 135–7

Tegyra, battle of 153, 158
Thermopylae: battle of (191) 30; battle of (480) 72, 79–80, 83, 86–7, 90, 92, 99, 127
Torone, battle of 110
Trench, battle of the 59
Tyre, siege of 180, 198